encyclopedia of

.northwest
music

From Classical Recordings
to Classic Rock Performances,
Your Guide to the Best
of the Region

SASQUATCH BOOKS
SEATTLE

For my mother,

Catherine Gibbons Bush

Printed in the United States of America
Distributed in Canada by Raincoast Books Ltd.
03 02 01 00 99   5 4 3 2 1

Grateful acknowledgment is made on page 325 to persons and organizations for permission to reproduce their photographs within this book.

Cover design: Karen Schober
Cover illustration: John Hillmer
Interior design: Kate Basart
Copy editor: Patricia Draher

Library of Congress Cataloging in Publication Data
Encyclopedia of northwest music : from classical recordings to classic rock performances, your guide to the best of the region / by James Bush
        p.   cm.
ISBN 1-57061-141-6
1. Musicians—Northwest, Pacific Biography Dictionaries.
    2. Music—Northwest, Pacific Discography. I. Title.
ML106.U4N93 1999
780'.9795'03—dc21   99-16791

SASQUATCH BOOKS
615 Second Avenue
Seattle, Washington 98104
(206) 467-4300
www.SasquatchBooks.com
books@SasquatchBooks.com

Contents

Jazz   173

American Roots/World 239

Classical 275

Great Records Not to Miss 293

Music Festivals 317

Photo Credits 325

Index 327

Acknowledgments

The first round of thank yous for this book must go to the folks at Sasquatch Books, especially my editor, Kate Rogers, for her amazing patience and encouragement throughout the process (and for never once striking me, although I'm sure she thought about it). Also deserving of much credit are editorial assistant Novella Carpenter, copy editor Patricia Draher, art director Karen Schober, designer Kate Basart, and proofreader Sherri Schultz.

Next, I would like to thank the wonderfully talented writers who contributed to this project. Their work speaks for itself, but their great effort and enthusiasm was downright inspirational.

Another great contributor to the success of this project was the Internet. Without band Web sites, e-mail, and the very helpful *All-Music Guide*, I have no idea how anyone could complete an ambitious undertaking such as this one. Special kudos to the guy/gal at amazon.com who decided to include release dates in their album listings.

A very special thank you to the folks who sat for long interviews about their musical careers: Mark Arm, Jim Basnight, Kurt Bloch, Duffy Bishop, Dave Dederer, Jack Endino, Jack Hanan, Orville Johnson, Peter Litwin, Ben McMillan, Ron Nine, Jim Page, Steve Pearson, Andrew Ratshin, Marv Ross, Bill Stevenson, Kim Warnick, and Rusty Willoughby.

A few more musical thanks: Ron Bailey, Jan Celt, Bill Freckleton, Mary McFaul, and everyone who provided photographs.

Other thanks: Richard Gibbons and family, Anne and Dave Tipton, Stephen Bush, Cecilia and Chris Gray, Stevan and Kathleen Morgain, John Fox, Gary Clark, Skip Berger and the *Seattle Weekly*, Emily Baillargeon, Catherine Tarpley, Sumi Hahn, John Longenbaugh, Terry Denton and Elizabeth White, Tim and Renee Muir, Michelle C. Buetow, Dan "Mr. Art" Ballard, and everyone at Pazzo's.

And now for a few words of thanks from the major contributors:

Dawn Anderson: I'd like to thank all who patiently helped me rehash a history they'd probably rather forget: Blaine Cook, Dave Crider, Kurt Danielson, Tad Doyle, Loud Fart, Steve Fart, the Murder City Devils, Tom Niemeyer, Joe Newton, Tom Price, Jim Sangster, Kim Thayil, and especially Jack Endino.

Andrew Bartlett: At various times many Northwest musicians have been both an inspiration to me and a source of great writing opportunities. These include Bill Frisell and Eyvind Kang (who each sat for long, colorful interviews), Rob Blakeslee, Rich Halley, Michael Monhart, Dennis Rea, Wally Shoup, Mike Bisio, Bob Nell, Al Hood, Julian Priester, Andrew D'Angelo, Chris Speed, Briggan Krauss, Wayne Horvitz, Jay Clayton, Bud Shank, Robin Holcomb, and many, many more. Without the music, we're all speechless. As a recently completed Ph.D. and a full-time–plus music critic, it's also vital that my wife, Leslie, knows how much her patience, forthrightness, and unconditional love mean to me. They mean the world, as do my kids, Allison and Benjamin, who delight me with impromptu dances and a great ear for the difference between saxophones, trumpets, guitars, pianos, and other instruments I'm certainly forgetting.

Norm Bobrow would like to thank all the artists who graciously provided information for these profiles.

Gavin Borchert thanks everyone who sent information when asked.

Neal Skok would like to thank: Ted Shreffler, Dick Powell, Lee Graham, Jim Plano, John Gaborit, Linda Lewis, Steve Lalor, Jon Keliehor, Doug Hastings, Don Caverhill, Jim Valley, Ned Neltner, Jeff Beals, Barry and Roxanna Curtis, Bill Engelhart, Buck Ormsby, Mark Lindsay, Phil Volk, Drake Levin, Mike Smith, Andy Parypa, Larry Parypa, Jerry "Zu" Matheson, Brad Miller, Mike Cox, Fred Zeufeldt, Marv Jensen, Joe Ross, Howard and Liz Monta, Gaye Winsor, Gordon Kjellberg, Jeff Kelly, Steve Lawrence, Keith "Hudson Brothers Expert" Queensen, Dave Baroh, Kevin Marin, Kim Marin, Phil Klitgaard, John Soltero, Rich Dangel, Pat Gossan, Kim Eggers, Mom, Steve Fossen, Roger Fisher, Mike Derosier, Don Wilhelm, Richard Gerber, Neil Rush, John Berg, Janet Durand, Cathy Whaley, Jeff Simmonds, Phil Kirby, Pat Mason, Roger Hart, Tim Tennis, Dudley Hill, Stacey Christenson, Mick Flynn, Linda Waterfall, Burl Barer, Pat O'Day, Scott Soules, and Toby Bowen.

And thanks to you, the reader, for coming along for the ride.

Introduction

My first contribution to this book was to almost talk my way out of it.

Just before signing the contract for the project, I noted in a weekly newspaper column that all-encompassing music guides were a bad idea, arguing that authors should limit themselves to profiling a specific style of music or a brief historical era. My soon-to-be editor at Sasquatch Books, Kate Rogers, was quite amused by that piece (she probably should have been horrified). But, after almost two years of writing, research, editing, editing, and editing, I can't deny a bit of sympathy for my original opinion that the job was too big. I'm quite pleased, however, with the ultimate results.

"A book on Northwest music?" That's the comment that invariably resulted when people learned of this project. Note the question mark at the end of the sentence—when it was delivered, peoples' faces registered surprise, wonder, and a bit of confusion. How does one go about writing a book about all the music from a geographic area? The obvious solution was to profile individual artists and groups. The designated gatekeepers for this process were the writers themselves, who had to choose whom to include. The most successful artists in each genre certainly had to be represented, but significant artists could be added at will.

Some guidelines had to be set: "The Northwest" was defined as Washington and Oregon, thus excluding the vital Vancouver, British Columbia, music scene (and a couple dozen more "must-include" groups) and including only those Idaho bands who had the sense to move out here. Given the rise of Northwest rock bands over the last decade, the book was likely to be heavily devoted to rock music. As such, the mid-1950s was chosen as our starting point—around the time of that musical genre's birth.

The individual writers each brought his or her own balance between musical critique and biographical detail to the profiles. Even with differing voices, however, each profile strives to answer three questions:
—Who was (or is) this artist?
—What did they accomplish musically?
—Why are they important to the region?

Obviously, given limitations of space, none of the profiles can be definitive. The important thing was that the third question be answered. Why was this artist important? Jimi Hendrix, for instance, established a new standard for the lead guitarist in rock, both as artist and as personality. Jim Basnight's band, the Moberlys, represented the leading edge of the late 1970s return of original music to Seattle clubs. Robert Cray, Paul deLay, and Curtis Salgado are the products of a simmering Portland blues scene that leapt to national prominence. Jim Page is the heart—and the conscience—of the Northwest folk scene. Not all equal accomplishments, perhaps, but all significant accomplishments.

Nobody's perfect, though. A project organized in Seattle, under the direction of a

Seattle music writer, and featuring the contributions of many of his Seattle music writing colleagues is bound to carry some bias in favor of Seattle acts. The remainder of the writers were recruited from Portland, which means the region's two big cities had an edge over the small towns. Recent artists also had a better shot at making it in than older artists.

The record or two listed at the end of most profiles are the writer's recommendations. These are not necessarily the musicians' most successful or critically acclaimed works, but the ones that the writer felt you, the reader, most need to hear. Admittedly, functionality was among our aims in choosing pick records. Many of the older bands are represented by "best of" retrospectives, which not only make more effective primers for the uninitiated, but often are the only albums available on CD. This is changing, of course. During the life of this project, the only-on-vinyl works of the Heats and Cowboys, two of Seattle's best bands from the early 1980s, were re-released on CD (as were those of Portland's Billy Rancher); individual albums by earlier bands like the Sonics and Wailers are also seeing reissue. Still, there are a few records cited here that will be available only to the well-heeled vinyl record collector until someone, somewhere, deems them worthy of a CD release.

Things have changed in the Northwest since my first record reviews for the Seattle University paper and my first concerts at the Paramount Theater and Seattle Center Arena. In our interview, vocalist/guitarist Kim Warnick, of Seattle's punk/pop immortals The Fastbacks, reminded me of how national bands would print their tour itineraries in ads in *Rolling Stone* or *Creem*. The bands would start on the East Coast, swing through the Midwest, hit the South, travel up the West Coast to San Francisco and stop. We Northwest kids would look sadly at the obvious gap. Well, after Nirvana, Pearl Jam, and Soundgarden, nobody's ignoring this corner of the country anymore. But these past slights worked in our favor: our isolation helped Seattle and Portland develop distinct, talent-laden rock music scenes that could then be "discovered" by national magazines and record companies with great joy and wonder.

Perhaps efforts such as this book will show the world there are Northwest discoveries to be made across the whole musical spectrum. And as these artists continue their careers, more great music is sure to follow.

Our Music Critics

Author/editor **James Bush** has written about Seattle music since relocating to the city in 1979. His work has appeared in local publications *Backfire, Backlash, Hype, The Rocket*, and *Seattle Weekly*, often under the pseudonym "J. R. Higgins." Formerly an avid rock photographer, he retired the camera with his final *Backlash* cover assignment in March 1991, traveling to Olympia to take photos of the not-yet-famous Nirvana. He also served as associate editor of *Backlash* and *Hype*. An award-winning news writer and columnist, he is employed as a staff writer for *Seattle Weekly*.

Major contributors

Dawn Anderson was Nirvana's first cheerleader, at least in the local music press. As editor of the Seattle rock 'zine *Backlash* from 1987 to 1991 and writer for *The Rocket* since 1981, Anderson has been a steadfast defender of "true rock" in all its forms, whether it be punk rock, heavy metal, or that thing we're not supposed to talk about anymore. She is current editor/publisher of *Backfire*, a quarterly rock 'zine.

Andrew Bartlett spent years as a freelance writer championing jazz of all stripes, but especially the most raucous, spirited kind. He completed a Ph.D. in a combined cultural study of African American literature and history and modern jazz in 1999 and has published academic essays on hip-hop, free jazz, and more. He is currently a music editor and project manager at amazon.com. Bartlett has lived in Seattle since 1989 and has a lovely family consisting of his wife, Leslie, and his kids, Benjamin and Allison.

Norm Bobrow has been a performer, promoter, and supporter of the Seattle jazz scene for the last six decades. He argues that the level of jazz talent in Seattle equals or exceeds that found in all the so-called jazz capitals—a sentiment he used to express on the programs for his jazz concerts with the phrase, "The names are everywhere else, there's only talent here." Still active as a singer/percussionist, he recently assembled an all-star band for Bainbridge Island's prestigious Spring Swing. The participation of multi-horn player Jay Thomas, pianist Bob Hammer, and tenor sax player Bill Ramsay reflects the high regard with which he is held among local jazz performers.

Gavin Borchert is the classical music critic for *Seattle Weekly* and an active composer in the Seattle area. His works have been performed by the Cincinnati Symphony, Indianapolis Symphony, and Seattle Youth Symphony. He has also written for the *Cincinnati Enquirer, Vancouver Sun*, and *Contemporary Music Review*, and is a contributor to the new edition of *Grove's Dictionary of Music and Musicians*.

Neal Skok has been writing about music for more than 20 years. His work has appeared in *Goldmine, Discoveries, Rolling Stone, Ugly Things*, and *Ptolemaic Terrascope*. The Redmond-based writer has also contributed liner notes for numerous albums and CDs. His label, Epilogue Records, has released several CDs of legendary Northwest rock acts of the 1960s and plans to reissue more historic music from the region.

John Chandler heads the Portland bureau of *The Rocket*, the Pacific Northwest's largest music magazine.

Michael Cox has followed the Seattle rock milieu for way too long. He is currently the editor-in-chief of the Strikethree.com baseball Web site, possibly as overcompensation.

Dan DePrez is a Portland-based blues writer.

Mark Fefer is a staff writer for *Seattle Weekly*, where he writes about jazz and municipal finance.

Matthew Fox is a Seattle rock guitarist and music writer, who has played with the bands Bitter End, Dr. Unknown, and Dinsdale.

Corinne Hollister is an award-winning arts and environmental writer based in Seattle.

Veronika Kalmar is the former editor of *The Rocket* and author of the book *Start Your Own Zine* (Hyperion). She now edits and publishes her own quarterly magazine, *The Iconoclast*, and is working on a book about independent record labels.

Jackie McCarthy is a former editor of the *Willamette Week* in Portland. She is currently a staff writer at *Seattle Weekly*, where she also served as music editor for two years. She has never owned any flannel shirts.

Kristen Schurr has fled Seattle for New York City, where she plays in a band, tends bar, and attends classes at Sarah Lawrence College. Her music reviews and articles have appeared in *Seattle Weekly* and *The Iconoclast*.

Rock/Pop

NORTHWEST ROCK AND POP

the arrival of rock 'n' roll in the mid-1950s both puzzled and excited those in the music industry. Some considered the new music a fad and tried to wring a few more hits out of Rosemary Clooney while jealously eyeing Elvis Presley's record sales. But visions of money danced in the heads of radio DJs and concert promoters, including several in the Northwest. And, as always, art followed commerce. A circuit of Washington and Oregon dance halls soon developed, and a slew of young bands formed to meet the demand for "teen" music. By the early 1960s, the "Northwest sound" was blasting forth; local record labels were producing singles by the dozens; and several big regional bands were developing large, rabid fan bases. The results occasionally leaked out to the rest of the world—the Kingsmen with their hit "Louie Louie," the mighty Paul Revere and the Raiders.

The psychedelic era scattered this carefully constructed situation to the winds. As they grew older, music fans "graduated" from teenage dances to more complex rock music performed in coffee houses and taverns. Bands could no longer make a living from the teen dance circuit. By the close of the 1960s, national labels and promoters had honed in on the regional scene. Big touring bands started using second-echelon national acts as openers, not the top local groups. As rock music became an album-oriented art form, the singles-dominated local labels began to disappear. The early and mid-1970s were ruled by bands that played cover versions of hit songs.

Although British-born punk rock was a commercial bust at first in the United States, the underground cult popularity of the music left its mark. The do-it-yourself ethic inspired bands to put on their own shows, release their own records, and—most important—write and perform their own songs. Bands like Portland's Billy Rancher and the Unreal Gods and Seattle's Heats and Cowboys re-created the regional circuit—selling records and selling out shows.

The Northwest remained a music-industry backwater, and bands took advantage of their obscurity: They created original music and built a culture around it, which the record companies lapped up after a few big albums: Nirvana's *Nevermind*, Soundgarden's *Superunknown*, and Pearl Jam's *Ten*.

The rest, of course is history. Here are a few terms to think about while you're reading it:

Northwest Sound. Think Sonics or Wailers circa 1960: raunchy guitar, chugging organ, honking sax, shouting vocals. The early teen dance bands played the circuit throughout Washington and Oregon and were inspired by each other's performances, covered each other's songs, and gradually coalesced into a recognizable musical genre.

Seattle Scene. This term arrived about 1985 or so, when the city had developed enough good bands yet was still undiscovered by the national rock press. This state of affairs allowed a goodly amount of musical cross-pollination, a common style of thrift-store-inspired dress, and a general surliness that made people snap at you when you mentioned the "Seattle scene" or, worse yet, used the term . . .

Grunge. There, I said it. More of a local joke than anything, this term went national to describe the distorted, 1970s-inspired guitar rock coming out of Seattle in the early 1990s. Bands like Nirvana, Soundgarden, and later, Pearl Jam got tagged with the "G-word"; the fashion socialites even institutionalized the flannel-shirt and torn-jeans look. Everyone hated the G-word at the time; now nobody can talk about early-1990s Seattle music without tossing this term around.

Lo-fi. Short for "low fidelity," naturally. Used to describe the unfinished, underproduced rock style pioneered in the late 1980s and early 1990s by Olympia, Washington, labels K and Kill Rock Stars and later adopted by national acts such as Pavement and Sebadoh.

Thrash. Like "speed metal," one of the many terms that sprang from the gradual merging of fast, aggressive heavy metal and fast, aggressive punk rock music during the mid- and late 1980s.

Trashrock. Think early Iggy Pop, the New York Dolls, Johnny Thunders, Hanoi Rocks, et al. Pretty much your standard rock 'n' roll, except it's gaunt, shiny, and dressed up in glamorous rags. Sample lines: "Oh yeah!" "Let's rock!"

The Accused

Formed 1982, Whidbey Island, Washington

as one of the Northwest's only true speedcore bands, the Accused knew just one trick, but they did it better than anyone else for more than a decade. They called it splatter rock—or heavy metal, or punk rock, depending on whether they were talking to European metal magazine *Kerrang!* or California punk publication *Maximum Rock 'n' Roll*. For most Seattle punk bands in the 1980s, rediscovering metal meant slowing down to a grinding dirge, but as the Accused honed their skills, they merely became harder and faster.

The main members were guitarist Tom Niemeyer and vocalist Blaine Cook, a diminutive, bug-eyed kid with a giant wrecking ball of a voice. Cook joined up with Niemeyer after leaving the Fartz when Seattle's original hardcore punk band changed directions and mutated into Ten Minute Warning.

The Accused released eleven albums and EPs throughout the 1980s and early 1990s, but were best remembered for their cartoon mascot, Martha Splatterhead. The cadaverous, slime-dripping, buxom Martha pulverized rapists, child molesters, and other lowlife, allowing the Accused to appeal to their fans' more morbid interests and be politically correct at the same time. Cook came up with the concept; then Niemeyer drew the original Martha Splatterhead, and various underground artists contributed their versions to later LPs.

The band's recording legacy begins with a virtually unlistenable LP shared with Seattle's Rejectors, and continues with the EP *Martha Splatterhead*, later rereleased with new songs as the LP *The Return of Martha Splatterhead*.

On tour the Accused quickly built up a national cult following among underage thrashers. As their reputation grew, they caught the attention of the hardcore metal label Combat Records, which signed them as a token punk band. Combat released *More Fun than an Open Casket Funeral* (1987) and *Martha Splatterhead's Maddest Stories Ever Told* (1988) before dropping the band in 1989.

Meanwhile, the folks at Nastymix, a Seattle rap label best known for breaking Sir Mix-A-Lot, were taking note of how well the national label Def Jam Records was doing with the new Slayer album, and began to show interest in the Accused. They signed the band and released the Accused's best album, *Grinning Like an Undertaker*, in 1990.

After numerous personnel changes the band settled into their most solid lineup yet: Niemeyer, Cook, bassist Alex Sibbald, and drummer Josh Sinder. By the early 1990s Niemeyer had developed into a ferocious heavy metal guitarist, and Sinder's intense drumming drove the band to new heights of amphetamine thrash. But this proved to be the band's peak. Niemeyer had begun to devote more time to his second band, Gruntruck. Sinder bailed after the next record, the EP *Straight Razor*. Nastymix fell on hard times when it was forced to defend itself in a lawsuit by its former star artist, Sir Mix-A-Lot. The label did manage to finance one last Accused album, *Splatter Rock*, before going out of business.

After Niemeyer quit the band completely, Cook kept it going through a few more personnel changes and two European tours before finally giving up. Both Sibbald and Sinder eventually joined Niemeyer in Gruntruck. But the guys can't resist the occasional reunion show, and their now-aging fans can still be counted on to put dignity aside and whip themselves into a communal frenzy. **DA**

Martha Splatterhead's Maddest Stories Ever Told

(1988, COMBAT/RELATIVITY)
This release takes the usual thrash and burn in unexpected directions: guest appearances from Metal Church's Kurdt Vanderhoof and rapper Sir Mix-A-Lot, and a cover of that great song by the Angry Samoans, "Lights Out."

Grinning Like an Undertaker

(1990, NASTYMIX)
A massive, raging geyser of puke and vinegar—the first recording to approach the intensity of the band's live shows. If you can't get into this, you are hopelessly lame.

Alice in Chains

Formed 1987, Seattle, Washington

heavy metal influences abounded in late 1980s Seattle rock, but unlike their grunge counterparts, Alice in Chains weren't trafficking in repackaged irony—these were actual metal boys gone legit. Guitarist Jerry Cantrell came from a South Seattle hairspray 'n' eyeliner outfit called Diamond Lie, while original bassist Mike Starr was a veteran of Gypsy Rose and the early 1980s satanic rockers Sato. When they joined singer Layne Staley and drummer Sean Kinney, they first called themselves Diamond Lie, then adopted the name of one of Staley's former bands—Alice in Chains. Tired of playing the metal/glam scene on bills with bands named Nasti Habitz and Ruff Toiz, the Alices dirtied their sound and image a bit and—surprise!—passed muster with the real scenesters.

Call it timing: These hefty-riff virtuosos appeared right when the Seattle bands were most enthralled with heavy rock. Cantrell, an accomplished guitarist, possessed a mastery of the wah-wah-pedal sounds then in vogue; Staley's vocals cheated low (often sweetened by Cantrell's harmonies) but kept their metal edge. Since Soundgarden had spawned some crossover of metal fans, Columbia Records was impressed enough by Alice in Chains to offer a contract (and mindful enough of the buzz around the band to release a limited edition, three-track tease of an EP entitled *We Die Young*). Good call. Alice in Chains' debut record, *Facelift*, released in 1990, helped kick open the big tent of Seattle music; Nirvana would knock the damn thing over the following year with *Nevermind*. The same critics who had sniffed at

Soundgarden's metal turn on *Louder than Love* a year earlier were appalled by Alice in Chains. The kids loved them. The heavier-than-heavy "We Die Young" was a radio staple; "Man in the Box" was nominated for a Grammy Award. (Alice in Chains would eventually notch a total of three Grammy nominations, but no wins.)

The band was caught enjoying its newfound fame a bit too much on the forgettable follow-up EP *Sap*, which features guest appearances by Soundgarden's Chris Cornell, Mudhoney's Mark Arm, and, believe it or not, Heart's Ann Wilson. They would not make the same mistake on their second full-length release, the bleak and frightening *Dirt* (1992). Heroin references abounded as Alice in Chains confronted listeners with their gloomy view of life (and death). Unhappy junkies were just fine with rock fans, apparently, as *Dirt* quickly rose to no. 6 on the U.S. charts. The album eventually sold 3 million copies; in its wake, *Sap* reached gold record status (500,000 copies sold), and *Facelift* was certified platinum (1 million copies). Starr became the first original member to leave the group in early 1993; new bassist Mike Inez joined up in time for a European swing and the summer Lollapalooza tour.

Although still unhappy (the group's two songs on the soundtrack for *The Last Action Hero* soundtrack were entitled "A Little Bitter" and "What the Hell Have I?"), the band took a more bittersweet angle and a semiacoustic approach on their next recording, the seven-song EP *Jar of Flies*. Recorded in seven days at Seattle's London Bridge studios, *Jar of Flies* jumped to the no. 1 spot on the *Billboard* charts after its release in early 1994, the first EP ever to accomplish that feat. But the band splintered over Staley's drug use; Cantrell and Kinney quit on the eve of a 1994 tour as openers for Metallica. Staley then recorded an album with Mad Season, a side project with Pearl Jam guitarist Mike McCready, bassist John Baker Saunders, and Screaming Trees drummer Barrett Martin. Alice in Chains re-formed in mid-1995 for their self-titled comeback recording. Despite a raucous opener ("Grind") and several slightly more uplifting lyrical efforts ("God Am"), the band sounds a bit tired on *Alice in Chains*. The next year the group that once set trends was following them with an acoustic record entitled *MTV Unplugged*. After a long idle period (even the Columbia Records timeline for the group stops in July 1996), Cantrell announced "a temporary break" from the band. His solo record, *Boggy Depot*, was released in early 1998, and his tour band included Kinney and Queensrÿche refugee Chris DeGarmo. **JB**

Facelift

(1990, COLUMBIA)
Heavy, high-energy songs. Jerry Cantrell stages a rock guitar clinic on the record that broke Alice in Chains nationally.

Jar of Flies

(1994, COLUMBIA)
Some of Layne Staley's most restrained, and best, vocal performances are included on this seven-song gem.

Beat Happening

Formed 1983, Olympia, Washington

Halo Benders

Formed 1994, Seattle/Olympia, Washington

Dub Narcotic Sound System

Formed 1994, Olympia, Washington

C alvin Johnson has the kind of voice kids use when imitating their dads. Droning solemnly in an exaggerated bass tone, that voice has been the focal point of all his bands, most notoriously Beat Happening.

Olympia, Washington, has become well known among underground music fans as a haven for riot grrrls as well as a breeding ground for sparsely instrumented, lo-fi pop bands that claim Beat Happening as their spiritual totem. Formed in 1983 and consisting of Johnson, Heather Lewis, and Bret Lunsford trading off on guitar, vocals, and drums, Beat Happening created rudimentary, childlike pop songs that the rock press dubbed "cuddlecore."

Johnson also founded K Records, known mostly for its huge stable of lo-fi bands but also for hardcore punk (Fitz of Depression), experimental-classical (Timothy Brock), and even a Beck album.

Lacking a bass player and a surly attitude, Beat Happening would seem to be the antithesis of Seattle steroid rock. But on closer listening, it's clear that these guys were hardly "anti" anything; they were merely playing the kind of music they liked, satisfied to not reach beyond their grasp. Plenty of imitators took up this simplicity as a religion, but minimalist pop minus songwriting chops equals "weakcore." Few of their imitators could match the songwriting cleverness of Johnson and Lewis.

Beat Happening's first full-length recordings were cassette-only releases on K, the first two of which were rereleased, along with their first single, on *1983–1985*, a retrospective CD. Beat Happening released two more albums on K, *Jamboree* (1988) and *Black Candy* (1989), both of which were later rereleased in 1992 after the band had signed to Seattle's Sub Pop Records. The band produced two full-length CDs coreleased on Sub Pop and K, *Dreamy* (1991) and *You Turn Me On* (1992).

Bret Lunsford eventually moved back to his native Anacortes, Washington, and formed the band D+ with bassist Karl Blau and drummer Phil Elvrum. Lunsford's tunes are understated and sometimes somber, but the startlingly loud, exuberant drumming makes for an overall happy noise. The band's sensitive, sincere pop music is best enjoyed on the long-player *Dandelion Seeds* (1998, K/Know Yr. Own).

In 1994 Johnson teamed up with Doug Martsch and Ralf Youtz from Built to Spill, Wayne Flower from Treepeople, and producer and all-around experimental wacko Steve Fisk to form the Halo Benders. This band continued the Beat Happening

Olympia

"This town is our town / This town is so glamorous / I bet you'd live here if you could / And be one of us." Maybe that Go-Go's song isn't specific to Olympia, Washington, but the incestuous little town rightly fits the bill as another Hipsterville, USA. It's ten blocks of hell or good clean alternative living, depending on your perspective.

Besides the State Capitol Building and loggers, a few famous fundamentals can be found in Olympia—the Positively 4th Street record store, riot grrrls, the festival YoYo A Go Go, and the labels K Records and Kill Rock Stars. Most Northwest rock types live, lived, or at least slept in the town at some point.

Olympia is as easy to mock as any place where people are trying to do more than emulate sitcoms. Half the folks just sit around looking alternative, but many are politically and socially active. Things to do: Have coffee at the Smithfield, drink liquor at the Reef, play pool and dance at Thekla, and see bands at the Capitol Theatre and Aerospace.

In the early 1980s in Olympia, Bruce Pavitt was publishing the *Sub Pop* fanzine, which preceded the record label. The Capitol Theatre was called the Backstage; the Surf Club was new wave and sat where Thekla is now. In 1982 Calvin Johnson's nascent K Records put out its first recording, *Supreme Cool Beings*. If you ordered a record from K and it wasn't available, Candice Petersen—an intern in 1986, a business partner now—sent a postcard signed "Love, Candice." People were nice.

The town has a hippie college, the Evergreen State College, where Lois Maffeo, then of the band Courtney Love, had a regular radio show on the campus station KAOS. While she played women-led and alternative rock, the other KAOS people were publishing *OP*, a small music magazine. Their festival in 1984 brought many more bands than they expected.

Pat Maley (of YoYo Recordings and the band Courtney Love) put out his first new wave record in 1987. Although hardly anyone knows about it, it was aptly called *Big Idea*. Slim Moon's Kill Rock Stars label has become a grumbly alternative to the generally perky K Records. The fanzine *Punk in My Vitamins*, published by Vern Rumsey (Unwound and Long Hind Legs), metamorphosed into a record label. Nirvana and the Melvins, both of next-door Grays Harbor County, recorded with Kill Rock Stars. The label put out a fairly influential compilation in 1991, *(Kill Rock Stars)* which got the town more notice. The next compilation that relied heavily on Olympia bands was YoYo's *Throw* (1992).

K Records' International Pop Underground Convention brought a lot of attention and people to Olympia in 1993. An inspired Pat Maley started up Yo-Yo A Go Go, which took the festival's place the next year. The festival still brings local and international bands, but now swarms with the same tired music industry routine that goes on everywhere.

Olympia was a better town than most in which to be a female artist. The hippie ideal of equality spilled over from Evergreen State College into the community at large. Later came the whole riot grrrl movement—mostly just some young women wanting to figure out how to play guitar without getting harassed for being girls. The riot grrrl movement may have been formed in Washington, D.C., but the attitude had Olympia written all over it: you can do anything; art is yours for the taking even if you've never done it before.

One of Olympia's best qualities for a music fan is its devotion to all-ages shows. Since so many kids could see bands, they found it easier to start playing their own music. Olympia's kid action thrived at party houses, while the Tropicana, a hardcore all-ages club, and the Central and Glass Houses put on punk shows. The Mushroom House in nearby Lacey was a haven to dancing punks and alternative types. The Capitol Theatre is the most consistently good place for all-ages shows. These places are the main reason so many new young bands have popped up in the last ten years. Dub Narcotic Sound System, Team Dresch, Sleater-Kinney, Unwound, Mecca Normal, Beat Happening, Fitz of Depression, plus many others have been the band of the day at varying times. K Records and Kill Rock Stars are thriving, Yo-Yo A Go Go has gotten international attention, and Slim Moon recently opened a new record store. A great deal is still happening in the music scene, despite a few personal conflicts. But there's no point in being critical; I'd rather live in Olympia than Spanaway.

—Kristen Schur

aesthetic with a fuller sound (including bass) and prettier vocals courtesy of Martsch. The Halo Benders released two CDs on K, *God Don't Make No Junk* (1994) and *Don't Tell Me Now* (1996).

Johnson's more recent project is a white-boy art-funk band called Dub Narcotic Sound System (also the name of his new recording studio). Its recorded output includes two full-length CDs, *Boot Party* and *Out of Your Mind*, as well as several EPs and 12-inch singles.

Dub Narcotic's personnel has changed over the years, but the constant elements are Johnson's distinctive vocals and his spastic onstage flailing, which can rouse even the most dour alternative rockers in the audience to gyrate, knowing they at least won't look more ridiculous than the man onstage. **DA**

Dreamy

(1991, K/SUB POP)
Of all the Beat Happening albums, this features the best songwriting, including the near-hit "Red Head Walking."

God Don't Make No Junk

(1994, K)
The Halo Benders' high point features pretty guitars, psychedelic moments, and vocals that range from melodic (Doug Martsch) to atonal (Calvin Johnson). It's all worth it just to hear Johnson solemnly intone, "Don't touch my bikini."

Out of Your Mind

(1998, K)
Dub Narcotic Sound System is James Brown meets wavo funk meets Johnson's running commentary of non sequiturs. The music is not quite the same without the visuals, but this is Dub Narcotic's best recorded work so far.

Bighorn

Formed 1970, Seattle, Washington

the annual Pain in the Grass outdoor summer concerts at Seattle Center have been going strong for years, but few people remember that, two decades ago, one local band drew crowds of ten thousand in their several appearances there.

Bighorn was Seattle's most popular band during the 1970s. Early members were Robb Clarke (vocals), Bob Anderson (drums), Marv Jensen (piano, organ, keyboard bass), Rusty Williams (guitar), and Bob Marcy (sax, flute, congas, vocals). In 1970 the band recruited a manager: Scott Soules, then a University of Washington student looking for groups to play keg parties.

Bighorn's first paying gig ($100 for the whole band) was December 31, 1970, at the Flightline, a club in the south end of Seattle. The band's early set lists included songs by Santana, the Doors, Jethro Tull, and Neil Young. A former member of the band Second Coming, Clarke was a brash, aggressive vocalist who excelled on Bighorn's stunning Rolling Stones covers. Keyboardist Jensen used effects pedals, reverb, and feedback to produce an amazing array of sounds. Marcy, an immediate attention grabber with his flowing red hair and wild stage antics, resembled Robert Plant or Roger Daltrey. An original song from this era was "Mr. M," usually the opener for the band's second or third set. Jensen, sometimes wearing a cape, would sneak out to the keyboards and start a hypnotic, spooky "Phantom of the Opera" organ line, and then be joined by the rest of the band as the stage lights came on.

In mid-1971 the band made its first personnel changes, adding bassist James Kenfield and guitarist Toby Bowen, and took its first extended road trip, playing clubs in Eastern Washington and Oregon. By that fall, Bighorn had added Vancouver, British Columbia, to their show resumé and picked up a new drummer, Fred Zeufeldt. A former member of several big acts of the 1960s (the Viceroys and the later lineups American Eagle and Surprise Package), the well-connected Zeufeldt got the band a month-long residency at Harvey Wallbanger's, a prestigious San Diego club. Soules and Zeufeldt began making aggressive plans for the band—and original songwriting was at the top of their list.

Starting in 1972 with more out-of-town gigs, the band recruited the multitalented Rick Randle—a lead vocalist, guitarist, and keyboardist—to replace Jensen. After Randle's original songs quickly worked into Bighorn's sets, and Marcy emerged as second lead vocalist, former frontman Clarke became redundant and left the band. Norm Lombardo was brought in on bass but was soon replaced by Portlander Ken Steimonts. The new-look Bighorn that opened for Foghat at Seattle's Paramount Theatre was well received.

In 1973 and 1974, Bighorn was the top draw among Northwest bands. They picked up more opening spots, including 1974 shows with Bachman Turner Overdrive at the Moore Theatre and Iron Butterfly and Sugarloaf at the Paramount. In 1974 the group released its first record, the single "I Get High"/"Takin' Me Down."

Although Seattle radio stations refused to play "I Get High," the song and the band became a hit with DJs in Yakima.

During the next few months, Randle left to form Child (he would later play with the Randle Rossburg Band and with Striker), and Bowen and Steimonts also departed (their band Aviary released an album on CBS/Epic in 1979). Their replacements were Steve Isham (keyboards), John Lucas (guitar), and former Bighorn bassist Kenfield, returning for his second stint with the band.

As manager Soules still had a firm grip on Bighorn. He and Zeufeldt, who shared his business-oriented outlook, carefully structured the band's set lists with odd progressive tunes by Yes and Kansas. The band also played a Jeff Beck medley and performed the entire second side of the Beatles' *Abbey Road* in concert. In July 1975 Bighorn headlined a show at Seattle's Seward Park that drew six thousand people. The opening act was Heart (some of the cover photos on Heart's *Dreamboat Annie* album were taken at this show).

The band played on during 1976 with an eight-week tour featuring dates in five Western states. The year also brought a few odd experiences: Bighorn was to perform with international acts Blue Oyster Cult, Bachman Turner Overdrive, and Rainbow at a three-day outdoor festival in Stateline, Idaho, but the show was canceled after the crowd rioted and burned the stage to the ground. One of the band's Seattle Center outdoor shows was marred when a stagehand accidentally overloaded their flashpots and the resulting explosions damaged not only equipment but people's hearing.

Bighorn underwent another major transition in early 1977 with the arrival of keyboardist Peter Davis, a melodic player and songwriter in the Elton John mold. As a major record deal seemed to be in the works, management cleaned house and rebuilt Bighorn around Davis, keeping only the band name and Marcy as second vocalist. The other slots were filled by Davis's friends Joe Shikany (guitar), Michael Ipsen (bass), and Steve Adamek (drums).

The Davis-led version of the band released its debut album on Columbia Records in early 1979. Featuring only original songs (Davis and Adamek did most of the writing), it was a fine effort but somewhat at odds with the group's live performances. In concert Bighorn was a high-powered, showy guitar band, but the album's heavily produced songs were more melodic and keyboard oriented.

Despite the national exposure the band received by opening for arena acts such as Van Halen, Boston, the J. Geils Band, and Journey, Bighorn was still playing the same clubs in their native Northwest. When their paychecks couldn't even cover the cost of hauling around the huge onstage setup, the band went into debt.

Realizing that their brand of showy rock was being displaced by a whole new breed of music, the members of Bighorn re-created themselves in 1979 as the Allies, a new wave pop act; the original lineup was Ipsen, Adamek, Shikany, and David Kincaid (guitar, vocals). With Soules still managing the band, the Allies continued as a major Seattle draw well into the 1980s. Bighorn is remembered for their unusual ability to evolve and reinvent themselves over and over, each incarnation better than the last. **NS**

Bighorn

(1978, CBS)
This major label release shows off progressive hooks reminiscent of Styx and Boston. The instrumental highlights are Bob Marcy's woodwinds, Joe Shikany's melodic guitar, and Peter Davis's keyboards.

Billy Rancher and the Unreal Gods

Formed 1981, Portland, Oregon

every rock scene has its tragic figures, but few can compare with Portland's Billy Rancher, a local rocker who actually attained the Holy Grail of a major label contract but ended up losing everything, including his life.

Rancher and his younger brother, Lenny, had a successful bar band called the Malchicks in 1980, but musical and personal tensions between the two split the band in early 1981. That was fine with Billy—tired of the Stones-ish Malchicks and intrigued by many musical styles (including new wave, rockabilly, and ska), he had a master plan for his next band. Unlike normal groups, who hung around with friends before and after their set drinking beer and smoking cigarettes, Rancher's new band was going to be professional: show up backstage at the club in time for the set and leave, just like the out-of-town bands that Billy and Lenny used to meet by staking out the Portland Motor Inn after shows. The members would wear stage costumes, not their street clothes. Completing Rancher's wish list: tight shows, carefully followed set lists, and even onstage go-go dancers (the Goddesses A-Go-Go). Needless to say, a few punk rockers were appalled, but Portland had never seen anything like Billy Rancher. Lanky and good-looking, the blond-haired Rancher was an awesome stage performer—charismatic, impulsive, and always "up." The band—ex-Malchick David Stricker on bass, Jon DuFresne on guitar, Billy Flaxel on drums, and Alf Ryder on keyboards—had dozens of songs to choose from, as Rancher was a prolific songwriter unlimited by musical styles.

Debuting in June 1981, the Unreal Gods were the hot band in Portland by the end of the year, making the trip up Interstate 5 to play the Seattle clubs as well. But during this heady period of quick popularity, Rancher had been diagnosed with testicular cancer. After two operations, everyone was hopeful the disease had been halted. Rancher, a canny promoter, found a Chinese restaurant with a huge lounge (converted from an old bowling alley) and started promoting weekend shows there, with all-ages performances held on off-nights to let the kids experience the Unreal Gods. In June 1982, the long-awaited album was released: *Boom Chuck Rock Now!* featured many favorites from the band's club sets, although it is probably best remembered by Northwest rock fans for its eye-catching cover photo of the shirtless, makeup-wearing Unreal Gods. Even though they couldn't crack the heavy metal–dominated rotation of Portland's top radio station, KGON, everybody else loved the album. On a side trip to New York that fall, the band recorded five songs and entertained the locals at a few live shows (an impressed Bruce Springsteen attended one performance). The band's next project, in spring 1983, was a video. The results never made MTV but, again, their Portland following loved it. By the end of the year the band had inked a contract with Arista Records.

The Unreal Gods didn't realize it, but they had entered the downhill portion of their career, even as they were celebrating their newfound success. First the band was matched with an unsympathetic producer, Peter McIan (then a hot name for his contribution to Men at Work's no. 1 album, *Business as Usual*). Next McIan and the Arista executives tried to get the Unreal Gods to "focus" their sound, ditching the ska excursions and other oddities that made the band so interesting live. Their long visit to Los Angeles in summer 1984 to record for Arista led to growing frustration between band, producer, and label. Worse yet, Rancher's cancer had returned. During his long hospitalization, the band tried to play as a four-piece group, then split in early 1985 after a few last gigs with Rancher. Arista shelved the record and released the group from their contract. Weakened by the advancing cancer, Rancher threw himself into solo projects, even singing onstage from a chair with his final band, Mr. Groove. Rancher died December 2, 1986, at age 29. **JB**

Boom Chuck Rock Now!

(1982, LOCALS ONLY RECORDINGS)
Boom Chuck Rock Now! is now available on CD, thanks to a surge of interest in Billy Rancher and the Unreal Gods set off by *Rocky Road*, journalist Bill Reader's excellent book about the band. Don't miss this album; Rancher was a fine songwriter and singer, and his work shows, above all, an impish sense of humor.

Bluebird

Formed 1968, Mercer Island, Washington

mercer Island, one of Seattle's wealthiest suburbs, has produced few rock 'n' roll musicians of note, but the members of Bluebird are an exception. The band's music looked to the future and the past. Deeply influenced by the Northwest's resident folkies-gone-psychedelic, the Daily Flash, Bluebird also demonstrated their love of the Byrds in their sound. Another key influence came through a chance meeting with fellow Mercer Island musician Jeff Beals, who told guitarist David Baroh that country rock was huge in Los Angeles. The comment encouraged Baroh to learn pedal-steel guitar and made Bluebird the first Northwest rock band to embrace country rock.

In August 1968 Baroh and bassist Kevin Marin formed Bluebird with friends Phil Klitgaard (drums) and Tony Pugel (guitar). In early 1969 another friend, John Soltero, replaced Pugel; the band's classic lineup was in place. All four shared deep friendships and common musical interests, and—perhaps most important—had played together over the years in various bands, including the Scarabs, the Loose Chippins, the Thymes, and Punch.

By late 1969 Bluebird was firmly entrenched as a top Northwest act. They played the Sky River Rock Festival and opened for national acts such as Joe Cocker, Bread, Golden Earring, and Rick Nelson. They were the house band at Seattle's Trolley Club. Among the many national stars who stopped by to hear them or even join them onstage for jams were members of the Flying Burrito Brothers, Buffalo Springfield, and Poco.

Other people were essential to the creativity and success of Bluebird: Chet Tozer, another old friend, was their longtime road manager and advisor. He would later serve as a roadie for Heart in the mid-1970s. Burl Barer, one of Seattle's top DJs (for the "hip" station, KOL), took the group under his wing and went on to manage and produce them for their entire career.

Bluebird's first single was released in September 1969. The A-side, "Billy Drake," was a clever original song about an outlaw (a theme that the Eagles would develop later); the flip side was a cover of Bob Dylan's "I Shall Be Released." Vancouver's Terry Jacks produced the next release, "Country Boy Blues" (June 1970).

The band's third single, "Modessa," a magical song about pirates, oceans, and love, proved to be their recording high point. Released in early 1971, the song's twelve-string riff, subtle orchestration, explosive percussion, and hypnotic bass line made this Baroh and Klitgaard composition unforgettable. Radio was good to "Modessa"— it received substantial airplay throughout Washington and Oregon. Two subsequent singles—"Whatever Happened to Rock & Roll" and a cover of the Searchers' "Needles and Pins"—earned some airplay but couldn't compete with "Modessa."

In 1972 Bluebird took a sharp turn. With their tight harmonies and intricate musicianship, they were falling out of fashion as audiences started favoring heavy metal bands like Deep Purple, Black Sabbath, and Grand Funk Railroad. The band responded with their elaborate parody, Grand Theft Auto. Baroh was billed as "Crowbar Mahoon," Marin was "Riley Sedgemont III," and Klitgaard took the name "P. K. Skins" (Soltero declined to participate). An album was recorded in 1972 by Barer (renamed "D. B. Fader" for the occasion) and was even played on local stations. Overdistorted and muddy power-trio riffing accompanied Baroh as he screamed lyrics skewering subjects from Michael Jackson to drug use to fast food.

Grand Theft (they dropped "Auto" when Grand Funk dropped "Railroad") played a couple of gigs but soon went back to being Bluebird exclusively. The parody album was rediscovered by record collectors in the 1980s (original copies can bring up to $500). The Grand Theft tapes were released on CD in 1996 as *Hiking into Eternity*, and strangely enough, the album was nominated for a Grammy Award in 1997.

Bluebird soldiered on. Soltero left in early 1973. Emerson Hoefs, another old friend, joined on guitar, and the band dropped country rock for a more commercial Top 40 approach. This was probably the most successful period for the band, but it was obvious Bluebird was becoming nothing more than a job.

In July 1973 Marin and Hoefs left and were replaced by Tom Chapman (guitar) and Ric Niemer (bass), who were in turn replaced by Craig Critchfield and Gary Barnes. At the end of 1973, Bluebird called it quits. Baroh and Klitgaard continued a few months more as Nash Rambler.

All the principal Bluebird members have continued in music and, more important, remained good friends. The band performed in 1997 for their thirty-year Mercer Island High School reunion and sounded as tight and harmonious as ever. Bluebird was an anomaly in the rich history of Northwest music. They were originators, unique in their blending of rock and country, and we have to be grateful for their unprecedented adventure into the fun of Grand Theft. **NS**

Hiking into Eternity

(1996, EPILOGUE)
This is the entire legendary 1972 album by Bluebird as Grand Theft, and includes another 45 minutes of practices, demos, and unreleased studio sessions. A slamming brew of heavy blues, psychedelia, and madness.

Built to Spill
Formed 1992, Boise, Idaho

Treepeople
Formed 1988, Boise, Idaho

a lthough guitarist Doug Martsch is Treepeople's most noted alumnus (and the only member of that band most people can name), he started out as the band's least famous member. That's because the other three original Treepeople members—guitarist and vocalist Scott Schmaljohn, bassist Pat Brown, and drummer Wayne Rhino Flower—were all veterans of State of Confusion, a well-known mid-1980s Boise punk band. When State of Confusion split in 1988, weary after years of touring and a bad experience with a record company, they hooked up with Martsch and released a three-song EP on Boise's Silence Records. They headed for Seattle the following year.

The band's live shows in Seattle received a positive reception, as did their two 1990 releases. *Guilt, Regret, Embarrassment*, released on Westworld Records (later rereleased on K Records), is still Martsch's favorite Treepeople record; *Time Whore* (1990) was recorded in Seattle by ace producer Jack Endino and released on vinyl by

Silence Records. The following year *Time Whore* was paired with the seven-song EP *Something Vicious for Tomorrow* (1992) and rereleased on CD by Seattle's C/Z Records.

By this time, Martsch's guitar style was well formulated. Neither rock flash nor punky note spewing, his melodic, angular lines were the lead instrument on most Treepeople tunes. (Martsch's and Schmaljohn's playing on the twin-guitar middle section of *Time Whore*'s "Radio Man" especially invokes the interplay of Television's Tom Verlaine and Richard Lloyd.) Rhino Flower left the band before the release of *Something Vicious for Tomorrow* and was replaced by T. Dallas Reed. Martsch's final Treepeople record was *Just Kidding* (1992), which featured Reed on bass and Eric Akre on drums. (The band, minus Martsch, released a final album on C/Z in 1994, *Actual Reenactment.*)

Returning to Boise, Martsch joined with guitarist/bassist Brett Netson and drummer Ralf Youtz to record the first Built to Spill record, *Ultimate Alternative Wavers.* Released on C/Z in 1993, it introduced to the world Martsch's plaintive, slightly high-pitched singing voice and reintroduced his talent for intelligent, tasty guitar lines. Most surprising was the exposure of his songwriting chops, especially longer, multisection pieces featuring sharp changes in tempo and feel. Having established a sound, Martsch tossed it aside blithely on the second Built to Spill long-player, *There's Nothing Wrong with Love* (1994), a selection of shorter, more focused songs about his youth.

Along the way, Built to Spill also released several singles, collected on *The Normal Years* (1996). The credits of this album sum up the band's ever-shifting lineup—nine different supporting players are cited. Martsch's most common rhythm section is bassist Brett Nelson (who has played with him in bands since junior high school) and drummer Andy Capps; other common collaborators include guitarist Brett Netson of Caustic Resin, drummer Scott Plouf, and cellist John McMahon. Martsch also recorded an EP with Netson and his bandmates, entitled simply *Built to Spill/Caustic Resin* (1995).

Built to Spill's *Perfect from Now On* (1997) features another load of gorgeous guitar work and unusual song structures. Take the album opener, "Randy Described Eternity," which starts with meandering, languid guitar lines, picks up intensity through a verse and chorus, and continues switching from quiet to intense, as guitars fade in and out of the mix. The group's next album—and the second in a row featuring Martsch, Nelson, and Plouf—was *Keep It Like a Secret* (1999). **JB**

Something Vicious for Tomorrow; Time Whore

(1992, C/Z)
Double up with these excellent Treepeople EPs available as a team on CD.

Perfect from Now On

(1997, WARNER BROS.)
A Martsch guitar show for Built to Spill, with some of his best songs yet.

Candlebox

Formed 1991, Seattle, Washington

a s Soundgarden underwent the gradual transition from ironic metal-edged punkers to full-blown arena rockers, and Pearl Jam offered the winning combination of three-quarters 1970s guitar rock and one-quarter alternative influences, the explosion of Candlebox's self-titled 1993 debut onto the national charts was probably inevitable. Although the guys had obviously listened to a few Pearl Jam and Soundgarden discs, Candlebox's triple-platinum status completed the curve of the Seattle sound from alternative back to mainstream rock. This band could've opened for Golden Earring or Uriah Heep back in 1976. Frontman Kevin Martin's phrasing shows signs of Robert Plant and Paul Rodgers, and, while the band isn't afraid to play slow and bluesy, the emphasis is on straightforward big-riff rocking. "Far Behind" cracked the Top 20 as a single, and several other tracks got comparable radio play.

The band (Martin, bassist Bardi "No relation" Martin, guitarist Peter Klett, and drummer Scott Mercado) naturally caught crap from the locals for signing to Madonna's Maverick label, for sounding somewhat derivative, and especially for being ill-mannered enough to become big stars while far more credible hipsters were selling thirty thousand copies of their latest independent-label releases. None other than Courtney Love, a noted carpetbagger herself, confided to the rock press that Candlebox were just a bunch of out-of-town guys transplanted to Seattle to cash in on the grunge thing. Wrong. The Candlebox guys were legit locals who had deftly managed to avoid any degree of success in their previous musical experiments. Mercado brought the most recognizable resumé, including a brief stint with revolving-door combo Sky Cries Mary and a tour of duty with the First Thought, a band best remembered for having included singer/songwriter Kristen Barry in an early incarnation.

Candlebox played it safe with their second effort, *Lucy* (1995). The album, a respectable seller, never strayed far from the style established on *Candlebox*. Although arguably more musically adventurous, it included fewer catchy radio songs. The band's next release, *Happy Pills* (1998), was produced by veteran Ron Nevison (Led Zeppelin, the Who) and features a new drummer, Dave Krusen, known for his work on Pearl Jam's album *Ten*. **JB**

Candlebox

(1993, MAVERICK)
Don't hate them because they're popular. Instead, listen to songs like the mesmerizing "You" or the riff-heavy "Arrow" and get in touch with your inner arena rocker.

Cherry Poppin' Daddies

Formed 1989, Eugene, Oregon

While everybody else in Eugene, Oregon, was busy excavating flannel shirts from the dark recesses of their closets, singer Steve Perry was experimenting with something a little more dapper. Already bored with what he perceived as artless guitar rock, Perry (no relation to the Journey guy) assembled a crack squad of frisky young jazzbos (including a horn section of University of Oregon music school students) to help him expand on his love of big band and Dixieland music. At first they were called Mr. Wiggle, but this rather pedestrian moniker was canned in favor of the Cherry Poppin' Daddies, a name Perry copped from an old Dixieland tune.

The name proved to be a source of friction for the band, even to this day. The more politically sensitive members of the community felt the band was somehow celebrating incest and rape, so for a short time, Perry and his cohorts backed down, calling themselves the Bad Daddies. Finally, egged on by other members of the local music community, Perry brought back "Cherry Poppin'," figuring the name would determine who the really dedicated fans were.

There was simply nothing like the Daddies during the early part of the decade; the so-called swing-revival and cocktail-nation flags had yet to be unfurled. The band's incendiary performances were equal parts jump blues, funk, ska, insouciant lounge jazz, and sophisticated big band glitz, always gilded by a streamlined groove you could hang your wash on. Through ceaseless touring, the Daddies developed faithful audiences who came out to shake some serious tail feather whenever the band came to town. In 1990 the Daddies released *Ferociously Stoned*, probably their most swinging album until the *Zoot Suit Riot* compilation came out. Tunes like "Master and Slave," "Doctor Bones," and "Drunk Daddy" shake uncontrollably with Cab Calloway–like "hidey-hos" and first-rate horn charts that blast the room like last call at the Savoy Ballroom. Add to the mix Perry's unflinching lyrics about society's underbelly ("I can't chew my food my face is sore / Momma didn't come home last evening / Neighbors say that she's a whore"), and you have an alcohol-burning dance machine.

Throughout the next several years, the Daddies became one of the biggest draws in the Northwest, even though they appeared to be the only representatives of the swing society in the region. Bands came and went, but the Daddies continually found themselves on bills with grungers, greasers, and goons. And still they persevered, easily bewitching crowds with their crazed rhythms, reminding dormant dancers that a little activity does wonders for the cardiovascular system.

They continued to record, releasing two more studio albums, *Rapid City Muscle Car* (1994) and *Kids on the Street* (1996). Though the records sold fairly well, it was the unbridled velocity of their live shows that knocked out the crowds. At the behest of their manager (who sold albums at their concerts), Perry and company assembled a compilation of their liveliest swing numbers and recorded a few new ones; *Zoot Suit Riot* was the album that brought them to Mojo Records and gave them furious chart escalation and the eagerly hoped-for "regular rotation" status. The majority of the band has been replaced more than once, though bassist Dan Schmid and trumpeter Dana Hiteman have remained constant. **JC**

Zoot Suit Riot

(1997, MOJO)
A super sampler record, featuring the most swing-oriented moments of the Daddies' early career.

City Zu

Formed 1965, Bellevue, Washington

modeled after Paul Revere and the Raiders and Don and the Goodtimes, with nods to the Righteous Brothers and classic R&B, City Zu, based in Bellevue, Washington, fit in perfectly on the area's teen dance circuit.

Led by Jerry "Zu" Matheson (vocals, sax), City Zu was a hotbed of 1960s Northwest talent. Other founding members included Doug Heath (guitar), Brad Miller (guitar), Mike Cox (bass), Mike Garland (drums), and Chuck Harcus (keyboards). All would later achieve individual musical success: Cox and Garland became one of the hottest session rhythm sections in the Northwest, and played live dates backing such luminaries as Merrilee Rush and Barney Armstrong. Heath and later City Zu bassist Ron Foos played with Paul Revere and the Raiders for more than two decades. In Miller's post–City Zu career, he led a band that developed an impressive body of original material over the years.

City Zu was extremely well rehearsed yet spontaneous enough to become one of the Northwest's most entertaining live acts. They wore classy matching suits, and the audiences—especially the girls—loved them. Matheson and Miller had perfect onstage chemistry, and everyone's musicianship was impeccable. Dance promoters knew City Zu was a top draw—their first few years saw them booked constantly throughout Washington and Oregon. In 1967 City Zu won a Seattle "Battle of the Bands" competition; the prize was a Los Angeles recording session and a release on Columbia Records. They cut the song "Give a Little Bit," written by Glen Campbell and Jerry Fuller. The Knickerbockers (best known for their 1966 hit "Lies") helped out musically, and the song was a Northwest smash. Fuller, who had worked with Rick Nelson and would soon produce Gary Puckett, didn't push the single enough nationally, but City Zu had a taste of fame. Manager Mac Keith got them a deal with Dot Records, which released two subsequent singles.

Matheson, one of the most energetic frontmen to come out of the Northwest, had far-ranging talents, from endless stage antics to gritty saxophone work to an uncanny Mick Jagger impersonation. And, perhaps above all, he knew how to keep a band together and make a living at it. The late 1960s were extremely busy for City Zu, both on the dance circuit and in high-profile concerts. Major acts they opened for included the Association, the Beach Boys, the Raiders, the Who, and Buffalo Springfield. Among their especially memorable concerts were a gig near Centralia with the Jimmy Page–era Yardbirds and a giant rock festival in Eugene, Oregon, on July 26, 1969, with such stars as Them, Alice Cooper, the Youngbloods, the Byrds, and the Doors.

By the early 1970s, the teen dance circuit was winding down. Matheson broke away from the band's Far West Entertainment booking agency and went with promoter Terry Schmidt. City Zu became a favorite on the lucrative lounge circuit and regularly played such Seattle venues as Golden Tides and Pier 70. Musicians came and went, although ex-Wailer Neil Andersson's stint with the band was a definite highlight.

In the early 1980s, Matheson folded City Zu and joined the Neil Rush Band. With two fine sax players (Rush had been playing professionally since the late 1950s), the act was excellent. City Zu was reactivated in 1983 and began playing in a five-state area as featured entertainers for the classy Greenwood Inn chain. The last decade has been even better for Matheson and City Zu. The band added a new co-frontperson in Kathy Childers, a striking lead vocalist and spot-on guitarist. They have broken into the ultracompetitive and highly lucrative Nevada casino circuit.

Jerry "Zu" Matheson is an anomaly in the music business—a full-time musician for more than thirty years with no plans to quit. He and City Zu are Northwest treasures. **NS**

Coffin Break

Formed 1987, Seattle, Washington

Coffin Break's classic punk sound made them the odd men out in grungetown. But in the late 1980s, the band introduced the concept of do-it-yourself touring to Seattle bands—unquestionably aiding the region's climb to national recognition.

New York City transplant Peter Litwin (guitar, vocals) and Bremerton homeboy Rob Skinner (bass, vocals) formed Coffin Break with pals Brad Jones (guitar) and Steve Corless (drums) in 1987, and immediately set to work recording and distributing their first crude demo tape. The band just as quickly became a three-piece, subtracting Corless and Jones and stealing drummer Dave Brooks from the band Cat Butt, which was practicing in the rehearsal room across the hall from Coffin Break's space.

The conventional wisdom at the time was that a band needed to get an album out to justify a tour. But while bigger bands were sitting on their thumbs in Seattle, Coffin Break went up and down the West Coast twice, peddling copies of their cassette along the way.

The band's first single ("Noise Patch"/"Boxes" and "Obsession") was due to be released on Sub Pop Records in 1988, but the label backed out, citing creative differences. They were right: Coffin Break's pure punk stand didn't quite jibe with the Sub Pop formula. The band had a streak of humor in both their stage shows (they always played barefoot) and their habit of writing tunes that cheerfully parodied the style of other bands ("Noise Patch" was a cheeky take on the band Soundgarden). The single eventually came out on C/Z Records, and the band marked its release with a full U.S. tour.

The band released the EP *Psychosis* (1989), the LP *Rupture* (1990), and three fine singles on C/Z, all the while burning up the road with long national tours. The band's favorite gigs were all-ages shows—ironically, because a repressive Seattle law kept them from playing many in their hometown. Curiously enough, the first Coffin Break single was recorded "live" at the OK Hotel (then a Seattle all-ages spot, now a bar) without an audience—before they could start their set, the cops had busted the show and sent all the kids home.

Coffin Break recorded their second full-length record, *Crawl* (1991), on Epitaph Records, but not before finally releasing a single on Sub Pop ("Lies"/"Pray," 1990). Their final LP, *Thirteen* (1992), also featured a second guitarist, Jeff Lorien. But things were clearly winding down in the summer of 1993, when the band took an "indefinite break." The break became definite when Skinner quit to form the band Pop Sickle; Litwin later formed his own band, Softy. **JB**

Psychosis

(1989, C/Z)

Coffin Break's first EP and best record features some of the band's finest straight-ahead punk originals, plus several cheeky songs parodying other Seattle bands. The CD release also includes *Rupture*, Coffin Break's first LP.

No Sleep till the Stardust Motel

(1992, C/Z)

Sure, it's a compilation of singles and rare tracks, but *Stardust Motel* is a delightful documentation of the band's musical progress. It includes some of Coffin Break's best (and hardest-to-find) songs, all the way back to the double-time cover of the Beatles' "We Can Work It Out" from their original demo, which first earned them airplay on college radio stations in 1987.

The Cowboys

Formed 1979, Seattle, Washington

Ian Fisher was born to be a rock star, but life didn't cooperate. The former singer of the Feelings, an early Seattle punk band, this spiky-haired stage dynamo had a solo single ("Girls Like That"/"It's a Riot") to his credit. In April 1979 his Feelings bandmate Jack Hanan (bass) invited him to join a band he was forming with buddy Dean Helgeson (drums). "There wasn't a lot of people involved in the scene at that time," recalls Hanan. "Ian was like one of the only guys that knew what we were trying to do." Original Moberlys guitarist Jeff Cerar completed the band.

If the Heats were the kings of the bars and the Moberlys' Jim Basnight the godfather of the nascent Seattle new wave scene, Fisher was the cool little brother, the one who listened to Clash records and trod the stage with a Jagger-esque swagger ("I pack a pistol in my pants," he sang on "Rock 'n' Roll Cowboy"). Although a few of Fisher's old friends bemoaned his loss of punk purity, the 'Boys were a major bar band and the top school dance attraction at the height of their popularity. They were also a popular import in Portland clubs, once challenging P-town heroes Billy Rancher and the Unreal Gods to a massive "dance-off," a battle of the bands viewed by a sellout crowd. And it didn't hurt that this cadre of fine musicians also looked good onstage. "Too pretty to punk" screamed one headline in the local rock magazine *The Rocket*.

Helgeson, who suffered from cystic fibrosis, lasted only about a year in the band, as the cigarette smoke in clubs aggravated his illness (he died in 1987). Marty Waychoff, formerly of the Girls, was brought in as his replacement. This cemented the classic lineup. Although a punk-influenced rock band, the Cowboys also liked to stir their reggae/ska influences into the mix on songs such as "Jet City Rockers."

Seattle Power Pop/1979–84

Perhaps they were just a bit before their time, given the recent movie remake of the British television show *The Avengers*, but the Allies released their tribute to the beautiful Emma Peel in mid-1982. Formed a year earlier, when two former members of Seattle's 1970s-era showbands Bighorn (Steve Adamek) and Pegasus (Dave Kincaid) joined forces, the Allies were the consummate Seattle new wave pop band. With Adamek as the John Lennon bad boy and Kincaid as the cute Paul McCartney clone, they became a popular club band and convinced their management to invest in a full-length album when such a thing was still a major event. *The Allies*, a well-produced record that demonstrated their musical range, was a regional hit, but Adamek soon left the band—and that's when things got weird. With a new lineup of Kincaid, original drummer Larry Mason, guitarist Carl Funk, and bassist Andy Pederson, the group decided to make a video of their most popular song, once again Kincaid's "Emma Peel." The Seattle-produced video managed to make the finals of MTV's "Basement Tapes" competition, which led to the release of an EP that opened with—you guessed it—"Emma Peel" again. By this time, Seattle audiences were feeling far less love for Emma Peel. The Allies released another single ("Heartbroken Man"/"Show Me How You Love") in early 1983 and disappeared for good.

Although the Heats and the Cowboys ran power pop–era Seattle (sharing the clubs with occasional visitors from the south, including Portland's Billy Rancher), there was no shortage of good bands that never quite got their due.

Pledging to avoid cheesy cover songs even if it meant sacrificing gigs, singer/guitarist Steve Aliment named his band No Cheese Please. The popular power pop band released a well-received EP in early 1983 ("Mary Ann" was the radio song) and broke up the following year. Aliment moved to San Francisco and formed Yanks with ex-members of SVT and Das Blok.

The thinking fan's local power pop band was Hi-Fi, a group that included two out-of-town rock stars (David Surkamp, formerly of the St. Louis band Pavlov's Dog, and Iain Matthews, a Fairport Convention vet). The band began working with Matthews when he was producing their first demos, and as the sessions progressed, he was invited to join. By mid-1981 Hi-Fi were staples of the power pop bar circuit, and later that year they released the highly praised EP *Hi-Fi Demonstration Record*. But the band ran its course quickly; it barely outlasted the July 1982 release of the seldom-seen album *Moods for Mallards*. Matthews returned to his solo career; Surkamp and bassist Garey Shelton joined Big Fun.

Ah, Big Fun. Now here's a *really* unusual story. When pioneering Seattle punk band the Enemy caught on to the growing popularity of new wave acts on a national level, they decided to retool. Singer Suzanne Grant bleached her hair à la Blondie's Debbie Harry and the band filmed a video of a song called "Radio Dance," calculated to ice their switch from punks to "wavers." When Surkamp and Shelton joined, the band dropped their former name and became Big Fun. By December 1992, bassist Morgan Blackwood had signed on, making Big Fun Seattle's first new wave supergroup. Here's the unusual part: lacking funds for more than one major project, the band decided to skip putting out a single, and instead issued a cassette and a full-color poster. The cassette is now forgotten, but the posters, featuring sexy Suzanne and the gang licking ice cream cones, are a collector's item.

—James Bush

The band's enduring reputation, however, was as a group that never quite managed to get it together on record. Their fine 1981 single sold well and passed muster with critics, but the ska-fueled A-side, "Rude Boy," and the countryish flip, "She Makes Me Feel Small," failed to conjure up the Who-meets-the-Clash fury of their live performances. "If we would have known what we know now, we could have recorded a lot better," says Hanan. "We were just young guys doing what we were told." Their debut EP, *Jet City Rockers*, featured four original songs that had long been staples of their live shows, but it wasn't released until early 1983, when the band's enthusiasm was starting to fade. Waychoff left just before the record's release; Cerar split a few months later, and was replaced by another former Moberly, guitarist Ernie Sapiro. By the summer of 1984, Fisher was ready to dissolve the group, although the breakup turned out to be a brief hiatus.

The Cowboys were back the following year with a new lineup: Fisher, Hanan, Sapiro, drummer Mark Guenther, and keyboard player Paul Brownlow. They continued to be a popular live draw under the management of Robert Bennett (the ex-fanzine editor and manager of the Lonesome City Kings and Rangehoods) and even released a fine album, *How the West Was Rocked*, in late 1985. But by then their time was definitely past and, not wanting to become a career club act, the members agreed to call it quits. The Cowboys have reunited a few times since then for revival shows, most notably with guitarist Dave Dederer of the Presidents of the United States of America (who never missed an all-ages Cowboys show when he was 14). **JB**

Jet City Rockers

(1998, CHUCKIE-BOY)
This lovingly assembled reissue includes "Rude Boy," the EP *Jet City Rockers*, and five songs from *How the West Was Rocked*. Essential stuff.

Crazy 8's

Formed 1982, Corvallis, Oregon

Looking at the success of the Cherry Poppin' Daddies, the Eugene, Oregon, swing band, some Northwest music folks are probably saying, "The Crazy 8's were doing that ten years ago. What's the big deal?" While the 8's never claimed to be a swing band, their hefty horn-and-percussion emphasis attracted some of the best players in the region. And they consequently proved that one can have a horn section and still be a modern-sounding party band.

Hailing from "the other college town," Corvallis, Oregon, the band originally leaned toward straightforward ska but soon mutated its sound, twisting a George Clintonesque funk beat into an up-tempo reggae-punk number. Lead vocalist Todd Duncan kept the action moving like an expert ringmaster, never drawing attention solely to himself but instead directing it toward the action of the moment.

As these lads from Oregon State University became less and less clean-cut, the group became more and more fun to watch. Horns were handled by Duncan (alto sax), Joe Johnson, Jr. (tenor sax, vocals), and Tim Tubb (trombone, vocals). The rhythm section was made up of Mike Regan (bass), Rick Washington (drums), Casey Shaar (keyboards), and Carl Smith (percussion). The group was led by imaginative manager Marc Baker.

The band label, Red Rum Records (motto: "Every hit's a killer"), faithfully supplied fans with album after album, although each was expected to be the last before a major label finally got the message and signed the lads. At one point *Rolling Stone* named the Crazy 8's one of America's top unsigned bands. But while the labels may have been ignoring them, America's college students certainly weren't. Constantly in demand in college towns from Bozeman, Montana, to Boston, Massachusetts, the 8's whipped students into a sweaty, frothy frenzy at every show.

Their breakthrough album, *Law & Order* (1984), featured a cover by syndicated political cartoonist Jack Ohman. Next came *Nervous in Suburbia* (1986), *Out of the Way* (1987), *Big Live Nut Pack* (1988), and *Doggapotamus World* (1989).

Near the band's final days, its personnel changed. Sax player Danny Schaufler joined, then left to follow quieter pursuits. He was replaced by Jay Collins, a monstrously talented player, who eventually left the group to carve out a niche in the neobop jazz scene, first in Portland and now in New York. The Crazy 8's released a greatest hits album of sorts in 1998, *Still Crazy After All These Beers.* **DDP**

Still Crazy After All These Beers

(1998, BDC)
A selection of tracks from each Crazy 8's release, this album is the way to introduce yourself to the band's blend of the tight horn runs of ska, the political savvy of reggae, the impact of rock, and the audience participation of a conga line.

Crome Syrcus

Formed 1966, Seattle, Washington

Crome Syrcus toured in both the United States and Europe, which set them apart from other Northwest psychedelic groups. And unlike most psych players, they didn't come from the folk or blues scenes. They were seasoned professionals, playing music jazzier and more complex than that of their local (and national) peers.

The group's origins lay in an early 1960s rock 'n' roll band, the Mystics, which performed mainly at dances and hops in south Seattle. Three of the Mystics were Dick Powell (keyboards, vocals), John Gaborit (guitar), and Jim Plano (drums). In

1962 Plano joined the military and was stationed in Hawaii. Powell and Gaborit, in the meantime, joined with a pair of jazz veterans—keyboardist Ted Shreffler and bassist/multi-instrumentalist Lee Graham—and Rod Pilloud, a businessman, artist, free spirit, and drummer, to form Crome Syrcus. The band immediately established a residency at a club in Seattle's Pioneer Square, the Gallery, which continued for the next eight months. The first shows comprised mainly cover tunes—but their high-quality original songs (mainly by Graham and Shreffler) began to attract attention.

Seattle's psychedelic scene in 1966 and 1967 was embryonic compared with the activity in Vancouver, British Columbia, to the north or the Bay Area to the south. But word travels fast, and soon the Syrcus's reputation began to spread. They were spotted at a concert at the Eagles Auditorium in Seattle by John Chambless, coordinator of the Berkeley Folk Festival, who immediately booked them for a July show. Although it was their first out-of-town gig, they were warmly embraced by the California audience.

Things started to move at lightning speed. The band met Robert Joffrey of the renowned Joffrey Ballet, who hired them to adapt Teo Macero's twenty-six-piece score for the ballet *Opus 65,* which the company performed at the Eagles Auditorium. This led to a two-year association with Joffrey.

Their first trip to New York, during the fall of 1967, led to the release of *Love Cycle,* the most psychedelic album to come from a Seattle band. The album was recorded in New York and released on ABC's Command Records label (they were signed by Peter Katims, son of Seattle Symphony Orchestra director Milton Katims). The first side of the record is Shreffler's 17-minute title cut, which incorporates everything from Gregorian chant to Gaborit's jazzy guitar figures to spooky organ lines and Graham's spacy flute. The other side is no less adventurous: Graham originals such as "Crystals," "Never Come Down," and "Take It Like a Man" are top-shelf 1967 psychedelia.

Joffrey wanted the Syrcus to follow the successful *Opus 65* with something even more ambitious—they wrote an original score to his new ballet *Astarte,* which premiered in New York in late 1967. Pilloud quit the band at this point and was replaced by old friend Jim Plano, whose drumming gave the band a tighter, more expressive sound. The new lineup of the band debuted at a Columbia University gig.

By early 1968 Crome Syrcus was getting worldwide exposure through their work with Joffrey, and the band was hot news on both coasts—especially at Bill Graham's New York and San Francisco clubs, Fillmore East and Fillmore West. They had powerful people behind them: their manager was Boyd Grafmyre, who managed and promoted the Eagles Auditorium. San Francisco promoter Richard Ward was also a major supporter.

Crome Syrcus toured nationally with major acts, playing multiple dates with the Doors, Jefferson Airplane, Traffic, Steve Miller, Creedence Clearwater Revival, the Byrds, Iron Butterfly, and Led Zeppelin. Often the Syrcus, with their unique twin keyboard sound, would steal the show from the headliners.

In September 1969 they completed their work with the Joffrey Ballet and returned to the hectic world of concerts, clubs, and one-nighters. Shreffler quit the band and moved to Los Angeles. Crome Syrcus was one of two local bands to appear at the illustrious Seattle Pop Festival in the nearby town of Woodinville (the other was Floating Bridge) and by all accounts was well received.

Crome Syrcus released a pair of singles on the Piccadilly and Jerden labels in 1971. One of them, "Lord in Black," is a Northwest psychedelic classic. Plano and Graham drifted out of the band in 1971, but the name was still a draw. Gaborit and Powell kept going until 1973.

With the exception of Pilloud, all the members have been musically active in the years since: Powell is considered one of the top West Coast harp players; Gaborit's guitar work is always in demand; Shreffler has an ongoing musical career in Los Angeles; Plano plays regularly in blues and rock bands; and Graham, now proficient on even more instruments, has released a CD.

After a chance meeting at a reunion party for the earlier local psychedelic band the Daily Flash, the Joffrey-era Syrcus members came together for the first time in almost twenty-five years. Striking up the old chemistry, they've been rehearsing together sporadically since, have played publicly several times, and plan to release a CD. Judging from their new material, Seattle's psychedelic legends may have more magic in them. **NS**

Love Cycle

(**1967**, COMMAND)
Adventurous psychedelia from a band at its creative peak.

Daily Flash

Formed 1965, Seattle, Washington

In the 1950s and 1960s, the rock 'n' roll teen dance circuit in the Northwest was thriving. Change was slow—and financially unfeasible—for local musicians; the bands that dressed in uniforms, followed choreographed steps, and belted out R&B standards continued to make the highest wages well past 1965.

It was out of this scene that the Daily Flash, arguably Seattle's first psychedelic band, coalesced in the University District in the summer of 1965. The leader was Steve Lalor, a successful folkie with a respectable West Coast following. Lalor, who collaborated with Alice Stewart, Billy Roberts (writer of "Hey Joe"), and Lynn Hughes, and had a weekly gig on the local *Hootenanny* television show in 1963. But when he relocated to San Francisco the following year, Lalor found that former folk performers were creating electric bands like the Jefferson Airplane, Grateful Dead, and Quicksilver Messenger Service.

Lalor and Don MacAllister, another transplanted Seattle folkie (formerly of the Willow Creek Ramblers), returned to Seattle, planning to perform amplified folk music, somewhat along the lines of what was happening in the Bay Area. The two joined with flashy, Yardbirds-influenced lead guitarist Doug Hastings and drummer Don Stevenson to form the Daily Flash. Lalor was the frontman on lead vocals and twelve-string guitar; MacAllister played bass and contributed high harmonies. But Stevenson soon left the band to join the Frantics on tour after that band's drummer, Jon Keliehor, was injured in an automobile accident. (Ironically, after Keliehor recovered, he took Stevenson's place in the Daily Flash.) In December 1965 the band debuted at the Door, a hip Seattle coffeehouse. They promoted and staged their early shows in rented halls. In early 1966 their first single ("Queen Jane Approximately"/ "Jack of Diamonds") was released on the Parrot label. Although the single faded quickly, the band started attracting attention up and down the West Coast. Old-time managers Charlie Green and Brian Stone (Sonny and Cher, Buffalo Springfield, Iron Butterfly) put the Flash under contract, and they were off to Los Angeles in the spring of 1966. Their first California gig was at San Francisco's Avalon Ballroom on May 6, opening for Big Brother & the Holding Company.

The Daily Flash was warmly accepted in California. Aided by Green and Stone's promotional push, coupled with the Flash's eclectic mix of harmonies, feedback, twelve-string guitar, and classically oriented percussion, they were soon opening for hot Los Angeles bands such as Love, the Byrds, and the Doors. The band started to headline shows in San Francisco's psychedelic ballrooms, and for the next year, fans couldn't get enough of the Daily Flash. They even had a local television show in Los Angeles, on which they performed their own versions of Top 40 hits. The band played steadily up and down the coast, making side trips to New York and Denver. They played shows with Them, the Yardbirds, Country Joe & the Fish, and virtually all of their old Northwest and San Francisco cohorts. Treated as hometown heroes in Seattle, they were regulars at the Eagles Auditorium, the city's psychedelic ballroom.

The Daily Flash released their second (and last) single in early 1967. "The French Girl" was a magnificent slice of baroque psychedelia led by the harpsichord of session player Gabriel Meckler (who recorded with Steppenwolf and Three Dog Night), anchored by Lalor's haunting guitar and sweetened by MacAllister's descending harmony vocal line. It was a smash, at least in Seattle.

But the band was rocked by the departure of Keliehor and Hastings in early 1967. Keliehor became a session musician, later playing with James Brown and the Doors; Hastings filled Neil Young's lead guitar slot in Buffalo Springfield in summer 1967, including a triumphant appearance at the Monterey International Pop Festival in California. He later played with the psychedelic band Rhinoceros, which released three albums on Elektra.

Meanwhile, Lalor and MacAllister added guitarist Craig Tarwater and drummer Tony Dey, and the Flash continued, but the magic wasn't quite there. Still drawing gigs on the strength of their name, the band changed drummers yet again, but packed it in by the spring of 1968.

Lalor and MacAllister regrouped as Popcorn, renamed the band Bodine, and recorded a fine album for MGM, but never caught fire commercially. MacAllister played as a session musician with Dr. John and Jackie DeShannon; he died in 1969. Lalor and Keliehor have since played together quite regularly and joined Hastings in 1994 for a reunion gig. **NS**

I Flash Daily

(1982, Psycho Records)

No Daily Flash recording is available on CD yet, but this British vinyl release includes both their singles and a few studio cuts. The flip side showcases a pair of long psychedelic jams, which, unlike most, are tight, cohesive, and melodic. A must-have for anyone interested in Northwest psychedelia.

Dan Reed Network

Formed 1984, Portland, Oregon

d an Reed Network had it all wrong. Existing during a period in the rock world when one simplistic lily-white musical style (teased-haired glam metal boys) was giving way to another (shaggy-maned alternative rockers), Dan Reed Network piled rock guitars, chiming keyboards, and pop vocals on a funk-rock base. A multiracial group, the band had a lineup of two white guys, two black guys, and one Asian American guy, all of whom dressed rock-star casual and loved playing to big audiences. At least they were big in Europe. They were also Portland's best band of their era—a dominant force through the mid-1980s until they broke up in 1993.

Transplanted Midwesterners Dan Reed (guitar, vocals) and Daniel Pred (drums) had played together since their teenage years. The Network took shape in early 1984, first picking up Seattle guitarist Brion James, then replacing their original bassist with Melvin Brannon II. The original keyboardist was Rick DiGiallonardo (ex-Quarterflash), who departed after playing on their self-released debut EP, *Breathless* (1986).

The band's stellar musicianship and impressive local drawing power earned the attention of major labels, with Mercury/PolyGram winning the battle. Their Bruce Fairbairn–produced debut album, *Dan Reed Network* (1988), featured a new keyboard player, Blake Sakamoto, and a hit single in "Ritual," which briefly penetrated the Top 40. A busy touring schedule probably helped: the Network did a full U.S. swing in early summer, then returned to the road as openers for the British reggae band UB40 in August.

Dan Reed Network spent much of the following spring in the studio with legendary New York producer Nile Rogers, working on the tracks that would become *Slam* (1989), their second full-length recording. Not a safe rehash of their first record,

Slam mixed in new rhythms and softer moments (guitarist James, in particular, displayed an incredible musical range—from scratchy funk to metallish rock lines to slide) but produced little airplay. The band also began to concentrate on its enthusiastic European fan base, touring the continent in support of Bon Jovi and the Rolling Stones.

The winter of 1990–91 found Dan Reed Network reunited with producer Fairbairn at the Little Mountain Sound studio in Vancouver, British Columbia. The resulting recordings, dubbed *The Heat*, were the band's final Mercury release (a "best of" package, *Mixin' It Up*, followed in 1993). Most of the band's later dates were either in the Northwest or in Europe. They toured Australia in 1992 and mounted a nineteen-date tour of Sweden (with stops in Denmark and England) in 1993, splitting shortly thereafter. A thirty-three-track CD compilation of the band's performances, entitled *Live at Last! Halfway Around the World*, was released in 1998.

Reed, who has worked as an actor as well as a musician, still lives and performs in the Portland area. Pred and Sakamoto both play in the band Generator with lead singer and guitarist Rob Daiker. James has relocated to Los Angeles, where he has found success as a songwriter, studio guitarist (including tracks with rap artists Coolio and Snoop Doggy Dogg), and producer. **JB**

Dan Reed Network

(1989, MERCURY/POLYGRAM)
One fan speculated in an Internet posting that Dan Reed Network could have been much bigger if they'd reprised the radio-friendly rock-funk of their debut album at least once before delving into the experimentation of *Slam* and *The Heat*. There's no way to test this theory, but another album like *Dan Reed Network*—with the classic songs "Ritual," "I'm So Sorry," and "Forgot to Make Her Mine"—would have been quite welcome.

Dandy Warhols

Formed 1993, Portland, Oregon

While the Dandy Warhols would have you believe they sprang full grown from the head of Warhol darling Edie Sedgwick, the truth is they started like every other Portland band: playing Satyricon (the local version of the seminal New York punk club CBGB) and the now-defunct annual AIM Fest, two days of independent-rock shows organized by Pond drummer Dave Triebwasser.

Courtney Taylor was the drummer for the Portland glam band Beauty Stab before forming Andy Warhol's Wet Dream in 1993 with his then-girlfriend Gretchen on keyboards, his longtime friend Peter Holmstrom on guitar, and drummer Eric Hedford. By the time the Velvet Underground–influenced band renamed itself the

Dandy Warhols, singer-guitarist Taylor and his girlfriend Gretchen had broken up, and 17-year-old Zia McCabe, who had no previous musical experience, replaced her. Managed by regional rock promoter Mike Quinn (the co-owner of Portland's large rock venue La Luna), the four-piece group became a fixture on the local club circuit, often sharing bills with friends and fellow psychedelic popsters Swoon 23 and Sugarboom. In a region known for its angsty hard rock bands, the Dandy Warhols garnered a devoted following by boasting of their appetites for alcohol, drugs, and debauchery of any kind—and sometimes disrobing midshow.

The band recorded its first album in Taylor's basement with local producer (and Heatmiser drummer) Tony Lash behind the mixing board. *Dandys Rule OK* was released in 1995 on the Portland indie label Tim/Kerr. The grammatically challenged album title aside, the band's droning guitar pop made a splash in the national music press. Describing the sound of *Dandys Rule OK*, *Rolling Stone* gushed, "Sonic Youth meets early Stone Roses," and other publications—from *Option* to *Alternative Press* to *Detour*—also raved.

When hype happens, major-label scouts are never far behind. After six months of entertaining offers—and being entertained by label representatives—the band signed with Capitol Records, and Taylor gave up his day job at a downtown Portland boutique. The band won the opening slots on national tours by Electrafixion and Love & Rockets, and MTV played the videos for the kazoo-embellished "T.V. Theme Song" (and used snippets of the song on its show *The Real World*) and "Ride," the second single. "Ride" was also used in the soundtrack of cult filmmaker Bruce La Bruce's *Hustler White*.

When the Dandy Warhols began to record their Capitol debut, however, they hit some bumps in the road. Feuding in the studio led McCabe and Hedford to take a walk, leaving Holmstrom and Taylor to indulge their love for effects pedals and knob tweaking. The resulting demos were deemed noncommercial—by both the band and the label—and the band, chastened and reunited, returned to the basement for a second try. Producer Lash bowed out of the final mixing, so the band brought in Tchad Blake (who worked with Cibo Matto and Los Lobos) for a more radio-friendly finish.

The Dandy Warhols Come Down finally appeared in August 1997, and the band was rewarded with more press and MTV rotation for the video of the first single, "Not If You Were the Last Junkie on Earth." They promoted the record on tour in Europe and the United States (at shows they sold singles of the original version of "Junkie" from the initial *Come Down* sessions). And the group became subjects of a musical riposte from the psychedelic band Brian Jonestown Massacre in the form of "Not If You Were the Last Dandy on Earth."

Aside from achieving some commercial radio airplay, *Come Down*'s second single, "Boys Better," appeared on the soundtrack to Gus Van Sant's Academy Award–nominated film *Good Will Hunting*. In the summer of 1998, the band contributed another single from the record, "Every Day Should Be a Holiday," to the soundtrack of *There's Something about Mary.*

Drummer Hedford left the band in March 1998 to pursue his dance-music solo work as DJ Aquaman; he went on to form the trio Magic Fingers with members of Brian Jonestown Massacre and fellow Portlanders Swoon 23. To fill Hedford's shoes for their 1998 European tour, the Dandy Warhols enlisted their longtime friend Brent DeBoer, who later became a permanent band member. **JM**

Dandys Rule OK

(1995, TIM/KERR)

Having released only two full-length records, the Dandy Warhols should have their best work ahead of them, but if you must choose, go for their debut, on the strength of the dense, layered, effects-heavy "Ride," which is, along with "Honey" by the Jesus and Mary Chain, among the definitive songs of the psychedelic pop genre. Better yet, buy the single and avoid getting stuck with the album's pointless 16-minute closing song.

Dead Moon

Formed 1988, Portland, Oregon

d ead Moon's Fred Cole has left his mark on the Northwest rock scene with various and sundry projects dating back to the late 1960s, when his band, the Weeds, transformed themselves into the Lollipop Shoppe during the dog days of psychedelia. When punk rock became the thing to do in the latter part of the next decade, Fred (guitar) and his wife, Toody (bass), formed the Rats, a dark little trio with enough raw edges to slice and dice a vegetable garden. Drummer Andrew Loomis eventually became their steady third, and the band evolved into Dead Moon, returning to the bristling sounds of powerhouse garage rock. Fred, now in his 50s, is a living link between Northwest rock's past and present, distilling the spirits of 1960s *Nuggets*-style proto-punks like the Sonics and the Wailers through his no-nonsense, three-chord sensibility.

Fred and Toody's record label, Tombstone, is a veritable do-it-yourself blueprint of self-reliance: they press their own records (always mixed in their beloved mono), produce all the cover art, and handle the mailing themselves while still finding time to record other artists, book the occasional local gig, and tour Europe. They are treated like genuine rock royalty abroad, playing shows to standing-room-only crowds before returning to the indifferent United States, their pockets crammed with money.

While Dead Moon is active in the recording studio, the live performance setting favors their leather-tough approach. Here Fred's phlegmy screaming, Toody's bruised and tender harmonies, and Andrew's crashing drum kit work in all their raging, ragged glory. The albums *Live Evil* (1991), on Germany's Music Maniac label, and *Hard Wired in Ljubljana* (1997), available domestically on eMpTy Records, feature killer live material and some choice covers. Fred's nervous tales of working-class defiance and dancing with destruction, like "Going South" and "54-40," shine brightest when he's feeding off the energy of a stoked houseful of frenzied folk. Dusty covers like "Play with Fire" and "Milk Cow Blues" are revitalized and honed to lethal sharpness. Onstage the band shares a whiskey bottle and a joint sense of duty to the moon gods of real rock, always delivering the crucial goods. There is nothing phony or contrived at a Dead Moon show, just raw power and rock action, the way it was meant to be. Let your parents grow old gracefully—Dead Moon grows old fearlessly. **JC**

Hard Wired in Ljubljana

(1997, EMpTy)
A double-live checklist of Dead Moon's finest songs (in mono, of course).

Dharma Bums

Formed 1986, Portland, Oregon

Like good mystic wanderers, the Dharma Bums were a tad ahead of their time. Predating resurgent country by more than a decade, the band formed on Christmas Eve 1986 outside Portland, in the home of guitarist Eric Lovre's grandmother. The four sweet-faced youths had already played together in various formations. Drummer John Moen and vocalist Jeremy Wilson had previously performed in Perfect Circle, while Wilson, Lovre, and bassist Jimmy Talstra played in the Watchmen.

Using rural imagery to convey simple spirituality, the Dharma Bums proved the antithesis of grunge but succeeded in spite of it. They packed clubs in Portland and Seattle by weaving threads of hope into the nihilism of the late 1980s. Not a bad trick for four 18-to-21-year-old kids from the Oregon countryside audacious enough to lift their name from a Jack Kerouac novel.

What proved so attractive about the Dharma Bums was not only their perceived naiveté but their ability to portray their own existence in nonurban America. Lovre grew up on a 500-acre farm (which his family lost during the Reagan era), while Wilson spent his childhood listening to protest folk music and watching traditional hootenannies in North Carolina. Those Southern sing-alongs inspired him to develop a trademark nasal twang.

The band's first album, *Haywire* (1988), was recorded in Seattle and released on producer Conrad Uno's PopLlama Products. Although the band had long since relocated to Portland, they returned to a rural setting to produce their sophomore release, *Bliss*. The album was recorded in a grange hall outside their hometown of

Silverton, Oregon—the band had to adjust their schedule to accommodate two square dances. Using a 24-track mobile unit, they recorded without studio effects, using only instruments and microphones to create reverb and acoustics by placement. The bass was recorded in a woodshed.

In contrast to the rustic lust and spirit of *Haywire*, *Bliss* dealt with issues including rape, suicide, and death. It also marked a turning point for the band. Talstra, who sang and wrote "Stayed Up Late," decided he wanted to take a more active role. The Dharma Bums made one more album, *Welcome* (Frontier), and broke up in 1991. Additional recorded material includes two singles ("Haywire"/"Shake" and "Givin' In"/"Shake Some Action") and contributions to the Northwest compilations *I-5 Killers*, *Satyricon: The Album*, and *On the Run*. All four members are still active in regional bands. Wilson plays in Pilot, Lovre fronts Spring Tooth, and Talstra and Moen perform in the Maroons. **VK**

Haywire

(1988, POPLLAMA)

Recorded at Egg Studios and produced by Conrad Uno and Scott McCaughey, *Haywire* provides the best example of the Dharma Bums' barnyard spirituality. A dreamy mix of twangy ballads and high-powered pop that respect both the earth and the atmosphere.

Don and the Goodtimes

Formed 1964, Portland, Oregon

In any region with a thriving music scene, a healthy competition always exists—bands constantly form, change members, and break up. Many Northwest bands, such as the Royal Notes, the Imperials, and Hawk and the Randellas, remained obscure. Some, like the Viceroys and Merrilee and the Turnabouts, earned considerable regional success. And others, such as the Kingsmen and Paul Revere and the Raiders, achieved national recognition. All of the above-mentioned acts have one thing in common—Don and the Goodtimes.

The story begins with Don Galluci, an ex–Royal Note and the talented 15-year-old keyboard player for the Kingsmen. When "Louie Louie" hit for them in 1963, Galluci was too young to tour. Original Kingsmen lead singer Jack Ely had been kicked out of the band, so he and Galluci formed the Goodtimes in 1964 with guitarist Pete Ouellette (a former Raider), drummer Bob Holden, bassist Dave Childs, and former Imperials sax player and vocalist Don McKinney. Their first effort was the Northwest instrumental hit "Turn on Song." Other songs from the early band include "Money," "The Witch," "Tall Cool One," and a few Galluci-penned originals, which would later be released on the LP *Where the Action Is* (1966, Wand).

Live, Don and the Goodtimes were a force to be reckoned with. They had something for everyone: top hat and tails for a touch of elegance, hot instrumental licks in the tradition of the Wailers and the Sonics, onstage hijinks and steps much like the Raiders. Their musical career would span brash Northwest R&B, killer garage punk, and polished 1967 pop rock. Don and the Goodtimes started out solidly in the Northwest sound niche, à la the Wailers or Sonics, but evolved through better songwriting and production. By the time of their 1967 demise, they sounded like a more adventurous version of the Turtles or Beatles.

As the band's live reputation grew, Jim Valley of the popular Seattle-based Viceroys replaced Ouellette on guitar. Valley's first effort with the Goodtimes was "Little Sally Tease" (which he claims to have written in 20 minutes), a Northwest hit featuring call-and-response vocals from Valley and McKinney. By now, other bands were covering the Goodtimes (the Kingsmen and the Standells in Los Angeles both released their own versions of "Little Sally Tease"), and the group was playing shows up and down the West Coast. Signing with Dunhill Records, they worked with legendary songwriter/producer P. F. Sloan on such material as "Hey There, Mary Mae" and "Sweets for My Sweet."

Valley split from the band in early 1966 to join the Raiders, enticed by Paul Revere's promises of riches, fame, and travel. His last effort with the Goodtimes was the scorching rocker "I'm Real," which includes a cryptic reference to the Los Angeles DJ Don Steele. Valley didn't forget his former bandmates, however; he helped them sign to ABC's *Where the Action Is*, the daily television show that featured the Raiders.

After drafting former Raider Charlie Coe to replace Valley, the Goodtimes retreated to the Northwest and were as big as ever. The personnel changes continued: Joey Newman (a Peter Noone lookalike who added to the band's visual appeal) from Merrilee and the Turnabouts replaced Coe while McKinney and Childs were replaced by vocalist Jeff Hawks and bassist Ron "Buzz" Overman, the nucleus of the Walla Walla, Washington, band Hawk and the Randellas. This new blood gave the Goodtimes a creative jolt—Overman's "You Were Just a Child" is indisputably one of the band's best.

In early 1967 the band hooked up with Epic Records and released "I Could Be So Good to You," a massive hit in the Northwest, though it fizzled nationally. An album produced by Jack Nitzche got national distribution, although fans noted it was not as powerful as the band's earlier work. But the Goodtimes were touring nationally, getting write-ups in teen magazines, and enjoying their television success. Surely they were on the verge of following the Raiders out of the Northwest to national success. But it was not to happen. The cancellation of *Where the Action Is* was just part of the problem; in late 1967, strobe lights, psychedelia, and drugs were in, and bands like Don and the Goodtimes were out.

The band, which had relocated to Los Angeles, released a few more singles before regrouping as Touch, with drummer John Bordonaro and bassist Bruce Hauser. Embracing the psychedelic culture, Touch's music was an ethereal blend of progressive keyboards, pyrotechnic guitars, and spaced-out lyrics. Financial need forced the band to occasionally play as Don and the Goodtimes in the Northwest—where their old material went over, but the new material didn't. Touch released a self-titled album on the Coliseum label in 1969, which was rereleased on CD by Renaissance in the late 1990s.

Touch didn't tour and soon broke up. Newman, Hauser, and Hawks formed Stepson, which released a self-titled 1974 album on ABC (with Galluci guesting). Something of a hard rock classic, it too—like everything connected with Don and the Goodtimes—has become a collector's item. Galluci made his mark in music production in the early 1970s, working with Iggy Pop and Tom Waits. Newman went on to become a respected session guitarist, most notably with Shaun Cassidy and Sheena Easton.

Interest in Don and the Goodtimes is still keen—the "Little Sally Tease"–era lineup has reunited on three occasions in Seattle, and in the late 1990s they were inducted into the Northwest Music Hall of Fame. **NS**

Don and the Goodtimes

(1994, JERDEN)
Hits, misses, and unreleased gems are in this twenty-one-song compilation (which includes a blistering Sonics cover and the obligatory "Louie Louie"). An essential slice of Northwest music history.

Pete Droge

after playing with two Northwest bands bearing memorable names (March of Crimes, Ramadillo), Bainbridge Island, Washington, native turned Portland immigrant Pete Droge decided to make a name for himself. Garnering label interest with an impressive performance at the South by Southwest music festival in Austin, Texas, in 1993, Droge became an overnight success with his American Records debut *Necktie Second* (1994), which included the alternative rock radio staple "If You Don't Love Me (I'll Kill Myself)." He opened shows for the likes of Neil Young, Tom Petty, Sheryl Crow, Melissa Etheridge, and Pearl Jam (whose guitarist, Mike McCready, produced Droge's original demo tape). Droge also collaborated with Eurythmics veteran Dave Stewart on the title track to the movie *Beautiful Girls*.

Droge is a rare link between rock's past and its present. His work mixes and matches any number of classic rock influences (in response to one interviewer's question about who he was listening to, he cited Van Morrison, Badfinger, R. L. Burnside, and Ali Farka Toure). In a society that scorns its roots, Droge's nods to the Beatles, Stones, Tom Petty, et al. are reassuring, even though his homage sometimes slips into tribute territory (like the borrowed Beatles background sounds on his single "Spacey and Shakin").

Droge's second album, *Find a Door* (1996, released under the band name "Pete Droge & the Sinners"), was aimed at establishing his backup musicians as a group and giving Droge's alternative singer/songwriter fare a slightly harder edge. Although the record disappointed American by selling poorly, it was highly regarded by critics and Droge fans alike. Several writers put it on their yearly Top 10 lists of 1996 albums.

Droge's third try is *Spacey and Shakin* (1998), a record that continues the musician's transition into more band-oriented material. Like his previous two records, *Spacey* was produced by Brendan O'Brien (best known for his work with Pearl Jam) and released on O'Brien's 57 Records. Although not billed in the title, the Sinners (now called the Millionaires) are still prominent in the mix, especially guitarist Peter Stroud's expert lines. The rest—acoustic guitarist Elaine Summers, bassist Dave Hull, and drummer Rob Brill—stay in a support mode, bursting out in spots like the graceful background choruses on "Eyes on the Ceiling" and the heavy rock flourishes on "Mile of Fence." **JB**

Spacey and Shakin

(1998, 57 RECORDS)
A nice sample of Pete Droge's stylings backed by his band's best work to date.

The Dynamics
Formed 1959, Seattle, Washington

the Dynamics were a hot, horn-driven band that left a long legacy of instrumental recordings and fondly remembered performances. Formed around the Adfem brothers—Terry on keyboards and 13-year-old Jeff on sax—their earliest incarnation also featured Dave Williams (guitar), Pete Borg (bass), Larry Smith (drums), and vocalist Tom Larson. Their first single, "Baby"/"Aces Up," was released in 1959 on the local Penguin label.

The following year held big changes for the Dynamics. The lineup shifted dramatically with three newcomers: Larry Coryell (formerly of the Checkers, based in Yakima, Washington) on guitar, Ron Woods on drums, and Mark Doubleday on trumpet. Randi Green was a featured vocalist. The same year the band also signed with the local record label Seafair-Bolo (later just Bolo). Their first release for Bolo was a pair of tough instrumentals, "Onion Salad" and "Lonesome Llama." The record earned the band some airplay and gigs on the burgeoning teen dance circuit. The follow-up single was a cover of "J.A.J.," a standard by local great Dave Lewis (the flip side was "At the Mardi Gras"); the song became one of their most popular numbers.

In 1961 the Dynamics were joined by new frontman Jimmy Hanna. Making the most of his striking good looks, intense stage presence, and smooth, soulful voice, he led the band to another level. The two horns added elements of soul and funk to the Dynamics' hard-rockin' guitar backbeat—a sound that would be more fully explored a decade later by such acts as Chicago and Blood, Sweat & Tears.

With their classic lineup in place, the Dynamics were now in big demand. They played all the dance halls and ballrooms and received more bookings than they could handle. Other local radio hits included "Wild Child" and "Tennessee Boy." In 1964 Bolo released a hot live album recorded at Parker's, the north Seattle nightspot. *The Dynamics with Jimmy Hanna* was an immediate smash; it contained a mix of covers and originals, the standouts being two Dave Lewis tunes ("J.A.J." and "Candido"), "Busybody," and "Come On" (a Northwest standard later covered by Jimi Hendrix on *Electric Ladyland*).

In 1965 the band released its final single with Jimmy Hanna. "Leaving Here," an obscure Motown song, was transformed into a powerful, propulsive cruncher that was a big Northwest hit at the time and still sounds torrid today. Carrying on the regional tradition, Pearl Jam had the good sense to cover it on the 1995 sampler album *Home Alive: The Art of Self Defense* (Epic).

Hanna formed the Jimmy Hanna Big Band to focus on the horn-driven sound he so dearly loved. Standout guitarist John Carmody and ex-Dynamic Pete Borg (who had been replaced by Gary Snyder) joined a lineup of trombone, trumpet, and sax players. The Big Band backed many national stars, including the Temptations, the Four Tops, Jimmy Ruffin, and Stevie Wonder. Hanna now lives in Texas, where he teaches music and owns a recording studio.

In 1966 the core Dynamics—the Adfem brothers and guitarist Harry Wilson— added bassist Bob Perry and drummer Joe Cavender and rechristened themselves the Springfield Rifles (the "s" was soon dropped). The Springfield Rifle released a series of singles on Jerry Dennon's family of labels. A fine trippy effort was "100 or Two" from 1966, with its chorus of "Got to be high." ABC picked up the novelty release "The Bears" for national distribution, and the new Quicksilver Messenger Service also covered the song. The group received a modest amount of national airplay with "That's All I Really Need." The band, which was evolving in a softer, loungier direction under the leadership of Jeff Adfem, later released a self-titled album containing many of their previous singles. The Springfield Rifle recorded singles into the early 1970s before calling it a day.

The younger Adfem brother later released an album entitled *Jeff Adfem and the Springfield Flute*, a collection of soft rock reworkings of older Top 40 songs. He and Wilson have reunited in Play It Again Sam; Coryell is a world-class jazz guitarist; and Doubleday has worked extensively as a national session player. **NS**

The Dynamics with Jimmy Hanna

(1964, Bolo)
A swaggering, soulful mix of originals and covers. Hanna's vocals are swank and the instrumentals are thick, passionate Northwest R&B.

Easy Chair

Formed 1967, Seattle, Washington

asy Chair's 1968 three-song EP is one of the most sought-after Northwest records of all time. Band members still receive phone calls from rabid collectors around the world, and a copy of this rarity can bring a four-figure price.

Led by north Seattle drummer turned bassist Jeff Simmons, the band burned brightly during 1968 and almost made the big time in Los Angeles. Simmons's first professional band had been the Prophets, a teen dance band complete with matching uniforms and choreographed moves.

In 1967 Simmons joined an existing band, the Blues Interchange (future new age star David Lanz played in an early lineup). Regulars on the new ballroom circuit, they wowed audiences with their trippy renditions of psychedelic blues and shared stages with Country Joe & the Fish, among others. Like many bands of that era, the Blues Interchange lost members to the military draft, and by the fall of 1967, newcomers Phil Kirby (guitar), Peter Larson (guitar), and Al Malosky (drums) had filled the vacancies. Kirby—at 17, still a high school student—was the youngest. Malosky had played with the popular Emergency Exit, while Larson had been in several bands in the Spokane, Washington, area, including the Chancellors. Strengthened by the change in chemistry, the band became more popular than ever. A highlight of this juncture was opening a Portland show for Blue Cheer, then hot with their hit "Summertime Blues."

The Blues Interchange then hooked up with ex–Bay Area scenester Mathew Katz, who was opening a new "San Francisco sound" club on Seattle's Capitol Hill. It was an important move, as Katz's savvy and the band's talent got them high-profile gigs as openers for touring Bay Area bands. Katz, who had been instrumental in the early successes of Jefferson Airplane and Moby Grape, renamed the group Indian Puddin' and Pipe.

The band dropped the name and cut ties to Katz in the spring of 1968 when Glen Harmon took over as their manager. The name Easy Chair came from a song by Simmons of the same name. A Boeing employee and enthusiastic fan of the band, Harmon was a born promoter, and he kept the group quite busy. Unlike the other Northwest psychedelic bands, Easy Chair played only to hip audiences, refusing to play school dances or roller rinks.

Easy Chair's style featured the unique guitar chemistry of Larson's psychedelic leads and Kirby's fluid lines and hypnotic chording. The two were tight players, yet their excursions into the unknown were always satisfying. The band played lots of original material, as Simmons was becoming quite a proficient songwriter. Easy Chair played many gigs in Vancouver, British Columbia, as well as Eastern Washington venues such as Spokane's Sadir Con Grotto and Yakima's Electric Angel. In May 1968, they opened for Jimmy Page's Yardbirds at Casey's in Lewiston, Idaho. When fans sent their Yardbirds albums backstage for autographs before the show,

Page, the only band member present, suggested that Easy Chair sign for the absent Yardbirds.

The band's famous 1968 release was recorded in April at the Ripcord Studios in Vancouver, Washington. Produced by Rick Keefer (soon to establish the cutting-edge Seattle studio Sea-West), the record included three originals, "Easy Chair," "My Own Life," and "Slender Woman." Definitive 1968 psychedelia, the songs are haunting and unforgettable. The record was sold in Seattle-area head shops and record stores—either five hundred or a thousand were pressed (no one is sure now)—and, as a bonus for buyers, each jacket contained one of four promo photos.

On Memorial Day weekend 1968, Easy Chair opened for Cream in their only Seattle appearance at the Eagles Auditorium. This appearance, along with another big show with the Chambers Brothers, represented the peak of their career. The band was offered a recording contract on Tetragrammaton Records, a new Los Angeles label. Easy Chair passed on the offer, not realizing that Bill Cosby was a label founder (Tetragrammaton later released Deep Purple's first American record). Not wanting to make the same mistake again, the band vowed to accept the next offer they received.

Larson was replaced during the summer by Burke Wallace (previously with Jack Horner and the Plums), whose flashy, driving guitar style was quite compatible with Kirby's playing. The band was busy that summer, with several outdoor festivals and their usual ballroom shows. In late August Simmons hustled a gig opening for Frank Zappa's Mothers of Invention at the Seattle Center Arena. Zappa liked what he heard and wanted to work with the group.

The match seemed perfect: the Mothers were a major undergound band, and Zappa's nascent Straight/Bizarre label was establishing street credibility through releases by such talent as Alice Cooper. Easy Chair headed south to Los Angeles in the winter of 1968, taking up residence in a Hollywood hotel and rehearsing constantly. They played a few gigs with Zappa and company—one of which was recorded professionally—but the promised studio sessions didn't happen, and by the end of the year Easy Chair began to disintegrate.

Simmons and Malosky remained behind and recorded a movie soundtrack album (*Naked Angels*) and followed it up with the long-awaited Straight/Bizarre album. For this project, Simmons recruited several Northwest players—Jon Keliehor (Daily Flash), Ron Woods (Dynamics), and Craig Tarwater (Hawk and the Randellas, Daily Flash). Zappa even played guitar.

Multi-instrumentalist Simmons has been the only member of Easy Chair to remain a high-profile musician. He played bass with Zappa's Mothers of Invention for a few years (appearing on three albums) and has backed or played with such luminaries as Mark Lindsay of Paul Revere and the Raiders, Paul Rodgers, the Wailers, Bo Diddley, and Etta James. Kirby and Simmons still occasionally play together, and the possibility of an Easy Chair reunion is being discussed.

Easy Chair crammed an amazing career into a year or so of activity. They are correctly remembered as Northwest psychedelic pioneers. **NS**

Easy Chair

(1968, Self-released)
Spooky, ominous melodic music vaguely reminiscent of Vanilla Fudge or Iron Butterfly. Easy Chair's masterpiece remains killer thirty years after its release.

Everclear

Formed 1992, Portland, Oregon

a triumph of will over originality, Everclear's success is a credit to the hard work of singer, guitarist, and songwriter Art Alexakis. The Los Angeles native had his share of personal adversity to overcome; both his brother and girlfriend died of drug overdoses in the mid-1980s, convincing Alexakis to get rid of his own cocaine habit. He moved to San Francisco in 1987 and formed Colorfinger, a rockabilly-tinged punk band. They released an album (*Deep in the Heart of the Beast in the Sun*) and an EP on Alexakis's own Shindig Records before breaking up.

In 1992 Alexakis moved with his future wife, Jenny, to her hometown of Portland. Once there, he joined up with bass player Craig Montoya and drummer Scott Cuthbert to form Everclear. For $400 the trio recorded their debut EP for Portland independent label Tim/Kerr Records. Alexakis soon decided that the label didn't have enough promotional muscle, so he launched his own marketing campaign, personally mailing out copies of the record to press and retailers. Everclear eventually added more tracks to the EP and rereleased it as the full-length *World of Noise* on their own label, Fire Records.

Everclear toured for nearly a year straight, building an audience of mostly teenage fans and earning a "Nirvana Lite" label from many critics. In the summer of 1994, Cuthbert was replaced by Greg Eklund, and Everclear signed a contract with Capitol. Along the way, they released another EP, *Fire Maple Song*.

Alexakis produced the band's major-label debut, *Sparkle and Fade* (1995). Despite being released when angst-filled hard rock was waning in popularity, the record yielded three hit singles, "Heroin Girl," "Santa Monica," and "Heartspark Dollarsign," which was notable not just for tackling the topic of interracial romance but also for having a video directed by controversial photographer and filmmaker Larry Clark, director of *Kids*.

As Everclear received national attention, so did claims that Alexakis had failed to credit others' work during his band's early Portland years. On top of these charges, a 1996 article in *Spin* magazine discussed accusations from fellow Portland musicians that Alexakis had abused his wife. Alexakis admitted that he'd had violent tendencies but said he'd gotten help, and Jenny vehemently denied that he'd ever struck her.

Apparently wanting more controversy, Alexakis became involved in politics. He reported on the 1996 political conventions for MTV and drew fire for his antiwelfare comments after it was revealed that he had once been a welfare recipient. Either because of or in spite of the attention—not to mention more exhaustive touring—*Sparkle and Fade* was certified platinum.

Bassist Montoya relocated to Atlanta, Georgia, but Everclear returned to Portland to record most of its third record, *So Much for the Afterglow*, for which Alexakis again handled production duties. Following the album's October 1997 release and the success of the first single, "Everything to Everyone," the band mounted a national tour, temporarily adding Steven Birch, an alumnus of Portland's Sprinkler, to fill out its live sound. Selling out most of its shows, Everclear rewarded fans across the country with free performances at record stores. **JM**

World of Noise

(1993, FIRE)
By virtue of its rawness, vitality, and undisguised anger, *World of Noise* is Everclear at their most endearing. Subsequent records repeat their full-length debut's melodic punk formula, but with less satisfying results.

The Fastbacks

Formed 1979, Seattle, Washington

It seems like the Fastbacks have always existed and will last forever—a curious situation, given the Seattle band's tenuous existence during most of their two decades as a group.

Ironically, the best-known band outside of the fictional Spinal Tap to have trouble keeping a regular drummer got together around a set of drums. Guitarist Kurt Bloch's first band, the Cheaters, had just broken up, and the drummer had left his kit in Bloch's basement. He took advantage of the situation by inviting high school pals Kim Warnick and Lulu Gargiulo over to play. The band, with Warnick on guitar and Gargiulo on bass and lead vocals, debuted at an all-ages show at a neighborhood recreational center in May 1980. After a few shows with this lineup, another friend, Duff McKagan (later to become famous as the bassist for Guns N' Roses), offered to play drums, allowing Bloch to switch back to guitar. Warnick, who was originally too intimidated to sing onstage, accompanied Gargiulo's vocals on most songs. The band's first four-song demo got them onto two records—the *Seattle Syndrome* compilation LP ("Someone Else's Room") and the band's debut single, "It's Your Birthday"/"You Can't Be Happy." These songs showcase the style that has survived to this day: happy, upbeat punky pop tunes with Bloch's well-crafted leads and the sing-songy yet wistful vocals of Warnick and Gargiulo.

McKagan soon became the first Fastbacks drummer to quit the band. Belying

Rock/Pop

Early Seattle Punk/1977–83

In the Seattle of the late 1970s, "punk" meant anything that didn't sound like Styx or Kansas. Only about fifty people in the city dared to listen to it, much less play it. Early punk bands like the Enemy, the Mentors, the Telepaths, and the Lewd boldly entertained crowds of twenty, made horrible recordings, and probably got beaten up a lot.

The Enemy eventually polished up their act, changed their name to Big Fun, and essentially became an MTV-style new-wave band. The Mentors moved to Los Angeles and took to wearing Grim Reaper hoods onstage and posing as violent woman-haters, which was supposed to be funny. In 1997 frontman Eldon Hoke, "El Duce," was hit by a train and killed.

Inspired by Iggy Pop and the New York Dolls, the Telepaths metamorphosed into the best art-spaz band of the early 1980s, the Blackouts. Drummer Bill Rieflin eventually joined Ministry. The Lewd featured the fabulous "Blobbo," who later took back his real name of Kurdt Vanderhoof and formed Metal Church. The Lewd's entire recorded output was rereleased as *Kill Yourself . . . Again* (1998, Chuckie-Boy).

By the early 1980s, the definition of punk was narrowing as the music became faster and louder and devolved into hardcore. One of Seattle's first hardcore bands was Solger, best remembered for their single "Raping Dead Nuns." Guitarist Paul Solger has since played in numerous bands.

Another constant presence in the punk scene was Upchuck (born Charles Garrish) of the group the Fags, perhaps Seattle's first Goth band. From the beginning, the darker, more somber sounds have infected Seattle punk, and early grunge was influenced by the experimental style of bands like the Fags as much as it was by heavy metal. The Fags also featured Solger and Jane Playtex, who eventually left to form the hardcore DTs with Mike Refuzor (of the Refuzors) and Duff McKagan. McKagan has played in more bands than he can count, most famously Guns N' Roses—but of course, that came much later. Garrish played in many other bands and appeared in the movie *Desperately Seeking Susan.* He died of AIDS-related illness in 1990.

Another early band of note, the Refuzors, lasted for years and played numerous shows but, thanks to a *Seattle Post-Intelligencer* article, will forever be remembered as the band that swung a dead cat around onstage. (Band members emphasize they were not the ones who killed it.) At this writing the Refuzors have re-formed and released an LP on the local punk label Idol Records.

Perhaps the most notorious of Seattle's third wave of punk bands were the Fartz, featuring Paul (Solger) Fart, Steve Fart, Loud Fart, and future Accused vocalist Blaine (Cook) Fart. This group was one of the first in Seattle to follow the example of England's Crass, eschewing mere shock tactics in favor of lyrics that espoused left-wing political causes. But few people tried to understand what they were screaming about, and the Fartz's furious sound drove youngsters into frenzies of vandalism, causing some to rip out the bathroom fixtures of the rental halls, much to the band's dismay.

This curious trend of violence against sinks was not limited to Fartz shows, but their vulgar name made the band especially visible and venues increasingly hard to come by. The Fartz made up for the lack of live shows by recording two EPs, a self-release entitled *Because This Fucking World Stinks,* which reached no. 7 on the British alternative charts, and *World Full of Hate* on Alternative Tentacles, both impossible to find today.

When drummer Loud suffered burnout and left the band (only to remain stuck with the name Loud for the rest of his life so far), he was replaced by the ubiquitous Duff McKagan. Steve Fart was followed by David Garriques on bass, McKagan switched to guitar, Greg Gilmore took over on drums, Blaine Fart was replaced by Steve Verwolf, and the band evolved into Ten Minute Warning. The group was considered one of the first punk bands to shamelessly incorporate metal riffs, though another band, a curiosity known as Malfunkshun, may have been the true trailblazers.

Ten Minute Warning recorded an EP's worth of material that was never released, and a later version of the band, featuring future Skin Yard bassist Daniel House, recorded an entire album that similarly failed to see the light of day. The band re-formed in 1997 with a new singer, Christopher Blue; signed to Sub Pop Records; and released a self-titled EP of powerful steroid rock (not punk) before calling it quits again a year later.

—Dawn Anderson

their happy music, the Fastbacks at the time were an argumentative group of people. Bloch says that McKagan "just wanted to play music, have fun, and be in everyone's band." The next drummer was Richard Stuverud, then a 16-year-old high school student, who played on the EP titled *Fastbacks Play Five of Their Favorites* before being replaced by Danny Zakos. The band was already starting to get a reputation for having a revolving door at the drum kit when Zakos quit. When his replacement didn't work out, Stuverud returned to play on the EP *Every Day Is Saturday*.

During the mid-1980s the band continued to record little-noticed demo tapes, breaking the monotony with the odd gig (usually their outdoor summer performance at the Seattle Center Mural Amphitheater) and a few West Coast minitours. Live shows during this period were sporadic, and the Fastbacks were often mismatched with bands that played only cover songs, recalls Warnick: "Some of the places you had to play were so depressing, and the crowds that would be there just didn't understand about bands that wrote their own songs."

In 1986 the band finally came up with a solution for their drummer situation. Nate Johnson, a former Seattle boy who had moved to Minneapolis, was talked into moving home and joining the band for their PopLlama label debut, *Fastbacks . . . and His Orchestra* (1987). But later that year, Gargiulo quit the band. The three-piece Fastbacks (with Warnick on bass) recorded the live *Bike Toy Clock Gift* (originally a 1988 cassette-only release, but now available on CD) and the set of demos that later became *Very, Very Powerful Motor* (1990). On hiatus from the band in 1990, Bloch toured as a member of the Young Fresh Fellows and discovered that, everywhere he went, people talked to him about the Fastbacks—driving home an important truth they had missed during their Seattle struggles. "We said, 'Hmmm. People do like our band,'" he recalls. With respectable sales of a four-song single ("In the Summer," 1990) and the release of *Very, Very Powerful Motor*, the band—including Gargiulo—re-formed to record a single for Sub Pop Records. The success of the releases revived the band and began a long association with Sub Pop, including *The Question Is No* (a 1992 compilation of rare tracks), *Zücker* (1993), *Answer the Phone, Dummy* (1994), and *New Mansions in Sound* (1996). By now, the drummer problem had turned full circle: for *Answer the Phone, Dummy*, Seattle's best drummers (including Dan Peters of Mudhoney, Jason Finn of the Presidents of the United States of America, and Mike Musberger of the Posies) lined up for the honor of playing on a track or two. The band's next release was *Win Lose or Both* (1998), an EP on the PopLlama label. **JB**

Very, Very Powerful Motor

(1990, PopLlama)
Every Fastbacks fan has a favorite record, and this one's mine. Doubters might note this album was recorded during the band's sans-Gargiulo phase and took almost two years to be released. My reply: Lulu sings on several songs, and it contains "In the Summer," "Trouble Sleeping," and "Better than Before." So there.

Answer the Phone, Dummy

(1994, Sub Pop)
Lulu's back, everybody's happy, and the Fastbacks have drummers to spare. The world is okay after all.

The Fleetwoods

Formed 1958, Olympia, Washington

a group of singing teenagers gets snatched right out of high school by talent scouts, and their first record becomes a no. 1 national hit. A movie plot? No, it's the true story of the Fleetwoods.

In 1958 Olympia, Washington, high school friends Barbara Laine Ellis and Gretchen Diane Christopher were seeking a third member for their singing group. After trying out several female singers, they decided to take a different tack, and recruited trumpet player Gary Troxell as an accompanist. The trumpet didn't work out, but Troxell did. Soon the trio—originally known as Two Girls and a Guy—was the hit of their high school and popular with teenagers all over Olympia. Along with vocal takes on popular standards of the day, the group dabbled in songwriting. Their best original song, "Come Softly to Me," featured Troxell's doo-wop opening, with Ellis and Christopher chiming in on the chorus. On the verse, Troxell takes the lead over a backing of "ooh's" and "aah's" from the others.

Bonnie Guitar, who had hit the Top 10 herself as an artist ("Dark Moon," 1957), was seeking talent for her new label, Dolphin Records. Tipped off by an Olympia talent scout, Guitar auditioned the group and was knocked out by the hit potential of "Come Softly to Me." The song was quickly recorded, the group rechristened the

Fleetwoods, and the single released in February 1959. Already on its way to becoming a regional hit, the initial Dolphin release encountered a pair of snags—another company named Dolphin was challenging its use of the name, and the small label couldn't produce enough records to keep pace with growing sales. Through an agreement with Liberty Records, the singles kept coming (until Dolphin Records could be renamed Dolton Records). Aided by appearances by the Fleetwoods on the Dick Clark and Ed Sullivan television shows, "Come Softly to Me" hit no. 1 on the *Billboard* chart on April 13 and held the perch for four weeks. Despite the trio's mellow vocal style, the innovatively sparse arrangement and Troxell's opening vocals caught the attention of the doo-wop crowd, as the song crossed over to the R&B charts, reaching no. 5.

For their next single, the group chose another song from their original repertoire, "Graduation's Here." The record was popular (cracking the Top 40 at no. 39) but hardly on the same level as "Come Softly to Me." The group's search for a new hit song led them to DeWayne Blackwell's "Mr. Blue" and their second no. 1 chart slot in September 1959.

But the Fleetwoods' fortunes dimmed in 1960 when Troxell was drafted into the Navy. Stationed in California, he spent his shore leaves in the recording studio with Ellis and Christopher. The group continued with a string of six Top 40 hits—their best showing being "Tragedy" (1961), which climbed to no. 10. Another particular highlight was their take on the Sharon Seeley and Jackie DeShannon song "(He's) The Great Imposter" (no. 30). The Fleetwoods' final Top 40 appearance was "Goodnight My Love" (1963), a 1956 R&B hit for Jesse Belvin that Two Girls and a Guy had included in some of their original Olympia shows. The group continued to release albums (a total of eight for Dolton) and singles, but their low-key vocal harmonies were ignored after the 1964 arrival of the British invasion guitar groups.

After Dolton dropped the group in 1965, the Fleetwoods recorded a pair of unsuccessful albums, *In a Mellow Mood* (1966, Sunset) and *The Look of Love, Sound of Soul* (1967, Verve), and then called it quits. But, although gone, the Fleetwoods were hardly forgotten. "The Great Imposter" was featured on the soundtrack for the 1973 movie *American Graffiti*, the film credited for kicking off the 1950s revival. The group re-formed in the late 1970s, but first Ellis and then Troxell departed; Christopher continued to tour with two other singers as the Fleetwoods. An excellent greatest hits album on Rhino Records (*The Best of the Fleetwoods*, 1990) made sure their songs would be heard by a new generation of listeners. **JB**

The Best of the Fleetwoods

(1990, RHINO)
All the Top 40 singles are here, mixed with an equal number of well-chosen but lesser-known Fleetwoods songs.

Floating Bridge

Formed 1968, Seattle, Washington

floating Bridge is fondly remembered as one of the quintessential late-1960s Northwest guitar groups, and their many appearances at festivals and psychedelic ballrooms are the stuff of legend.

Floating Bridge evolved from a 1967 group called Unknown Factor. Featuring Rich Dangel (guitar), Joe Johansen (guitar), Joe Johnson (bass), and Michael Marinelli (drums), Unknown Factor basically provided backup for vocalists Ron Holden and Patti Allen. Holden was a Northwest fixture—in 1960, his doo-woppish "Love You So" became a national smash (reaching no. 7 nationally).

Unknown Factor wasn't content to remain a backup band for long. Dangel had been a founding member of the Wailers, leaving that band in 1963 to study guitar and get deeper into jazz and blues. Multi-instrumentalist Johansen was already playing drums, trombone, tuba, upright bass, and steel guitar as a high schooler in the small town of Mossyrock, Washington. His band credits included the Adventurers (which, with local hero Little Bill of the Bluenotes as frontman, recorded one of the first versions of "Louie Louie"), the Checkers (a Yakima, Washington, band that toured with teen stars like Bobby Rydell, Freddy Cannon, and Bobby Vee), the Frantics, and the Dave Lewis Trio. Johnson, originally from Texas, had played locally with Sir Walter Raleigh and the Coupons (featuring future Buffalo Springfield drummer Dewey Martin). Marinelli came from the East Coast as part of a duo with organist Howard Wales.

The band changed its name to Floating Bridge in 1968, but was still singerless when a house gig came up at Mr. P's, a tavern-cabaret in Seattle's Ballard neighborhood. Underage Pat Gossan, in a fit of bravado, joined them onstage one night and was immediately asked to join the band. Gossan may have been young, but he was no beginner. He had previously played in the Ambassadors as organ player and vocalist, fronted the psychedelic Papa Bear's Medicine Show (which opened for the Grateful Dead at Seattle's Golden Gardens Park in 1967), and spent a year and a half with Punch (a band from suburban Mercer Island featuring future Bluebird members John Soltero and David Baroh). Floating Bridge played bluesy hard rock with blazing twin lead guitar work everywhere. Some jazz influences crept in, but overall their melodies and hooks were quite psychedelic.

Floating Bridge's timing was solid. Their first gig with Gossan was a slot at the much-anticipated 1968 Sky River Rock Festival in Sultan, Washington on Labor Day weekend. Their manager, Frank DeQuilla, had assured them that talent scouts from major labels would be there, and in fact, a representative from Liberty/Vault Records liked what he heard and quickly signed the band.

Floating Bridge played a few more local shows, blowing audiences away with the guitar interplay of Johansen and Dangel. Many of their songs were lengthy instrumental improvisations, as Marinelli's thundering drums and Johnson's tight bass work held down the rhythm. Gossan didn't play any keyboards (how could he, with so much guitar work going on), but his wild lyrics and frenzied percussion made him a manic focal point.

In October 1968 Floating Bridge went to Los Angeles to record an album with producer Jackie Mills. Through Vault's efforts, the band played several high-profile Los Angeles shows, including an opening spot at the Forum for British rockers Ten Years After on their first American tour. Other opening gigs matched them with Iron Butterfly and Albert King.

Coming back to Seattle for the new year, band members were treated like stars. They weren't entirely happy with the finished album, which came out in early 1969; they didn't have enough good original material, but their take on the "Eight Miles High"/"Paint It Black" medley is excellent, as are the originals "Crackshot" and "You've Got the Power." Floating Bridge played a memorable December 27 show at the Seattle Center Arena with headliners Vanilla Fudge. Also on the bill was Led Zeppelin, in their first Northwest appearance.

Despite regular gigs at the popular Eagles Auditorium and opening slots for national acts like the Moody Blues, the money wasn't enough for Dangel, who had a family and needed more security. He left Floating Bridge to join a lounge trio called Sledgehammer, which, while not as musically adventurous, at least paid well.

Guitarist Denny McCleod replaced Dangel, bringing with him a slight country influence. After hooking up with the promoters Far West, the band started getting better shows. Floating Bridge opened the second day of the Seattle Pop Festival (Crome Syrcus was the only other local band on the bill), and they also played the Vancouver Pop Festival, in British Columbia and the Buffalo Party Convention in Eatonville.

Vault Records was reasonably happy with the first album (also released in England and Japan). In the fall of 1969, Floating Bridge journeyed to San Francisco to record a second one. Their new manager, Eric Nelson, financed the recording (at Columbia Studios in the North Beach neighborhood), and everyone involved was pleased with the results. The original material was strong—the 21-minute "Ode to Crazy Ray" is a psychedelic classic—and the band was allowed to participate in mixing and production. But Vault decided to pass on the album; it remains unreleased to this day.

McCleod's subsequent departure kicked off the band's most adventurous era. He was replaced by Michael Jacobsen on electric cello and sax and Andrew Lang, Jr., on trumpet. But the band's "hip" status was slipping, and their gigs were mostly teen dances.

In the fall of 1970, Floating Bridge suffered a double blow from which it never recovered. Their van rolled over on the way to a gig, damaging the vehicle and causing minor injuries to band members. Soon afterward, the van itself was stolen—with all of Floating Bridge's equipment inside. Old friends in the band Bluebird headlined a benefit show to help finance new equipment, but the group broke up in December 1970.

Of the band members, Gossan and Dangel have remained the most active musically. Gossan has been in a variety of country blues and rock acts, including Wagon Wheel Willie and the Five Spokes, the Woodpeckers, Freddie and the Screamers, and Fat Cat. Dangel led the Reputations for years, is involved in regular Wailers reunions, and is a prolific solo performer. Sadly, Johansen and Johnson have both died. Johansen had worked regularly as a session guitarist in Los Angeles, playing with acts such as Bobby Sherman and Delaney and Bonnie.

Floating Bridge's short career produced some memorable shows and one long-out-of-print album, and their blend of bluesy psychedelia and fiery guitar interplay will long be remembered. **NS**

Flop

Formed 1990, Seattle, Washington

Pure Joy

Formed 1986, Seattle, Washington

When all of Rusty Willoughby's high school friends moved to Seattle in 1984 to attend the University of Washington, he went too—except he skipped the school part. Working in a Burger King in the University District, Willoughby (guitar, vocals) joined friends Scott Sutherland (guitar), Lisa King (bass), and Jim Hunnicut (drums) to form the Dwindles. The band lasted about a year and a half, playing dorm parties and the rare bar gig. Having finally booked studio time to make a record, Sutherland suddenly quit to form his own band, Chemistry Set. Undaunted, the now three-piece band played the session anyway, stealing their new name from a song by the Teardrop Explodes—Pure Joy.

This session resulted in "The Attempt" and "Words Conceal," two of the four songs on the band's self-titled debut EP. Rusty's brother, Randy, who had just been discharged from the Air Force, showed up in town and was recruited to play keyboards on the last two tracks. Among the record's admirers were DJs at the University of Washington radio station KCMU, who provided the airplay through which *Pure Joy* is still fondly remembered by many Seattle rock fans, not including Rusty. "It's still embarrassing—it sounds stupid to me," he says.

The band's lineup remained the same until 1988: when brotherly feuding led to Randy's departure, Craig Montgomery took over on guitar and keyboards. A friend of their manager at the time played benefactor, paying for hours of studio time at Ironwood Studios. He'd also promised to pay for the pressing of the record, but Montgomery and Willoughby had nagging doubts. During the mastering process, the two taped their own copy of the twelve songs. When they returned from a tour, their would-be benefactor had disappeared. Unfortunately, even with the copy of the tape, the band lacked the money required to release the album. (In 1994, the "great lost Pure Joy record," minus three of the slower tracks, was released on Flydaddy Records as *Unsung*.)

After a few more shows, both Hunnicut and Montgomery decided to leave the band. Drummer Andy Davenhall (later of Sister Psychic) was recruited, and Pure Joy became a three-piece band with a darker, stripped-down sound. They released a single ("Now I Know"/"All the Stupid Things") on Fatbald Records in 1989 and the album *Carnivore* (1989, PopLlama), showing a band with pure pop instincts, yet influenced by the harsher sounds then being produced by their Seattle brethren.

A disastrous tour and Willoughby's general lack of interest in continuing Pure Joy led to the creation of Flop. Pure Joy was scheduled to appear on the cover of the Seattle rock magazine *Backlash*. Unbeknownst to the writer, Willoughby had started practicing with ex-Fastbacks drummer Nate Johnson, bassist Paul Schurr, and guitarist Bill Stevenson, so when the writer arrived for the interview, he found waiting for him not Pure Joy but Flop. "We came up with the name riding on the bus to the interview," recalls Stevenson.

The band quickly recorded the four-song EP *Flop* (1990, Lucky) and a single on the Dashboard Hulagirl label in 1991 ("Drugs"/"Action") before signing with Frontier Records. Their first two releases on Frontier were both pop classics: *Flop & the Fall of the Mopsqueezer* (1992) and *Whenever You're Ready* (1993). Flop mounted three major U.S. tours and several minitours, often built around their concentrations of college radio play—spots like St. Louis, Austin, Houston, and Lawrence, Kansas. They also toured with Redd Kross, the Posies, and the Lemonheads. In fact, it was on a British tour with the Posies that they met up with Dave Fox (then a Posie), the bassist they recruited to replace the departing Schurr. He played on Flop's swan song, *World of Today* (1995).

But the story doesn't actually end there. After a hiatus, Seattle clubgoers again began to spot "The Dwindles" in the club listings—it was Willoughby and two original members of Pure Joy/Dwindles, bassist King and drummer Hunnicut. The band returned to the name Pure Joy in early 1997 and released an album, *Getz, The Worm*, later that year. **JB**

Carnivore

(1989, POPLLAMA)
A snapshot of a great time in Seattle music, Pure Joy's *Carnivore* features a ripping good collection of Willoughby songs, played with clenched-teeth intensity. Also included on the CD release are three tracks from the rare vinyl-only EP *Sore Throte, Ded Goat* (1990, No Threes Records), an aural momento of Pure Joy's last live performance.

Flop & the Fall of the Mopsqueezer

(1992, FRONTIER)
Okay, it would have made just as much sense to choose Flop's *Whenever You're Ready* (1993). But *The Mopsqueezer* has more power pop garage spirit than its somewhat Beatlesque follow-up, plus it opens with a four-pack of the band's best songs. Rave on.

Foo Fighters

Formed 1994, Seattle, Washington

dave Grohl had no intention of becoming a drummer for hire following the death of Nirvana singer Kurt Cobain. A veteran of the Washington, D.C., bands Mission Impossible, Dain Bramage, and Scream, he had relocated to Seattle to join Nirvana in late 1990. During the eventful years that followed, Grohl had been recording songs of his own on the side, planning to release them under a pseudonym. After Cobain's 1994 suicide, Grohl decided to book time in a 24-track studio and make a professional-quality recording with producer Barrett Jones. Starting with the drums, he built each track by adding guitars, bass, and finally vocals. Grohl made one hundred copies of the resulting mixes.

Copies of the tapes started making the rounds in Seattle. Record companies were interested. So was Pat Smear, the former Germs guitarist who had toured with Nirvana and played on the album *Unplugged in New York*. When Grohl finally decided to release the tapes and form a band, he snagged the rhythm section from the crumbling Sunny Day Real Estate—Nate Mendel (bass) and William Goldsmith (drums). The resulting band was dubbed Foo Fighters, World War II Air Force lingo for unidentified flying objects. Although poised to tour in support of the *Foo Fighters* album, Grohl's fellow band members had actually made just one contribution to it—posing for their photographs. Except for one guitar track by the Afghan Whigs' Greg Dulli, Grohl played it all.

Although the music was carefully examined for similarities to Nirvana, few were readily apparent. While Cobain's punk edges obscured his sense of melody and pop song construction, Grohl is a pop singer who churns out speedy radio-worthy thumpers at will ("This Is a Call," "Good Grief"). He's also good for one scorching screamfest per album—check out "Weenie Beenie" on *Foo Fighters* for the proof. Despite a torrent of friendly press, all touting Foo Fighters as a band of equals and great pals besides, Goldsmith split from the band before the release of *The Colour and the Shape* (1997). His "pal" Grohl erased most of his drum parts and rerecorded them himself. Smear has since left the band and been replaced by Franz Stahl (guitar). Taylor Hawkins played drums on a recent Foo Fighters tour. Mandel says he'll stay a Foo Fighter, although he appeared on the Sunny Day Real Estate reunion record. Stahl quit the band in mid-1999, squelching their plans to play a set at the Woodstock '99 festival. **JB**

Foo Fighters

(1995, ROSWELL/CAPITOL)
This "one-man show" album demonstrates Grohl's adept touch at alternative pop.

Forced Entry

Formed 1986, Seattle, Washington

mention the name Forced Entry to anyone familiar with the Northwest thrash metal scene of the late 1980s and early 1990s, and images of intoxicated postadolescent males butting heads in a rolling mass immediately spring to mind. To this day, no other Northwest independent metal band has had a more fanatical (or inebriated) following. Beyond their hard-driving party image, though, Forced Entry showed that a local underground metal band could become a success through promoting their own shows and marketing their own music.

Forced Entry was formed by high school buddies Tony Benjamins (bass, vocals), Brad Hull (lead guitar, vocals), and Colin Mattson (drums) in 1986. Their first indie release, *All Fucked Up*, came in early 1987 and featured "Get Fucked Up," a great party tune that was to remain a staple of their live set.

Things really started moving for the band after their rehearsal room burned down, reportedly because Benjamins's cat got too close to a space heater. With the resulting insurance money, the group was able to finance its second release, *Thrashing Helpless Down* (1987), which ultimately sold thousands of copies and garnered considerable underground radio airplay worldwide.

On the strength of this indie effort, as well as their fanatical regional following, Forced Entry was signed by Combat/Relativity in 1989. Their first album, *Uncertain Future*, featured better recordings of previously released tracks such as "Anaconda" and "Unrest They Find," and cemented Forced Entry's place at the top of the Northwest thrash metal pantheon.

Like many bands of the thrash/speed metal genre, Forced Entry was clearly influenced by heavyweights such as Metallica and Slayer, but their hypnotic rhythms and occasionally melodic vocals also predate more successful (and sometimes uncannily similar) later efforts by groups such as Prong, Helmet, and Tool. And Forced Entry was blessed with an exceptional lead guitarist in Brad Hull, who had the rare ability to fit his considerable playing chops into tasteful and coherent solos.

Following several tours in support of *Uncertain Future*, Forced Entry reentered the studio in late 1990 to record their second album for Relativity, *As Above, So Below*. While this album continued in the same brutal vein, the band was taking more chances sonically. This was especially true on "Bone Crackin' Fever," which featured a demonic riff that predates the later and widely heralded noise guitar of Rage Against the Machine's Tom Morello.

While this album did well among Forced Entry's local and international following, it came out at a time when label and media attention was shifting away from metal bands and toward the new and more radio-friendly wave of postpunk acts emerging from the Northwest. This shift, combined with internal problems at Relativity, led to Forced Entry's departure from the label in 1992.

Sans record deal, the band continued on for another three years, releasing a four-song CD, *The Shore*, in 1994. Fittingly enough, it was produced independently, a hallmark of a band that truly did things its own way.

While one doesn't hear much Forced Entry on local radio anymore, their influence is present in the work of the current generation of Northwest musicians, many of whom drank their first beer and slammed in their first mosh pit at one of Forced Entry's legendary all-ages shows. **MF**

As Above, So Below

(1990, RELATIVITY)
Great tunes, including "Bone Crackin' Fever" and "Macrocosm, Microcosm," as well as a new recording of longtime band staple "Get Fucked Up," retitled "How I Spent My Summer Vacation" to avoid distribution problems with uptight retailers.

The Frantics

Formed 1957, Seattle, Washington

One of the Northwest's most influential early rock acts, the Frantics broke new ground in the 1950s and have a sterling reputation more than forty years after their inception. They were among the most popular of Seattle's original rockers and, to this day, their first few singles are treasured finds.

Before rock 'n' roll (read "Elvis") hit the airwaves, 1950s radio was staid and conservative, featuring the likes of Mitch Miller, Rosemary Clooney, and Perry Como. Among the Northwest stations that jumped on the new rock bandwagon was KTAC in Tacoma, Washington. Their top DJ was Bob Summerrise, who played an eclectic blend of jazz, R&B, and the embryonic rock 'n' roll; a wild mix of Freddie King, Faye Adams, Fats Domino, Clyde McPhatter, and B. B. King.

It was this sort of ambiance that the young future Frantics were soaking up. Formed in 1957 as the Four Frantics by guitarist Ron Peterson, the band added his childhood friend from Seattle, Jim Manolides, later that year and became simply the Frantics. Manolides's "audition" with the band was at a dance at the nightspot Parker's, where he wowed everyone with Elvis Presley's version of "Let's Have a Party."

The band's lineup quickly solidified with Bob Hosko (sax), Chuck Schoning (keyboards), and Dick Goodman (drums). In 1957 there were only a few local rock 'n' roll acts—Seattle's Dave Lewis Combo and Tacoma's Wailers and Little Bill and the Bluenotes. With the burgeoning demand for "teenage music," the Frantics became popular quickly and effortlessly.

In the summer of 1958, the band got their first big break. Art Simpson, a DJ at Seattle's radio station KOL, allowed them to record a catchy instrumental, "Straight Flush," which they had composed on his station's equipment. After playing the demo tape and receiving favorable listener response, Simpson introduced the Frantics to

Bob Reisdorff, whose Dolton label would soon be in the money with a series of chart smashes by Olympia's Fleetwoods. "Straight Flush" was rerecorded at local producer Joe Boles's West Seattle basement studio and released in 1959. While getting lots of local airplay, the song barely nudged into the national charts, spending three weeks at the bottom of the Top 100.

Necessity Is the Mother of Invention

Before Seattle became the early-1990s answer to the Swinging London/Haight-Ashbury of the 1960s, it had a thriving underground scene on which many later-famous musicians cut their teeth.

Keep in mind that through most of the 1980s, the main venues in town for original music were 21-and-over clubs such as the Rainbow and Astor Park, and they weren't exactly friendly to up-and-coming glam, metal, or punk bands. Later on, the Central, Squid Row, and the Vogue began promoting original music for the over-21 crowd. But laws designed to separate young people and live music left underage Seattle kids without a regular live music venue to attend (unless they were willing and able to drive an hour or more to the Community World Theater in Tacoma or Natacha's in Bremerton).

This situation led to a thriving do-it-yourself underage music scene. Bands such as Forced Entry, Alice in Chains, and Mother Love Bone would rent spaces like the Veterans of Foreign Wars hall in the Ballard district, as well as the Musicians Hall in Renton, and the Skate King in Kent, both south of town. At their self-produced shows security was lax, which meant that underage drinking was tolerated, if not encouraged, and hundreds of kids came to check out the up-and-coming bands (and each other).

The other key element in this mix was a number of party houses, the sites of weekly gatherings: the Dog House in the Capitol Hill neighborhood, the Tramp House south of Seattle in Federal Way (home of glam band Tramp Alley, and well known to county health authorities as a nexus for the spread of, um, social diseases). Then there was my residence, the House of Death in the University District, the site of weekly gatherings to hear Jeff Gilbert's *Brain Pain* radio show on local station KCMU. In this way, young musicians spent many late nights together listening to new music, jamming in basements and bedrooms, and bonding over cheap beer.

Perhaps the most important outcome was that the once-clear boundaries between metal, glam, and punk were broken down. While these were discrete cliques in say, 1985, by 1989 what we had learned from one another led to a new fusion of genres that the world would eventually label "grunge."

Shortly after we started turning 21, new clubs such as the Off Ramp and RKCNDY were opening in Seattle, creating many more opportunities to play and party in a "legitimate" setting (that is, no worries about cops or eviction notices). For the most part, the new venues eventually supplanted the do-it-yourself and house-party scenes.

In retrospect, what surprises me most is how many of my contemporaries ultimately got record deals, from bands that did a few records and tours to full-on rock stars such as Alice in Chains, Nirvana, and Pearl Jam.

—Matthew Fox

Meanwhile, the Frantics were earning good money playing to rock 'n' roll–hungry teen audiences, often drawing up to 1,500 people to their dances. At one of these late 1950s dances, a skinny left-handed guitar player sat in with the Frantics—worldwide fame would come later to Jimi Hendrix.

Another single, the jazzy-sounding "Fog Cutter," was released in 1959. But it was their third single, "Werewolf" of 1960, that should have broken the act nationally. Over a rhythmic bed of haunting percussion, Peterson's guitar sounds vaguely like Link Wray's on the classic rockabilly instrumental "Rumble," only spookier. Reisdorff begins the song with a Boris Karloff–style tale of turning into a werewolf, and snarls and growls punctuate throughout. Pretty strong stuff, especially for a label that had just had a national no. 1 hit with the Fleetwoods' "Come Softly to Me." Feeling "Werewolf" was too intense for national radio consumption, rereleased it as "No Werewolf," minus the narration and sound effects. Not surprisingly, the cleaned-up version flopped.

In the late 1950s and early 1960s, touring solo stars would use local acts as backup bands. After the Frantics played a set with Bobby Darin, the singer asked if they could back him on his next single. The day after the show, they spent several hours at Boles's studio recording "Dream Lover," a no. 2 smash for Darin.

In 1961 the Frantics got their biggest break yet. They scored a house gig at a downtown Seattle lounge, Dave's Fifth Avenue. Core band members Peterson, Manolides, and Hosko remained, and the residency lasted six months. They were each earning about $600 a month—excellent money by 1961 standards. But the band had to tone down their music for the over-21 crowd, and their instrumental scorchers gave way to adult contemporary standards including "Never on Sunday" and "Misty." Yet the Frantics remained one of the most popular Northwest rock acts, releasing ten singles through 1963, all of which received local airplay.

By 1964 the band's membership was changing again. Peterson had left, and Manolides was in the Army. The band's name was still valuable, and they could attract top local musicians. Joe Johansen (ex–Dave Lewis Trio and later a member of Floating Bridge) played guitar alongside Jerry Miller during the mid-1960s. The Frantics drummer at this time was Jon Keliehor, who would later anchor the Daily Flash. But musically the band was becoming something of an anachronism, playing more lounge gigs.

In 1965 the Frantics decided to relocate to San Francisco. On the drive down, the band got in a serious car accident near Eugene, Oregon. Keliehor was hospitalized in Seattle, and the drummer for the local band the Daily Flash, Don Stevenson, went to the Bay Area to join the Frantics. After Keliehor recovered, he took Stevenson's place in the Daily Flash.

Miller and Stevenson remained in San Francisco as the Frantics, but by 1966 they had changed the band's name to Luminous Marsh Gas, which would in turn evolve into Moby Grape. The two led Moby Grape through their critically acclaimed career. While in Moby Grape, they played many Bay Area shows with Quicksilver Messenger

Service, whose keyboard player was old Frantic Chuck Schoning.

Peterson continued in the Northwest music scene for a while, leading a mid-1960s band called Ron Peterson and the Accents. Manolides has been quite prolific musically. He fronted James Henry and the Olympics during the mid-1960s, was a founding member (with Hosko) of Jr. Cadillac in 1970, and has since played with such bands as the Hardly Everly Brothers and the Bowling Stones.

The Frantics have re-formed their early lineup a few times in the 1970s and 1980s. Their reunion in June 1987 produced spirited renditions of "Fogcutter" and "Werewolf" that sounded as fresh and dynamic as in 1959. **NS**

Gabriel

Formed 1970, Seattle, Washington

abriel was one of the bigger local Seattle bands of the 1970s, lasting from 1970 through 1981. The only constant throughout their career was drummer Michael Kinder. Other longtime members were founder Stacy Christenson (keyboards), Gary Ruhl (bass), Terry Lauber (guitar), and Frank Butorac (guitar). Lauber was a veteran of Merrilee and the Turnabouts; Christenson had played with the Statesmen. Managed by Don McKinney of Entertainment Authorities (former Don and the Goodtimes singer), Gabriel was one of the few Northwest acts of the era to release albums on national labels: *This Star on Every Heel* (1975, ABC), *Sweet Release* (1976, ABC), and *Gabriel* (1978, Epic). All three sold respectably, and the band even notched a couple of Top 5 hits in Europe. National record promoter David Krause was instrumental in hooking the band up with these major-label deals.

The albums, however, were far softer and more radio-friendly than Gabriel's live shows, which generally featured an intriguing mix of sophisticated R&B, hard rock, and good old rock 'n' roll. The band was also supplemented on their albums by session musicians—ranging from Philadelphia's legendary MFSB Orchestra to local friends such as Danny O'Keefe, Kim Eggers (Viceroys), and Kell Houston. Gabriel also managed national tours with Sha Na Na, Bread, and George Thorogood. Various Gabriel members have remained active in music: Kinder has played with the Wailers during much of the 1990s, and he and Ruhl are the rhythm section in the Blues Power Review (with ex-Static Richard Gerber). Christenson played with funk/soul band Epicentre and currently runs a successful north Seattle recording studio. **NS**

Gas Huffer
Formed 1988, Seattle, Washington

The U-Men
Formed 1982, Seattle, Washington

In the early 1980s, damn few people rocked at all, but no one rocked more majestically than the U-Men. Tom Price's creepy, jerky guitar lines, John Bigley's gut-busting vocals, and the band's improvisational spirit made the rudimentary rantings of most early-1980s bands sound wimpy by comparison. Some have compared them to the Cramps, the Birthday Party, and Screamin' Jay Hawkins, but in Seattle, the U-Men had no peer.

Through most of their existence, the lineup consisted of Price, Bigley, bassist Jim Tillman, and drummer Charlie Ryan. There were many times when the four of them took the stage drunk and out of tune, which annoyed folks who paid the cover charge, but at least each U-Men show promised a spectacle, often featuring performance art, barbecue, horror movies, souvenir barf bags, anything manager Larry Reid could think up. Reid was the reigning king of the art punk scene at that time and owned two of Seattle's coolest live music venues, the Graven Image and Ground Zero art galleries. His innovative publicity efforts turned every U-Men gig into a carnival.

But the band came up with the flaming moat idea all by themselves. The U-Men performed on a stage surrounded by a pond at the Seattle Center Mural Amphitheater in what was unquestionably their most memorable gig. Friends of the band poured lighter fluid into the water, and Bigley set it on fire, looking as shocked as everyone else when 20-foot flames shot up and surrounded the stage. They were not invited back.

The U-Men released their first EP in 1984 on Bombshelter Records, Bruce Pavitt's label before he went on to found Sub Pop Records. They recorded another EP, *Stop Spinning*, for Homestead Records in 1985, and two excellent singles in 1987 and 1988, all of which are out of print. Sub Pop has considered rereleasing the whole mess on a CD someday; if and when they do, the world will be a happier place indeed.

But life was not so happy for the U-Men, who suffered in poverty for their art. After a couple of grueling tours, the band members grew sick of each other, and of wondering where the grocery money would come from. Tillman left the band in 1988 and was replaced by Tom Hazelmeyer, now the owner of the Amphetamine Reptile label in Minneapolis.

Hazelmeyer was in turn replaced by Tony Ransom, whose youth and enthusiasm temporarily injected new life into an increasingly burnt-out band. Their first and only full-length LP, *Step on a Bug: The Red Toad Speaks*, was released in 1988, but interest in the band was waning, and the gigs became further apart.

Price recalls that the third time he showed up for practice and found no other band members there, "I finally got the hint that someone was trying to tell me something." After striving for eight years to sound dark and sinister, Price was ready for a different direction. "I just wanted to punk out for a while," he says. Price's next band, Gas Huffer, evolved from the Kings of Rock, which played mostly jokey versions of garage rock classics. At the same time, Price worked at getting a more serious band together. He and Don Blackstone, the Kings' bassist, got together with drummer Joe Newton and began jamming.

At first Price tried to sing. Newton tactfully suggested he concentrate on his guitar playing. When it came to finding a singer, Price thought of Matt Wright, an Eastern Washington college student who had previously sung in the Walla Walla–based Holy Ghost People. Tom had been amazed when he first saw that band open for the U-Men the year before. He thought the mutton-chopped Wright was the best punk singer in the Northwest.

Before the release of their first real album, Gas Huffer released an album's worth of singles. They seemed unable to turn down any small label, cutting records for Regal Select, Black Label (both coincidentally named after a cheap brand of beer), Estrus, C/Z, Amphetamine Reptile, and the Steve Priest Fan Club, run by the Fastbacks' Kurt Bloch.

In 1991 Gas Huffer left for a national tour with Mudhoney the week before their LP *Janitors of Tomorrow* was released. Price found himself playing in some of the same cities the U-Men had tried and failed to win over, only this time at 1,200-seat theaters. Wright's spastic stage presence complemented his goofball lyrics, which, over the years, have covered subjects from sand fleas to weighty topics like "The Sin of Sloth."

After the tour, the band members kept their day jobs and continued to play Seattle gigs. In 1992 they recorded *Integrity, Technology and Service*, and the fledgling eMpTy Records went directly to work to book more tours for them. Their quest for fame, fortune, and decent road food has been captured in the Gas Huffer comic books, four so far. Drawn by all four band members, the books are included as free bonuses with the vinyl releases of all their LPs.

In 1993 Epitaph Records, which until then had focused on thrash music, managed to convince Gas Huffer of their benevolence and released *One Inch Masters* (1994), *The Inhuman Ordeal of Special Agent Gas Huffer* (1996), and *Just Beautiful Music* (1998). The band began touring and enjoying the moderate benefits of backing from a larger independent label.

The 1998 album careens off in unexpected directions, including the sort of wild, experimental guitar that longtime Price fans always knew he was capable of. Wright addresses the usual wide range of topics, from Viking attacks to homemade explosives, greed, and anger, with a new, disturbing note of pensiveness in a couple of the love songs.

They haven't abandoned punk "rawk" by any means, but one can only speculate about what strange new sounds these four will come up with next—either in Gas Huffer or in their inevitable future bands. **DA**

Step on a Bug: The Red Toad Speaks

(1988, BLACK LABEL)

A screaming art punk psychotic seizure. Call Sub Pop Records every day and pester them to rerelease the early U-Men stuff.

Integrity, Technology and Service

(1992, EMPTY)

All five Gas Huffer records are pretty rockin', but this one has the cool song about sand fleas on it.

Green Apple Quick Step
Formed 1991, Seattle, Washington

Inspector Luv
Formed 1989, Tacoma, Washington

Green Apple Quick Step traces its history back to the summer of 1987, when Tacoma, Washington, boy Dan Kempthorne talked Ty Willman out of five bucks to accompany him to a Jane's Addiction, Soundgarden, and Mother Love Bone show up in Seattle. A couple of years later, the two (along with pal Steven Ross) were living in the basement of Tacoma promoter Jim May's rented theater, playing in a band together. A tape of four songs from their first recording session was released on Aroma Records as a vinyl EP. The group (including drummer Bob Martin and bassist Eric) decided to move north to Seattle after a club owner there explained he only bothered to book bands that had friends in town.

This first incarnation of the band, called Inspector Luv for short (the complete version of the name was Inspector Luv and the Ride Me Babies), quickly established themselves in Seattle as a fun-loving fivesome of musical pranksters and a great, if sometimes unfocused, musical outfit. Despite a big-talking manager, Inspector Luv never hooked up with a major label.

Fast-forward to 1992: with new bassist Mari Ann Braeden, the band has rechristened itself Green Apple Quick Step and taken to the studio to experiment with new twists on their typically heavy Seattle sound. By this time the band is tighter, the new songs better, and fellow Seattle homeboys Pearl Jam and Soundgarden are big rock stars—major-label bidding war, anyone? After allowing themselves to be wined and dined by record company representatives (Dan got a signed copy of Madonna's book *Sex*, but the band still didn't sign with the famous singer's Maverick label), the band signed with the New York–based label Medicine.

Green Apple Quick Step's first Medicine release, *Wonderful Virus* (1993), showed a band with ideas to spare and no great loyalty to Seattle's heavy rock tradition. Songs not only fire up ("Bottle" is an obvious exception) but also float along ("Feel My Way") and percolate (the graceful "Dirty Water Ocean"). But the overall sound was judged similar enough to their bigger-selling Seattle brethren to earn the band a cool reception from critics.

The 1995 follow-up, *Reloaded*, was an obvious attempt to wean themselves from Seattle-sound life support. It worked. Producers Stone Gossard and Nick Didja supervised the set; the band provided the different sounds, as Braeden took a higher-profile vocal position (lead vocal on "No Favors" and major background contributions), the guitarists found some funky positions on the fretboard, and Willman stretched out as a vocalist ("T.V. Girl").

If this band's career had been an up-and-down affair, its last days were a roller-coaster ride. Green Apple Quick Step revamped its lineup, replacing Ross and Martin with guitarist Dana Turner and drummer Jeff Reading, and signed to Columbia Records. Their third album, *New Disaster* (1998), was fully completed and advance copies had been distributed to the media, but it was suddenly withdrawn before final release, and the band was dropped by Columbia. The group originally intended to shop the album to other labels, but the project was never heard from again, and Green Apple Quick Step drifted apart. In early 1999 Willman released a solo EP on Loosegroove Records by the name *Calm Down Juanita*.   **JB**

Reloaded

(1995, MEDICINE)
A superior showcase for Green Apple Quick Step's guitar prowess and Ty Willman's vocals. Don't worry about the slow start—it gets catchy after a while.

Green Pajamas
Formed 1983, Seattle, Washington

n ot a whole lot was happening musically in Seattle during 1983, but a chance meeting at a summer party changed things. Multi-instrumentalists Jeff Kelly and Joe Ross met and discovered a mutual love for edgy 1960s psychedelic pop. Both were veterans of several bands, and Kelly already had a backlog of dozens of highly crafted demos of original songs.

The two collaborated on the home-recorded *Summer of Lust*. Drummer Karl Wilhelm was added, and the Green Pajamas (fondly known as the PJ's) began to get a reputation. Guitarist Steve Lawrence joined in late 1984, and the foursome rapidly became a popular live draw.

Producer Tom Dyer cut three tracks with them in early 1985—"Jennifer," "Peppermint Stick," and "Kim the Waitress"—and soon their first full-length album,

Book of Hours, was recorded. Ross then left, to be replaced by keyboard player Bruce Haedt. With Kelly and Lawrence sharing bass duties, *Book of Hours* was released in 1987 to excellent critical response. Favorable comparisons to the psychedelic eras of the Beatles and Rolling Stones were lavished on the band, as writers from Europe and England heaped praise on them.

In early 1988 Haedt left and Ross returned. Various cassette-only projects were issued, while Kelly's remarkable moody psych-pop creations continued to amaze. That same year saw a new single, "Sister Anne"/"Emily Grace." The album *Ghosts of Love* was released the following year, with ten more Kelly gems. Orchestration, bagpipes, and psychedelic effects only served to heighten the brilliant songwriting.

After *Ghosts of Love*, the band went on hiatus. All continued to record their own projects, but live performances were a thing of the past. Ross and Kelly kept writing high-quality songs, and many of Kelly's songs were nothing short of amazing, even in home-studio demo form.

In 1993, the Green Pajamas were back with a moody single, "I Have Touched Madness"/"Song for Christina," released on Ross's Endgame Records. The band began performing live again. Another multi-instrumentalist, Eric Lichter, was added to the core of Kelly, Ross, and Wilhelm, and his songwriting, percussion, keyboard, and guitar abilities make this lineup the strongest yet. Averaging a show every month or two, the band has been gaining a new fan base.

The Green Pajamas have been very prolific in the studio since the mid-1990s. In 1997 alone they released three CDs on different labels: *Indian Winter* (East Coast independent label Get Hip), *Strung Behind the Sun* (Camera Obscura), and *Strung Out* (Endgame). Plans are being formulated to release the band's back album catalog on CD with lots of unreleased bonus tracks.

More than fifteen years after their formation, the Green Pajamas are more popular than ever. In 1995, the decade-old track "Kim the Waitress" was covered twice, by Material Issue and Sister Psychic. In 1998, Laura Weller (who played with Ross in the band Capping Day) joined on vocals and acoustic guitar. While a European tour is discussed, new fans keep discovering their magic. **NS**

Ghosts of Love

(1989, Bomp)
The last full-length effort with Steve Lawrence. Jeff Kelly's writing is melodic and morose here; his lyrics are true poetry, and the density of the production is breathtaking.

Indian Winter

(1997, Get Hip)
A retrospective compilation covering the Green Pajamas' history, this gem collects their singles and rarities. *Indian Winter* is the best place to start, but once you've heard the band's shimmering psychedelia, you won't be able to stop. CONTINUED...

Strung Behind the Sun

(1997, CAMERA OBSCURA)
The first effort with Eric Lichter. Moody, glittering, and impassioned, this material is some of the best of their career.

Green River

Formed 1984, Seattle, Washington

after high school noise-rockers Mr. Epp & the Calculations ended a four-year assault on the eardrums (and sensibilities) of unsuspecting new-wave Seattle in 1984, Epp's two guitarists, founding member Mark Arm and late addition Steve Turner, "decided that we still wanted to keep on rockin'," as Arm tells the story. Their first recruits were bassist Jeff Ament and drummer Alex Shumway. Ament, then playing with Deranged Diction, made the cut because "he played through a distortion box, and he jumped up in the air a lot," confides Arm. Guitarist Stone Gossard, who had played with Turner in the Ducky Boys, was the last original member to join, signing on just before the band's debut show in late 1984. His arrival allowed Arm to put down his guitar and concentrate on vocals.

The arty noise-rock leanings of Mr. Epp were long gone by this time. Arm was influenced by hardcore punk, and suburban boy Gossard brought in metal influences. All were enthralled by the trashrock revival of the period: vintage tracks by the New York Dolls, Iggy Pop and the Stooges, and Alice Cooper were constantly on their turntables. The first album, *Come on Down* (1985), released on Boston's Homestead Records, showed the band making the transition from simpler songs like the title track and "Swallow My Pride" to the extended multisectioned "Tunnel of Love." Turner didn't like it. "Steve quit for that very reason," says Arm. "He just discovered Billy Childish and the Milkshakes and [minimalist] stuff like that." With Turner refusing to accompany the band on tour, Bruce Fairweather took his place in mid-1985, in time to play on the two tracks Green River contributed to the legendary sampler LP *Deep Six* (1985, C/Z). By this time, it was clear the band had little future on Homestead, says Arm. "I remember calling Homestead a lot and not getting past the receptionist."

By late 1986 Green River held the title of Seattle's best band, had self-released the single "Together We'll Never"/"Ain't Nothing to Do" (November 1986; a different version of "Together" was included on *Rehab Doll*, 1988), and had five great tracks on tape but no way to get them out. Local college radio guys Bruce Pavitt and Jonathan Poneman stepped into the breach, forming Sub Pop Records and releasing the two EPs that would define the Seattle scene for years to come, Soundgarden's *Screaming Life* and Green River's *Dry as a Bone* (both 1987).

With these two records, Seattle's reputation as an alternative music town began to grow, and Green River was able to schedule tours. Arm remembers the band's visit to New York well. "We played CBGBs to the staff and four Japanese tourists. But we were so jazzed—the Dead Boys played here, and the Ramones!" The band also made it to California twice and were a van breakdown away from playing shows in Texas. However, there was another big breakdown in that van: on the final tour down the coast, the band battled over the tape player. "On the drive down there, I remember trying to listen to the Scientists and Feedtime and everyone else being really bummed out about it," says Arm. "And [the other members] cranking the first Guns N' Roses record and the new Aerosmith, which was kind of at odds with what I wanted to do." The final Green River album, *Rehab Doll*, was finished by January 1988 but not released until June. By then the band had splintered over their musical differences—the pieces later became Mudhoney (Arm and Turner) and Mother Love Bone (Ament, Gossard, and Fairweather). **JB**

Dry as a Bone/Rehab Doll

(1987/1988, Sub Pop)
The CD release includes both these records, plus three extra tracks unavailable on albums. This is the best and most essential recording of the early Seattle scene. Why don't you have it already?

Hazel

Formed 1991, Portland, Oregon

hazel had an attitude. They clashed with audiences who didn't care for their music or their stage antics. Their Web site brims with pages of vitriolic press criticism. Although a musical trio, they had a fourth member onstage, dancer Fred Nemo, who once told a magazine interviewer: "My job is to upset the audience, really. That's the central thing."

The band—guitarist and vocalist Pete Krebs, drummer and vocalist Jody Bleyle, bassist Brady Smith, and Nemo—was a musically prolific member of the early 1980s Portland scene. They contributed tracks to four compilation albums and released a single on Cavity Search before being caught up in the Portland shopping spree of Seattle's Sub Pop Records. The band released two more singles ("Jilted" on Sub Pop and "Heida" on Candy Ass) before their first full-length album, *Toreador of Love*, came out in August 1993. This well-received debut showed their swirl of influences—sitting on the waning edge of Northwest sludge rock and the leading edge of lo-fi, but with a pop edge. Bleyle and Krebs sounded awfully good when they sang together in a yin-yang of sharply different voices that fit together. The band's live performances made many converts and a few enemies—some folks just couldn't figure why the trio was accompanied by an oddly dressed gray-haired guy flailing around to the music.

After a few more singles, the band released *Are You Going to Eat That* (1995), their second and final Sub Pop long-player. The record further developed the Bleyle-Krebs vocal partnership and had some pretty moments, including "Ringing in My Ears" and "Crowned." Curiously enough, unlike most every album released in the CD format, the better songs are clustered near the end. The record received a tepid critical response (most writers preferred the first record, or complained that Hazel were becoming tired "indie" rockers).

By this time, Bleyle was also drumming with Olympia's Team Dresch and running Candy Ass Records, so the band's future was in question. (Fred again, from another interview: "It's an anti-industry stance, having it blurred whether you have broken up or not.") Hazel answered the question in two ways, by releasing the EP *Airiana* (1997) and by actually breaking up. They re-formed in early 1998 for a few shows. **JB**

Airiana

(1997, CANDY ASS)
It's only a five-song EP, but this is the best recorded sound Hazel ever achieved, and there's lots of Jody Bleyle singing on it. She even gets a solo vocal turn on the title track.

Heart

Formed 1967, Kenmore, Washington

mentioning the name "Heart" immediately brings to mind two legendary forces in Seattle music. That's right—Roger Fisher and Steve Fossen. Although most music books trace Heart's history back only to 1974, when Nancy Wilson joined her sister Ann in the band, the group actually dates back to 1967 as Army. Ann Wilson joined a later version of the band in 1971. But it was only after the band tallied two Wilson sisters that Heart became known outside the Northwest, eventually selling twenty million albums in the United States alone.

The band that would become known as Heart was formed in the Seattle suburb of Kenmore by Inglemoor High School buddies Roger Fisher (guitar, vocals), Steve Fossen (bass), and Don Wilhelm (vocals, keyboards, guitar), along with drummer Ray Shaefer. Known as Army, the band had an entrepreneurial flair from the start. They put on their own dances, promoting shows with such slogans as "The Army of Love," "The Army of Music," and "Come Join the Army."

A major factor in Army's early success was manager Mike Fisher, Roger's older brother. A gifted artist, he designed logos and psychedelic posters for the band, and his construction worker salary helped finance expensive equipment purchases.

The band also had a load of talent. Roger Fisher was a keen student of the white blues phenomenon, and Fossen's bass lines were equally influenced by Northwest bassists like Andy Parypa and Buck Ormsby and the usual British rockers. Wilhelm alternated on organ and guitar and provided soulful, passionate lead vocals. The band was known for their vocal prowess—they spent hours creating and practicing their intricate harmonies. Their renditions of Beatles songs were the highlight of their sets.

In mid-1968 the band underwent two major changes relating to the Vietnam War. Mentor Mike Fisher moved to Vancouver, British Columbia, to avoid the draft. The name "Army" was starting to attract complaints from peace-loving fans, so in December it was changed to Whiteheart. This was a golden era for the band. The members had finally graduated from high school and could now travel. What's more, they were young and cute enough to attract teenage girls, but musically proficient enough to please more serious music fans.

A bit of musical meddling by new managers Entertainment Authorities temporarily halted Whiteheart's rise. Pairing the existing members with guitarist/vocalist Carl Wilson (formerly of Portland's Mr. Lucky and the Gamblers and Merrilee and the Turnabouts), management rechristened the band Carl Wilson and Heart. With management-imposed matching suits and Wilson's songs dominating the set list, the new band debuted at a Bellingham, Washington, show. For the first time in their career, they got booed. Wilson departed in early 1970.

The Wilson-less Heart played a six-week stand in 1970 at the Warehouse Tavern in Bellevue, a suburb of Seattle; the gig cemented their local popularity. Drummer Shaefer departed later that year and was replaced by Ron Rudge. The next original member to go was Wilhelm, who quit that summer. At that point the band expanded to six members by adding vocalist Gary Ziegleman (ex–Buffalo Clancy), percussionist Ken Hanson, and 15-year-old Bellevue guitar prodigy James Chirillo. With the new lineup, Heart became more musically adventurous, experimenting with odd time signatures, strange tunings, and even more mysterious original songs. In the process of recording an album of original material with producer Don McKinney, the band scored a coveted spot playing on a live television broadcast on the Seattle station KIRO. Sounding like no one else and looking like the Mothers of Invention, the group saw what should have been their big break turn into a disaster. The station was deluged with complaints about the hippie weirdos, the album was shelved, and this version of the band drifted apart.

Fossen and Fisher tried to carry on Heart with different musicians, but in 1971 decided to reunite with original frontman Wilhelm in a new band called Hocus Pocus. The other members were guitarist Mick Etchoe (formerly of Raisin' Cain and the Funn Company) and three members of the defunct band A Boy and His Dog— drummer Chris Blaine and vocalists Gary Humphries and Ann Wilson. The new band resulted in two romantic matches—Ann began to date Mike Fisher, and Ann's younger sister, Nancy, and Roger Fisher became an item.

When Hocus Pocus broke up in mid-1972, Ann moved to Vancouver to be with Mike. The following year Fossen and Roger Fisher joined them (the immigration issues were finessed when producer Mike Flicker obligingly wrote to tell the authorities that their studio musical skills were badly needed). The Fisher brothers, Fossen, and Ann Wilson vowed to assemble a band that would become Vancouver's biggest within two years. Adding drummer Brian Johnston and keyboardist John Hannah, the band spent the winter of 1972–73 building sound and lighting equipment, practicing, and developing their new concept.

The new band with an old name—Heart—debuted at Vancouver's Cave in early 1973. Their two-year plan was accomplished within a year as they became the hit of the city's clubs. Among the highlights of their stage show were covers of Led Zeppelin songs, with Fisher note-for-noting Jimmy Page licks and Ann Wilson matching Robert Plant's bluesy howls. Several members of Led Zeppelin even caught a Heart show at Oilcan Harry's. Once Heart was established as a band, Nancy moved north to join the group. Heart became that much more exciting with the addition of Nancy's blond good looks, haunting vocals, and acoustic guitar playing, which balanced Fisher's guitar pyrotechnics. The band also made swings south to Seattle in 1974, playing clubs such as Bellevue's Hatchcover and the Aquarius Ballroom (the renamed Parker's). Mike Fisher reprised the role he had with Army, developing an elaborate quadrophonic sound system and manning the mixing board himself. He also briefly regained Heart's management, before handing the reins to Ken Kinnear and Albatross Productions in 1975.

Heart's first album was *Dreamboat Annie* (1975) on Vancouver's Mushroom Records. Producer Flicker decided to use some session players on the record, which led to the departure of Hannah and Johnston, but at least he provided replacements. Guitarist and keyboardist Howard Leese (who had played with Flicker in the mid-1960s Los Angeles rock band Zoo) and drummer Michael Derosier were recruited into the band after contributing to *Dreamboat Annie*. Ironically, Derosier was a veteran of two Seattle bands (Waterwheel and Blizzard), that had opened shows for Army years before.

Also released by Mushroom in the States, *Dreamboat Annie* sold two million copies and eventually made the U.S. Top 10. "Crazy on You," the first single, barely cracked the Top 40, but "Magic Man" rose all the way to no. 9 on the U.S. charts in mid-1976.

With Derosier and Leese officially full-time members, the band began work on their second album, *Little Queen*. This is the version of Heart that burned its image into the minds of rock fans. Fronted by fiery, dark-haired Ann and quiet, acoustic-guitar strumming Nancy, the band dressed as rock gypsies and featured a melodic combination of chugging riff rock and ringing female vocals. But Heart's surprising success also brought problems. As the band signed a new U.S. record contract (with Portrait/CBS) and began recording *Little Queen*, Mushroom Records was preparing its own Heart album, a collection of half-finished tracks and demos it called *Magazine*. Both turned out to be million-sellers, although the legal battle between band and old

Heart Redux: A Scholarly Rock Debate

James Bush and Dawn Anderson

JB: To fully appreciate the 1976–77 version of Heart, you had to be a teenage boy. In the summer of 1977, when "Barracuda" was ruling the airwaves, most of the other so-called "women in rock" were wimps like Stevie Nicks and Christine McVie of Fleetwood Mac or Linda Ronstadt. But Heart rocked like a pocket-sized West Coast Led Zep. One critic wrote that seeing Ann Wilson sing live was the closest thing teenage boys would ever get to duplicating the experience of females watching Mick Jagger onstage.

DA: James, you ignorant slut. In order to truly appreciate Heart, you had to be a teenage girl in the late 1970s. Seeing Ann Wilson live was the closest a girl could come to duplicating the feeling boys got when they were fantasizing about being Mick Jagger. And Heart was the first solid evidence that women could rock hard and boys would still want them. It is impossible to overestimate this achievement.

JB: It's clear the "girls 'n' boys together" theme of Heart resonated with members of both sexes. A female friend of mine says she used to gaze for hours at the gypsy camp photos on the cover of *Little Queen,* perhaps imagining Heart as an egalitarian society where all were equal (although the girls got the big pictures on the front cover). And speaking of archetypes, could any band have collected a more perfect selection: the fiery dark-haired singer (Ann), the shy, spiritual acoustic guitarist (Nancy), the macho guitar god (Roger Fisher), the curly-haired stoner boy drummer (Michael Derosier), the intense, handsome bass player (Steve Fossen), and . . . well, Howard Leese. I don't have a theory yet about Howard Leese.

DA: You know, I never really appreciated Roger Fisher until he was gone. *Bebe Le Strange* was an okay album, but from there the band grew progressively more lame and simpering throughout the 1980s. By that time there were plenty of women rockers on the charts, and at least a few of them rocked harder than Heart. In retrospect, the only thing that would've held my interest at that point would've been if they had hired ex-Runaway and MTV glamour girl Lita Ford to replace Fisher. Can you imagine what might have been?

JB: That would have made for better videos, at least.

label continued until 1978, when a court allowed Heart to remix and modify several tracks on *Magazine.* Meanwhile, the band continued to score on the U.S. singles charts; the Zeppelin-ish "Barracuda" (from *Little Queen*) hit no. 11, and "Heartless" (from *Magazine*) advanced to no. 24. The band's first minor stumble was *Dog and Butterfly* (1978). Intended as a concept record pairing a rock (dog) and an acoustic (butterfly) side, the record was Heart's weakest to date, despite good sales and a Top 20 single in "Straight On." Cracks were developing within the group as well. Roger Fisher ended his romantic relationship with Nancy Wilson and quit the band; road manager Mike Fisher and Ann also broke up. But their first Fisher-less recording, *Bebe Le Strange,* was another commercial success, rising to no. 5 in the U.S. charts.

Without their Jimmy Page–style guitar hero, however, Heart lost their hard edge and stumbled around looking for a new direction. The band's next two albums, the quieter *Private Audition* (1982) and the weepy love-song-dominated *Passionworks* (1983), although brave stabs at finding a new postmetal direction, were commercial disappointments. Fossen and Derosier departed the band after *Private Audition* and were replaced by Mark Andes and Denny Carmassi. (Fossen, Derosier, and Fisher later collaborated in the band Alias, which produced the no. 2 single "More than Words Can Say" in 1990.) The band's 1985 comeback album, entitled simply *Heart*, completed their transition from rockers to radio-friendly pop stars, selling five million copies. Heart also notched four straight Top 10 singles, "What About Love?", "Never," "These Dreams," and "Nothin' at All." This version of the band released two more studio albums (*Bad Animals* in 1987 and *Brigade* in 1990), a live release (*Rock the House Live* in 1991), and several hit singles (including the no. 1 hit "Alone"). The Wilsons and Leese have released one subsequent Heart album, *Desire Walks On* (1993), and the obligatory acoustic greatest hits record, *The Road Home* (1995), but these days they more often perform with their acoustic side project, the Lovemongers. Ann Wilson went on the road in the summer of 1998 with a new version of Heart, performing the band's greatest hits at summer festivals and fairs; Nancy skipped the tour. **NS AND JB**

Little Queen

(1977, Portrait/CBS)
Although people most remember the kick-ass rock singles "Barracuda" and "Kick It Out," this is a breathtakingly gorgeous album as a whole, with layers of acoustic guitar and mandolin on softer gems like "Love Alive" and "Dream of the Archer." Heart's finest hour.

Greatest Hits

(1998, Legacy/Epic)
Including live records, this album is actually the band's sixth take at a greatest hits collection (and their second one in two years entitled *Greatest Hits*!). This effort wisely relies heavily on tracks from Heart's first five albums and is therefore the most deserving of your attention.

Heatmiser

Formed 1991, Portland, Oregon

Elliott Smith

erhaps Portland's greatest should've-been, Heatmiser disbanded just as they were releasing their best record and major-label debut. The quartet's origins lay in the late-1980s meeting of guitarist-vocalist-songwriters Neil Gust and

Elliott Smith at famously arty Hampshire College in Amherst, Massachusetts. After four years of playing in local coffeehouses, they relocated to Gust's hometown of Portland in 1991. They soon formed Heatmiser (named after one of the villains in the television holiday special *The Year without a Santa Claus*) with bass player Brandt Peterson, a refugee from a Stooges-inspired bar band, and drummer Tony Lash, a high school bandmate of Gust's.

After one self-released, self-titled cassette, Heatmiser signed with the renowned Los Angeles independent label Frontier, the home of fellow Portlanders the Dharma Bums. On two full-length CDs, *Dead Air* (1993) and *Cop and Speeder* (1994), and an EP, *Yellow No. 5* (1994), Heatmiser refined their angular, winding indie rock, and major labels eventually came calling. Just as *Cop and Speeder* was coming out, Smith drew national attention with his solo debut, the acoustic *Roman Candle* (1994), on Portland indie label Cavity Search.

So far, so good, and Heatmiser clinched a deal with Virgin Records. But the band was crumbling. Peterson had returned to school, leaving them without a bass player. Smith released a second solo record in 1995 on the Kill Rock Stars label, in Olympia, Washington; the morosely beautiful self-titled effort earned him even more acclaim (including several comparisons to Nick Drake, the mysterious early-1970s British folk artist) and encouraged him to tour as a solo act. In the meantime, he and Gust had stopped writing songs collaboratively. Lash had become an in-demand producer, working on records by Eric Matthews, Skiploader, and the Dandy Warhols, among others.

Pulled in different directions but obligated to record an album for Virgin, Lash, Smith, and Gust enlisted former Donner Party frontman Sam Coomes (half of the avant-pop duo Quasi) to play bass in the studio. Once recording was finished, however, Virgin got wind of Heatmiser's shaky status. The label balked at the idea of releasing a CD from a band that might not be around to tour, so Caroline Records stepped into the breach, releasing Heatmiser's *Mic City Sons* in 1996. The band stayed together long enough to play a few dates of a planned national tour before they called it quits.

After releasing his most successful solo effort to date, *Either/Or* (1997, Kill Rock Stars), Smith signed to DreamWorks as a solo act. In August 1998, the major label released his fourth record, *XO*, a lovely effort that highlighted Smith's pop songwriting skill with more diverse instrumentation than on any of his previous works.

"Rest My Head Against the Wall," a song from *Mic City Sons*, made a post-Heatmiser appearance on the soundtrack to the 1998 film *Zero Effect* (shot in Portland). Yet Smith again overshadowed his former band when "Miss Misery," one of his contributions to *Good Will Hunting*, directed by Portland filmmaker Gus Van Sant, was nominated for an Academy Award for Best Original Song. Smith sang "Miss Misery" at the awards ceremony and, in an incongruous moment, took his bow while holding hands with fellow nominees Celine Dion and Trisha Yearwood. **JM**

Mic City Sons

(1996, Caroline)

Heatmiser refined its muscular sound into textured, melodic guitar rock on *Mic City Sons*. Full of lyrics about departures and disappointing arrivals, the songs also function as a nice metaphor for the band's career.

Either/Or

(1997, Kill Rock Stars)

Elliott Smith's third solo album contains haunting snapshots of melancholy moments; this time around, however, his songwriting is less diffuse, and his voice is even stronger.

The Heats

Formed 1978, Kenmore, Washington

Once billed as Seattle's "soon to be famous" rock band, the Heats never got the national success they coveted, but they proved that bands playing original material could draw crowds—edging cover bands out of the major area clubs and paving the way for the city's vibrant late-1980s rock scene.

Originally known as the Heaters, the band—singer and guitarist Steve Pearson, singer and guitarist Don Short, bassist Keith Lilly, and drummer Kenny Deans—had to drive all the way to Sequim High School on Washington's Olympic Peninsula to play their first gig in February 1979. By that summer, they were a successful tavern attraction, catching the attention of both Seattle's news media and Albatross Productions, which signed them to an exclusive management deal. Although touted by some as Beatlesque, the band played a straightforward rockin' brand of power pop, with Pearson and Short trading off lead vocal and backup harmony duties.

Not that the rock dinosaurs succumbed easily. Pearson recalls an out-of-town gig opening for Bighorn, a classic 1970s big-amplifier, cover-song showband. "There was a struggle for a little while between the Bighorns of the world and us," he jokes. The Heats arrived at the club to find the stage filled with Bighorn's equipment, "and we'd have to open for them on this little postage stamp–sized area." The Heats offered to just pack up and go home, but to everyone's surprise, "the club owner supported us and told them, 'Those days are over with. You've got to share the stage with these guys,'" says Pearson. The Heats compounded the joke by advising Bighorn that the way to make it in Seattle was to play the Shire Tavern, a tiny West Seattle club.

But events conspired against the band. As they were preparing for a national tour opening for the Knack, news broke that a Los Angeles band had already been using the name "The Heaters." The band decided on "The Gears" and did the tour, but then learned that name was also taken. Settling on "The Torpedoes," Albatross purchased an expensive ad in *Billboard* magazine to promote the change—and soon heard from another band called the Torpedoes. It was March 1980 before the newly renamed Heats released their first single ("I Don't Like Your Face"/"Ordinary Girls"), a regional hit that sold more than 14,000 copies. Albatross was still hopeful that a national recording contract could be arranged, but finally bit the bullet and self-released the band's first album, *Have an Idea*. Produced by Heart guitarist Howard Leese, *Have an Idea* featured rerecorded versions of the two songs on the single, plus a host of catchy, hummable three-chord pop tunes.

Despite scoring solid regional sales and grabbing the best headlining gigs in Seattle, the Heats proved unable to take their success beyond the bars. Local rock stations KISW and KZOK gave the single airplay, but it didn't really fit into their heavy metal–dominated rotations. Seeking to expose the Heats to an underage audience, KZOK sponsored a show at the Paramount Theatre, but the teenage concertgoers were much more receptive to the opening band, Foreigner-soundalikes Loverboy. The lone Seattle rock magazine, *The Rocket*, was far more interested in promoting the city's tiny art-rock scene than praising the Heats. "Kill the Heats" was spray-painted on walls all over town.

As the Heats faded from "next big thing" status to merely a successful bar band, Lilly and Deans started to lose interest. Lilly, with a family to support, was the first to quit.

Their early 1982 single, "Count on Me"/"Rivals," featured new bassist Wayne Clack and two songs that Pearson considered a departure for the band. " 'Rivals' was the only song that Don and I really sat down and just swapped lines," he says. And "Count on Me" was the band's first studio take on a slow song. The single sold respectably, but wasn't a huge success. By the time the Heats were ready to release their second album (a live set played at Astor Park, then the top Seattle club), Rick Bourgoin was the drummer, and the band members were jaded enough by the whole process to consider calling the 1982 record "Kill the Heats Live" (they instead called it *Burnin' Live*). During this period, the Heats were touring regularly, playing taverns around the Northwest—a working musician's life that suited Pearson just fine, but Short wanted the band to move to Los Angeles and take one last shot at the big time.

The Heats' final near-brush with fame came when Heart's Ann Wilson offered to produce a demo for the band and, on the strength of her name, Geffen Records funded the studio time. A three-song demo was produced, but the label wasn't interested. Short was disappointed enough with the Heats' failure to break through commercially to quit the band at the end of 1983.

Pearson quickly formed the Rangehoods with guitarist Pat Hewitt of the Pins (another early Seattle power pop band), bassist Tony Lease, and drummer Don Kammerer (later replaced by Bill Shaw). Although they released a fine rockin' debut EP, *Rough Town*, in 1985, their biggest subsequent break was their 1986 selection as one of the Miller Genuine Draft–sponsored touring bands. The Rangehoods played gigs in small Northwest bars well into the 1990s. **JB**

Smoke

(1998, CHUCKIE-BOY)
Don't let the title fool you: this is the Heats' first self-released album, *Have an Idea*, with a couple of extra tracks (an awe-inspiring "Let's All Smoke" from the album sessions, and an Ann Wilson–produced "In Your Town" from the Geffen demo). Named one of the Top 50 power pop records of all time by *Goldmine*—for good reason.

Hellcows

Formed 1986, Portland, Oregon

noise. Performance art. No wave jazz. Art punk. Call it what you will, Portland has a seriously strange and powerful history in this nebulous area that traces back to the Northwest progenitors of sound science, Smegma, who have been at work off and on for twenty-odd years. Almost all of the Hellcows played in Smegma at one time or another. Their lone album, *Toothless*, was recorded at Smegma Studios by Mike Lastra in 1988.

The Hellcows formed in 1986 from the collective ashes of earlier groups like Spike, Porkycarcas, Carrion Commandos, and FDM. The first lineup consisted of Mike King (Portland's premier rock graphic artist) on percussion, Jerry Ostrem on guitar and sax, Eric Stotic on guitar, Carl Annala on bass, and Brian Koelling on voice (definitely an instrument of destruction). The sound was a meltdown of free jazz, metal, punk, and primal scream therapy enclosed by a wall of confusion. You've heard of the three B's in music (Bach, Beethoven, and Brahms, for you classical purists)? For the Hellcows these roles were probably filled by Black Sabbath, (Captain) Beefheart, and the Birthday Party. Their daring dash toward the extremes of music took many people with them, as did their fearless disregard for rock. The Hellcows were undoubtedly the first socially acceptable misfit musical act that many young Portlanders were exposed to. After the departure of Eric Stotic, a frisky youngster named Sean Croghan (later of Crackerbash and Jr. High) was eventually taken into the fold. When vocalist Koelling left (as did his replacement, Firefly Wreck's Mike Martinez), Annala and Croghan took up the vocal slack.

Not content with just playing weirdo music, the Hellcows would dress and act the part, starting with cross-dressing and then extrapolating from there. And the band would throw things at the crowd to get a show moving (everything from flower petals to carrots to parts of the drum kit, according to Annala). In their wanderings they played with noisy notables like Sonic Youth—who dedicated a song to the Hellcows when they played Memorial Coliseum as the opening act for Neil Young— White Zombie, Scratch Acid, Butthole Surfers, and the Meat Puppets.

Even with several lineup changes, the Hellcows produced a barrage of singles and compilation tracks. Their album *Toothless* (1988, Black Label), by virtue of its density alone, is the place to start when grappling with their legacy. The twenty songs are loaded with real menace, from Ostrem's bleating sax squalls to Koelling's maniacal and mostly indecipherable screeches and growls: this isn't just barely structured caterwaul, it has a sound that's almost evil.

There have been a great many bands in Portland that have incorporated noise and song deconstruction as an integral part of their modus operandi—Hitting Birth, King Black Acid, and Moustache come to mind—but few if any have equaled the artistic audacity of the late, great Hellcows. **JC**

Toothless

(1988, BLACK LABEL)
This twenty-song opus opens with the stuttering "Shut Up" and includes such high points as the aptly titled "Snort Honk" and "Harmonica" as well as "Ape Grave," which served as the band name for a free-jazz and noise outfit formed later by Annala, Croghan, and former Hitting Birth drummer David Parks.

Jimi Hendrix

Jimi Hendrix himself would be a little uneasy with—and probably somewhat amused by—his stature as the patron saint of Seattle rock. Although he was born and raised in Seattle, Hendrix left the city after high school, returning only to visit his family and play concerts.

James Marshall Hendrix was born in Seattle on November 27, 1942, the son of Al Hendrix and his wife, Lucille, a Cherokee. The two split while Al was in the military and later divorced. Their son lived with various friends and relatives until age 3; after his release from military service, Al took custody of the boy. Jimi's first guitar was purchased from a friend of his father for $5. A left-hander, he turned the guitar over, with the neck pointing to the right, and taught himself songs by playing along with records of favorite artists such as B. B. King and Chuck Berry. At Seattle's Garfield High School, he was a shy, strange guy who seemed to care only about his guitar, which he played in a local band, the Rocking Kings.

Joining the Army in the summer of 1961, Hendrix received a medical discharge a year later after injuring his ankle. He was a gypsy musician for the next three years, touring the country backing soul singers and living at various times in Vancouver, British Columbia, Tennessee, and New York. The soul and blues licks and chord progressions he picked up through his self-study served him well: he recorded with Lonnie Youngblood, the Isley Brothers, and Curtis Knight. His big break came in late 1966, when Chas Chandler, Animals bassist and producer, saw Hendrix play in a New York club and convinced him to move to London.

Within a month's time, he had formed the Jimi Hendrix Experience with bassist Noel Redding and drummer Mitch Mitchell; by December the band had released their first single, "Hey Joe," which hit the British Top 10 in early 1967. Their debut album, *Are You Experienced?*, was released in May and rose to no. 2 on the U.K. charts, behind the Beatles' *Sgt. Pepper's Lonely Hearts Club Band*. More than thirty years later, *Are You Experienced?* still amazes. The production by Chandler and engineer Eddie Kramer is stunningly modern, building dense sonic structures through multiple Hendrix overdubs. Feedback-laden guitars dart in and out of the mix on "I Don't Live Today"; Mitchell's drums duel Hendrix's lead parts on "Manic Depression." And has any group since created a more beautiful, elegant track than "The Wind Cries Mary"?

Although they couldn't compete for attention with their charismatic guitar hero frontman, Redding and Mitchell, in their performances on the Experience's albums, justify Hendrix's boast, "I came to England [and] picked out the two best musicians." Mitchell had played with Chris Sandford's backing group, the Coronets, which had a British hit with "Not Too Little, Not Too Much." He also played with Georgie Fame's Blue Flames before hooking up with Hendrix through a chance meeting with Chandler. Redding, earlier a guitarist with several British groups, including the Loving Kind, was hired to play bass with the Experience through an open audition.

The Jimi Hendrix Experience's arrival in America came in June 1967 with a bang (the guitar-burning appearance at the Monterey International Pop Festival) and quickly became a whimper (an ill-advised U.S. tour opening for the Monkees, which lasted just eight gigs before the two groups parted by mutual consent). The Experience's second album, *Axis: Bold as Love*, was released in December, rising to the Top 10 on both the U.S. and U.K. charts. In 1968 the Experience completed a three-month U.S. tour in June and started an even longer North American tour in late July. By this point, Hendrix had reached a rare dual status: a brilliant guitar technician worshiped by fellow musicians, and a bankable hit maker. The double album *Electric Ladyland* was released in October and hit the Top 10 on both sides of the Atlantic, including two weeks at the no. 1 spot on the American charts. The long touring schedule increased tensions within the band. The Experience split temporarily at the end of 1968, and permanently in June 1969 after another long U.S. tour.

Hendrix went to New York and began recording with drummer and vocalist Buddy Miles and bassist Billy Cox; the same lineup is featured on the live album *Band of Gypsys*, recorded at a New Year's Eve gig. Hendrix, who had been arrested for heroin possession in mid-1969, began to exhibit unpredictable behavior, walking offstage during the final *Band of Gypsys* show in January 1970 and insulting the audience during his final Seattle show at Sicks' Stadium in July. By this time, Mitchell had returned on drums, and he, Hendrix, and Cox began a long European tour, starting with an appearance at the Isle of Wight Festival in August. The tour was canceled after a few dates when an ill Cox flew back to New York. Hendrix's return to

London ended tragically on September 18, 1970, when he died after taking barbiturates and choking on his own vomit. *The Cry of Love*, the last Hendrix-sanctioned release (featuring Cox and Mitchell), was issued in early 1971 and, like his earlier albums, became a Top 10 smash in both the U.S. and Britain.

Even after his death, Hendrix remained both musical icon and marketable commodity. As a generation of Hendrix-influenced guitarists ascended to the height of the rock world, they readily acknowledged his influence. All the while, record companies cashed in. Several live Hendrix performances were released as albums, as were outtakes, in-studio jams, unfinished tracks, and other substandard tracks, a situation that undoubtedly would have horrified the meticulous Hendrix. The nadir of this musical grave-robbing was reached in 1975, when producer Alan Douglas used studio musicians to overdub new parts on unfinished Hendrix tracks. The repackaging continued well into the CD era, with new compilations and live recordings. In a macabre sidelight, so did rumors that his death was not a simple overdose. British authorities responded to the publicity by reopening the inquiry into his death in 1993, but they found no evidence of foul play.

In his hometown of Seattle, Hendrix retained an unusual status: revered but publicly unacknowledged. An early-1980s attempt to organize public support for a Hendrix monument fell short (the only result being a rock with a plaque on it, oddly sited at the city's zoo). A statue of Hendrix was finally placed on Broadway in the Capitol Hill neighborhood in 1996. Proceedings in Seattle's federal courthouse led to the happiest event of all—a 1995 settlement that returned control of Hendrix's music to his father, Al, and surviving family members. Under the direction of the Hendrix family, the guitarist's classic studio albums were remastered and reissued in 1998 on the Experience Hendrix label (distributed by MCA) with bonus tracks, liner notes, and rare photographs. **JB**

Are You Experienced?

(1967, TRACK)
The record that made guitarists around the world sit up and take notice. The classic tracks come in bunches—"Hey Joe," "Red House," "Manic Depression," "Fire," "The Wind Cries Mary," "Purple Haze."

Electric Ladyland

(1968, TRACK)
The band's the same, but everything else has changed on this double album, the final studio release of the Jimi Hendrix Experience. Miles away from the song-oriented approach of *Are You Experienced*, this album mixes brilliance and self-indulgence (despite some great Hendrix licks, the 15-minute blues "Voodoo Chile" typifies the latter). Hendrix, the credited producer, was also getting comfortable in the recording studio, experimenting with effects and multiple overdubs. Among the highlights: the funky "Crosstown Traffic" and Hendrix's dramatic take on Bob Dylan's "All Along the Watchtower."

Hole

Formed 1990, Los Angeles, California

despite the band's inclusion of several talented players, Courtney Love is Hole. The band has been Love's vehicle from day one. Never mind her run-of-the-mill megalomania, fits, tantrums, and nasty case of drug abuse; kicking her out is a sheer impossibility. But it's also her band because she writes good songs and can win any stare-down contest with music industry types. Although Hole was considered a Portland, Los Angeles, and Olympia, Washington, band at different points, Love long had her sights on Seattle, often to the chagrin of local music folks. Sometimes one town isn't big enough for everyone.

Hole's first release was recorded in Los Angeles, the 1990 single "Rat Bastard" on the aptly named Sympathy for the Record Industry label. A year later, Love, Eric Erlandson (guitar), Caroline Rue (drums), and Jill Emery (bass) released the nasty punk record *Pretty on the Inside* (Caroline), the first semblance of an influential release, if only in a sexpot, little-girl way. At its worst, the record came off as self-serving ranting; at its best, as convincingly punk rock and craggy. The album was made more notable by its incongruous producers, Don Fleming and Kim Gordon, Sonic Youth bass goddess.

But it was Love's association with Nirvana's Kurt Cobain that put her, and in turn Hole, clearly in the public eye. In early 1992 papers were reporting that Cobain was to marry Love, and the rumors took off from there. Hole was inactive in the wake of the scandalous write-ups, the most harmful being a *Vanity Fair* article that lambasted Love for using heroin while pregnant.

Shortly after a publicized cleanup and the birth of a healthy daughter, Frances Bean Cobain, Love was nearly ready to revive Hole. Patty Schemel of Kill Sybil was the new drummer, but Leslie Hardy played bass only long enough to record a single, "My Beautiful Son." Love had long wanted Kristen Pfaff of the Minneapolis band Janitor Joe to play bass, and eventually she got her.

Soon Hole released a record that Love deserved and earned respect for. With the lineup of Erlandson, Pfaff, Schemel, and Love, the band recorded *Live Through This* (1994, Geffen). By then Hole was fairly successful and was playing big shows, where Love showed off baby Frances Bean to the crowds. The timing of the record's release, however, was unfortunate: Cobain had committed suicide a week earlier.

Live Through This seemed haunting in the wake of Cobain's death. It moves like a biography of Love, documenting her horribly troubled childhood, including an inside-cover photo of her as an unkempt, sweetly disturbing child. She sings, "I want to be the girl with the most cake" on the song "Doll Parts." Her delivery drives home the lyrics: she sings "I fake it so real I am beyond fake" in a tired and raw voice, and then she nearly screams the first half of the line "Someday you will ache like I ache," and ends nearly speaking the last few words. Strangely foreshadowing Cobain's death are the lyrics "If you live through this with me / I swear that I will die for you,"

Love for All

(Reprinted from *The Rocket*, September 27, 1995)

Courtney Love, Seattle's goodwill ambassador to the world, took time from her busy court schedule to charm the residents of Ephrata.

Love visited the Central Washington town to plead guilty to a charge of fourth-degree assault stemming from an accusation that she punched Kathleen Hanna, singer for Bikini Kill, during an onstage incident at the Lollapalooza festival. Love's band, Hole, also performed at the July 4 concert at the Gorge Amphitheater.

The singer's Sept. 25 appearance at the Grant County Courthouse is unlikely to be soon forgotten. "She was coming up the courthouse steps followed by TV cameras and her entourage and she flipped us the bird with both hands," reported Randy Bracht, managing editor of the *Grant County Journal*.

Fortunately, Love's gesture of greeting was captured on film by *Journal* staffer Shannon Lowry and shared with the entire county via its appearance on the twice-weekly newspaper's front page. Bracht admitted that printing the photo was a bit out of character for the paper, but noted that he thought it summed up the "media circus" atmosphere of the event.

"A lot of local folks disliked it," he said. "Which is understandable."

Grant County District Court Judge Rich Fitterer was equally unimpressed with Love's bad-girl act, imposing a one-year jail term but then suspending the entire sentence and assessing a $150 fine and $285 in court costs. She was also required to complete an anger management course.

—James Bush

from "Asking for It," and "With a bullet, number one / Kill the family, save the son," from "Jennifer's Body." The nasty rumor that Cobain wrote much of Hole's material is more than likely untrue.

More death followed the band. Pfaff died of a heroin overdose a month after completing drug rehab. Seattle and Love were momentarily blamed, as they had been for Cobain's suicide, although the city still didn't claim Love as its own. (Love called *The Rocket*, a Seattle-based music magazine, to complain that Hole's records weren't listed on its chart of top-selling Northwest releases.) Shaken by Pfaff's death, the band members picked up slowly and moved on. Pfaff was replaced by bass player Melissa Auf der Maur from Montreal. *Ask for It*, a not very good live EP consisting of several covers and prereleased originals, was issued in 1995 on Caroline. The same year another Hole EP came out, *Softer, Softest* (Geffen Australia).

The band's next full-length record, *Celebrity Skin* (1998), took a more commercial stance, with lighter material and heavier rock star posturing. The record marked the departure of Schemel, the band's last Seattle native. Love now lives in Los Angeles with Frances Bean, and is a movie star and designer-dress-up doll—a rather ironic development, considering all the time she spent insisting Hole is a Seattle band. **KS**

The Hudson Brothers

Formed 1964, Portland, Oregon

although the Hudson Brothers haven't lived down the bad rap from their late-1970s incarnation as television pretty boys, their roots are an essential part of Northwest music's glory days.

Originally part of the early 1960s Portland band My Sirs, they got the attention of Jim Bailey, a Chrysler executive, who became their manager. Offered the chance to record a promotional single, they released their Beatlesque "Things Are Changing" on the Santana label and were rechristened the New Yorkers to tie in with the auto manufacturer.

Bill Hudson, the oldest, played guitar; multi-instrumentalist Mark concentrated on drums; and the youngest brother, Brett, played bass. All three sang lead and provided harmonies (although Mark was the primary lead vocalist), and their genetic vocal blend was a high point of their early efforts, sounding like the Beach Boys or early Bee Gees. Another early band member was guitarist Kent Fillmore, later replaced by Bob Haworth.

Northwest producer Jerry Dennon, flush with success from placing the Kingmen's "Louie Louie" on Wand Records, was able to release several Hudson Brothers singles on Scepter, Wand's sister label. The band's sound at this time had more in common with the new British sounds than with classic Northwest rock. "When I'm Gone" (1967) had a minor-key psychedelic feel to it and caused quite a stir locally. The band's first high-profile show, on July 15, 1967, saw them in the opening spot for Herman's Hermits at the Seattle Center Coliseum. The other acts on the eclectic bill were the Who (in their first Seattle appearance), Jim "Harpo" Valley (fresh from Paul Revere and the Raiders), the Blues Magoos, City Zu, Springfield Rifle, and Emergency Exit. Other big names the New Yorkers appeared with during this era included the Spencer Davis Group, Glen Campbell, Harpers Bizarre, and the Supremes.

Their next single, "Mr. Kirby" (1968), is the Hudsons' most-remembered early record. Driven by a hypnotic sitarlike lead line, this psychedelic cut has been a standout on several compilations of 1960s gems. Telling the sad story of a doomed man, "Mr. Kirby" is still an attention grabber today. It was a sizable Northwest hit, yet despite Dennon's and Scepter's promotion, little happened nationally.

After one more Scepter single ("Show Me the Way to Love") and two hopelessly rare Jerden releases—"Ice Cream World"/"Adrianne" (1968) and "Michael Clover"/

"Land of Ur" (1969)—the band missed a break when their cover of Harry Nilsson's "I Guess the Lord Must Be in New York City" (Decca) failed to make the cut for the soundtrack of *Midnight Cowboy*. The band changed its name to Everyday Hudson and released a final single on Decca, the bubblegumish "Laugh Funny Funny" (1970). A 1971 single, "The World Would Be a Little Bit Better" (Lionel), was released under the name Hudson.

The Hudson Brothers' story kicks into high gear during the early 1970s. After releasing an album (*Hudson*) and single ("Leavin' It's Over"/"Someday") on Playboy Records in 1970, they hooked up with Bernie Taupin, Elton John's songwriting partner. Taupin produced the album *Totally Out of Control* (1974) for them on John's Rocket Records.

Having relocated to Hollywood, the band landed a summer-replacement television series in 1974, the Saturday morning kiddie program *The Hudson Brothers Razzle Dazzle Show*. The show provided the national exposure the band had always sought, but stereotyped them as a teenybopper act. In any case, the show was a short-term aid to record sales: their album for Casablanca, *Hollywood Situation* (1974), was their best seller to date. They also cracked the Top 40 with the single "So You Are a Star," which reached no. 21.

Despite aiming at the adolescent market, the Hudson Brothers were coming up with a lot of good music. They were respected by their peers (both John Lennon and Paul McCartney were fans) but treated indifferently by most critics.

Their next album, the curiously titled *Ba Fa* (1975), featured contributions from Beach Boys Brian Johnston and Carl Wilson, as well as their second national hit, "Rendezvous," a rollicking, hook-laden stomper that reached no. 26. Meanwhile, the teenybopper press machinery was in full gear for them. The mass exposure in magazines like *Flip*, *Tiger Beat*, and *16* brought them short-term adolescent popularity but ultimately hurt their credibility as musicians.

A few more albums were released, *Truth About Us* (1976, Arista), *Brothers* (1978, First American), and *Damn Those Kids* (1980, Elektra), but the songwriting and performances weren't up to previous standards. They didn't even play on *Truth About Us*, although their trademark vocals are very evident.

The band dissolved in the early 1980s, but all three brothers are still active in entertainment. Mark produced a recent Ringo Starr release and has written and produced for artists such as Cher, Aerosmith, Hanson, and the Scorpions. Given their family and musical bonds, one would suspect a reunion is likely. **NS**

So You Are a Star: The Best of the Hudson Brothers

(1995, VARÈSE SARABANDE)
A stunning twenty-cut retrospective that contains the high points of their 1970s career, this disc even has a couple of new recordings and one unreleased cut.

Johnny and the Distractions

Formed 1979, Portland, Oregon

Jon Koonce, former drummer with 1970s favorites Sleazy Pieces, put together a rock and R&B band and hit the bar scene with a vengeance. With Bill Feldman (also a Sleazy Pieces alum) on guitar, Greg Perry on keyboards, Kip Richardson on drums, and Larue Todd on bass, Johnny and the Distractions had a sweaty, funky urban sound and tightness. At the time, this type of band—especially when fronted by a singer with a soulful voice and a sense of showmanship—automatically called up a comparison to Bruce Springsteen.

As with most easy analogies, this one was woefully inadequate. Because of the group's close ties with old R&B records and meat-and-potatoes rock, the Distractions were accessible in a way that new wave–influenced or heavy metal–oriented bands were not. Koonce's vocals ran the gamut from macho soul shouts to velvety crooning, and the singer's stage presence was impeccable. Onstage, Koonce was perhaps the most athletic performer of the time. After becoming a top attraction in both Seattle and Portland clubs, the band recorded and released its self-titled album in 1980; the record sold well enough in the Northwest to garner the Distractions a three-album deal with A&M Records, hot on the trail of Quarterflash's successful leap from local success (as Seafood Mama) to platinum sales for Geffen.

In 1981 guitarist Feldman left the band and was replaced by Mark Spangler, and drummer Richardson switched to the new wave power pop band the Odds, while Odds drummer Kevin Jarvis became a Distraction. The two new members brought a more contemporary groove and feel to the songs, without sacrificing any precision. This was the lineup that signed to record *Let It Rock*, the first Johnny and the Distractions album for A&M. Spangler became a writing partner for Koonce and went on to cocreate some of the group's biggest crowd pleasers.

Promotional budgets at that time were spent on bands from New York and Los Angeles with skinny ties and quirky names; *Let It Rock* sold well in a few spotty markets but poorly overall. A&M decided that a change was necessary and dropped the Distractions from the picture, so Koonce recorded two albums as a solo act to satisfy his contract. By the time the third album came out, produced by Al Kooper, the only intact element of Johnny and the Distractions' success was Koonce's gutsy, roaring voice (laid on top of overproduced, soulless tracks).

By the late 1980s, Koonce needed to recover not only from the A&M experience but also from serious damage to his voice. The singer concentrated on his songwriting and guitar playing skills. Since 1993 he has fronted a trio, the Gas Hogs, which has done well with two CDs: *Forever Faithful Rockin' Daddy* (1995) and *Pump Sausage* (1996). Koonce plans to move to the Nashville area, where he will continue writing and recording the roots rock sound of his current band. **DDP**

Let It Rock

(1981, A&M)

The closest picture one can get of the true Johnny and the Distractions sound. "Shoulder of the Road" features one of the top five rock 'n' roll screams of all time.

Pump Sausage

(1996, Moon)

The stripped-down Gas Hogs sound, one that will appeal to Blasters fans.

Jr. Cadillac

Formed 1970, Seattle, Washington

While never breaking nationally, Jr. Cadillac has been a Northwest institution for almost three decades. Ignoring the musical fads of the 1970s–1990s, they continue to do things their way—and are revered as the party band of Seattle.

Taking their name from an obscure Norman Greenbaum song, Jr. Cadillac was originally a casual band formed by several local rock legends to play their favorite songs. The leader was Spokane, Washington, native Ned Neltner (Mark V, Gas Company); other early recruits were Andy Parypa of the Sonics, former Frantics Bob Hosko and Jim Manolides, and drummer George Rudinger from the nationally known Fireballs. By the time their 1971 debut album was recorded live in a local tavern, Buck Ormsby (Wailers) had replaced Parypa on bass. Fittingly, this sweat-driven LP opens with a Chuck Berry song—Jr. Cadillac would go on to back Berry more than a dozen times throughout the Northwest (they also backed Bo Diddley at several shows).

The band's early sets drew heavily on older covers, causing some to incorrectly stereotype them as a 1950s retro act. But with Neltner's smoky vocals and the soulful sax and keyboard lines, Jr. Cadillac had much more in common with the real raunch and soul of classic R&B revues. Neltner and company rapidly became popular in the Northwest, kicking off the successful 1970s tavern circuit. By their third album, *Hamburgers to Go* (1975), former roadie Tom Katica had replaced Manolides on keyboards, and Neltner's Spokane cohort Les Clinkingbeard was the sax player. The band was also adding tasty originals that sounded just as legitimate as the oldies they lovingly covered.

During the mid- to late 1970s, Jr. Cadillac was everywhere. They opened for the Beach Boys, Fleetwood Mac, Jethro Tull, Ten Years After, the Electric Light Orchestra, and the Kinks—and it was not unheard of for Jr. Cadillac to blow away the headliners. Neltner and publicist Rhoda Mueller were masters of public relations. Local papers couldn't write enough about the band, and Jr. Cadillac's legendary "sea cruises" (alcohol-fueled dance parties held on boats) are still remembered with awe today.

By the early 1980s, Jr. Cadillac's repertoire was becoming dominated by Neltner's original songs—which were requested as often as their well-chosen covers. Ormsby, a professional musician since 1956, retired in 1983. He was replaced on bass by Garey Shelton, who then gave way to bassist Don King. Steve Flynn replaced Katica on keyboards. Other key personnel over the years have included soundmen Ron Winters and Billy Genevese, vocalists Lily Wilde and Nancy Claire, early drummer Roger Hyuke, and guest guitarist Larry "Rube Tubin" Richstein. Many nationally known players have sat in with the band from time to time, including Larry Coryell, Freddie Hubbard, Steve Miller, and Julian Priester.

Although Jr. Cadillac bar gigs have been scarce recently, the band still plays corporate functions and summer festivals. They also continue to record and have added ex-Kingsman Jeff Beals on baritone sax. As they approach their thirtieth anniversary, it's likely Jr. Cadillac will still be pumping out old Northwest classics twenty years from now, when grunge and rap are merely memories. **NS**

Jr. Cadillac Is Back

(GREAT NW, 1971)
Despite the title, this is the group's first album. Recorded live at a tavern, the playing evokes the mythical 1960s Northwest legends. Of the Northwest standards included here, "Lucille" and "High Blood Pressure" are standouts.

It's a Rock and Roll Party

(1995, ENTERTAINMENT DISTRIBUTION)
A three-disc set covering Jr. Cadillac's entire career. Included are their timeless covers of early Northwest R&B standards, several killer originals, and two versions of "Louie Louie."

The Kingsmen

Formed 1959, Portland, Oregon

The Kingsmen will forever be linked with their hit recording of "Louie Louie," but the full story is far more complex and controversial.

Taking their name from a brand of aftershave lotion, the original Kingsmen were Mike Mitchell (guitar), Jack Ely (vocals, guitar), Lynn Easton (drums), and Bob Nordby (bass). Playing supermarket openings, school dances, and private parties, the band had an early repertoire of instrumentals, with a few vocal turns by Ely. In the fall of 1962 the band lured 15-year-old classically trained pianist Don Galluci away from the Royal Notes and became a five-piece.

The one song every rock band of the era was required to play was "Louie Louie," first recorded by "Little Bill" Engelhart of Tacoma, Washington. The Wailers had a local hit with the Richard Berry doo-wop song in 1961. The Kingsmen cut their "Louie Louie" in March 1963 in the same week and at the same Portland studio (Northwest Recording) where Paul Revere and the Raiders did their version. The Kingsmen's finished product was, well, unique. At various places, it sounds as if each player is trying to solo over everyone else. The drummer's timing is certainly suspect, Galluci's keys are distorted, the guitar wheezes and strains, and Ely's muddied vocals can barely be understood. The band's original intention was to use "Louie Louie" as an audition tape, but instead it made rock 'n' roll history.

That summer, the Kingsmen were all but disbanded, and their Jerden single of "Louie Louie" was getting soundly outsold in the Northwest by the Raiders' version. But Portland disc jockey Ken Chase and Jerden owner Jerry Dennon promoted the Kingsmen's version, and it started to get attention in, of all places, Boston. Meanwhile, Easton announced he had registered the band name and was taking over as frontman (Gary Abbot became drummer but was soon replaced by Dick Peterson). Original vocalist Ely quit—he would later tour with his own version of the Kingsmen, record with the Courtmen, and play bass with the psychedelic Portland Zoo. Also out was Nordby, who was replaced by Norm Sundholm. Keyboardist Galluci, still in high school and unable to tour, was replaced by Yakima, Washington, native Barry Curtis.

"Louie Louie" entered the national charts in November 1963, and by the end of the month it was a no. 2 hit and the whole nation was "Louie" crazy. College students spent late-night sessions trying to decipher the allegedly dirty lyrics obscured by the slurred vocals (or they made up their own—the Stooges, whom Galluci later produced, featured a profane "Louie" in their live set, which showed up on the famous *Metallic KO* bootleg album). Indiana's governor actually banned the record, and the FBI investigated the band. Ignoring the perceived threat to their morals, kids everywhere wanted to hear the Kingsmen. Booked by William Morris, the band toured the country. They chose another Northwest R&B standard, "Money," for their next single. Featuring a protometal sludgy guitar line, the all-out rocker scored the band's second Top 20 hit (reaching no. 16 in April 1964). The Kingsmen appeared on all the era's teen television shows (*Upbeat, Where the Action Is, Hullabaloo*) and even got into a Frankie Avalon and Annette Funicello beach movie (*How to Stuff a Wild Bikini*, 1965). The Kingsmen scored their third (and final) national hit in early 1965 with a reworking of the Olympics' 1960 hit "Big Boy Pete." The band "updated" the song with hilarious lyrics about canned vegetables and called it "Jolly Green Giant." The vegetable company was unamused, but the controversy was mild compared with the "Louie Louie" uproar, and the likable tune hit no. 4 on the U.S. charts.

The Kingsmen were quite prolific in the studio. Many of their albums were overdubbed with crowd noise and applause to create a party ambiance; most included a combination of Northwest R&B standards, Top 40 cover versions, and a few originals. Their final LP, *Up and Away* (1966), had a decidedly British feel. Some of their last 1960s songs, such as "Just Before the Break of Day" and "I Guess I Was Only Dreaming," embraced psychedelia but didn't sell well.

More personnel changes followed before the band went on hiatus in 1968. Curtis served in Vietnam, and Sundholm went into electronics (his company produced the Sunn amplifiers, popular with 1970s rockers). Among the members during this phase of the band were Kerry Magness, J. C. Reick, Pete Borg, Jeff Beals, and Steve Friedson. Regrouping in the early 1970s, the trio of Mitchell, Peterson, and Curtis joined bassist Freddie Dennis and reestablished themselves as a live act; this version of the band cut some songs for Capitol, but they were never released. After a short break, the band debuted another new lineup. Kim Nicklaus was added on keyboards, and ex-Sonic Andy Parypa took up the bass so that Dennis could move to frontman. Marc Willett replaced Parypa in 1984 and was in turn replaced by Todd McPherson in 1992. Steve Peterson (no relation) also joined in 1992. The current lineup (Mitchell, Peterson, Curtis, McPherson, Peterson) tours the country with a variety of old and new acts, still churning out sets of classic Northwest R&B interspersed with British invasion material, including "Gloria" and "Shakin' All Over."

The Kingsmen were back in the national news in 1998, when a U.S. District Court judge gave the band the rights to the original master tapes of "Louie Louie." The former owners of the song were two companies that hadn't paid the group a penny in royalties for three decades. The U.S. Supreme Court later affirmed the decision. Interestingly, "Louie Louie" songwriter Berry had also managed to collect his back royalties, receiving a $2 million settlement in 1986 (he died in 1997). It's good that justice has prevailed—we all want to hear "Louie Louie" again by the original party band. **NS**

Plugged

(1995, SELF-RELEASED)
A raucous live compilation featuring material from 1988 and 1994. Loud, raunchy, and wailing—everything the Kingsmen represent. Curiously, no "Louie Louie."

The Very Best of the Kingsmen

(1998, VARÉSE VINTAGE)
A carefully annotated, well-chosen eighteen-song compilation, this disc gives us all the Kingsmen's garagy, pregrunge classics. Mastering is superb, and the sound is thick with early Northwest atmosphere.

Dave Lewis

d ave Lewis is widely acknowledged as perhaps the most influential Northwest musician of any era. His thick, melodic lines on the Hammond B-3 organ were the blueprint for the quintessential Northwest sound so revered today.

Lewis began his professional career with the instrumental Dave Lewis Combo and Five Checks vocal group. With Lewis on piano, Barney Hilliard and J. B. Allen on saxophones, John Gray on double bass, and George Griffin on drums, the Combo became the most in-demand group in Seattle during the early to mid-1950s. Their sound was heavy on the backbeat, rhythmic and energetic, with a wild mix of bluesy shuffles, R&B, and seductive counterpoint. Many aspiring musicians were in awe of Lewis and religiously journeyed to the Central Area clubs where he reigned.

By the late 1950s and early 1960s, Lewis was in constant demand throughout the state and a true star in the Puget Sound area. He headlined many local clubs—the Black and Tan, China Pheasant, Four-Ten Supper Club, Mardi Gras, Birdland, Embers, and Dave's Fifth Avenue. He also played lucrative teen dances at Parker's, the Spanish Castle, and various roller rinks. Perhaps the most important event in his career, however, occurred at a late-1950s show at Seattle's Palomar Theater—Wild Bill Davis introduced him to the Hammond B-3 organ. The early Northwest teen rock scene was exploding, and many classic groups including the Wailers, the Kingsmen, and the Dynamics were influenced by Lewis's new sound.

In 1961 his song "J.A.J." was released as a single by the Dynamics and became a sizable regional hit. The same label, Tom Ogilvy and Joe Boles's Seafair-Bolo Records, put out Lewis's debut single ("Candido"/"Untwistin'") in 1962. The record got solid airplay, but it was the follow-up on Jerden Records, "David's Mood," that cemented Lewis's success. A hypnotic, midtempo instrumental based vaguely on the "Louie Louie" chord changes (Lewis was one of the first Northwest musicians to cover the song), "David's Mood" anticipated the material that Booker T. and the MG's later recorded. Suddenly, it seemed like all the Northwest bands were covering Lewis songs.

While Lewis was playing Dave's Fifth Avenue in 1963, Los Angeles impresario Herb Alpert happened to see the musician and took a liking to him. Alpert signed Lewis to his new A&M label and released several albums during the 1960s. All told, Lewis had over a dozen single releases and nine albums to his credit.

By the mid-1960s, he had formed the Dave Lewis Trio with master guitarist Joe Johansen, and the group played gigs up and down the West Coast. Still anchored by Lewis's haunting organ work, the band had a more jazzy, soulful sound. The trio was as influential as Lewis alone had been. Young keyboard players especially enamored of Lewis's magic included Mike Rogers (Viceroys, Surprise Package), Clyde Heaton (Dimensions), and Marv Jensen (Bighorn). Other prominent Northwest musicians involved with Lewis during the 1960s include Mike Burk (Wailers) on drums and Jim Manolides (Frantics, James Henry and the Olympics) on bass.

The 1970s and 1980s were up and down for Lewis. Although he was still widely recognized as an essential architect of the classic organ-drenched Northwest sound, his style was no longer connecting with younger audiences. But he was the arranger for the fifty-piece house orchestra at the Paramount Theatre, and received plenty of well-deserved accolades. Performing at the Seattle Center Coliseum during the 1984 Bumbershoot festival, Lewis was the obvious highlight in a star-studded lineup of 1950s and 1960s Northwest performers (many of whom watched in awe from the side of the stage). In 1989 Lewis was one of the first inductees in the Northwest Music Hall of Fame.

The 1990s saw more activity from Lewis. He played the occasional club date and sat in with local stalwarts Jr. Cadillac from time to time. He died on March 13, 1998.

Dave Lewis will long be remembered as an excellent songwriter and arranger—and the man whose trademark abilities on the Hammond B-3 organ helped shape a whole musical genre. **NS**

Little Bill and the Bluenotes

Formed 1959, Tacoma, Washington

When guitarist and vocalist "Little Bill" Engelhart joined a group of older musicians—already known as the Bluenotes—in 1956, the result was the Northwest's first rock 'n' roll band. The original Bluenotes didn't last long. Engelhart kept the name and brought in John "Buck" Ormsby (steel guitar, bass), Frank Dutra (sax), and Lassie Aanes (drums) as his new Bluenotes. During the next couple of years the band grew, adding Buck Mann on baritone sax, Tom Giving on tenor sax, and "Rockin' " Robin Roberts on vocals.

Despite this promising start, Engelhart's career took an unwanted U-turn. Dolton Records owner Bob Reisdorff decided to market him as a white-bread teenybop idol in the mode of Frankie Avalon or Fabian. The Bluenotes disbanded, and Ormsby and Roberts joined Tacoma's Wailers. Needless to say, R&B fan Engelhart didn't fit well as a budding pinup boy. Despite high-profile national tours with the likes of Brenda Lee, Roy Orbison, and Ricky Nelson, Engelhart soon retreated to his old Northwest stomping grounds. His band was the first to record "Louie Louie," although, ironically, the Wailers' version was the local hit. Forming a new band with drummer Tommy Morgan and keyboardist Buck England, Engelhart recorded his now-rare 1963 album *Live at the Fiesta Club*. The band continued to play dates, but their bluesy R&B was being edged out by the new Beatles-influenced groups. Engelhart quit music for several years, paying the bills with jobs as an accountant, counselor, and DJ. But after a successful one-night gig in the late 1970s, he formed a band with Morgan and guitarist Joe Johansen, playing a four-year residency at the Mint, a Seattle club. Vocalist Patty Allen fronted the band for a while, and when she left, the band harkened back to the glory days of the late 1950s by adding a horn section of

Robby Jordan and Randy Oxford.

Since then, Little Bill and the Bluenotes have been mainstays on the Northwest's ultra-competitive R&B/blues circuit. Engelhart has a reputation for attracting great guitarists (including John Carmody, Hans Ipsen, and Rich Dangel)—and lead player Marak Riley is as hot as they come. Other players during the past decade have included keyboardist Pat Hues and tenor sax player Brian Kent. With a core of Engelhart, Riley, Morgan, and England (plus a horn section of Oxford, Jim Pribenow, Greg Parman, and Hadi Al Saadoon), the band continues to produce some of the area's choicest music, a haunting blend of rich keyboards, tasty guitar, and Engelhart's musky vocals and solid bass lines. **NS**

Respectively Yours

(1995, MONKEY HAT)
This compilation contains the classic early singles, including the Northwest's first "Louie Louie," most of the extremely rare *Live at the Fiesta Club* album, and some unreleased 1970s and 1980s material. Essential.

Live at the Spar

(1995, MONKEY HAT)
A ripping live set of well-chosen R&B obscurities, featuring harpist extraordinaire Dick Powell and a great performance from Marak Riley. Another must-have.

Love Battery

Formed 1989, Seattle, Washington

Lots of bands can claim that they never got their due, but few possess the recorded evidence of Love Battery. Serving up a lumpy sonic soup of psychedelia, pop jangle, punk energy, and singer/guitarist Ron Nine's likably surreal lyrics, Love Battery was the oddball band on the heavy guitar and scraggly hair label Sub Pop. Like labelmates Mudhoney, who did the same trick with "Touch Me I'm Sick"/"Sweet Young Thing (Ain't Sweet No More)," Love Battery arguably reached their peak with their first single, "Between the Eyes."

Nine formed Love Battery with drummer Jason Finn, bassist Tommy "Bonehead" Simpson, and guitarist Kevin Whitworth, all three of whom were sharing a house in Seattle's Capitol Hill neighborhood. Down-the-street neighbor Nine rolled his Twin Reverb amp over to his bandmates' house for the first practices. Nine had fronted the thoroughly psychedelic Room Nine from 1982 to 1988. Finn had played briefly with several local bands, including Skin Yard. Simpson was the former bassist for trashrockers Crisis Party; Whitworth replaced him in that band, and split his time between Love Battery and Crisis Party (he played on their lone LP, *Rude Awakening*).

Like many of the other early Seattle scene luminaries, Nine had a day job at Muzak sorting tapes. His coworker there, Sub Pop Records founder Bruce Pavitt, had promised to release a single on his label if Nine got a band together. That record, "Between the Eyes"/"Easter" (1989), caused a minor sensation among the Seattle rock community, although Sub Pop hardly seized the moment. Love Battery had already been on the road several times before the release of the awesome EP *Between the Eyes* (1990), an Australia-only Sub Pop corelease with Aussie label Waterfront—on 10-inch vinyl, no less. About this time, Simpson became the first original member to depart the band (he later played with Alcohol Funny Car), and was replaced by former U-Men bassist Jim Tillman. The recording of Love Battery's first full-length record, *Dayglo*, was sandwiched around a tour of the United States and Canada. The Conrad Uno–produced *Dayglo* comes off a bit scattered in retrospect, but remains a band favorite. Pleased with the results, Sub Pop added three leftover tracks from the *Dayglo* sessions to the EP *Between the Eyes* and released the result in this country as a CD album (also called *Between the Eyes*, 1991).

When Tillman quit the band in mid-1992, Bruce Fairweather was added on bass. Already a well-known Seattle guitarist from his stints with Green River and Mother Love Bone, Fairweather was frustrated by the breakup of his post–Love Bone band, Blind Horse, and wanted to go on tour with an established group. With just one record remaining on their Sub Pop contract, the band enthusiastically allowed themselves to be courted by major labels. Sub Pop released a poorly mixed version of their third LP, *Far Gone*, and washed their hands of the band. Love Battery released the EP *Nehru Jacket* (1994) and the ambitious full-length *Straight Freak Ticket* (1995) on Atlas Records. By the time the album was released, Finn had gotten tired of splitting time between Love Battery and his second band, the Presidents of the United States of America, and he left to become a full-time chief executive. So-so sales led to Love Battery's parting ways with Atlas, but the trio of Nine, Whitworth, and Fairweather has hung together, playing gigs around Seattle and releasing an EP, *Snipe Hunt* (1998), featuring Mudhoney's Dan Peters on drums), and an LP, *Confusion Au Go Go* (1999, C/Z), with drum contributions by Finn, Peters, and former Posies member Mike Musberger.   **JB**

Between the Eyes

(1991, Sᴜʙ Pᴏᴘ)
The album-length version of the debut EP features both sides of Love Battery's classic first single, two more world-class tracks ("Highway of Souls" and "Before I Crawl"), and a trio of decent outtakes from the *Dayglo* sessions (the best being "67").

Nehru Jacket

(1994, Aᴛʟᴀs)
Intended only to fill the shelves until *Straight Freak Ticket* was completed, this four-song EP is probably the most successful snapshot of this version of the band. Includes two non-LP tracks, most notably a great cover of the Telescopes' "Please, Before You Go," and charming cover art by Ed Fotheringham.

The Makers

Formed 1990, Spokane, Washington

t he Makers look like mods, roar like punks, and call themselves a soul band. Most people would probably call them a garage rock band, and defined broadly, that's exactly what they are. But the Makers aren't interested in striving for authenticity; the band's love for 1960s protopunk, old R&B, the Velvet Underground, and basic dirty rock 'n' roll is genuine and often shows itself in unexpected ways.

Brothers Mike and Don formed the Haymakers with a guitarist named Jay and a harmonica player named John, who all took on the last name "Maker," just as the members of the Ramones had renamed themselves about fifteen years before.

They wore black suits and Beatles boots in a town that was best known for hairspray metal. Their Spokane audiences were irony deficient and easily provoked, and the Haymakers loved to taunt them from the stage. Early shows were marked by violence, earning the band a reputation as badasses that would plague them (and bolster them) throughout their career.

They soon shortened their name to the Makers and began touring the country in their 1965 Bonneville hearse. The combination of their ferocious music, sneering stage presence, and lack of tact led to violent incidents that further enhanced the band's reputation. In Austin, for instance, they made the mistake of calling Texas "small."

After releasing a slew of independent EPs and singles, the Makers were picked up by Estrus Records in Bellingham, Washington, which has released five Makers albums: *Howl*, *All-Night Riot*, *The Makers* (best known as "the middle finger album" due to its tasteful cover art), *Hunger* (1997), and *Psychopathia Sexualis* (1998). John left the band in 1993, and Jamie replaced Jay on guitar some time later, making his debut on *Hunger*.

The cover of *Psychopathia Sexualis* depicts the band in full glam regalia, impenetrable black sunglasses, and male-model pouts.

Onstage, Mike Maker's catlike moves eerily resemble those of Prince, though his voice is in-your-face punk. His oversexed lyrics ask such piercing questions as "Are you on the inside or the outside of your pants?" They rhyme "sicko sexual" with "skin-tellectual" (or is it scintillectual?). The ladies love them. The guys grumble, "That singer thinks he's so cool."

He doesn't think: he knows. **DA**

Psychopathia Sexualis

(1998, Estrus)

This is the Makers' most soulful album to date, containing a couple of unapologetically tender ballads and even a spoken-word bit by Mike and Don's brother Vic Mostly (must be a half brother). But their crazed rock is still what does it for me, and here it's more furious than ever.

Melvins

Formed 1984, Montesano, Washington

t he Melvins are the only group from the 1985 Northwest compilation *Deep Six* that is still intact. Formed in the tiny logging town of Montesano, Washington, and named after an old boss at the local grocery store, the band is most known for being a major influence on Nirvana, which is nothing short of a travesty. With slow, metal-edged songs and distorted guitars, the Melvins were an undeniable influence on countless bands in the Northwest and beyond.

Although guitarist/vocalist Buzz Osborne and drummer Dale Crover are apparently the only two Northwest artists to develop during the pregrunge era who didn't achieve monumental success, the Melvins possess an underground following that will carry them much farther than temporary fame.

The Melvins never resided in Seattle; they merely moved from Montesano to Aberdeen, a short drive from their birthplace. In 1989 Osborne broke up the band to move to San Francisco and live with his girlfriend at the time, Lori Black. Crover followed, and the band re-formed with Black on bass. Original bassist Matt Lukin moved to Seattle and joined Mudhoney. He recorded only one album with the Melvins, *Gluey Porch Treatments* (1986, Alchemy).

The Melvins released four records on the San Francisco–based independent label Boner. Black played on the first three: *Ozma* (1989), *Bullhead* (1991), and the EP *Eggnog* (1991). Joe Preston, who owned Boner, filled in on *Lysol* (1992) and performed with the band until he was replaced by long-term bassist Mark Deutrom in 1994. Although Deutrom didn't play on the Melvins' major label debut, *Houdini* (1993, Atlantic), he was on board in time for the subsequent tour. He also performed on the band's Atlantic releases, *Stoner Witch* (1994) and *Stag* (1996).

During their Atlantic tenure, the band also released a CD (entitled *Prick*) under the moniker Snivlem on the Amphetamine Reptile label. After fulfilling their obligations to Atlantic, the band rejoined the Amphetamine Reptile roster to release the album *Honky* (1998). **VK**

Gluey Porch Treatments

(1986, ALCHEMY)
A must-have simply because it shows the beginnings of genius. It's an excellent peek into the early development of Buzz Osborne's guitar wall. You also get to hear Dale Crover before he developed his not quite minimalistic drum style.

Stoner Witch

(1994, ATLANTIC)
Undoubtedly the most beautiful record the Melvins ever released. This CD goes the farthest in balancing heaviness with unique drum, guitar, and vocal inflections. Certain songs, like "Queen" and "Sweet Willy Roll Bar," even have a sort of pop structure (but not too much).

Metal Church

Formed 1982, Seattle, Washington

Seattle's second most famous metal band of the 1980s never lived up to the sales numbers of the more successful Queensrÿche, but earned higher ratings from headbangers and thrash devotees. Guitarist Kurdt Vanderhoof, who had played with Seattle protopunks the Lewd, formed the band after moving back to Seattle from San Francisco (he borrowed the name from one of his Bay Area groups). The original lineup was Vanderhoof, singer David Wayne, guitarist Craig Wells, bassist Duke Erickson, and drummer Kirk Arrington. Already stars in the tape-trading metal underground, the band was featured on a pair of metal sampler records (*Metal Massacre V* and *Northwest Metalfest*) before releasing their self-titled debut record on the independent label Ground Zero in 1984.

After selling an impressive fifty thousand copies and getting noticed by such luminaries as Metallica, the album was picked up for national distribution by Elektra. Still recognized as a classic of the genre, *Metal Church* incorporated the increasingly popular speedy thrash riffs and threw in a bit of sword 'n' sorcerer mysticism ("Many, many years ago on a distant shore / Men did gather secretly beyond the hidden door"). Add to those elements the ace knob twirling of up-and-coming producer Terry Date and Wayne's otherworldly screeching, and you have a massive slab of metal perfection. Not a Satanic metal band per se, the group still catered to the dark-side needs of teenage boys with heavy hits like "Beyond the Black," "Merciless Onslaught," and "Gods of Wrath." And has any band ever had a cooler theme song than "Metal Church," with its mesmerizing guitar riff and Arrington's immense drum sound?

After a couple of years on the road with the likes of Metallica, the Church recorded its second studio offering, *The Dark* (1987). Producer Mark Dodson replaced Date and was observant enough to maintain the aural emphasis on Arrington's rock-solid drumming. Overall, the songs seem faster, reflecting the growing popularity of speed metal. Fans weren't disappointed. You can almost see the hair flying when you listen to headbangers like the album-opener, "Ton of Bricks," and the chantlike "Start the Fire."

The band was in for major changes in 1988: after a few abortive attempts to leave the band, Wayne was gone for good. Vanderhoof, weary of touring, announced his intention to leave Metal Church to concentrate on songwriting and producing. (He would remain as the band's nonplaying sixth member, writing or cowriting most of the songs on the next three records.) Vanderhoof's career change quickly worked to the band's advantage—while producing *The Breaking Point* for the Los Angeles metal band Heretic, he was impressed by singer Mike Howe and recommended him as Wayne's replacement. The new guitarist was John Marshall, a Metallica roadie who played onstage with that band after singer James Hetfield broke his arm skateboarding. The new lineup debuted on *Blessing in Disguise* (1989), which featured a

Suburban Metal/Early 1980s

It sounds unbelievable today, but once upon a time in the Northwest, satanic speed metal bands often shared the stage with hairspray-encrusted pop metal bands, and nobody got hurt!

During the first half of the 1980s, Seattle heavy metal bands played to underage suburban audiences almost exclusively, and the kids were out to have a good time, dress in leather, rock mightily, and not judge each other too harshly. This attitude was in stark contrast to Seattle's punk clubs, in which feigned indifference was the strictly enforced social code, broken only by occasional bouts of violence against plumbing fixtures.

Much of the action took place at the same skating rink circuit that once supported the garage bands of the 1960s, including the Lake Hills Roller Rink in Bellevue, an affluent, sprawling suburb of Seattle on the east side of Lake Washington. Promoter Craig Cooke took over the band nights in 1982 and began hosting weekly Battles of the Bands on two separate stages so that one band could rip into a set immediately after the last band finished, with no loss of momentum between acts. Well-groomed teens in leather and chains began packing the place.

Much has been made of the Seattle all-ages rental hall gigs where future members of now-famous bands practiced their chops, but those who hung out on the "other side" of the lake had the chance to watch future members of Alice in Chains, Pearl Jam, Queensrÿche, and several more modestly successful bands make their live debuts.

Defining the parameters were Shadow, a kiddie metal-pop band featuring 16-year-old future Pearl Jam guitarist Mike McCready, and Overlord, who played dark, sinister, dirge metal that could only be called grunge. Some of Overlord's members later formed My Eye, who often shared bills with the likes of Green River and Soundgarden at what were then considered the underground music gigs.

Sato was an insipid imitation of Mötley Crüe, but nevertheless featured future Alice in Chains bassist Mike ("It's my real name") Starr. Myth's singer, Geoff Tate, eventually split that band to join Queensrÿche. The Bondage Boys featured Taime Downe, later of the Los Angeles hairspray band Faster Pussycat.

The most venerated forefathers of the metal scene were Rail and TKO, both of whom started out on the high school/skating rink circuit and went on to release albums and tour nationally.

Everyone thought the next breakthrough band would be Culprit, who put on ferocious live shows featuring lots of original material at a time when most bands were too timid (or untalented) to showcase more than a handful of their own songs. Culprit released their LP *Guilty as Charged* in 1983, featuring a slew of powerful songs but lackluster production. Shortly after the album's release, two members jumped ship to join TKO, and Culprit disbanded. The two other most talked-about bands during this period were Metal Church and Portland's Wild Dogs.

Enthusiasm for local metal reached a peak in 1984 with the release of the *Northwest Metalfest* compilation album on Ground Zero Records, the label of future rock journalist Jeff Gilbert. The album featured ten bands representing the entire spectrum from glam to hardcore, including Metal Church, Sato, MACE, Lipstick, Overlord, and the Bondage Boys. The sold-out release party at Seattle's Moore Theatre, featuring all ten bands, proved that teenagers' attention spans are actually far longer than adults'.

> But all good things must come to an end, and by the mid-1980s the metal scene was beginning to change shape. A major rift was forming between thrash metal and glam metal bands, fragmenting audiences and causing general grouchiness all around.
>
> Then there was the Queensrÿche problem: after this band rose to national prominence practically straight from the basement, the skating rink gigs began to look like an embarrassing waste of time, and fewer of the good bands even bothered. Eventually the venues closed down (or remained open only to roller skaters), and the remaining heavy metal bands either made the switch to urban clubs or continued in their own basements, waiting forever to be discovered.
>
> —Dawn Anderson

more mainstream collection of Vanderhoof songs. The album's standout cuts were epics in the Led Zeppelin mold—"Badlands" and "Anthem to the Estranged"—but there were enough speedy shouters to keep the kids happy.

As heavy metal's hold on the nation's musical consciousness faded, Metal Church released two more albums—*The Human Factor* (1991, Elektra) and *Hanging in the Balance* (1993, Blackheart). Although the band survived for a time, Arrington has since signed on with Vanderhoof's new band, called simply Vanderhoof. Wayne reappeared as the singer for Reverend.

The first four Metal Church records remain in print and, when heavy metal ends its current hiatus, the Church will be recognized as one of the genre's best practitioners. **JB**

Metal Church

(1984, GROUND ZERO; 1985, ELEKTRA)
Still fresh and energetic more than a decade after its release. A power primer for riff-happy guitar heroes to come.

Steve Miller

although the Steve Miller Band and Heart were the best-known Northwest acts of the mid- and late 1970s, Miller was actually an adopted son of the region. Shortly after scoring his first major national success with *The Joker* in 1973, Miller bought a farm in Medford, Oregon, where he built a 24-track studio. Thus his Northwest credentials were established during his memorable eighteen-month assault on the U.S. charts, in which the albums *Fly Like an Eagle* (1976) and *Book of Dreams* (1977) combined to sell more than seven million copies and spawned a string of six Top 25 singles, including gold-record hits "Rock'n Me" (no. 1), "Fly Like an Eagle" (no. 2), and "Jet Airliner" (no. 8).

At the time of his arrival in the Northwest, Miller had already amassed a solid career. Born in Milwaukee and raised in Texas, he formed his first band at age 12 with school friend Boz Scaggs. He followed Scaggs to the University of Wisconsin, where they played in an R&B cover band. After a stint in Europe studying literature at the University of Copenhagen, Miller moved to Chicago, where he formed the Goldberg Miller Blues Band with Barry Goldberg. After releasing one album, that band split, and Miller moved to San Francisco in late 1966. His Steve Miller Blues Band shared bills with major bands like the Doors, Buffalo Springfield, and Quicksilver Messenger Service; played a set at the 1967 Monterey International Pop Festival; and signed a long-term contract with Capitol Records. Curiously enough, the Miller Band's first appearance on record was as the backup group on Chuck Berry's LP *Live at the Fillmore.*

Scaggs rejoined the band for their first Capitol release, *Children of the Future* (1968), a well-received record that earned radio play but sold poorly. After *Sailor* (1968), Scaggs departed and the band dropped "Blues" from its name. With an ever-shuffling lineup (including stints by future Rolling Stones keyboard player Nicky Hopkins and bassist Ross Valory, later of Journey), Miller released four more albums on Capitol (plus a 1972 two-album retrospective, *Anthology*), all of which sold respectably and were popular with FM radio DJs, but his big commercial breakthrough was yet to come. Sidelined by an auto accident and a subsequent illness, Miller wrote the songs for his first Top 10 album, *The Joker* (1973); its title track was a no. 1 single. Rather than capitalize quickly on his newfound success, he retreated to his Oregon farm for the next three years, playing just a few live shows before the May 1976 release of *Fly Like an Eagle.*

Although sometimes classed as a 1970s guitar hero, Miller offered ringing guitar lines that were spare and chord-based, and he often shared the stage with two other guitarists. The real attraction was Miller's uncanny skill for catchy chorus hooks that rattle around in the listener's head long after the song ends.

Miller's chart success continued into the early 1980s: *Circle of Love* (1981) was a gold record with a Top 25 single ("Heart Like a Wheel"), and *Abracadabra* (1982) gave Miller his last platinum album, with the title track his third no. 1 single. He also notched a British no. 1 single in 1991 when his record company rereleased "The Joker," then featured in a popular Levi's jeans commercial. Although he released four more albums in the 1980s, most of Miller's subsequent record sales were earned by greatest hits collections. His 1993 release, *Wide River*, marked a return to his blues roots. **JB**

Fly Like an Eagle

(1976, CAPITOL)
Not just Miller's best-seller, but also a great commercial rock record. Includes Miller's two best singles, "Rock'n Me" and "Take the Money and Run."

The Moberlys

Formed 1977, Seattle, Washington

C an any rock scene boast of a contentious relationship with one of its founding fathers to match Seattle's continuing joust with Jim Basnight? After all, Basnight was far enough ahead of his time as a Roosevelt High School student to love the New York Dolls and form a band called the Loverboys (who played at a school talent show, only to get booted off the stage and beaten up by jocks in the parking lot). He also played with a pioneer punk band (the Meyce), recorded and released his own single ("Live in the Sun"/"She Got Fucked," 1977, still considered a Seattle classic), and kicked off the city's prolific early-1980s power pop scene with his band the Moberlys. Still, Basnight's self-promotional drive and his general puzzlement that he isn't considered an icon of Seattle rock means he takes his lumps in the local rock press. Take this classic from *The Rocket*'s Johnny Renton gossip column circa 1982: "Richard Pleasant, lead singer for Shatterbox, lost his voice at a recent Hibble & Hyde's gig. Luckily, Jim Basnight was in the crowd trying to explain to people who he was and what he did. He saw his chance and jumped on stage to sing a set of '60s material."

Well, Basnight doesn't have anything to explain. Although it was the Heats and the Cowboys who ended up flirting with fame, the Moberlys were Seattle's first all-original power pop practitioners. After the Meyce broke up, Basnight journeyed to New York, a visit he recalls as "sort of a cross between the early CBGB's scene and *Midnight Cowboy*—I was lucky to survive." Inspired by the vibrant music scene there, he returned to Seattle determined to start a group that played only original songs. During the Moberlys' formative stages, Jeff Cerar of the Cowboys and both Heats guitarists (Don Short and Steve Pearson) served time with Basnight's evolving original music project. "So all the guitar gods in town were in the band at one point or another," says Basnight.

The Moberlys got off to an auspicious start, debuting at the Paramount Theatre as openers for the Greg Kihn Band in December 1978. Before the band broke up in late 1979, they recorded *The Moberlys*, the album that made them the first of the big three to get onto vinyl, albeit posthumously (the record came out in April 1980). The lineup on the album was guitarist Ernie Sapiro (later of the Lonesome City Kings and the Cowboys), drummer Bill Walters, and bassist Steve Grindel. "We kind of spearheaded this ridiculous idea that a band from Seattle could do original music and people might actually come and see them," says Basnight.

As the Heats grew in popularity, bar bookers became willing to hire power pop groups, and Basnight joined forces with Pat Hewitt, Bill Shaw, and Bruce Hughes to form the Pins. This was admittedly a cash-money gig for Basnight, who was saving up for his 1980 move to New York.

After splitting from the Pins and moving cross-country, Basnight started playing solo acoustic shows and eventually formed a new version of the Moberlys with New York musicians. He also ended up living in a building where several bands practiced, including the pickup groups of ex–New York Dolls guitarist Johnny Thunders, and even sat in on bass at a couple of shows with the New York legend. He also played with Alan Vega of the band Suicide. The new Moberlys, supplemented by Seattle transplants Al Bloch (bass) and Dave Drewry (drums), were getting good gigs and had a shot at a record deal, but it didn't pan out, and Basnight and Drewry returned to Seattle in 1983. The band added Toby Kiel on bass and performed several times before returning to New York. Basnight found that things had changed dramatically. "The disco-Madonna thing had kind of blown the rock scene out of the water," he recalls. Back in Seattle, the Moberlys, which now included guitarist Glen Oyabe, managed a series of regular shows at Pioneer Square's Central tavern (later a center of the late-1980s Seattle rock scene), but couldn't compete with the established bands.

Deciding to split town again, the Moberlys relocated to Los Angeles in 1985. Again, the band was a poor match for the times. "It was not so hip to be in a pop band," says Basnight. "L.A. had the Plimsouls," he says, "but the rest was Mötley Crüe." Even so, the Moberlys managed to get gigs and earned a recording contract with EMI in 1987, resulting in studio sessions with R.E.M.'s Peter Buck at the helm. But before the group could get an album released, EMI went through a merger and decided to clean house. The Moberlys were first out the door—record company executives were interested in dance pop bands and Guns N' Roses–style metal, explains Basnight, not jangly two-guitar pop. The band recorded with other producers (the results can be found on Basnight's two compilations, *Pop Top* and *Retro*), but the Moberlys never issued a record and split up in 1989.

Meanwhile, Los Angeles resident Basnight had gotten a real job (as a stockbroker) and tried his hand at a few other bands (including the Skyscrapers, with former bandmate Al Bloch) before returning to solo acoustic performances. After some business reversals, Basnight returned to Seattle in 1992; he expected to stay a few months but ended up playing music again. He released *Pop Top*, a mixture of Moberlys recordings and new solo material, and ended up forming a band, the Rockinghams, with Seattle veterans Chris Crass (the Muffs) and Jack Hanan (the Cowboys). That band released a five-song EP in 1995 and *Makin' Bacon* (1999, Not Lame), a retrospective CD. Basnight has also composed music for television and theater, including the music for the acclaimed children's play *Little Rock*.

His more recent project is the Jim Basnight Band, which released its debut album, *The Jim Basnight Thing*, on his own Precedent label in 1997. With an unusual lineup of players and instruments—Jim Knodle (trumpet), Jeffrey Sick (six-string violin), Mike Rollins (bass, flute, sax), Mike Slivka (drums), Susan Sims (vocals)—backing the singer/guitarist, the album finds Basnight miles away musically from the Moberlys' powerful pop. **JB**

Sexteen

(1995, ATM)

Although Basnight has rereleased the first Moberlys album on Precedent, this thorough German compilation includes all those songs, plus both sides of the "Live in the Sun" single, the excellent "We'll Always Be in Love" (featured on the 1981 sampler LP *Seattle Syndrome*), live tracks, and demos.

Modest Mouse

Formed 1992, Issaquah, Washington

the members of Modest Mouse are showing definite signs of surviving their short spell as the Seattle music scene's child prodigies. With their second longplayer, *The Lonesome Crowded West*, out on Up Records and a godlike reputation among critics and serious listeners, Isaac Brock (guitar, vocals), Jeremy Green (drums), and Eric Judy (bass) are getting attention across the country.

The band formed when all three members were teenagers. After Judy left for a time, the band experimented with other lineups, and Brock made solo tapes on his own. The first Modest Mouse single, "Dukes Up"/"It Always Rains on a Picnic," was released in 1995 on K Records with Dann Galucci on second guitar and John Wickert on bass. The band also released singles that same year on Sub Pop ("Broke") and Suicide Squeeze Records ("A Life of Arctic Sounds").

By this time, Judy was back and Modest Mouse was again a trio. The band's early recordings captured the attention of Chris Takino, head of Seattle's Up Records. He sponsored the studio sessions that produced the group's first album, *This Is a Long Drive for Someone with Nothing to Think About* (1996). The album name was inspired by the band members' daily drive from Seattle to the Olympia, Washington, studio where the tracks were recorded. The band recorded and released its second record, *Interstate 8*, later that year. This record, although billed as an EP, contained 56 minutes of music (which, come to think of it, was nothing compared with the 74 minutes of *This Is a Long Drive*). Modest Mouse released another EP in 1997, *The Fruit That Ate Itself*, this time on Olympia's K Records. *The Lonesome Crowded West* was released on Up that October.

Describing Modest Mouse's music is a tough task: Brock's vocals and guitar ride atop the din created by the fluid, active rhythm section. Sometimes the band steps up into screaming rock, or vamps endlessly on some chunky, funky riff; other times the music is just a drone behind Brock's introspective vocalizing. This is a man who can sound smart speculating about space travel (his impression: it'd be boring as hell), and who produces couplets that just scream to be quoted ("I had a drink the other day / Opinions were like kittens, always giving them away"). Now that all three guys are finally old enough to drink legally, things can only get better. **JB**

(1997, Up)
A portrait of a band whose talents are maturing before their fans' very eyes.

The Mono Men

Formed 1987, Bellingham, Washington

The antithesis of tall "skinny" lattes and overpriced microbrews, the Mono Men stand for cheap beer, sticky floors, and blaring lo-fi rock, taking up where Northwest garage bands like the Sonics and the Wailers left off in the late 1960s.

In addition to garage rock, frontman Dave Crider is also a fan of old surf rock instrumental bands, especially the Ventures. He and future Mono Men bassist Ledge Morrisette (no relation to Alanis) formed a surf band called the Dentures, which later evolved into the Roof Dogs. Crider started up an independent label as a vehicle for his own music, dubbing it Estrus after the state of a bitch in heat. A few personnel changes later, the Roof Dogs renamed themselves the Mono Men and decided to add vocals. Crider couldn't sing, so he learned to scream his head off instead, which he did divinely. The first Mono Men album, *Stop Dragging Me Down*, was released in 1990 and featured Crider, Morrisette, guitarist/vocalist Marx Wright, and drummer Eric Roeder.

Meanwhile, Estrus Records was becoming more than a hobby to Crider, who released a storm of garage rock records by bands from all over the world. Employing every gimmick he could think of to jerk the chains of fellow record collectors, Crider had the vinyl pressed in colors nature never intended, packaged them with comic books, and tucked them in cardboard "lunch buckets." The numerous compilations and tribute LPs in the Estrus catalog include the reverent *Here Ain't the Sonics*, a corelease with PopLlama (the Mono Men got to do the Sonics' hit "The Witch," of course).

After Wright left the band in 1991, John "Mort" Mortensen began sharing guitar and vocal duties, the group released its second full-length recording, *Wrecker*. Like many of their releases, it's available with two different covers, a clean one and a dirty one: in this case, the same woman with and without clothing. As a concession to critics of their singing (Mort's voice wasn't quite as raunchy as Crider's, but it came close), the Mono Men put out an all-instrumental LP called *Shut Up* (a later, alternate version was titled *Shut the Fuck Up*). Subsequent releases were the LP *Sin & Tonic* (1994), *Live at Tom's Strip n' Bowl*, released as a 10-inch EP and CD (1995), and a collection of singles called *Bent Pages*; the group has appeared on more than sixty recordings all together, including singles, EPs, and compilation tracks.

In 1997 Crider's offices caught fire, destroying much of his record collection. A very grouchy Crider next recorded *Have a Nice Day, Motherfucker*, the band's most powerful CD yet. By this time the Mono Men had become a power trio, although Crider is vague about whether Mortensen actually left the band, explaining that "he never officially joined."

Bellingham, a small college town 80 miles north of Seattle, had little musical history to speak of before the Mono Men appeared, armed and ready to blow everyone out of a Grateful Dead–induced trance. (The Posies are from Bellingham, but they fled to Seattle fairly early in their career.) The town more or less slept through the punk era but snapped out of it in time to get a college alternative radio station going, and a group of bands began gigging at the one or two taverns that featured live music. These bands included Mortenson's alma mater Game for Vultures and the famously awful Dust Blair. Every year around Labor Day, the Mono Men and their pals host the Garage Shock festival at Bellingham's 3-B Tavern, which drummer Eric Roeder now owns. About twenty bands a day play for four days to a largely inebriated crowd of blissed-out trashrockers.

Despite their obvious love for their forefathers, the Mono Men have proven themselves to be no mere imitators. If they had the chance to travel back in time and share a bill with the Sonics and the Wailers, they'd stand a good chance of blowing those bands off the stage. And that's not greasy kid stuff. **DA**

Wrecker

(1992, ESTRUS)
Dave Crider's slash-and-trash vocals are balanced by the more sensitive John Mortensen's. This album features garage rock and nonwimpy surf riffs, a couple of well-chosen cover tunes, and just a few minutes of Farfisa organ. A cool, trashy record.

Have a Nice Day, Motherfucker

(1997, ESTRUS)
Raging from start to finish, without a single polite moment. Song titles express the band's current world view: "Off My Back," "Hate Your Way," "Hey (You With the Face)," and a cover of the Zeros' "Wimp" that decidedly improves on the original.

Mother Love Bone

Formed 1988, Seattle, Washington

Malfunkshun

Formed 1982, Bainbridge Island, Washington

before Nirvana's *Nevermind*, before Sub Pop Records, and arguably even before grunge, there was Landrew the Love God.

Landrew, born Andy Wood, was the closest thing Seattle had to a star for a long time. He never played to coliseum-sized crowds, but even when he looked out at an audience of 12, Wood always visualized a Kingdome full of lit Bic lighters.

One of the first in Seattle to welcome the 1970s revival that heavily influenced grunge, Landrew began baffling punk rock audiences back in 1982, wearing white face paint and publicly worshiping Kiss. Fronting his band Malfunkshun, he draped himself in fake fur, scarves, and spandex in a parody of cock-rock excess.

Malfunkshun consisted of Landrew on bass and vocals, his older brother Kevin Wood on guitar, and longtime Bainbridge Island, Washington, buddy Regan Hagar on drums. Their music ranged from the sublime to the excruciating, a numbing, gloppy mass of purely delightful noise. The band could have been Kiss if they weren't so loose and runny.

In 1988 Landrew teamed up with three ex-members of Green River, guitarists Stone Gossard and Bruce Fairweather and bassist Jeff Ament, and the ex-drummer of Ten Minute Warning, Greg Gilmore, to form Mother Love Bone. An abrupt departure from Green River, Mother Love Bone played slick, midtempo hard rock, and their audiences quickly grew almost large enough to meet Landrew's expectations. He began referring to himself simply as Andrew Wood, but he had finally become the Landrew character he had invented.

Meanwhile, major label scouts began noticing a strange smell emanating from the Northwest and concluded it was money. Soundgarden was signed to A&M, and several labels began circling Mother Love Bone. The winner was PolyGram, which reportedly paid them the largest advance ever offered a Seattle band for a debut record. The EP *Shine* was released in 1989 on Stardog Records, the band's own label, which PolyGram distributed. Full of swagger and hard rock crunch, the EP also contained plenty of Landrew-style vocal excesses and immortal lyrics like "If you want a plate of my beef swellington baby / You're gonna have to pay the cover charge."

Mother Love Bone embarked on a forty-date club tour before settling down to record their next release, the LP *Apple.* Plans were being made for a video shoot and a national tour. But Andy Wood was never to play the coliseums he seemed destined for. On March 19, 1990, he was found dead in his apartment of an accidental heroin overdose.

Wood had been battling addiction since his years with Malfunkshun. Before his final relapse, he had reportedly been clean for almost four months. Predictably, a sickening media blitz followed his death, and Wood was canonized as an artistic visionary. But the depressing fact is that he never came close to realizing his considerable potential.

The remaining band members negotiated their release from the PolyGram contract, ending up in massive debt to the label. *Apple* received little promotion, and sales were unimpressive. PolyGram kept the Stardog name for its more "alternative" bands, like Ugly Kid Joe.

Gossard and Ament teamed up with Chris Cornell and Matt Cameron of Soundgarden to record the 1991 CD *Temple of the Dog* in Wood's memory. The CD also featured vocals by an unknown singer named Eddie Vedder. The project gave rise to the formation of Pearl Jam, which went on to achieve all the success Andy Wood had dreamed of. **DA**

Apple

(1990, POLYGRAM)
Mother Love Bone's power riffs and power ballads, which in retrospect sound unbelievably sad.

Return to Olympus

(1995, LOOSE GROOVE)
Former Mother Love Bone bandmate Stone Gossard dug up these gems from a 1988 Malfunkshun recording session and released them on his own label. The Seattle music scene has often been accused of being overly serious, but if you want to know how passionately silly it really was, listen to this.

Mudhoney

Formed 1988, Seattle, Washington

When musical differences split up trashrock kings Green River in late 1987, Mark Arm knew just who to call: Steve Turner. A founding Green River member, Turner had left after playing on that band's first EP, disgusted with his bandmates' growing fascination with complex song structures. Arm proposed a band that would stick to the basics—straight-ahead guitar riffs and a thunderous rock sound. Ex-Melvins bassist Matt Lukin and former Bundle of Hiss drummer Dan Peters completed the band. Their first recording session, with producer Jack Endino at the helm, resulted in the 1988 single that defined the term "grunge"—"Touch Me I'm Sick"/"Sweet Young Thing (Ain't Sweet No More)." The follow-up EP was the six-song *Superfuzz Bigmuff* (named after two popular guitar distortion units). By the time the EP was released, the band had already done their own East Coast tour, plus a West Coast swing with Sonic Youth.

Mudhoney released two albums on Sub Pop Records, *Mudhoney* (1989) and *Every Good Boy Deserves Fudge* (1991), all the while earning a reputation as touring wildmen. Their tenure with the Seattle independent label coincided with Sub Pop collector mania. As many always suspected, Arm says that phenomenon was another brilliant Sub Pop scam. He remembers the process: releasing singles, stashing about half the copies, and announcing that the records were sold out—waiting for the price to go up before selling the remaining records on the collector market. This ruse kept the label's coffers full during the lean years and made collector's items out of slabs like the brown vinyl "Touch Me I'm Sick" single.

The band departed for Reprise Records in 1993, releasing *Piece of Cake* (produced, as was *Every Good Boy*, by Seattle studio mainstay Conrad Uno). That record had its moments, although the most interesting thing about the follow-up EP was its name, *Five Dollar Bob's Mock Cooter Stew* (1993). More recently, *My Brother the Cow* (1995) marked the band's best effort since the first LP, especially the sarcasm-dripping "Into Your Schtick" and "Generation Spokesmodel."

Although its members have other projects to occupy them—Arm sang for Monkeywrench (which released an album in 1992) and has toured and recorded as a guitarist and keyboard player with Bloodloss, while Turner is a record moguel with Super Electro—the group hung together. After a series of bar gigs in 1998 (including several of those "secret" shows that Seattle insiders love so much), the band came back reenergized with a strong final album on Reprise, *Tomorrow Hit Today*.

Mudhoney's future as a band is now in question, however. As the band was working on a retrospective 2-CD set for Sub Pop (one disc compiling the band's greatest hits, the other comprising B-sides and rarities), Reprise dropped Mudhoney from their artist roster, and Lukin departed the band. **JB**

Superfuzz Bigmuff

(1988, Sᴜʙ Pᴏᴘ)
The CD version includes the original EP, the band's first two singles, and extra tracks. What more could you want?

My Brother the Cow

(1995, Rᴇᴘʀɪsᴇ)
Mudhoney's comeback effort reunites them with producer Jack Endino and features some of the band's most pointed songs.

The Murder City Devils

Formed 1996, Seattle, Washington

t he Murder City Devils lead the pack of reverential/pestilential 1970s-style punk bands currently infesting Seattle clubs. To old-timers their music recalls all that was dirty and exciting about those golden days of the New York Dolls and Cleveland's Dead Boys. Those bands were called punk then, but it was really only rock 'n' roll.

Vocalist Spencer Moody, guitarists Dann Galucci and Nate Manny, bassist Derek Fudesco, and drummer Coady Willis all got their start in hardcore punk bands, striving to play harder, faster, louder than everyone else using a by-the-numbers formula. There's only so far you can go with this, however, and by the time the five guys came together as the Murder City Devils they were ready for a change. They wanted to recapture a time when true rock was gritty and sleazy and played strictly for fun. Blaring guitars and exuberant, mostly tuneless vocals joined trashy drums and Farfisa organ to create a sound that was part 1970s New York punk, part 1960s Northwest garage.

In the late 1990s the record companies were once again pronouncing rock dead, and once again Seattle refused to cooperate. It took almost no time for the Murder City Devils to become one of the most popular new bands in town. They released two singles in 1997, followed by a self-titled album on Sub Pop's punk-oriented subsidiary label Die Young Stay Pretty. Although the CD was underproduced and thin sounding, it did give the band exposure and an excuse to hit the road touring. Their next album, *Empty Bottles Broken Hearts*, packed a bigger wallop. In 1998 they recruited Leslie Hardy from the Portland band Love Is Laughter to play Farfisa organ (the guys had previously traded off keyboard duties). Hardy plays on about half the songs; the rest of the time she looks very cool holding a cigarette.

In the 1970s the idea of a punk band playing coliseum shows was preposterous. Those with the nerve to dress punk in high school ended up with footprints on their faces. But the world evolves, and in 1998 the Murder City Devils were invited to open for Pearl Jam in front of some eighteen thousand people at several sold-out shows. They played fast and furious and exited the stage hoping nobody would throw bottles at them. Nobody did. **DA**

Empty Bottles Broken Hearts

(1998, DIE YOUNG STAY PRETTY)
You don't get to see them set the drum kit on fire, but other than that, this record captures all the cheese and sleaze of the Murder City Devils' live shows. Contains some very crunchy tunes, a couple tearjerkers, and a tribute to Johnny Thunders.

MxPx

Formed 1992, Bremerton, Washington

he Northwest's teen dream band earned a record contract through a private audition in their garage practice space, released their first album as high school juniors, and celebrated their graduation by going on tour in support of their second long-player. What more do you need to know about Bremerton's MxPx?

Originally the band was called Magnified Plaid, a joking reference to a plaid shirt owned by original guitarist Andy Hustad by bandmates Mike Hererra (bass, vocals) and Yuri Ruley (drums). The band got its new name when Ruley drew a show poster for "M.P." using little x's for periods, and the name stuck. Like many young punk bands, MxPx played coffeehouses, teen centers, and parties. Unlike many young bands, MxPx soon attracted the interest of a record company.

As the young MxPx's were all Christians, there was natural interest from Seattle's independent Tooth & Nail label, which is run by Christians and features many bands with Christian members. After their garage audition, MxPx was in, releasing *Pokinatcha*, their first album, in 1994.

Hustad quit the band and Tom Wisniewski of Evolution of Man was tabbed as his replacement. This version of the band debuted on *Teenage Politics* (1995), their second Tooth & Nail release. A eighteen-song punk/pop extravaganza, the record sometimes suffered from Hererra's attempts at lyrical profundity. (This is, after all, a record that includes the track "Like Sand Through the Hourglass . . . So Are the Days of Our Lives.") Far more successful were the band's takes on teenage life, such as "Teenage Politics" and "Punk Rawk Show."

For their next (and, as it turned out, their last) Tooth & Nail release, the band went back to the well and produced an upbeat soundtrack for adolescence, *Life in General*. This 1996 gem included a pair of charming singles, "Move to Bremerton" and "Chick Magnet," but every song was good. The band was far tighter than on earlier recordings; Wisniewski's guitar licks were especially memorable. The record sold more than the sixty thousand copies of *Teenage Politics*—solid enough numbers to draw the attention of A&M Records, which purchased the band's contract and rereleased *Life in General*. The split wasn't without unpleasantness—Tooth & Nail executives were disappointed with the band's defection to a major label, and some Christian fans were upset with the change to a secular label.

In the summer of 1997, MxPx was featured on the national Warped Tour with Bad Religion and Rancid. The first major-label MxPx recording, *Slowly Going the Way of the Buffalo*, was released in June 1998. The label planned to make amends with MxPx fans by selling the album both in record stores and in Christian bookstores. Tooth & Nail was also allowed to co-release the live MxPx album, *At the Show* (1999). **JB**

Life in General

(1996, Tooth & Nail; 1997, A&M)
Glorious teenage punk rock with poppy, sing-along choruses and great tunes about girls and growing up.

THE VICEROYS

THE POSIES

STEVE TURNER (MUDHONEY)

THE MOBERLYS

THE HUDSON BROTHERS

METAL CHURCH

SOUNDGARDEN

THE WAILERS

SIR MIX-A-LOT

SCREAMING TREES

SGM

PAT O'DAY AND THE KINGSMEN

NIRVANA

BLUEBIRD

TREEPEOPLE

EASY CHAIR

DAILY FLASH

INSPECTOR LUV

TAD

JR. CADILLAC

PAUL REVERE AND THE RAIDERS

THE WALKABOUTS

GREEN RIVER

POND

THE COWBOYS

DON AND THE GOODTIMES

THE FASTBACKS

CROME SYRCUS

LAYNE STALEY (ALICE IN CHAINS)

THE YOUNG FRESH FELLOWS

CHRIS NEWMAN (NAPALM BEACH)

GREEN PAJAMAS

MERRILEE AND THE TURNABOUTS

COFFIN BREAK

THE ACCUSED

THE HEATS

ROCKIN' ROBIN ROBERTS
(THE WAILERS)

BILLY RANCHER

HAZEL

CITY ZU

Napalm Beach

Formed 1983, Portland, Oregon

Snow Bud and the Flower People

Formed 1986, Portland, Oregon

Chris Newman is a one-man musical cottage industry. To call this Portland rock legend prolific would be a heinous understatement. Newman's trio Napalm Beach (with drummer Sam Henry and a rotating series of bassists) has been performing and recording off and on since the early 1980s. Snow Bud and the Flower People, his pro-pot "side project," is arguably the more famous band. In 1996 the marijuana magazine *High Times* named Snow Bud one of the five best bands of all time.

Newman first came to the attention of Northwest rock fans in the late 1980s, when the stocky, dark-haired guitarist/singer played with a bunch of skinny punk kids with dyed blond hair called the Untouchables. After that band split, he was working on a cassette-only record and asked Henry (ex-Wipers, ex-Rats) to help him finish a few tracks. The combination worked out, and the band released the 1985 album *Napalm Beach* (rereleased as *Teen Dream*), in addition to several cassette-only releases.

In 1989 Newman hooked up with a nascent Portland label, Flying Heart Records, which remains his recording home base. Newman played bass himself on *Liquid Love* (1989); Dave Dillinger toured Europe with the band and played bass on their next full-length release, *Fire Air and Water* (1990). Largely due to the efforts of an exchange student who became a big fan of the band and promoted them heavily upon his return home, Napalm Beach has a large fan base in Germany and has released two German-only albums, *Moving To and Fro* (1987) and *Thunder Lizard* (1991). The obliging Henry reportedly earned his footnote in cinema history by teaching actor Matt Dillon how to shoot heroin for his role in the film *Drugstore Cowboy*. In 1993 Portland's Tim/Kerr label released a collection of rare Napalm Beach tracks entitled *Curiosities*. Another set of Napalm Beach tracks was released by Seattle's CM Records as *In Our Tree*.

Before Napalm Beach was going strong in the late 1980s, dedicated pot-smoker Newman had formed Snow Bud with guitarist/bassist Greg Slyter and drummer Jeff Roth. The band released two cassettes worth of cannabis worship, which Flying Heart remixed and rereleased in 1990; *Complete Works* is the label's best-selling cassette ever. Guitarist/bassist Jan Celt joined the band (Celt also has produced many of Newman's records) as Snow Bud graduated to CD status with *Green Thing* (1991).

Despite the subject matter, Snow Bud is no joke band, as proven by the brilliant *Ripped Van Stinkle* (1994, Tim/Kerr). Originally recorded in 1991, the master tape for this album was destroyed in a fire. All the tracks were rerecorded the following year, but the tape sat on the shelf until Tim/Kerr stepped in. The lineup became

Newman, drummer Lance Paden, bassist Nathan Fong, and the ubiquitous Henry now playing keyboards. The songs shift effortlessly through musical styles from the heavy, grinding rock of the opener, "Tweakin' at Bob's," to the music hall bomp of "Lazy Days," to the intense skittering ska of "Burn Down the Meth Lab." Snow Bud also rated a release on Sub Pop Records' famous Single of the Month Club, "Killer Bud"/"Third Shelf."

Newman has also created two Snow Bud comic books and a coloring book for children. In 1995 he released the solo record *Volunteer* on Flying Heart. **JB**

Ripped Van Stinkle

(1994, Tim/Kerr)
Love for the bud drives Snow Bud and the Flower People through this likable hodge-podge of musical styles.

Volunteer

(1995, Flying Heart)
This solo effort (Lance Paden plays drums; Chris Newman does the rest) got lost in the flurry of Napalm Beach and Snow Bud and the Flower People releases—which is a crying shame, because some of Newman's best work is included here. His voice is a combination of Jim Morrison and Lou Reed on the creepy "Mr. Gus"; "Down in New Orleans" could be a lost Doors track.

Nirvana

Formed 1988, Aberdeen, Washington

orget all the "voice of a generation" crap. Nirvana's career was exceptional for two reasons:
1. They sold lots of records.
2. They didn't suck.

In the 1990s, Nirvana was the greatest rock band of its generation at a time when rock ruled. After a decade of vapid dance music masquerading as "new wave," Nirvana turned up at the right place at the right time—which inexplicably turned out to be Aberdeen, Washington, in the late 1980s.

The dreary white-trash town of Aberdeen was (and probably still is) dominated by mulletheads in El Caminos blasting Night Ranger. It was in this unlikely setting that Kurt Cobain and Krist Novoselic first began making noise together.

The Melvins, proto-metal punks from neighboring Montesano, were apparently the only other underground music fans in the area. Cobain and Novoselic idolized the Melvins. When the two recorded their first demo in Seattle in 1988, Melvins drummer Dale Crover sat in on drums. The three laid down several tracks with producer Jack Endino, who recorded the bulk of the Sub Pop releases that came to be known as early grunge. (Some songs from this session ended up on the 1992 LP *Incesticide*, a collection of demos and outtakes.)

Endino passed the tape on to Sub Pop's Jonathan Poneman. The band's excruciatingly heavy riffs and tortured vocals certainly fit in with what was becoming known as the Sub Pop sound, but something set Nirvana apart from the growing number of grunge bands in Seattle. Most were made up of hip urbanites who played the heavy trip as a joke. Nobody could think Nirvana was joking; Cobain's agony sounded uncomfortably real. And in a town reputed to be heavy on riffs and light on songs, he was already writing memorable tunes, the kind with hooks.

Nevertheless, the band's first single for Sub Pop was a cover, a criminally catchy version of Dutch band Shocking Blue's "Love Buzz" backed with Nirvana's own "Big Cheese." It featured Chad Channing, who remained the band's drummer for the next two years.

To fill out their sound while on tour, Nirvana picked up a second guitarist named Jason Everman. Everman lent them the money to pay the recording bill for their debut album, *Bleach* (1989, Subpop) but didn't play on the album, though he was credited. The only recording he actually appears on is a hideous version of "Do You Love Me" on a Kiss tribute album put out by C/Z Records. He quit or was fired after a U.S. tour.

By the time the band went on a European tour with Northwest labelmates Tad, the British press was convulsing with ecstasy over Seattle and Sub Pop, Nirvana in particular. Once again, the Brits proved their genius at selling an American concept back to America after grabbing it for themselves. First it was rock 'n' roll and now it was . . . rock 'n' roll, only this time folks were calling it grunge. As the raves continued, the mainstream media in Seattle finally began to take Nirvana seriously.

Around Puget Sound in the early 1990s, the pinnacle of success was selling one hundred thousand copies of an album on a larger independent label. Nobody, least of all Nirvana, could have predicted the breakthrough success of the "major label corporate sellout album" *Nevermind* (1991, Geffen), which sold almost fourteen million copies worldwide.

Suddenly a sensitive and socially awkward young singer/guitarist found himself the object of worldwide adoration, which was undoubtedly fun at first. Cobain's stage presence evolved from that of a cringing geek (albeit a cute geek) uncomfortable in his own skin to that of a guitar-smashing maniac. The band's subsequent sports dome concerts were uneven but always a spectacle worth wading through puke and broken glass for. (Songs from the *Nevermind* tour make up the majority of a career-spanning live album, *From the Muddy Banks of the Wishkah*, released in 1996.)

Nevermind marked the major label debut of future Foo Fighter frontman Dave Grohl, who replaced Channing and remained Nirvana's drummer for the duration. During this time, Cobain hooked up with his future wife, Courtney Love, about whom far too much has already been said.

As fans awaited Nirvana's third album, the rumors began to fly that Geffen hated it and had declared it unreleasable. The mystique grew as folks wondered what kind of abrasive, exciting noise the men in suits were trying to quash. The producer this time was Steve Albini, who wasn't exactly known for making slick, commercial records.

In Utero was released in 1993. Though not as immediately accessible as *Nevermind*, it was certainly not the commercial disaster some predicted. The album entered the *Billboard* charts at no. 1. The production sounded fine.

About this time the band picked up two new members, Pat Smear of the Germs as second guitarist and Lori Goldston on cello. Adding strings to rock music is usually an ominous sign of impending wimpdom, but in this case it worked. When Nirvana performed an acoustic set for MTV's *Unplugged* series, Goldston's presence added emotional depth to the haunting group of songs. (The live album from these sessions was released in 1994.)

By then, scandals surrounding Cobain's drug use and his marriage were being reported with mind-numbing regularity, not only in rock magazines but on television news and in mainstream press like *Vanity Fair*. The reporting seemed like the standard rock-star routine, and most fans tuned it out. But Cobain was growing progressively sicker. Nirvana's 1994 European tour was cut short, and in March, Love discovered her husband passed out on the floor of their hotel room in Rome. He was rushed to the hospital in a coma. Newspapers dutifully reported that he had suffered an "accidental overdose," which did not seem unlikely at the time. Later it emerged that he had taken as many as fifty tranquilizers and had written a suicide note.

One month later Seattle-area residents were subjected to a full-color photo of Cobain's body splashed across the front page of the *Seattle Times*. Cause of death: self-inflicted gunshot wound. The day after his death saw the arrival of staff for *A Current Affair, Inside Edition, Hard Copy*, MTV's Tabitha Soren, two *Rolling Stone* writers, *People* magazine reporters, and countless others. The consensus seemed to be that Cobain should have been happy because he was rich.

Though many Nirvana songs recalled both the power of 1970s heavy metal and the melodic ring of 1960s pop, older rock fans who came of age with the Beatles and Led Zeppelin remain strangely deaf to the band's magic. Cobain's death at the age of 27 guaranteed him eternal rock 'n' roll martyr status, but we'll have to wait for today's 23-year-olds to start lecturing their own kids about how there's been no good music since Nirvana to put the band's importance in perspective. **DA**

Bleach

(1989, SUB POP)
Still this writer's favorite, a harsh, uncompromising record with a couple of genuine pop tunes and some residual 1980s artiness around the edges. It introduced the world to that *gung-gung-gung* sound and showed off Kurt Cobain's genius at making the slightest annoyance sound like the end of the world: "NO RECESS!"   CONTINUED...

Nevermind

(1991, GEFFEN)
Back with an arena-sized sound courtesy of producer Butch Vig, Nirvana reluctantly conquered the world with a then-unique combination of jarring and beautiful sounds that every lame-brained stoner who could hold a guitar was soon imitating. This isn't Nirvana's fault. Pull this record out twenty years from now, and maybe "Smells Like Teen Spirit" will sound brilliant all over again. (Okay, so it didn't work with "Stairway to Heaven.")

In Utero

(1993, GEFFEN)
The quiet parts are more somber, the screams more agonized, the jarring shifts between hard and soft more extreme than ever. Cobain sounds resigned and occasionally bored but still can't manage to write a bad tune. The CD's closer, "All Apologies," is perhaps the most world-weary song ever recorded.

Paul Revere and the Raiders

Formed 1958, Boise, Idaho

One of Idaho's first rock 'n' roll groups, keyboardist Paul Revere's band was originally known as the Downbeats and included Bill Hibbard on bass, Jerry Labrum on drums, and guitarist brothers Robert and Richard White. Revere's next recruit was 16-year-old singer Mark Lindsay, then playing with the country and western Idaho Playboys; he joined the band after promising to learn how to play saxophone.

The band's first recordings as Paul Revere and the Raiders were released on California's Gardena label. The mainly instrumental first album, *Like Long Hair*, is dominated by boogie-woogie piano and Lindsay's raunchy sax lines, and includes nods to the Wailers and other early Northwest bands. The title cut edged into the national Top 40, hitting no. 38 in April 1961, but the young band's momentum was quashed when Revere was drafted. To honor their remaining contractual commitments, the band deputized a young Leon Russell as "Paul Revere" for a few dates.

Revere and Lindsay regrouped in Portland in fall 1962, adding drummer Mike "Smitty" Smith on drums, guitarist Steve West, and bassist Ross Alemang. Although they released only a few records during this period (for Jerry Dennon's Jerden label), they made two critical connections—their future manager, KISN radio personality Roger Hart, and Seaside, Oregon, booking agent Pat Mason, through whom the Raiders got dance and concert bookings in every corner of the Northwest. Like Portland's Kingsmen, the Raiders covered "Louie Louie" in early 1963. The Kingsmen got the national hit, but the Raiders' version was a Northwest smash, selling more than fifteen thousand copies. The pressures of touring led to the departure of West and Alemang, who were replaced by guitarist Drake Levin and bassist Mike "Doc" Holiday. The Raiders were the first rock band signed by Columbia Records; their debut, *Here They Come,* featured a live side of Northwest R&B standards and a ballad-oriented side of studio recordings (with another new bassist, Phil "Fang" Volk).

The band didn't adopt their familiar American Revolution uniforms until 1963, when they rented them from a costume shop as a gag before playing a high school prom. The kids went crazy over the Raider's new look, and the uniforms stayed as the band's visual trademark. The Raiders borrowed the habit of performing choreographed steps from other Northwest acts but quickly were executing more intricate moves than any of their rivals.

By early 1965 Paul Revere and the Raiders were poised for national stardom. They were the house band for ABC's daily show *Where the Action Is,* and had started getting major notice in teen magazines due to Lindsay's photogenic appeal and the talents of Beatles publicity agent Derek Taylor. Hooking up with producer Terry Melcher, the Raiders began their assault on the U.S. charts with "Just Like Me" (no. 11). Their next two singles, "Kicks" and "Hungry," cracked the Top 10 and earned gold record status. In 1966 the Raiders and the Beach Boys were the biggest acts in America (in Seattle, the Rolling Stones were the opening act for one Raiders show). But despite the triumvirate of national television exposure, radio airplay, and massive print coverage, the cracks were starting to show. That spring Levin was drafted and replaced by Northwest rock veteran Jim "Harpo" Valley (of the Viceroys and Don and the Goodtimes). Levin returned briefly the following year, but he, Volk, and Smith were becoming fed up with the wild colonial outfits and teen idol hijinks. The three departed to form the band Brotherhood, which released three albums but never approached the Raiders' commercial success. The new players were guitarist Freddy Weller, drummer Joe Correro, and ex–Don and the Goodtimes bassist Charlie Coe (replaced quickly by Keith Allison).

Meanwhile, the Raiders soldiered on with more Top 40 hits ("I Had a Dream," "Too Much Talk") and a new television show (Dick Clark's *Happening 68*), but although the songs approached their previous Northwest crunch, the band's audience was growing younger, and their reputation with serious music fans was slipping. Despite Lindsay's Top 10 solo album (*Arizona,* 1970) and no. 1 hit ("Indian Reservation," 1971), the band was now reduced to playing lounges and amusement parks. As the 1970s continued, the band added two ex-Sonics—bassist Ron Foos and guitarist Doug Heath—and Lindsay quit. The Raiders broke up for a time, but Revere re-formed the group in the late 1970s and, with the help of veteran Northwest manager Neil Rush (Statics, Merrilee and the Turnabouts), became a success again, playing Nevada casinos and county fairs. The band, which now includes Foos, Heath, drummer Omar Martinez, singer Carl Driggs, keyboardist Danny Krause, and Revere's son, Jamie, on guitar, recently celebrated forty years in the business. **NS**

The Legend of Paul Revere

(1990, COLUMBIA)

A magnificent fifty-five-cut overview of all the Lindsay-era singles, plus a generous dozen or so true rarities and unreleased cuts.

The Essential Ride

(1995, COLUMBIA)

A twenty-song compilation of the band's killer Northwest garage sound. Several unreleased tracks are here, including an amazing outtake of "Hungry" and a mesmerizing version of "The Great Airplane Strike." Bonus points for the brilliant liner book.

Pearl Jam

Formed 1990, Seattle, Washington

If Nirvana was the blade that lanced the emotional boil of Generation X, Pearl Jam was the salve that healed the wound. The group used their fame to raise Americans' awareness of social issues such as ticket distribution monopolies and underground radio, and they probably did more than any well-planned and well-financed media campaign to inform teenage boys about abortion rights.

After the death of Mother Love Bone frontman Andy Wood, guitarist Stone Gossard and bass player Jeff Ament hooked up with Gossard's childhood guitar buddy, Mike McCready. The trio went in search of a drummer and vocalist. Unable to recruit their first choice—ex-Red Hot Chili Pepper Jack Irons—the band chose Dave Krusen as drummer. He quit after recording *Ten* (1991, Epic), the band's debut album. His replacement, Matt Chamberlain, stayed long enough to appear in the video for "Alive" and then quit to join television's *Saturday Night Live* band. Enter Dave Abbruzzese. He played on *VS.* (1993, Epic) and was then fired for undisclosed reasons. Irons filled in on a couple of tour dates and eventually joined the band, solidifying Pearl Jam's original vision.

The debut album, *Ten*, sold more than eight million copies in the United States alone. This unanticipated success didn't sit well among independent-label purists. Locally, another reason for resentment stemmed from the band's importation of vocal virtuoso Eddie Vedder from the beaches of San Diego. Seattle was feeling inundated by outsiders relocating to cash in on the growing music scene. In addition, Vedder's voice was just too big; rather than whining about angst and prejudice, it boomed with pain and pride—completely out of sync with the "loser" mentality cultivated by Sub Pop Records.

Pearl Jam's success continued with two huge hit albums, *VS.* and *Vitalogy* (1994, Epic). Their fourth release, *No Code* (1996), didn't sell as well. Some attributed its comparatively low sales to Pearl Jam's limited touring and refusal to make videos.

More likely, the esoteric nature of *No Code* simply left average fans behind. Heavily influenced by the late Nusrat Fateh Ali Khan, a Sufi Muslim vocalist, the softer cuts on the record turned inward rather than reaching out the familiar, healing hand.

Since Pearl Jam had decided to fight the system from the inside, they faced an interesting quandary. The counterculture considered them sellouts and often viewed their political stances as publicity stunts. At the same time, tight-lipped music-industry executives weren't doing handsprings over the band's actions either.

Pearl Jam's first run-in was with MTV over the video for "Jeremy" (from *Ten*). The version that aired was a vignette of a disaffected boy who kills his classmates; in the original version, the boy kills himself. Although they agreed to alter the video's ending, Pearl Jam refused to produce any videos for television thereafter.

The band's larger fight came with Ticketmaster. Seeking to avoid what they considered exorbitant service fees, Pearl Jam tried to sell tickets through alternative sources. After Ticketmaster's pressure tactics blocked the effort, the band filed a complaint with the antitrust division of the Department of Justice. The tactic failed, and so did Pearl Jam's attempt to circumvent Ticketmaster. After four year of sporadic touring, Pearl Jam decided to once again play venues with exclusive Ticketmaster distribution agreements. Ironically, losing this battle further proved the band's point about the company's monopolistic practices.

The title of Pearl Jam's fifth release was telling. With *Yield* (1998), Pearl Jam returned to making songs accessible to the masses. (The band also released a live album in late 1998, the sixteen-track *Live on Two Legs*.) The lyrics of *Yield* revisited tales of change and the struggles of everyday human beings, though they were sung by someone temporarily elevated to mythic status. **VK**

Ten

(1991, EPIC)
This debut wraps all the intriguing elements of Pearl Jam into eleven tasty tunes plus a haunting introduction that repeats at the end of the album. Lots of driving guitar and bass ("Once") and lyrics leaning toward the social ("Why Go") and the spiritual ("Release," "Garden").

Vitalogy

(1994, EPIC)
Although the later, esoteric *No Code* is Pearl Jam's most spiritually affecting album, the blend of strong guitar and bass and the introspective ballads on *Vitalogy* rank it with the greatest rock records.

Poison Idea

Formed 1981, Portland, Oregon

oison Idea was formed as a no-wave jazz trio with "Jerry A." on saxophone, Chris Tense on bass, and future Helmet bassist Henry Bogdan on drums. But instead of sticking to their noisy, avant-garde jazz sound, Poison Idea—after sucking up platters by the Germs and Black Flag—swelled into Portland's premier beery, brawling punk rock band. They added massive Tom Roberts (known as "Pig Champion" or "Tom Pig") on guitar. Dean Johnson (later known as "Thee Slayer Hippy") took over the drums from Bogdan. Since there were no local punk clubs to speak of in Portland, the band often played a gay dance joint called the Metropolis before other little venues, like the Urban Noise Club and the 13th Precinct, began to show up. None of these establishments survived the 1980s.

While the classic image of the street-rat punker is an emaciated junkie scarecrow, Poison Idea was fronted by Jerry A. (300-plus pounds) and Pig Champion (about 450 pounds), a pair of malt liquor–swilling monsters—surly alcoholic misfits who never left home, much to their parents' dismay. They filled the stage with their bulk while filling the tiny venues they played with brain-blasting riffs and blistering lyrics about being young and defiant while living life face-down in the gutter. Jerry A.'s lyrics could be combative and venomous, but also occasionally poignant and introspective, qualities not often associated with the flailing chaos of punk rock: "View the world through a fisheye lens / Lost my face / Party at my place / But now you're gone and I feel like shit" (from "Out of the Picture"). Poison Idea in their heyday were drunk, damaged, and definitely dangerous; they once caused city officials to cut short the annual "Mayor's Ball" because Jerry A. was breathing fire from the stage.

One of the fiercest and finest recorded manifestations of Poison Idea's fury can be found on their first full-length album, the aptly titled *Kings of Punk* (1986); its classic cover photo shows Jerry A.'s shirtless torso with the band name jaggedly cut into it. The album is a snarling stew, anchored by an unrelenting rhythm section, as Pig's crushing guitar hosts a meeting of the minds between Black Flag and Judas Priest. Jerry A. was at the top of his game, spitting out odes to self-destruction like "Short Fuse" ("Another drink / Another fight / A drunken display of lust tonight") and rants against creeping stupidity ("Ugly American") and bucking the establishment ("Made to Be Broken," "Lifestyles"). Poison Idea recorded a ton of material, releasing nearly two dozen singles, EPs, and LPs. Another must-have record is *Pajama Party*, the band's 1993 compilation of cover songs by such disparate acts as British punks the Damned and soul instrumentalists Booker T. & the MG's.

The group was huge in Europe (actually, they were pretty large wherever they went), embodying the purely antiauthoritarian American characteristics demonstrated by deities of a bygone age like the MC5 and the Stooges. Poison Idea spent a significant chunk of their career motoring about the Continent keeping the punk fires burning.

After breaking up in 1995 (Jerry A. formed two other bands, Gift and Pisswild Horses), the band regrouped with Jerry, Dean, Chris, and Ian Miller, formerly of Portland's Apt. 3G, who replaced Pig Champion on guitar. Champion, meanwhile, has formed the Submissives with MDC vocalist Dive Dictor.   JC

Kings of Punk

(1986, TAANG!)

This record's despair, alienation, and general sense of pissed-off hopelessness positively boils over, making runts like Green Day or the Offspring sound about as threatening as the chatter at a Cub Scout softball game.

Pond

Formed 1991, Juneau, Alaska

I t figures that Portland's most interesting band would actually be from Alaska. Two-thirds of it, anyway. Bassist Chris Brady and guitarist Charlie Campbell fled south to escape the horror of having to play in cover bands and met up with ex-Thrillhammer drummer Dave Triebwasser. And before you could say "Bruce Pavitt," the resulting combo ended up with a debut on Seattle's Sub Pop Records that was among the musical high points of 1993 (and helped hide the fact that, at this late date, Seattle's musical well was running dry indeed). "We figured we were kind of a pop band and they'd never be interested in us," says Brady of the night when Sub Pop representatives showed up at a gig. "I said, 'Just play, and they'll go away'—and they didn't."

Pond's initial CD showed a band with two equal singer/songwriters and ideas to spare. Trading leads and harmonies, Campbell and Brady displayed pure pop instincts, backed by a dense instrumental landscape featuring both shimmer and drone. Producer Jon Auer (yes, that Posies guy) channeled the band's youthful exuberance into the tracks and built up the result with a big mix. "It seemed like [Auer] was young enough in his style . . . he was into making us happy and he wasn't real set in his ways," muses Brady. The great songs didn't hurt, either. "Tree" sounds familiar yet brims with discovery; "Agatha" captures the timidity of a shy teenager. Critics loved the band's attempt to put "pop" into Sub Pop—one inspired soul labeled Pond's sound "bubble grunge."

By the time their second album rolled around, the trio was set on doing something different. *The Practice of Joy Before Death* (1995) fit that bill; reflecting the low-fidelity experimentation of the time in its tinny production, *The Practice of Joy* unfortunately also incorporated the lo-fi trait of recording half-finished, half-baked songs. Sub Pop loved the record and couldn't figure out why it didn't sell; fans of the first album's triumphant pop just didn't get it.

The band did, however, and went for more of a middle ground on *Rock Collection* (1997). Although only "Scoliosis" hearkens back to the first album's sound, the band regains the intensity they ceded on *The Practice of Joy* and puts together a well-paced, thoughtful third effort. **JB**

Pond

(1993, Sub Pop)
Musicians are never charmed by lavish praise for their first album ("We're so much better now"), but there are just too many classic songs here to worry about making friends.

The Posies

Formed 1988, Bellingham, Washington

When buddies Jon Auer and Ken Stringfellow took to their Bellingham, Washington, basement in 1988 to record *Failure*, they couldn't have been expecting this would be the start of something big. For starters, although the music was Beatlesque power pop (with lyrics reflecting a sour attitude toward love), Auer and Stringfellow were a couple of Cure guys with big hair. Furthermore, folks in Seattle were definitely not looking for the next Beatles. However, Conrad Uno of PopLlama Products was impressed enough to fund a vinyl release of the formerly cassette-only product. So Auer and Stringfellow picked up a band (bassist Rick Roberts and drummer Mike Musberger), ignored the bleeding from a few cutting local reviews, and earned themselves a reputation as a boisterous live act. Signed to Geffen Records during the Seattle feeding frenzy, the Posies confounded expectations with *Dear 23* (1990). While people were expecting an attempt to translate their live edge onto vinyl, the Posies and producer John Leckie instead created a gentle, melodic set of detailed pop gems.

Despite issuing one of the year's best albums in a good year for Seattle bands, the Posies didn't set any sales records. The next release, with Dave Fox replacing Roberts on bass, aimed at including more of the Replacements-like rock crunch of the Posies' live performances. The result, *Frosting on the Beater* (1993), hit a good middle ground, satisfying longtime fans while showing the band's harder-edged side. The resulting tour took the Posies across the world—Europe, Japan, the United States. By the end of the long tour, Roberts and Musberger had thought of better ways to spend their time. When the Posies released their fourth record, *Amazing Disgrace* (1996), Brian Young was playing drums and Joe Bass was playing—you guessed it—bass.

During the break between *Frosting on the Beater* and *Amazing Disgrace*, Auer and Stringfellow also realized the ultimate ambition of pop revivalists by re-forming Big Star, the cult band from Memphis, with Alex Chilton and Jody Stephens for a

Kansas City reunion concert.

In late 1997 the Posies went full circle, releasing their (supposedly) final studio album, *Success*, on their original label, PopLlama. The band now says they plan to emulate their friends the Fastbacks, re-forming occasionally for shows and other projects while working full-time on their own music. **JB**

Dear 23

(1990, GEFFEN)
The Posies mature from their British Merseybeat youth with this elegant and shockingly underrated disc. "Golden Blunders" is pop perfection; "Flood of Sunshine" takes the listener on a matchless ride. Still their best effort.

Amazing Disgrace

(1996, GEFFEN)
A selection of amazingly pretty songs, despite the bitter topics explored lyrically. "Daily Mutilation" is an energetic and tuneful song about a relationship gone awry; "Precious Moments" is uplifting musically, yet depressing lyrically.

The Presidents of the United States of America

Formed 1993, Seattle, Washington

minimalism in rock is ordinarily associated with stern faces, depressing lyrics, and black clothing. Not so for the Presidents of the United States of America, three guys churning out punk/pop on five strings and no cymbals. Lead vocalist Chris Ballew (on two-string "basitar") had some national credibility: he used to play with Morphine's Mark Sandman in a band called Supergroup and had toured with Beck. He started playing with Dave Dederer (on three-string "guitbass") in 1991, although the band picked a new name for each gig until they came up with the longest name they could think of and decided to keep it. Jason Finn, a decorated veteran of the Seattle rock scene and regular drummer for Love Battery, joined the group in 1993 (he quit Love Battery two years later). The stripped-down guitars, minus the high strings and played in a lowered open-tuning scheme, were basically a tactic invented to allow the vocals to cut through the din at live performances, says Dederer. (Big cymbals, also in sonic competition with vocal frequencies, were banned at the same time.) Dederer later switched to an ordinary six-string guitar onstage. "Chris plays through a bass amp and plays more like a bassist, and I play through a guitar amp and play more like a guitarist," he notes.

The Presidents' sunny stage disposition and the childlike silliness of their songs about kitties, dune buggies, and canned peaches won them a large and loyal Seattle following, which snapped up their late-1994 self-titled debut on PopLlama. That album was in turn picked up by Columbia Records, which released its remastered version of *The Presidents of the United States of America* in July 1995.

To say the band struck a chord with American music listeners would be an understatement. The rereleased *Presidents* produced three Top 40 singles ("Lump," "Kitty," and "Peaches"), MTV fame, a Grammy nomination, dozens of magazine and newspaper articles, and sales of two million–plus copies. "It was a totally bizarre experience and, in terms of career longevity, not the way to do it," says Dederer. "We were a pop culture phenomenon for 12 months—but after that, what are you?"

With all the furor over the group's first record, their second seemed destined for disappointment. That prediction came true—in 1996 *II* didn't approach the sales of its predecessor, despite an around-the-world touring schedule and a promo push. "Our second record was a product of what we were doing at the time, which was playing bigger shows," says Dederer. "We had kind of turned into this big fast loud rock band, which was never what we had intended to be." Interviewed in fall 1997, Dederer was excited about the prospect of recording a third Presidents album, which he expected to show off a softer, acoustic side of the band. Alas, this was not to be. That December the band announced their imminent breakup, based on Ballew's desire to resign his presidency. A final concert was presented at Seattle's historic Paramount Theatre on the last day of January 1998. The band posthumously released *Pure Frosting*, a collection of live tracks, rare songs, and other odds and ends. **JB**

The Presidents of the United States of America

(1995, COLUMBIA)
Cute, catchy, and charming as all get-out, the first record by the Presidents of the United States of America set a standard the band unfortunately found hard to match. Don't let the nuttiness blind you to the fact that these chief executives could rock.

Quarterflash

Formed 1981, Portland, Oregon

although they never quite matched their debut single, "Harden My Heart," Quarterflash was no one-hit wonder—they produced three Top 20 hits, four albums, and more than a decade of live performances.

Guitarist Marv Ross and wife Rindie, a singer and ace sax player, were already well-known Portland musicians in 1980 as leaders of the band Seafood Mama (in existence from about 1977 to 1981). That band's first single, "Harden My Heart"/ "City of Roses," a smooth, radio-friendly rock gem on their own Whitefire label, cracked the tight playlists of Portland radio and became a huge local hit. The original "Harden My Heart" single sold about ten thousand copies before Geffen

Records asked Marv and Rindie to pull it from the market in preparation for signing a contract.

Marv and Rindie folded Seafood Mama and formed Quarterflash with four members of another local group, Pilot (no relation to the late-1990s Portland band of the same name). With a lineup of Marv, Rindie, Rich Gooch (bass), Brian David Willis (drums), Jack Charles (guitar, vocals), and Rick DiGiallonardo (keyboards), the band recorded their debut, *Quarterflash* (1981). Lacking any other major Christmas releases, Geffen decided to buck industry tradition and release the unknown Quarterflash's debut in time for the holiday season. "It was kind of a risky thing," recalls Marv. "But they felt like they had a hit single on their hands, so they decided to release it."

Score one for Geffen—Quarterflash was an overnight success on both the album and singles charts. A bitter midtempo breakup tale with an unforgettable sax introduction and a wistful yet sultry vocal by Rindie, "Harden My Heart" rose to no. 3 on the national charts in November 1981, earning a gold record for the band. The follow-up, the more up-tempo "Find Another Fool," hit no. 16 four months later. *Quarterflash* rose to no. 8 on the album charts and sold more than a million copies. The band hit the road, touring as both headliners and openers for the likes of Sammy Hagar and Loverboy. Quarterflash also joined Elton John's successful 1982 tour.

As if the band needed any more proof they'd made it, Quarterflash was recruited to perform the title theme for the movie *Night Shift*—a song cowritten by Marv Ross, Burt Bacharach, and Carole Bayer Sager. Not only that, "Don't Be Lonely," the B-side to the Geffen release of "Harden My Heart," showed up on the soundtrack of *Fast Times at Ridgemont High*.

Quarterflash's second Geffen album, *Take Another Picture* (1983), produced a further Top 20 hit in "Take Me to Heart" (no. 14). Despite strong songs, including the catchy but odd title track and "Make It Shine" (on the Geffen soundtrack for the movie *Gremlins*), sales were significantly lower than for the debut. *Take Another Picture* barely missed qualifying for gold record status with about 450,000 copies sold.

But without a record contract, the band went into hiatus and drifted apart. While Marv pursued other musical goals, Rindie recruited new labels. In 1988, with Epic Records showing interest, Quarterflash re-formed with a new lineup of Doug Fraser (guitar), Sandin Wilson (bass), and Gregg Williams (drums). Melanie Kubick was later added on keyboards. But before Quarterflash could produce their first record for Epic, the label was purchased by CBS Sony, which pruned its roster, dropping Cheap Trick, 'Til Tuesday, Cyndi Lauper—and Quarterflash. Curiously, before Quarterflash was dropped, advance copies of their album *Girl in the Wind* had been distributed to DJs and label representatives in Europe and Japan, and received a positive response. So *Girl in the Wind* (1981) was released overseas, although it never gained stateside distribution.

Quarterflash continued as a band through the early 1990s, playing mainly Northwest shows. After calling it quits once, the band re-formed in 1997 to play a summer benefit for the organization Cycle Oregon. Marv, who runs his own production company, still writes songs. Rindie returned to college and earned a master's degree in mental health counseling. The two play with Trail Band, a "folk and brass band" featuring an odd array of instruments. "It's music," says Marv. "But it's not Quarterflash." **JB**

Quarterflash

(1981, GEFFEN)
The record that broke Quarterflash nationally. Includes the Top 20 singles "Harden My Heart" and "Find Another Fool."

Harden My Heart...The Best of Quarterflash

(1997, GEFFEN)
Okay, it's probably cheating to select a greatest hits album when this band's first three albums are still in print. But Quarterflash was first and foremost a singles band, and this release includes all five of the original group's singles, plus the *Night Shift* theme.

Queensrÿche

Formed 1981, Bellevue, Washington

the dream of any self-respecting metal boy in 1981 was finding that special vocalist—a guy with a damn-near operatic range who could screech, scream, and hold high notes forever. When the four musicians from Seattle's Eastside suburbs who would form Queensrÿche—guitarists Michael Wilton and Chris DeGarmo, drummer Scott Rockenfield, and bassist Eddie Jackson—found singer Geoff Tate, they were so sure he was the real thing, they took a different approach to selling the band. Instead of playing bar gigs, the band retreated to the studio to create a professional-quality demo tape. The tape earned the attention of record store owners Kim and Diana Harris (who would become the band's first managers) and the European metal mag *Kerrang!*, which sang the Rÿche's praises when they still hadn't played a Seattle show. Whether owing to this tactical brilliance or (more likely) to Tate's superior pipes, EMI Records picked up the band after their independently released four-song EP *Queensrÿche* had sold 3,500 copies.

Their excellent first album, *The Warning* (1984), brushed aside the sword-and-mysticism clichés of the debut EP, injecting the socially relevant themes and intricate musicianship that built Queensrÿche's image as the band for thinking metal fans. Queensrÿche also established itself as a hard-traveling opening act, touring with headliners from Ronnie James Dio to Bon Jovi. Their second full-length record, *Rage for Order* (1986), found the band in a holding pattern—still rocking hard, but experimenting with foofy stage costumes and hairstyles (thus alienating more than a few of the leather-jacketed faithful). But loyalists were soon rewarded with the stunning concept album *Operation: Mindcrime* (1988), a critical favorite that is still a venerated relic of metalheads everywhere. Fans were so taken by the futuristic tale of drugs, murder, and mental manipulation that Queensrÿche began performing the album in its entirety live, accompanied by an elaborate stage show. (The band released a live recording of the tour, entitled *Operation: Livecrime*, in 1991.)

Also touted as a concept album, *Empire* (1990) was actually more of a set of songs exploring related themes and showing a softer side to the band. It started slow but received a boost from MTV. As the video for "Silent Lucidity" ruled the airwaves, *Empire* rose to no. 7 on the U.S. charts and notched triple-platinum status. Released as a single, "Silent Lucidity" ascended to no. 9 on the American charts.

After a four-year silence, Queensrÿche returned with *Promised Land* (1994), an album that resembled *Empire* in style and approach. There was a resemblance in sales too; the album debuted at no. 3 in the United States and reached platinum status. The band's next project was a 1996 CD-ROM adventure game, also called *Promised Land*, which was loosely based on the successful game *Myst*. Getting back to the music, Queensrÿche shook off their ballad-based chart success and trotted out the guitars for the varied rock/metal *Hear in the Now Frontier* (1997). DeGarmo became the first original member to depart the band the following year, when he quit to tour with the solo project of Alice in Chains guitarist Jerry Cantrell. His replacement is guitarist/producer Kelly Gray, best known locally for producing Candlebox's multiplatinum debut disc. **JB**

Operation: Mindcrime

(1988, EMI)
No question here. Producer Peter Collins gives the band a larger-than-life sound, layering details that make this record headphone heaven. All-but-forgotten Seattle metal vocalist Pamela Moore contributes a fine guest-star turn as Sister Mary.

Hear in the Now Frontier

(1997, EMI)
A masterful return to their rock roots after the ballad-heavy *Empire* and *Promised Land*. Wilton and DeGarmo thickly layer on the guitars on some of Queensrÿche's best songs ever.

Rail

Formed 1973, Bellevue, Washington

rail was one of the first Seattle bands to score a major label contract and have a video in heavy rotation on MTV. For more than a decade they toured regularly, opening for the likes of Van Halen and Ted Nugent across the country. Locally, they were one of Seattle's most popular hard rock acts.

They will be best remembered for the singer's fur boots.

Vocalist/bassist Terry Young, guitarists Andy Baldwin and Rick Knotts, and drummer Kelly Nobles began playing together in high school in 1973. They built a following within what was still called the teen dance circuit, though few teenagers actually danced anymore. Hair shaking and fist pumping had become the preferred mode of expression.

Like virtually all Seattle acts at that time, Rail was primarily a cover band, pumping out reverent renditions of Led Zeppelin, Queen, Styx, and Rush songs and gradually mixing in originals. But there wasn't much competition in those days, so Rail was often chosen to share the bill with arena acts seeking a local opener for their Seattle shows. Besides Van Halen and Ted Nugent, Rail opened for Three Dog Night, Pat Benatar, Krokus, and of course Heart. Their LP, *Arrival*, received some airplay on local stations.

Rail was a few years ahead of the heavy metal explosion in Seattle's surrounding suburbs in the 1980s. Rail's members were dubbed the "forefathers" of the Eastside metal scene, though they were still only in their 20s at the time. In those days, spandex and Aqua Net Super Hold were part of the required uniform for hard rock bands, and any musician bold enough to take the stage without makeup was thought to be making an audacious statement. The Rail boys wore red and black leather pants, black fingerless gloves, and strategically torn T-shirts, but all this was commonplace. Young's knee-high white fur boots became the focal point of the band, and later a symbol of 1980s excess.

In 1983 Rail entered and won the much-coveted grand prize of the MTV Basement Tapes competition—a recording contract with EMI. Viewers chose the winner by calling in their favorite of five finalists, and Rail's success was probably due to the enduring popularity of hard rock. Rockers voted as a bloc to snuff the new wave wussies who were Rail's competitors, and it was on to the majors.

During MTV's glory days it was impossible to imagine a band that had its video in heavy rotation not becoming an overnight success. It was assumed Rail would become the next Heart. Instead, EMI fulfilled its contractual obligation by releasing a four-song EP rather than an album, hiring outside songwriters to assist the band, and choosing a cover song as the pick hit, "1-2-3-4 Rock 'n' Roll."

The band went on to tour the country as they had been doing for years, but nothing more ever happened for them, and Seattle eventually moved on to more hardcore sounds. Rail never officially broke up, and in 1998, they released the album *Big World*, and surfaced to play a local reunion gig. Young still has the fur boots. **DA**

Rail

(1983, EMI)
That cover song really is pretty catchy.

Screaming Trees

Formed 1984, Ellensburg, Washington

t he members of Screaming Trees have wanted to kill each other for more than a decade now, but their music proves that beauty is often born from chaos. It started innocently enough in the small central Washington town of Ellensburg, where Mark Lanegan, Mark Pickerel, and the brothers Gary Lee and Van Conner shared an obsession for music and a dangerous amount of free time. The four began to hang out at Ellensburg's Velvetone Studios with Steve Fisk, writing and recording songs. A transplant from Olympia, Washington, Fisk created art-noise music under the name Anonymous, including a track on the compilation *Let Them Eat Jellybeans* (1981, Alternative Tentacles); he must have seemed exotically urban.

The band released a tape titled *Other Worlds* and managed to get some gigs around Washington State and eventually Seattle. Screaming Trees were immediately pegged as a psychedelic band, and for good reason. Lee Conner's amazing guitar spazz-outs and Lanegan's dreamy stoner vocals accompanied classic mind-blowing lyrics. Their live shows were always a spectacle, as the hefty Conner brothers hurled themselves to the floor and writhed while flailing at their instruments. But it was evident from the start that the Trees were not just another "neo"-psychedelic band; they were true originals who knew from experience what it was like to have one's mind constantly changing shape, and their knowledge had nothing to do with drugs (those problems came later).

Their 1986 debut LP, *Clairvoyance* attracted the notice of SST Records, home of Black Flag and other classic underground bands the Trees idolized. SST signed the band and released their next three albums, *Even If and Especially When* (1987), *Invisible Lantern* (1988), and *Buzz Factory* (1989), as well as a vinyl rerelease of *Other Worlds*. The band was thrilled about being part of SST and building up a small national following.

Their happiness was short-lived. Rumors that the band members were having personality conflicts began almost immediately. Van Conner left the band for a short time before the release of *Buzz Factory* and was replaced with Donna Dresch, later of Team Dresch fame. When he changed his mind, the band promptly hired him back.

It was widely assumed Screaming Trees were on the verge of a breakup when Epic Records grabbed hold of them in the Seattle feeding frenzy of 1990, set off by Soundgarden's success. Though sick to death of each other, the Trees managed to record *Uncle Anesthesia* (1991), a surprisingly beautiful, moody record. During their next tour, reports of fistfights between the Conner brothers on stage were "if anything, underexaggerated in the press," Van told *Rolling Stone*.

Pickerel left the band for good to join Truly, which also features Robert Roth and ex-Soundgarden bassist Hiro Yamamoto. Lanegan recorded a critically acclaimed solo album for Sub Pop, *The Winding Sheet*. The Conner brothers each recorded albums with their side projects, Van with Solomon Grundy and Lee with the Purple Outside.

In 1993 the Trees came back together to record their breakthrough album, *Sweet*

Oblivion, with new drummer Barrett Martin, formerly of Skin Yard. Meanwhile, the Seattle-hype volcano had erupted the world over, and the Trees were about to experience their own right place/right time harmonic convergence. The single "Nearly Lost You," included on the *Singles* movie soundtrack, was played ad nauseam on radio stations across the country, the band toured incessantly, and *Sweet Oblivion* became their biggest-selling album.

But by the time Screaming Trees reconvened to record their next CD, the thrill was gone—again. They recorded an album's worth of songs, decided it all sucked, and declined to release it. Lanegan recorded his next solo album for Sub Pop, *Whiskey for the Holy Ghost*. Martin joined up with Pearl Jam's Mike McCready, Alice in Chains' Layne Staley, and a bass player known only as Baker to form Mad Season. That band released the album *Above* in 1995.

After the break from each other, Screaming Trees put together another album, *Dust* (1997). It was their most complex album yet, its Eastern influences enhancing the band's trademark trippiness.

The band was still expected to call it quits, this time because of Lanegan's drug problems, which had reached the status of local legend. But at this writing the guys have once again pulled it together, playing some ripping shows with a second guitarist, Josh Homme from Kyuss, and sometimes a third if Pearl Jam's Mike McCready or R.E.M.'s Peter Buck decides to join them onstage. Lanegan still doesn't say much, but he's never looked healthier. **DA**

Invisible Lantern

(1988, SST)
Highest ratio of killer Screaming Trees tunes.

Dust

(1997, EPIC)
If anyone has earned the right to use Mellotron, tabla, cello, and sitar on a rock album, it's these guys. Take it all away and you've still got some terrific pop songs.

7 Year Bitch

Formed 1990, Seattle, Washington

Seattle's major contribution to the inventory of all-female rock bands, 7 Year Bitch often seemed as well known for the articles written about them as for the songs they performed. Although often compared with the female group L7 for reasons more visual than musical, 7 Year Bitch avoided that band's Girlschoolesque heavy metal leanings for an unaffected punk rock sound, which grew more diverse with each of their three albums.

Despite having little to do with the then-hip grunge scene (or because of that), the newly formed band—singer Selene Vigil, guitarist Stefanie Sargent, bassist Elizabeth Davis, and drummer Valerie Agnew—struck a chord with Seattle audiences. After releasing an EP on local label C/Z, they started to earn a national reputation for their frenetic live shows. The momentum was abruptly halted in 1992 by Sargent's death from a heroin overdose, just as the band's first long-player, *Sick 'Em*, was being prepared for release. Her successor, Roisin Dunne, joined the group for the subsequent tour. *Sick 'Em*, a sometimes crude punk rock document containing equal parts anger and humor, earned 7 Year Bitch serious attention. Also noticed was the band's political edge: they actively supported Home Alive, the self-defense program

(Young) Women in Rock

You might end up in a rock band because all your friends are in one, or because you've been to too many shows as a hanger-on fan, a friend-of, or a guest-list spot. Whatever the reason, you want a better reason to be there. You've got options: either become a journalist, sleep with the band, or be in your own band. Rock criticism is not that satisfying, and after a while the fun goes out of sleeping around.

Be in the band. That's it. That's all there is left.

Young women in bands have it tough. "Oh, are you in a girl band?" "You must be the singer." "Cute skirt." "Isn't that guitar heavy?" See, most boys grow up inherently knowing that they can do whatever the hell they want. Girls don't. So half the guys in high school practice guitar. Girls don't. My brother was in a couple of good power pop bands, my dad performed in folk and rock groups, and my grandfather made his living playing in a Dixieland band. Even my mom's boyfriend was in a band. He used to play the Pioneer Square bars in Seattle on weekends when I was a little kid. She used to watch. I was raised to be a groupie. Yeah.

Meanwhile, I didn't get to look past my little-kid fingers playing our living room piano or my flute in seventh-grade lessons. The only good music influence I had was Kim Warnick, who's been in the Fastbacks since I was 10. She told me any girl could learn to play guitar, just like any guy can. Sometimes the simple things need to be said out loud.

The next lesson is don't sleep with anyone in your band. Even though you've ascended from hanger-on status, just because you're playing doesn't mean you're an equal member. If something goes wrong, like he misses his old girlfriend or meets someone new, you look bad all the way around. Either you'll get kicked out, or the whole band will break up due to unspeakable tension.

And take note: you don't have to wear hooker outfits to belong on a stage. That's another lesson I learned the hard way. I actually wore a creepy gold skirt before I realized it made me look like I was overcompensating for a self-perceived lack of skill. When I started in a band that had a lot of undersold shows, my boyfriend at the time suggested, in a roundabout way, that I dress sleazier—like show off my breasts. That's a hell of a good way to play better.

Rock on, sister (no joke).

—Kristen Schurr

for women started after the murder of close friend Mia Zapata, singer for the Gits. Their other political projects included benefits to fund breast cancer research and strong prochoice support (which landed them on the "Enemies of the Unborn" Web site). Although puzzled by critics who equated a stand against rape with being anti-male, the group rocked on. The Jack Endino–produced *Viva Zapata!*, Dunne's first recorded outing with the band, showed a moodier side of the group—with a dark thoughtfulness crowding out the stark edges of *Sick 'Em*.

Having fulfilled their contract with C/Z, 7 Year Bitch signed with Atlantic Records. *Gato Negro* (1996), their first and only major label album, featured their strongest collection of songs yet. Dunne left shortly afterward and was replaced by Lisa Faye Beatty. The band broke up in late 1997. **JB**

Gato Negro

(1996, ATLANTIC)
No longer just angry, 7 Year Bitch is certifiably dark on this album. Billy Anderson's production sets a claustrophobic stage for Selene Vigil's inspired snarling.

Sir Mix-A-Lot

I n a genre that acknowledges just two cities—Los Angeles and New York—rap artist Sir Mix-A-Lot has always been a defiantly proud Seattle guy. On the cover of his first long-player, *Swass,* Mix and crew tower over the Seattle skyline; on his 1996 album, *Return of the Bumpasaurus*, he stands perched on a giant road map of Puget Sound.

His loyalty hasn't helped his career. Nor has his continuing interest in creating funny party raps about big-money cars and big-bottomed ladies at a time when the rap powers-that-be prized "gangsta" attitude and tales of ghetto violence. But Mix has managed some career high points, most memorably "Baby Got Back," his 1992 tribute to women with ample rear ends, which was a no. 1 single for five weeks and sold 2.5 million copies.

Sir Mix-A-Lot, born Anthony Ray, got started in rap because of his love for electronic music (Kraftwerk's *Computer World* was a significant influence) and his belief that he could out rhyme the rappers he heard on record. The Roosevelt High School grad started making his own tapes on a 4-track recorder and appeared at rap shows at the Boys Club in the Central District. A newly formed local label, NastyMix, released his first 12-inch single, "Square Dance Rap." The novelty song, which featured a squeaky, sped-up lead rap vocal, was a dance floor smash and rose to the top of the dance charts.

Swass was released in 1987, earning platinum record status and spawning the popular video "Posse on Broadway." Although the backing tracks sound a bit thin by today's standards, this album established several of Mix's trademarks, not least of which was his talent for the mean but funny attack rap ("Bremelo" mocks an ugly woman; "Hip Hop Soldier" takes on his fellow rappers). The record also included a rap over the Black Sabbath classic "Iron Man," featuring guitar lines from Craig Wells of Metal Church.

Mix-A-Lot released a second album on NastyMix in 1989, *Seminar*. Although this record also sold well, earning gold record status, financial disputes between the record company and Mix led to a lawsuit and a switch to Def American. His first album for the new label was 1992's *Mack Daddy* (1992), which featured his breakthrough single "Baby Got Back." The rapper says the song was based on a conversation with models on a music video shoot, who complained they couldn't get jobs because they didn't meet the painfully thin fashion-model ideal. Although blasted by critics as sexist, the song was a hit with the public—both the single and *Mack Daddy* went platinum. The song also won him a Grammy Award for Best Rap Solo Performance.

His next album, *Chief Boot Knocka* (1994), featured an even more outrageous single ("Put 'Em on the Glass"), but was poorly promoted and didn't come close to matching *Mack Daddy's* commercial success. Mix-A-Lot puts part of the blame on his immersion in his first major acting job on *The Watcher*, a UPN television series styled after the old *Twilight Zone* show.

The Watcher was canceled, and Mix-A-Lot returned to the studio in 1996 for *Return of the Bumpasaurus*. The self-proclaimed Pacific Time Zone's Head Honcho took aim at his critics ("Man U Luv Ta Hate"), wannabe gangsters ("Aintsta"), and sellouts ("Aunt Thomasina"). Three different producers (Mike Kumangai, Funk Daddy, and Quaze), a fuller sound, and heavy beats completed the package. Mix's high-profile appearances since then have been in bankruptcy court (he filed for Chapter 11 protection from creditors in 1997) and on the MTV television show *The Real World*, after he befriended one of the cast members and helped her record a song. **JB**

Mack Daddy

(1992, DEF AMERICAN)
Sir Mix-A-Lot's commercial high point includes his controversial hit single "Baby Got Back" and the equally infamous "Swap Meet Louie." His most hard-edged outing to date, both musically and lyrically.

Return of the Bumpasaurus

(1996, AMERICAN)
The loudest album from Sir Mix-A-Lot features a big studio sound and some great individual tracks.

Skin Yard

Formed 1985, Seattle, Washington

he term "punk rock," in its original sense, encompassed whatever styles of music were considered oddball at the time. Bassist Daniel House and guitarist Jack Endino were a couple of Seattle musicians with both an appreciation for new sounds and a fondness for the more twisted of the 1970s progressive bands. Their goal, as Endino remembers it, was to form a band to play music that was "kind of edgy and kind of nasty and kind of weird." That band was Skin Yard. Their first recruit was drummer Matt Cameron; at their unofficial debut show at a friend's party, they met singer Ben McMillan. Skin Yard's earliest recorded efforts, after only about six months as a band, ended up on the legendary sampler LP *Deep Six* (1985). The band's uncompromising self-titled first album, released in 1987, was Endino's first production job, recorded in a basement on a friend's 12-track board.

Cameron, soon to join Soundgarden, quit the band in early 1986. The band tried several drummers and eventually settled on Jason Finn (later of Love Battery and the Presidents of the United States of America). Finn lasted eight months (his only recorded appearances with the band are two single B-sides) and was replaced by Norman Scott. With this lineup, arguably their best, Skin Yard began their most active period as a touring band. Scott's first appearance was on the awesome "Stranger" single, followed by the album *Hallowed Ground* (1988). The band's ambitious post-*Hallowed Ground* touring schedule almost finished them. Six weeks on the road in a van that broke down daily led to personal friction; in the summer of 1989, the band straggled back into Seattle. For more than a year, they didn't play a show, "and nobody noticed," adds Endino.

Scott had quit, and McMillan was working with the band Gruntruck but took time to sing on the unfinished tracks for what would become the album *Fist-Sized Chunks* (1990). The band had arranged to release the album on Cruz Records, while Endino was putting together a one-shot live show based on his solo project, Endino's Earthworm, with drummer Barrett Martin. Coffin Break bassist Rob Skinner was set to play but had to cancel, so House stepped in. The resulting gig was successful enough that Skin Yard reunited, with Martin on drums, and toured in support of *Fist-Sized Chunks*. This version of the band also recorded *1000 Smiling Knuckles* (1991).

When House, busy with his family and record company (C/Z Records), quit the band, Martin recruited his former Thin Men bandmate, bassist Pat Pearson. He toured extensively with the band, including a European swing (their most enjoyable tour yet, marred only by the Italian thieves who ripped off their guitars, CDs, and T-shirts from their tour van). The band went on another hiatus when Martin joined Screaming Trees, but reunited briefly to record their final album, *Inside the Eye* (1993).

During Skin Yard's early career, Endino was establishing his reputation as producer at Reciprocal Recording, where he was responsible for a handful of records that established the "Seattle sound"—Soundgarden's *Screaming Life* (1987), Green

River's *Dry as a Bone* (1987), Mudhoney's debut EP, *Superfuzz Bigmuff* (1988), and the first Nirvana long-player, *Bleach* (1990). He also released his own solo records, *Angle of Attack* (1990, Bobok) and *Endino's Earthworm* (1992, Cruz). **JB**

Hallowed Ground

(1988, TOXIC SHOCK)
Skin Yard at their most rockin' and most accessible. Guitarist Jack Endino calls it "the band's artistic high-water mark." He's right.

Sky Cries Mary

Formed 1986, Seattle, Washington

the story of Sky Cries Mary begins in 1986 with Roderick Romero, a disenchanted premedical student who decided a foray to Europe and some graduate-level courses would lighten his mood. While there, Romero recorded a few tracks for an emerging French independent label, New Rose, under a name he got from fellow travelers on a Romanian train who misstated the title of the Jimi Hendrix song "The Wind Cries Mary."

Upon returning to the United States, Romero joined forces with Ken Stringfellow and Jon Auer to record an industrial music release titled, *Until the Grinders Cease* (New Rose), but the ensemble split when Stringfellow and Auer's other project, the Posies, took off. Romero was free to begin work with Anisa, a performance artist and painter he had met at the University of Washington in 1986. In 1989, he asked Anisa to help compose and record songs for an upcoming release. Over time the band was fleshed out with drummer Ben Ireland, keyboard player Gordon Raphael, and Todd Robbins. Sky Cries Mary was transformed from industrial grind to a cosmic mix of art rock, psychedelia, and ambient music visually enhanced by light shows (then produced by Cam Garrett) and theatrical garb designed by Seattle clothing artist Darbury Stenderu.

Sky Cries Mary's subsequent albums—*Exit at the Axis* (1992, World Domination), *Return to the Inner Experience* (1993, Capitol), *This Timeless Turning* (1994, World Domination), and *Moonbathing on Sleeping Leaves* (1997, Warner Bros.)—explored new ways to induce a musical trance; perhaps Anisa's numerous years as a hatha yoga instructor were an influence. When Sky Cries Mary returned to World Domination after a brief stay with Warner Brothers, they released *Fresh Fruits for the Liberation* (1998), a greatest hits compilation.

The entourage had gained the attention of Warner Brothers, as well as other major labels, when they broadcast the first-ever live musical performance over the Internet in 1996. But although their theatrics and dark, moody effects may have made the band appealing to major labels, their music proved too complicated to be mass marketed. Sky Cries Mary is best cared for by a label that respects their unique artistic experiments.

Through the years the band has changed members, losing keyboardist Raphael, who left on good terms, and adding guitarist Michael Cozzi. Truth is, Sky Cries Mary revolves around Roderick and Anisa Romero (they eventually married). From them springs a metaphysical union, which they enhance with other players, dancers, and visual artists who work with light, film, and fabric. Seeing the band perform live is essential to fully appreciate the hypnotically transformative effect of their music. **VK**

Exit the Axis

(1992, WORLD DOMINATION)
A must-have for "Elephant Song" alone. This EP is filled with trippy chants guaranteed to transport you to a union with the mighty mama matrix.

Sleater-Kinney

Formed 1994, Olympia, Washington

Sleater-Kinney got famous for being girls from Olympia, Washington. People jumped at a band that could play fairly well and came the closest to punk rock as anybody these days. The hype wasn't lost on the best of the independent label acts. Sonic Youth said they'd play Seattle's Bumbershoot arts festival in 1997 if Sleater-Kinney opened for them. They also opened for Guided by Voices in New York's Central Park and toured with the Jon Spencer Blues Explosion.

In 1994 Corin Tucker, from Heavens to Betsy, and Carrie Brownstein, formerly of Excuse 17, met to play music on Sleater-Kinney Road, a major thoroughfare between Olympia and the nearby town of Lacey. Tucker had moved to Olympia in 1990 because she liked Calvin Johnson's band, Beat Happening, and Lois Maffeo. Heavens to Betsy played their first show at the 1991 International Pop Underground festival, sponsored by Johnson's K Records.

As with any self-respecting Northwest band, Sleater-Kinney can't keep a drummer (although their current one is a gem). Misty Farrell of Bitchcore was the drummer on their first single, "You Ain't It"/"Surf Song," released in 1994 on the Villa Villakula label, which put three Sleater-Kinney songs on its compilation album. In Australia, Tucker and Brownstein made a self-titled record with Lora Macfarlane from the Sea Hags as drummer; *Sleater-Kinney* was released in 1995 on Donna Dresch's Chainsaw label and Villa Villakula. A year later the three recorded *Call the Doctor*, also on Chainsaw. They toured in the United States, but Macfarlane lived in Australia, so she dropped out and Toni Gogin took over the drums for a while. After parting with their next drummer, the band sent out press releases imploring that any promotional photo with said drummer be destroyed. The replacement photos included the

Riot Grrrls

Like any rebellion against the status quo, the riot grrrl movement is often derided, which shows how quickly we back away once the media seizes on a trend. Make a community look foolish, and they lose some of their driving force. (Just look at the sad example of "alternative" music.) But ideally, people who believe in what they're doing will continue regardless of the fallout. The riot grrrl movement, my dears, has a little of it all—both criticism and perseverance.

Although Olympia is generally thought of as the home of the riot grrrl concept, the name was actually coined in Washington, D.C., on the heels of the riots in the Mount Mt. Pleasant neighborhood there. It came to signify rock shows where more than one band with female members played and where workshops on subjects like body image and racism took place.

In Olympia these folks included Corin Tucker of Heavens to Betsy (and later Sleater-Kinney), drummer Tobi Vail of Go Team and Bikini Kill, Kathleen Hanna of Viva Knievel and Bikini Kill, Donna Dresch of Team Dresch and the label Chainsaw, and Molly Neuman of Bratmobile. They put together meetings for young women in their music/art world to create solidarity, wrote fanzines dealing with feminist issues, and played political music. That is a great thing.

Why, then, did some people snicker at the sign Kathleen Hanna posted reading, "Girls: Let's have a meeting about punk rock and feminism"? Well, some women don't equate calling yourself a girl with being a feminist. Just like society at large, the rock

Portlander Janet Weiss, formerly of Motor Goat and Jr. High. (She still drums as half of a great duo, Quasi, with her ex-husband Sam Coomes.) *Dig Me Out*, a full-length recording on the Kill Rock Stars label, was released in 1997.

As Sleater-Kinney, Tucker, Brownstein, and Weiss present an Olympia version of energized assault and bobbed hair. They're schoolgirl punk without falling back on trying to be cute. Tucker screams a sweet crowd pleaser, "I wanna be your Joey Ramone," with Brownstein right behind her (dueling vocals are a specialty); and Weiss plays hard while somehow maintaining perfect posture. They don't bother with a bass player.

Despite their charmed luck and power as players, the band still has to deal with general sexism. As one drummer said, "I think people are surprised when they come to a show and see three women who play well." One can only hope that in a few years, with Sleater-Kinney clearly doing their part, folks won't make such a fuss over a band being a bunch of girls. **KS**

Call the Doctor

(1996, CHAINSAW)
Produced by favorite John Goodmanson, *Call the Doctor* features Corin Tucker's hypnotically craggy high vocals, Carrie Brownstein's full backup, and Toni Gogin as power drummer of the day.

music community has been dominated by men. It doesn't matter how many of those men are decent people or how many cool musicians are women. Are guys ever implored to show their tits while playing a show? Riot grrrls helped women break into music by assailing the stubborn assumption that girls belonged in front of a stage instead of on it. When young women had the chance to play, they got better.

The riot grrrl movement also challenged attitudes by putting tough and girly-girl women in the same spot, whether that was the intent or not. Baby-doll dresses, barrettes, and lunch boxes were among the trappings, but the movement made it clear that we still need to talk about feminism in an age (and within a community) supposedly too evolved for that to be necessary.

Kathleen Hanna is regarded by many as the star of the riot grrrls. The name of her band, Bikini Kill, was hoisted from a party act performed by Olympia's Lois Maffeo and Margaret Doherty that involved dancing in fake fur and singing surf songs. (Bikini Kill usually records on Olympia's Kill Rock Stars label; check out *Pussy Whipped*, 1993.) In a weird case of co-opting, Hanna's practice of writing words like "slut" or "incest victim" on her stomach (to give substance to a static photo) led to the local popularity of tiny T-shirts saying things like "Porn Star" in glitter letters.

Riot grrrl chapters started popping up in different cities after Hanna said in a *Los Angeles Times* interview that they existed all over the country. When young women couldn't find the group, they formed their own chapters.

The first riot grrrl fanzine, *Girl Power,* was published in the early 1990s by Kathleen Hanna, Molly Neuman, and Allison Wolfe. *Girl Power* espoused changing the male-influenced ideal of cool to the expressive attitude of dorky: "Dorks die when bullets hit them and dorks cry real tears." Make fun if you want to, but regardless of your personal style, women working for more freedoms for women are not the enemy.

—Kristen Schurr

Some Velvet Sidewalk

Formed 1988, Olympia, Washington

While bands somewhere to the north of Olympia, Washington, were playing faster and louder, singing about being depressed, and flipping their hair around a lot, hometown boy Al Larsen was touting the virtues of "love rock." As practiced by Some Velvet Sidewalk and K Records labelmates Beat Happening, the music emphasized raw, primitive playing and singing and was built around themes too personal or too off-the-wall to be exploited elsewhere in rock.

First a duo (Larsen and drummer Robert Christie), then a trio (Larsen, bassist Don Bloom, and drummer Martin Bernier), Some Velvet Sidewalk spewed stop-and-start rhythms behind Larsen's vocal meanderings. Like a somewhat less chipper Jonathan Richman, Larsen lurches lyrically from childish ramblings to surprisingly pointed commentary, sometimes in the space of a single song. "One Bear Alone" starts like a nursery rhyme and then, without warning, segues into teenage catharsis. "I Blame You" is terse and punk-edged, as Larsen points the finger at some unknown enemy. Not that music and lyrics are always matched: "Ice Cream Overdrive" is a tough-rock celebration of everybody's favorite frozen dessert. As both a guitarist and vocalist, Larsen sometimes chooses the wrong note for effect; the tuning of his guitar is often suspect.

Perfectly matched with Calvin Johnson's K Records, the band has spent its entire career recording for the label (aside from a few singles and compilation appearances). *I Know* (1988) and *Appetite for Extinction* (1990) feature the original duo; *Avalanche* (1992) and *Whirlpool* (1994) are by the rockin' three-piece. The missing link in the Some Velvet Sidewalk collection, *Shipwreck*, was released in 1995 but recorded four years earlier with Larsen and guest stars including Tobi Vail of Bikini Kill and Donna Dresch of Team Dresch.

Much to everyone's surprise, the 1997 Some Velvet Sidewalk long-player, *Generate!*, presents a fourth band member (Paul Schuster) and a new emphasis on funky dance-style bass and steady drums with doodling, both vocal and instrumental, over the top (including keyboards and the flute of guest player Arrington de Dionyso). Larsen even turns rapper on "The Lowdown" ("Coming to you from the studio"). No telling what happens next. **JB**

Whirlpool

(1994, K)
A good collection of Al Larsen's various moods—producer Steve Fisk keeps the sound on an even keel.

The Sonics

Formed 1963, Tacoma, Washington

even taking into account their limited musical abilities, noisy recordings, and short life span, the Sonics remain one of the Northwest's most influential rock 'n' roll acts. More than thirty years after the original band's demise, promoters are still clamoring for reunion gigs, and the band's many singles and three albums are constantly being reissued on vinyl and CD.

In the late 1950s the Wailers, from Tacoma, Washington, were the biggest thing to hit the Northwest. The Sonics were formed from a group of young Wailers fans, including brothers Larry and Andy Parypa. Younger brother Larry loved gritty guitarists like Link Wray and Freddie King; Andy found classic R&B artists like Bill Doggett, Ray Charles, and Ike and Tina Turner more to his taste. Through various basement jams in the Parypa home, the Sonics emerged as a crude instrumental outfit, taking their name from the frequent sonic booms emitted by neighboring McChord Air Force Base. After a few gigs at parties and church dances, the Parypas joined the remnants of another Tacoma band, the Searchers, and formed the classic

Sonics lineup: Larry Parypa (guitar), Andy Parypa (bass), Bob Bennett (drums), Gerry Roslie (vocals, keyboards), and Rob Lind (sax).

Still emulating the Wailers, the early Sonics' set lists featured a gritty combination of black R&B, classic instrumentals, and Roslie's blood-curdling approximations of Jerry Lee Lewis and Little Richard. Shortly after getting together, Larry Parypa and Roslie begin writing original songs for the band. One of their first efforts, "The Witch," was originally an attempt to cash in on the various fad dances of the early 1960s. Thankfully, nobody recalls the dance, but most remember the song. It was released on the Wailers' independent Etiquette label, and Seattle's KJR-AM helped make it a Northwest smash—the best-selling record to that point by any Northwest artist.

Recorded at Seattle's Audio Records with Kearney Barton as producer, "The Witch" is poorly engineered and mastered, yet the energy and excitement in the grooves make it an instant classic. Larry's simple, haunting guitar riff is unforgettable, and his solo is pure teenage adrenaline. Bennett's meter is inexact, but his drum attack is nothing short of ferocious. Andy's bass line anchors the song, while Lind's sax follows the melody line. But "The Witch" belongs to Roslie, whose manic, screaming vocals warn us all to stay away from the girl "who's new in town with the big black car."

With a certified hit on their hands, things began to happen quickly. The album *Here Are the Sonics* was released, again produced by Barton at Audio Records. Although most of the tracks are punked-up covers of 1950s songs (impressive in their own right), the clear highlights are the originals "Psycho" (a paean to adolescent sexual frustration) and "Strychnine" (an ominous pounder about the joys of imbibing poison).

By 1964 the Sonics were big on the thriving Northwest dance circuit, packing roller rinks, clubs, and auditoriums in the three-state area of Washington, Oregon, and Idaho. The Sonics also served as the backing band for touring national stars, although it's hard to imagine their ferocity behind the frothy Lesley Gore, Johnny Rivers, and Shangri-Las. But, being young and inexperienced, the band quickly ran into problems. Members fought constantly, and onstage blowups sometimes interrupted shows. The band began to develop a reputation as troublemakers among some promoters.

A second album, *Boom*, was recorded in 1965, featuring a cluster of great originals ("He's Waitin'," a song about Satan, was the obvious highlight). As with all Northwest bands of the period, the Sonics included a version of "Louie Louie," but their version is certainly an anomaly—Larry subverts the chords, and it comes out sounding like embryonic heavy metal. During this era, the band played with virtually every touring national act. Surely bands like Them, the Byrds, the Yardbirds, and the Kinks must have wondered what was going on with their opening act. After the Sonics opened for the Rolling Stones, London Records (the Stones' label at the time) even took an interest in the band.

In 1966 the band left Etiquette to sign with Jerry Dennon's Jerden label. It seemed like a smart move, based on Dennon's connections and record of success (the Kingsmen's "Louie Louie" was a no. 2 national hit). The association started out well: Dennon arranged to have "The Witch" rereleased in several medium-sized radio markets (including Pittsburgh, San Jose, California, and Orlando, Florida) and set up a national tour that included an appearance on the legendary Cleveland television program *Upbeat*. Intended to break the band with a national audience, the title of their third album, *Introducing the Sonics* (1966), now merely seems ironic. The production (courtesy of famed Goldstar Studio in Los Angeles) was better this time, but the rereleased versions of their Northwest hits like "Psycho" and "The Witch" only served to show the weakness of the newer material. Lind's sax was largely replaced by a harmonica, and Roslie's vocals were a bit more controlled. Although still powerful, the record had more of a British invasion feel than the amped-up, over-driven Northwest sound of their earlier recordings. By the end of 1966 the band was still a big draw, but frustration over their failure to hit nationally was taking over. The Sonics' last recording with the original lineup, a version of Frank Zappa's "Any Way the Wind Blows" (mid-1967), featured innovative wah-wah guitar by Larry and a haunting Roslie effort ("Lost Love") on the flip side.

Bennett was the first to leave; Andy Parypa was the last. Talented people took over the band (solid Northwest musicians, including Jim Brady and Randy Hiatt), but the magic was gone when the original lineup splintered. The name was used for another ten years but had no connection to the seminal band.

The Sonics gained their national fame after the fact. The records from the 1964–67 band have never gone out of print, and early recordings are eagerly sought by collectors around the world. Their influence on the 1970s punk movement is unmistakable, and current Northwest rockers are among their biggest proselytizers. The Sonics records sound as raw and passionate today as they did then. **NS**

Here Are the Ultimate Sonics

(1994, ETIQUETTE)
The best of many Sonics compilations, this contains all their originals and their finest covers. Rarities include some live material, an exceptionally out-of-control outtake of "The Witch," and a radio ad and interview.

Soundgarden

Formed 1984, Seattle, Washington

Soundgarden's slow but steady ascent from the dives on the noise-rock circuit to arenas full of reverent metalheads is one of Seattle's only true success stories—they escaped with their sanity and most of their brain cells intact.

Soundgarden began as a three-piece band featuring guitarist Kim Thayil, bassist

Hiro Yamamoto, and drummer Chris Cornell. They were part of what nobody yet knew was a trend, a handful of new bands that played mind-numbing heavy metal riffs at an excruciatingly slow pace, baffling their mostly punk audiences. They soon picked up drummer Scott Sundquist, which allowed Cornell to scream and thrash, unfettered by an instrument (he didn't begin playing guitar onstage until a couple of years later). Sundquist was later replaced by Matt Cameron, the former drummer for Skin Yard. Cameron was heavily influenced by jazz, and his crushing yet meticulous beats added another layer of complexity to the band's already dense sound. Their contributions to the legendary 1985 compilation *Deep Six* established Soundgarden as central to this new genre that had no name. Bruce Pavitt loved the stuff and soon released the EP *Screaming Life* (1987) on his fledgling Sub Pop Records.

The EP was a primitive roar, nothing like the smart, polished metal the band later produced, but it established the underlying Soundgarden style that would remain at the root of their music—neither entirely head music nor cock rock, but a cosmic melding of the physical and the intellectual that later earned Soundgarden the dubious title of "thinking man's metal band." In 1988 they signed a one-album deal with the California label SST Records, which released the LP *Ultra Mega OK* (1988). Meanwhile, the tireless efforts of manager Susan Silver (Cornell's future wife) were paying off as several major labels began vying for the band's attention. They finally chose to sign with A&M Records that same year.

A so-called underground band signing with a major label was unprecedented in Seattle at that time; predictably, the accusations of selling out flew fast and furious. It didn't help that *Louder than Love* (1989) sounded so slick, just like commercial metal—albeit good commercial metal. But the riffs were crushing and the songs had instant impact, enough to gain Soundgarden an entirely new audience. They still hadn't gone platinum, but heavy metal fans embraced them like long-lost brothers.

Bassist Yamamoto left the band to pursue other interests and was replaced by Jason Everman, who had just left Nirvana. Nirvana hadn't hit it big yet, so to Everman, this seemed to be a giant step up; he had admired Soundgarden for years. Then began the cycle of endless touring that threatened to suck every ounce of the band's creative energy. Fortunately, they lived through it and were able to release *Badmotorfinger* (1991), an artistic triumph that showcased Thayil's imaginative guitar work and the band's general psychedelic weirdness overlying commercial hooks. By this time, Everman had been replaced by his old schoolmate, Ben Shepherd. The new lineup went on tour with Guns N' Roses and headlined the festival Lollapalooza '92.

Contrary to popular folklore, Seattle did not invent flannel, long hair, or distortion pedals, but one trend it probably can claim for its own is denial of rock stardom— genuine corporate rockers snarl incoherently about how corporate rock sucks, even as they rack up hit records, Grammys, and *Tonight Show* appearances. Judging from Soundgarden's interviews during this period, the band members still didn't think of themselves as rock stars, but the release of the next album would change all that. *Superunknown* (1994) debuted at no. 1 on the *Billboard* album chart; the song "Black

Hole Sun" became a huge radio hit; and suddenly the band members couldn't leave their homes without being approached for autographs. Up to this point, Soundgarden had been a moderately successful band, but suddenly they were outselling the Rolling Stones.

With nowhere to go but down, the band recorded their fifth and final album, *Down on the Upside* (1996), which contains several great songs and far too many boring ones. The somber mood pervading the CD seems to hint that not all was well with the band. When Soundgarden's management announced their breakup in 1997, the Seattle press clamored for an explanation, but the real reasons for the split were banal: the band members were sick of touring and sick of each other. This fan believes they exited the public world at the precise moment they should have. **DA**

Screaming Life/FOPP

(1987/1988, Sub Pop)
A rerelease of Soundgarden's first two EPs. They've never reached the level of primal intensity they so effortlessly achieved back then.

Superunknown

(1994, A&M)
Full of crashing crescendos, this album packs all the punch of the band's earlier release, *Louder than Love*, but with the kind of complex arrangements perfected on *Badmotorfinger*.

The Spinanes

Formed 1991, Portland, Oregon

rebecca Gates's first experience with the music business was as the manager of the popular Portland band the Dharma Bums. In May 1991 she stepped to the other side of the amplifier with drummer Scott Plouf to form the Spinanes. Experimenting with nontraditional guitar tunings, singer/songwriter Gates was able to make her single instrument sound as rich as a stageful of guitars.

The Spinanes made their live debut in August 1991 at K Records' International Pop Underground Convention in Olympia, Washington. This appearance yielded the duo's first recording, "Jad Fair Drives Women Wild," a track on the IPUC compilation.

In 1992 the band saw the release of their first single, "Suffice"/"Halloween Candy," followed that winter by "Rummy," whose B-side is the now-classic "Hawaiian Baby," a choral homage to the New Zealand alternative pop group the Verlaines. After two years of playing around the Northwest and an occasional brief tour, the Spinanes signed to Sub Pop Records and visited Minnesota to record. Their first Sub Pop single, "Spitfire"—with a B-side cover of "Bad Karma," a song by fellow

Portlanders Crackerbash—came out in the summer of 1993, followed a few months later by *Manos*, their full-length debut.

The record's second single, "Noel, Jonah and Me," became a minor hit on commercial radio and landed on MTV courtesy of a refreshingly plain black-and-white video shot in Portland. The song's success meant more touring, including a swing through Europe, and an appearance on the Conan O'Brien show.

A series of side projects for both Gates and Plouf followed. Gates provided backing vocals for Noise Addict singer Ben Lee's solo debut, *Grampa Would* (1995, Grand Royal), and for fellow Portland singer Elliott Smith's self-titled second record (1995, Kill Rock Stars); she also appeared as half of the Cradle Robbers, with Lois Maffeo, on the AIDS benefit compilation *Red Hot and Bothered* (1995, Kinetic/Reprise). Among other outings, Plouf drummed on Beck's record, *One Foot in the Grave* (1994, K).

The Spinanes' sophomore effort, *Strand*, was recorded in the summer of 1995 at Easley Studios in Memphis, and was released in February 1996. After the promising critical and commercial response to *Manos*—which landed in several year-end Top 10 lists—*Strand*'s reception was disappointing. While some reviewers applauded the band for branching out from their signature guitar-pop sound, others categorized the new material as unfocused, and sales were disappointing.

In July 1996 Plouf left the band to join influential rockers Built to Spill, who had just switched from their independent label to Warner Brothers. Gates soldiered on, touring under the Spinanes name with various friends backing her up (including former Crackerbash member Joanna Bolme and former Dharma Bum John Moen). She also honed her live guitar skills with solo shows in and around Portland.

No Northwest musician exemplifies the region's tight-knit music scene more than Gates, so her relocation to Chicago in mid-1997 surprised many. She returned to Easley Studios to record and produce the third Spinanes full-length record, *Arches and Aisles*, with Bolme contributing guitar and keyboard on some tracks. Additional work on the record was completed in Gates's new hometown with Chicago indie luminaries John McEntire and Sam Prekop (Sea and Cake, Tortoise). Released in April 1998, *Arches and Aisles* was a masterful, literate, and mature record. Despite—or maybe because of—its subtle beauty, the record failed to broaden Gates's audience beyond the already converted. **JM**

Arches and Aisles

(1998, Sᴜʙ Pᴏᴘ)
Rebecca Gates's third full-length album draws on the Spinanes' earlier releases: the ingratiating pop songwriting of *Manos* combines with the darker emotions and textured production of *Strand*. With her luminously poetic lyrics and intimate delivery, Gates says more about love and longing in a single line than a shelf full of records by any chart-topping alterna-diva.

The Statics
Formed 1960, Burien, Washington

Merrilee and the Turnabouts
Formed 1965, Seattle, Washington

t he Statics, along with featured vocalist "Tiny" Tony Smith, were one of the original architects of the Northwest sound. Their business-oriented approach to music was also ahead of its time, and they contributed greatly to our musical legacy.

Four high school students from Burien, on the outskirts of Seattle—Jim Spano (guitar), Rod Garrity (guitar), Dave Erickson (drums), and Randy Bennett (steel guitar)—formed the Statics in 1960. Playing mostly instrumentals, the band relied on the Ventures, Link Wray, and Duane Eddy for their repertoire. One of their favorite early venues was the community center in the little town of Roslyn (later famous as the town where the television series *Northern Exposure* was filmed). They always packed the joint.

Their friend Richard Gerber let the band practice in his basement, and when Garrity quit in 1961, 15-year-old aspiring guitarist Gerber replaced him. Spano also quit, Bennett switched to bass guitar, and the remaining trio began playing with a series of keyboard and saxophone players (including keyboardist Dennis Yaden, formerly of the local band the Exotics).

Erickson began aggressively promoting the band, courting the DJs at local youth-oriented radio stations KJR and KOL. In 1962, DJ Dick Curtis offered Erickson a deal—play for free at a dance he was sponsoring at Burien's McMicken Heights Hall and, if things went well, they could play the prestigious Spanish Castle. The regal old adobe structure, midway between Seattle and Tacoma, was generally reserved for top touring acts.

Their dance appearance was a hit and the Castle gig went well, but the band realized they needed a frontman in order to become a top act. Tiny Tony Smith, a black vocalist who had sung in a number of R&B and soul groups (most notably the Galahads) was recruited. Also added were Neil Rush (sax) and Merrilee Gunst (vocals, organ).

The band idolized the black artists who made tour stops at venues like the Evergreen Ballroom in Olympia, Washington. They loved to study, analyze, and assimilate the dance steps and stage moves of James Brown, Bobby Bland, Marvin Gaye, and the Ike and Tina Turner Revue. With the Statics' sharp stage uniforms, young Merrilee's good looks, and their hot instrumental chops, Erickson was able to land them high-paying gigs throughout the Northwest. In 1962 they released their first single on the Bolo label, "Hey Mrs. Jones," a cover of an obscure Jimmy Witherspoon song. The Statics' bluesy arrangement featured a call-and-response between Smith's lascivious lead vocals and Gunst's more innocent singing, punctuated by Rush's growling saxophone lines. The record was a local radio hit and remains a Northwest sound classic.

Erickson's radio connections came through again when KOL's Ron Baily hired them for his shows at West Seattle's Morrison Hall. They opened for Roy Orbison and Conway Twitty there, and backed up singers including Jackie DeShannon. Another memorable early backing gig paired them with Little Eva at a civic center on Seattle's Eastside—it turned out the one-hit singer knew only two songs. The band lost both drummer and manager in 1963 when Erickson left, but Carl Peters ably took over his onstage duties and Rush became the band's manager.

The Statics distinguished themselves as the best-sounding local band through a state-of-the-art PA system designed by Gerber's brother-in-law Carl Schultz. They also were one of the first local acts to have a roadie (or "band boy," as they were then known). Jimmy Johnson, their first roadie, later toured with Paul Revere and the Raiders, Chicago, and the Eagles.

The Statics next released three more singles: "Buster Brown Pt. 1/Pt. 2," on their own Bregg label, and two on the Seattle-based Camelot imprint (covers of Little Richard's "The Girl Can't Help It" and "Harlem Shuffle," and an original song, "Tell Me The Truth," which would be their last recording). Tiny Tony, billed as "300 Pounds of Twist," and the Statics were still doing big business in the Northwest, from British Columbia to Idaho. But their R&B act was becoming an anachronism. Rush and Gunst (now Merrilee Rush) were married and quit the Statics, becoming an immediate success as Merrilee and the Turnabouts. The Statics limped on for a few more months before breaking up.

But the story was just beginning for the former Statics. In 1966, Gerber and Bennett formed a psychedelic band, Patterns and Colors, which was hired as the house band at the Seattle club Mr. P's but lost the job because their music was considered too experimental. Gerber moved to Los Angeles in 1967 and formed a band with Texas guitarist John Ussery and bassist John Keske. They scored a gig at a Sunset Strip club but didn't have a name. On the phone with their agent, they borrowed the name of a factory across the street from the phone booth—International Brick. The band played in Los Angeles for a while before returning to Seattle, opening shows for stars like the Byrds and the Doors. International Brick released a single on Camelot, "You Should Be So High"/"Flower Children," which is a perfect slice of Northwest psychedelia.

At the same time Merrilee and the Turnabouts kept increasing in popularity. While on tour with Paul Revere and the Raiders, they went into a Memphis studio and recorded the song that became their biggest hit, "Angel of the Morning." The song reached no. 7 on the *Billboard* charts and became a standard for female vocalists—country singer Juice Newton scored a no. 4 hit with her 1981 cover version. The Turnabouts followed with a couple of minor hits ("That Kind of Woman," 1968, and "Reach Out," 1969), but nothing equaled "Angel." Still, Merrilee remained a major regional star and toured nationally throughout the 1970s. Many local musicians played in the Turnabouts over the years, including members of Heart, City Zu, the Sonics, the Raiders, and even the former Statics.

Neil Rush made good use of the experience he gained managing and promoting the Statics and the Turnabouts. In 1969 he formed two businesses, Artists Development Management and Entertainment Authorities, which groomed, booked, and managed rock acts. These companies were a major force in Northwest music during the late 1960s and 1970s and grew into the powerful Far West Entertainment agency, still active today. Rush served a stretch as bandleader for Paul Revere and the Raiders after leaving the Turnabouts and has led several popular club bands. He currently operates the West Coast Talent Agency.

The group's vocalist, Smith, died in the early '90s. Bennett has since moved to Hawaii, but most of the other ex-Statics still live in the Northwest. Gerber has been especially active and played in the psychedelic band Peece during the late 1960s and early 1970s. He later spent several years with the Raiders and performed with the 1980s country acts Shenandoah and the Unknown Band. In the last decade, he led the Union Blues Band and now plays with the New Blues Brothers Revue (along with former Peece cohorts Pat Hues and Gary Ruhl). **NS**

Sunny Day Real Estate

Formed 1992, Seattle, Washington

the arrival of another "next big thing" in 1992, courtesy of Seattle's Sub Pop Records, came as no surprise—the unusual part was Sunny Day Real Estate's ability to live up to their advance billing. Although the band released just two full-length albums, they earned a rabid cult following during their short life. The band re-formed briefly in 1998 to record and release a third album for Sub Pop, *How It Feels to Be Something On*; a CD of outtakes and rare tracks is also expected.

Sunny Day Real Estate was formed by Dan Hoerner (guitar), Nate Mendel (bass), and William Goldsmith (drums) in 1992. Early the following year, the band released a single, "Flatland Spider"/"The Onlies." When Mendel left the band briefly to tour with Washington, D.C., punks Christ on a Crutch, Hoerner switched to bass, and Jeremy Enigk joined as vocalist and guitarist. Upon Mendel's return, Hoerner returned to guitar and the band's classic lineup was set. They released a second single with Enigk on vocals (although the disc itself was called "Thief, Steal Me a Peach," its two tracks were known simply as "Song No. 8" and "Song No. 9") and quickly signed to Sub Pop.

The band's first Sub Pop record, *Diary* (1994), set the template for Sunny Day Real Estate's stylized music. Take "Song About an Angel," which starts with an understated Enigk vocal accompanied by Hoerner's chiming guitar as Goldsmith and Mendel doodle in the background during the verse; the band coalesces into a powerful unit on the chorus as Enigk's vocals rise and fall, plaintive and dramatic. Not all

Sunny Day Real Estate songs fit this mold: "Round" is a power tune from the first note; "Pheurton Skeurto" is a stark piano- and bass- backed track in which Enigk channels John Lennon up front. The band connected with their young audience—not only did they put on powerful live shows, but they insisted on playing all-ages venues.

Their heroic tenure was to be brief, however. In March 1995, as recording for the second album was completed, the band broke up. Among the tensions was Enigk's newfound devotion to the Christian faith, which some band members felt was excessively coloring his lyrics. Whatever the reason, by the time *Sunny Day Real Estate* (1995) was released, the group was irrevocably broken. Goldsmith and Mendel joined ex-Nirvana guys Dave Grohl and Pat Smear to form the Foo Fighters. After an underwhelming solo acoustic performance at a Seattle Sub Pop showcase, Enigk reversed fields and released *Return of the Frog Queen* (1996), a well-received debut record whose orchestrated arrangements neatly fit his vocal style.

Although they're still beloved by their rabid fans, their first Seattle reunion show didn't draw an article in either of the city's daily newspapers, and Sunny Day Real Estate's future as a band remains an open question. Enigk intends to maintain his solo career. Mendel didn't even make the reunion—he was replaced by bassist Jeff Palmer, formerly of San Francisco's Mommyheads. But don't count these guys out just yet. **JB**

Diary

(1994, SUB POP)
This is what all the fuss was about. *Diary* first and foremost introduces a young band with tons of style and a bright future—which, unfortunately, didn't last long.

Super Deluxe

Formed 1994, Seattle, Washington

I f Seattle hadn't already earned a reputation as a power pop paradise, the 1995 release of Super Deluxe's *Famous* surely would have brought it over the top. Although the band shrugs off the basement—recorded gem as a demo that ended up on CD, the record is a stunning collection of songs, mostly tunes by guitarist and vocalist Braden Blake that predated the band's formation. Played live on 8-track with only a few overdubs, *Famous* has more immediacy than Super Deluxe's big-studio follow-up, *Via Satellite*. Blake's perfect pop voice and the backing harmonies of guitarist John Kirsch make "She Came On" and "Holly's Dream Vacation" (with its catchy chorus, "I'll do anything for love") two gems of the should've-been hit parade.

Blake met drummer Chris Lockwood through a "vocalist seeking band" ad in the Northwest music magazine *The Rocket*. The rest was not history: the two never formed a band, and Blake went on to play as a solo performer. But a few years later, Lockwood and bassist Jake Nesheim showed up for one of Blake's gigs and decided to try the band thing again. Recruiting guitarist Kirsch, the band clicked quickly and had been together for only a few years when they went the basement-studio route with producer Martin Feveyear (Gavin Guss, of fellow Seattle pop band Tube Top, coproduced most of the tracks).

Released on Portland's Tim/Kerr label, the record was picked up by Revolution in 1996. Next up was *Via Satellite* (1997, Warner Bros), a less cohesive but ultimately satisfying effort. Highlighted by tracks including "Your Pleasure's Mine" (documenting an encounter with an obsessed fan) and "Farrah Fawcett" (an ode to she of the feathered hair). The duo of Kirsch and Blake, who wrote just one song on *Famous*, was now a prolific songwriting team. Although a bit less enthralled by love ("You can get fifty [negative] songs out of a good divorce!" says the knowing Kirsch), the band's tuneful ways emerged intact. **JB**

Famous

(1996, REVOLUTION)
What can you say about pop perfection?

Supersuckers

Formed 1985, Tucson, Arizona

heat beads gather under the nasty cowboy hats of the Arizona-born Supersuckers. When you grow up with musical aspirations in a place like Tucson, you stick with the folks you befriend or get out quick. The Supersuckers did both. High school buddies Eddie Spaghetti, Ron Heathman, Dan Bolton, and Dan Seigel graduated from Santa Rita High in 1985. As would-be rock legends traditionally do, the guys learned a bunch of chords, covered AC/DC's "Live Wire," Madonna's "Burnin' Up," and Chuck Berry's "Nadine," decided they sounded pretty good, and kept going. After a stint as Thai Pink and with a slightly different lineup, the current Supersuckers, along with singer Eric Martin, formed the Black Supersuckers. But there wasn't much doing for five free-thinking rock types in Tucson. When their present manager, Danny Bland, then a member of the Best Kissers in the World, left Arizona in search of a town where he could wear his leather jacket during the summer, he found Seattle. The Suckers followed, joining other rock groups in the mass migration to the city in the late 1980s and early 1990s.

Lead man Spaghetti, although always principal songwriter, was backup singer to Martin. When the Suckers lost Martin in 1991, they dropped the "Black" from their name and threw charmed grinner Spaghetti center stage. He played bass, as before, while guitar superstar Ron Heathman learned to sing rock harmony. Dan Bolton was the other guitar heavy. Both are known for guitar-pointing-to-the-sky salutes and rock-slinging cowboy etiquette. Historically the healthiest of the crew, Dan Seigel looms over his drum kit, reminiscent of Tarzan on a sweaty day.

As a four-piece group, the Suckers went to Seattle's Avast Studios in 1991 and recorded demos with Spaghetti singing lead and Heathman backup. Out of those tapes came the band's first three singles on three labels: Sympathy for the Record Industry, Lucky, and eMpTy Records. *The Smoke of Hell* began their official Sub Pop career in 1992. The cover art was the band's best to date, designed by underground cartoonist Dan Klowes. Ever prolific, the band continued to record singles, and the following year brought their rock highlight, *La Mano Cornuda* (that's "The Horned Hand" to us monolingual types). The record won them a Spanish Grammy for Best Rock Album in 1994. The next year, a rather bleak one in rock, the Suckers released *Sacrilicious* without Heathman. His temporary replacement was Rick Simms of the Didgits.

Although loud and libidinous, the Suckers are not one-trick ponies. Their first demos for Sub Pop, recorded by Jack Endino, were acoustic. The final full-length record for Sub Pop, which completed a five-year, four-record contract, embraced the sweet soul of country. *Must've Been High* was recorded in 1997 with minimal effects and equipment, using Nashville players and an ethereal telephone appearance by Willie Nelson. But everything in between was rock and roll.

Regardless of their many recordings, live is the best way to deal with the Suckers. Goofy phrases like "stage presence" come to mind. The Suckers and friends form a seasonal band, the Junk Yard Dogs, who play at Seattle's University District Street Fair every spring. Another noteworthy project is their Thin Lizzy cover band, for which the Suckers dress to the nines—wigs and all.

A celestial light continues to shine on our Arizona boys—oddly enough, considering the fate of most Seattle bands. They stayed with Sub Pop longer than any other group, scraping together a living without day jobs for five years. The band took on Danny Bland as manager in 1994, and the president of their new label, Interscope, is their artist representative. That's a pretty charmed life for such an unlikely Seattle band. **KS**

La Mano Cornuda

(1993, Sub Pop)
Rock 'n' roll. The definitive highlight is "Creepy Jackalope Eye" (the jackalope is compared to the biblical Adam and Eve). Also listen to the multiple-car-wreck sound of the guitar spinout at the end of "Nitroglycerine."

Must've Been High

(1997, Sub Pop)
Lyrical, rockin' campfire songs recorded during what sound like horseback rides of varying tempos.

Sweet Water

Formed 1992, Seattle, Washington

SGM

Formed 1986, Seattle, Washington

through two decades of rock trends, countless bar gigs, at least three distinct bands, and numerous pairs of stretch jeans, these four guys from Seattle's affluent Bush School have seen and done it all—and are still going strong.

High school buddies Rich Credo (guitar), Adam Czeisler (vocals), Cole Peterson (bass), and Paul Jewler (drums) were just four private-school punks playing music together when they formed the nucleus of what would become SGM in the mid-1980s. Czeisler had moved on by 1987, when SGM—fronted by singer Mike Loser and featuring guitarist Kris Quinn—finagled a record contract and released *Aggression*. A buzz-saw punk/metal amalgam, *Aggression* spotlighted Loser's astounding screaming vocals and the band's flat-out desire to rock. SGM, by the way, didn't stand for anything, although the band filled in the blanks with amusing one-shot names on gig posters, including Stoney Gossard Mania and Stupid Gnarly Men. Loser split the band to attend college; after a brief period with ex-Mace vocalist Kirk Verhey, Czeisler rejoined and the old gang was back together again.

During his early SGM days, Czeisler sang on a series of classic demos recorded with producer Jack Endino—songs that, unfortunately, exist for now only in Seattle's cassette-tape underground. The band decided they needed an actual name and chose Shot Gun Mama. Somehow record companies were able to resist them, and after a brief period with another vocalist, Shot Gun Mama packed it in.

But the breakup didn't last. Quinn split town to join the band Truly, pal Dudley Taft was brought in on lead guitar, and Czeisler returned. The new band dubbed itself Sweet Water and immediately began playing gigs and recording new songs. Without a record company yet on the hook, the band released ten songs from their original demo sessions on Seattle's New Rage Records. Titled simply *Sweet Water*, this now-rare 1992 CD release was impressive enough to get the band inked to Atlantic Records.

Working with several of the same songs (and, strangely enough, the same album title), the band released their Don Gilmore–produced major label debut, *Sweet Water*, in 1993. Although the record started to receive airplay, some of the rerecorded songs suffered when compared to their original versions. Much better was Sweet Water's follow-up, *Superfriends* (1995). This is ironically the band's most cohesive record, despite the turmoil surrounding it. Taft left the band during the sessions (his playing appears on a few cuts), and the group was officially a four-piece when *Superfriends* was released. Better production (by Dave Jerden), better songs ("Self Hater" and "Feed Yourself" in particular), and a straight-ahead rock-meets-glam approach make this Sweet Water's best release.

Superfriends was also a successful release, spawning radio airplay and good tour gigs. But, caught in the shaky world of record label realignment, Sweet Water found themselves without a contract in 1996, and the band splintered.

Nobody was fooled. In late 1997 the four blood brothers got together for a side project to be called the Parc Boys (for Paul, Adam, Rich, and Cole). But once they were in the studio with producer Martin Feveyear, the project caught fire. The resulting album, *Two Weeks to Live*, was released in early 1998. **JB**

Aggression

(1987, Restless)
SGM's first and only album may just be the most inspired combo of punk rock and heavy metal ever. Mike Loser's incessant screaming and panting is completely in context on this crashing power chord symphony.

Superfriends

(1995, Eastwest America)
An easy but eventful ride through Sweet Water's trashrock influences. A few slow spots, but just as many hits, including "Cake and Strychnine" and "Big Rock Show."

Tad

Formed 1988, Seattle, Washington

now, we've told you kids a thousand times not to get messed up with major labels, but do you listen? Never. Well, here's another story of how the music industry wreaked havoc on a band's career.

Tad is one of the heaviest bands ever to graduate from Seattle's Sub Pop Records. It began as a solo project when ex-H-Hour drummer Tad Doyle laid down some tracks at Reciprocal Studios with engineer Jack Endino (who was not yet calling himself a "producer"). Sub Pop's Bruce Pavitt got all excited when he heard the resulting tape, which he mistook for the new Killdozer album. When the truth came out, Pavitt released the first Tad single, and Tad the man proceeded to round up a band.

The group, which then consisted of Doyle, guitarist Gary Thorstensen, bassist Kurt Danielson, and drummer Steve Wied, became part of the second wave of what was later called grunge. They typified "the Seattle sound," combining heavy metal, punk, and industrial influences to create pure, primal noise.

Sub Pop released two Tad albums, *God's Balls* (1989) and *8-Way Santa* (1991), and one EP, *Salt Lick* (1990). The label cultivated a sort of redneck trailer-trash mystique for the band, which Doyle and Danielson encouraged in interviews. They presented themselves as inbred, illiterate woodsmen, though this bluff should have been transparent, as Danielson couldn't seem to resist quoting H. P. Lovecraft novels.

Tad began opening for Mudhoney and other fairly established heavy guitar bands in Seattle, then embarked on a European tour just in time for the British media blitz surrounding the so-called Seattle invasion. Tad coheadlined these shows with another promising new band, Nirvana.

Shortly after embarking on a U.S. tour in support of *8-Way Santa*, the band learned the record had been pulled from the stores. The controversy was over its cover, a photo of a long-haired, skinny hippie grabbing his girlfriend's breast. Both have insipid, stoned grins on their faces. The woman in the picture was not amused to see this 1975 photo of herself reproduced on albums being sold all over the world, and threatened to sue. Because Sub Pop was experiencing financial difficulty at that time, a new cover wasn't printed until a few months later, which pretty much killed the album's sales. Tad was forced to finish the tour without a record in the stores.

The band suffered a loss of momentum when Wied left, setting off a two-year search for a permanent drummer. They finally settled on ex-Accused basher Josh Sinder.

Just before leaving on a U.S. tour with Soundgarden, Tad was informed that the band would receive no funding from Giant. They had no choice but to break their contract with Mechanic, but they had to promise one last album. The result, *Live Alien Broadcasts*, contains in-concert versions of songs from *8-Way Santa* and *Inhaler*, plus a B-side from the *Inhaler* sessions and two entirely new tracks.

Meanwhile, a much larger label, Elektra, promised to rescue Tad from oblivion. The band parted ways with Thorstensen and became a power trio in an attempt to streamline their sound. The dual guitar assault on *Infrared Riding Hood* is all Doyle's work.

This should have been a happy ending, but instead, the Elektra representative who had championed Tad and other alternative bands left the company, and Tad was dropped from the roster just as *Infrared Riding Hood* reached the stores. No promotional copies were sent out, and Tad couldn't tour. Sucks, doesn't it?

At this writing, Tad is still playing to appreciative Seattle audiences and hopes to be around for the next rock revolution. **DA**

8-Way Santa

(1991, Sub Pop)
The songwriting here is top-notch. Along with the more crushing numbers, this Tad album contains actual melodies and hooks!

Infrared Riding Hood

(1996, Elektra)
The most pulverizing record Tad has ever recorded.

TKO

Formed 1977, Seattle, Washington

I t used to be okay to want to be a rock star, even in Seattle. But in the small Eastern Washington town of Yakima in 1973, it was considered a little weird for a guy to pluck his eyebrows and dye his hair blue. Glamour boy "Bad Brad" Sinsel must have been hard to miss in his hometown—where he wore glitter and worshiped David Bowie while his schoolmates threw rocks and called him a faggot.

Bad Brad didn't care. He was going to be a star. He moved to Seattle and, after playing in a couple of cover bands, hooked up with Ze Fabulous Whiz Kids, a cabaret troupe that by this time had metamorphosed into a rock band. With their face paint and flamboyant costumes, the Whiz Kids served as a fitting opening act for the glam New York Dolls at Seattle's Moore Theatre in 1974.

In 1977 Sinsel and fellow Whiz Kid Rick Pierce formed the first version of TKO and hooked up with Heart's management company, Albatross Productions. Sinsel had a strong, dramatic voice that would now be described as classic rock, falling somewhere between the vocal mannerisms of the Who's Roger Daltrey and Aerosmith's Steven Tyler and recalling a hundred other long-forgotten late-1970s rock 'n' roll bands. Their sound was the sort of earnest, overblown hard rock that ruled mainstream radio at that time.

The band released the LP *Let It Roll* on Albatross Records in 1979 and toured in support of Cheap Trick, Heart, and the Kinks. Seemingly poised on the brink of commercial success, the band broke up after a fight with their management. In 1981 another version of TKO was formed, featuring Adam Brenner, future frontman of the band Adam Bomb, on guitar. This TKO was short-lived and split apart just before landing a contract with Combat Records, which released *In Your Face* in 1984. This time the band went for the big-crunch approach with a muscular sound falling halfway between Def Leppard and AC/DC, once again perfectly in sync with prevailing fashion.

For the next version of TKO, Sinsel teamed up with two ex-members of the hardcore metal band Culprit, guitarist Kjartan Kristofferson and bassist Scott Earl, and future Sanctuary drummer Ken Mary. The three new members appeared on the *In Your Face* cover photo, although none of them actually played on the album.

The 1986 album *Below the Belt* was the band's slickest yet, in keeping with the listener-friendly MTV pop metal then in vogue. As Poison and Ratt can now testify, there was nowhere to go from there.

After disbanding TKO, Sinsel once again teamed up with the band's former guitarist and ex-Q5 member Rick Pierce to form Suicide Squad, which released a self-titled, fairly aggressive EP. Pierce now plays in the band Nightshade. Sinsel later formed War Babies with ex-members of the alternative rock band Black Is Black, which released a self-titled CD on Sony Music in 1992. They broke up a year or so later. Adam Brenner is still doggedly trying to make it big. His 1998 Adam Bomb CD,

1970s Rockers

Northwest music of the 1970s wasn't all artsy glam, snotty punk, disco, or arena rock. The crowds of the 1960s teen dance circuit had matured—and as the core baby boomer audience aged, taverns and lounges started to do a huge business with the ravenous rock-oriented clientele.

Cheyanne is a Northwest band that dates back to the mid-1960s yet still survives today. Formed in Spokane as the bluesy trio Cold Power, the band changed its name to Whiterock and released a catchy original single: "Mister Sun." The early lineup was Eric Burgeson (guitar), Gene Nygaard (guitar), Lee Perkins (bass), and Howard Walter (drums). The group soon changed its name to Cheyanne and added vocalist/keyboard player David Christensen. Their sound was good basic hard rock, supplemented by covers of songs by Elvis and the Rolling Stones. (Christensen's "Tribute to Mick Jagger" was a staple of Cheyanne shows throughout the decade.)

By the early 1970s, the band had relocated to Seattle and hooked up with the Far West Entertainment booking agency. After a swing to Los Angeles, the members changed the spelling of their name to "Shyanne" (sometimes "Shy Anne") and continued playing the rowdy Seattle tavern circuit. Among the members in this era were Scott Rosburg (Blue Sky, the Randle Rossburg Band/Striker) and Don Wilhelm (a founding member of Army, the group that evolved into Heart). In 1982 Shyanne released a self-titled album, a strong arena rock effort that showcased Burgeson's songwriting and all-around hot playing. But music styles had changed, and Shyanne called it quits a few years later. A revival version of the band has been back in the bars for several years playing "classic rock"—the same sort of material Whiterock and Cheyanne were playing in the late 1960s and early 1970s.

Fragile Lime was another big 1970s band with roots in the previous decade. Formed in Everett, Washington, in 1966, the band was fronted by the charismatic Mark Gallagher (the Mark Four). Fragile Lime had an initial burst of success after connecting with manager Jack Chesterfield: one early triumph was opening for Paul Revere and the Raiders at a 1966 Seattle Center Coliseum show. Fragile Lime released two singles on the local Sabrina label. The first, "Fairyland (When I Was a Little Boy)"/"I Know What It Is" (both written by Gallagher and drummer Ken Dammand), featured some great harmonies and Beatlesque chord changes. The second, "Day in the Sun"/"I Need Your Love" (both written by guitarist Howard Wiebe), showed the band's musical progression. "Day" has a psychedelic baroque feel (with a great harpsichord part by Tim Lee); the B-side was reminiscent of Cream. Fragile Lime hooked up with national acts the Grass Roots and the Lemon Pipers on their Northwest dates (including the memorable Tacoma, Washington, Grass Roots gig where someone fired bullets into the club from outside while Fragile Lime was playing).

As the 1960s drew to a close, Fragile Lime lost drummer Dammand to the military, and manager Chesterfield died in a plane crash. Dammand's replacement was Ed Young. For its management, the group chose the region's two biggest: Entertainment Authorities and Artists Development Management. The new lineup's first single was "Angie"/"I'm Gonna Get You" (1970) on the local Thunder Tummy label (the recording was supplemented in the studio by City Zu bassist Mike Cox and the horn section from Onyx). "I'm Gonna Get You" became a local radio hit and was rereleased nationally by

Warner Brothers. The 1972 follow-up on Thunder Tummy, a cover of Otis Redding's "Happy Song" backed by the Gallagher original "She's Got Me Shakin," also was picked up nationally, this time by Metromedia. Produced by Neil Rush and Don McKinney, these two soulful singles were some of the most sophisticated to be recorded and released locally at the time.

By 1973 Fragile Lime was winding down. The final version of the band, featuring new vocalist Barney Armstrong and hotshot guitarist Mike Vena, did several West Coast tours. Although the band soon broke up, Fragile Lime members have been musically active. Gallagher fronted Blue Mountain Eagle, Dammand has played in several jazz/swing bands, Vena released a fine solo album in 1980, and Lee is the longtime keyboardist/musical director for the Righteous Brothers.

The band Child brought an appreciation of the late-1960s British blues revival sound to Northwest clubs. Formed in West Seattle in the early 1970s, the hard-rocking, bluesy band was fronted by guitarist/vocalist Mick Flynn. Child had a full complement of Hiwatt amplifiers (favorites of English acts like the Who) and an eclectic set list featuring songs like Fleetwood Mac's "Albatross." In 1975 Bighorn's Rick Randle joined Child, bringing with him several excellent original songs and many of his former group's fans. This version of the band recorded an album, unfortunately never released. Randle split to form the Randle Rossburg Band, which changed its name to Striker and released an album on Arista in 1978.

Child released its own album on the local Ariel label in 1977, featuring several fine originals by guitarist Tim Turner (the other players on this release were Flynn, bassist Lance Baumgartel, and drummer John O'Conner). Flynn quit the band (he is now a well-known dealer in rare guitars), and Child continued into the early 1980s with vocalist Bruce Hazen. Child has reunited periodically since their breakup.

—Neal Skok

Je Suis Rock Star, was released on KBC Records.

Sinsel plans to raid his archives and release a new TKO album. Since the band always managed to stay in perfect tune with prevailing sounds on any given day, such a record could serve as a document of the evolution of commercial hard rock throughout the 1980s, before the alternative rock revolution crushed it like a gaudy, drunken insect. **DA**

TKO in Your Face

(1984, COMBAT!)
For those about to rock, they salute you.

The Ventures

Formed 1959, Tacoma, Washington

they were the contemporaries of the first wave of Northwest rock 'n' roll bands, yet the Ventures haven't been identified with the region. Although their style has little in common with the classical regional sound of thick organ, sax, guitar, and screaming vocals, the Ventures are one of the most successful acts to emerge from the Northwest.

A pair of Tacoma, Washington, bricklayers, Don Wilson and Bob Bogle, discovered their common talent for guitar playing and formed a duo in 1959 to play local dances and clubs. By late summer, they were proficient enough to record a demo tape, which Don's mother, Josie Wilson, tried unsuccessfully to place with several record companies. Believing in the duo, she started her own label, Blue Horizon. With the addition of two more members—bassist/guitarist Nokie Edwards and drummer Howie Johnson—the band dubbed itself the Versatones and began playing gigs in Tacoma. In February 1960 the band released their first single ("The Real McCoy"/"Cookies and Coke"), recorded at Seattle's Custom Recorders.But it was their next recording that would establish the band—now known as the Ventures. A cover of a tune by jazz guitarist Johnny Smith, "Walk—Don't Run" was released in April. Picked up nationally by Dolton/Liberty, the single peaked at no. 2 in July. By the end of the year, their first album (also titled *Walk—Don't Run*) was no. 11 on the U.S. charts. After just over a year as a band, the Ventures were bona fide stars.

The early 1960s were heady times for the instrumental band. Relocating to Los Angeles, they recorded a few more Top 40 hits ("Perfidia" and "Ram-Bunk-Shush"). Their twin-guitar melodic instrumental sound fit well with the surf music craze; the band's albums were a mixture of reinterpreted older songs, current hits, and their own catchy tunes.

By 1963 Johnson had left and was replaced by Mel Taylor. The Ventures enjoyed worldwide popularity and were special favorites with listeners in Japan, rivaling the Beatles in that country. The band began a parallel Japanese career, touring there constantly and releasing hundreds of songs specifically for the Asian market. Meanwhile, many American teens were learning to play guitar from instructional albums by the Ventures—several of which charted during the early and mid-1960s. The group took advantage of their association with the electric guitar by marketing their own guitar line—Mosrite (named for business partner Semie Mosrite). Produced until the mid-1970s, these instruments are highly prized.

In 1968 Edwards quit and was replaced by Jerry McGee. The band kept current during the late 1960s by adding keyboards. Their final U.S. hit was the theme from the television series *Hawaii Five-0* (the album of the same name was their last Top 40 album). In an unusual twist, the band had sixteen Top 40 albums but just six Top 40 singles (including two versions of "Walk—Don't Run").

In the early 1980s, when new wavers rediscovered the Ventures, the band started to gain much-deserved recognition for their influential career. They continue to play as the classic four-piece lineup, particularly in Japan. **NS**

The Ventures, On Stage

(1965, DOLTON)

Recorded in Japan, England, and the United States, this raving live album is among the first of its kind. The selections are light on the hits ("Walk—Don't Run" and "Perfidia" form a medley), but the audience's response is what we'd expect from a Beatles show. And, yes, they duplicate their studio sound perfectly.

Walk—Don't Run: The Best of the Ventures

(1990, EMI AMERICA)

With more than one hundred album releases and countless singles, it seems impossible that a single-CD collection could do the Ventures justice, but this twenty-nine-cut compilation does just that. Containing excellent liner notes and all the essential hits, it's the perfect introduction to the band (bonus points for radio ads and interviews).

The Viceroys

Formed 1958, Seattle, Washington

the Viceroys were formed in 1958 by north Seattle high school classmates Jim Valley (guitar) and Al Berry (keyboards). Other early members included Bud Potter (bass), Greg Thompson (drums), and Fred Rucker (sax).

Within a year the Viceroys were playing sophisticated Northwest R&B on the same circuit as Tacoma's Wailers and Seattle's Frantics. In a personnel shakeup, the band added 14-year-old drummer Fred Zeufeldt (who, a year later, was signing contracts on behalf of the band) and sax player Mike Rogers, who later switched to keyboards (the first Northwest musician to play a left-handed bass keyboard). The Viceroys' recording debut was "My Only Love"/"I Love a Girl" (1960). Although most of their early recordings were instrumentals, the band was frequently fronted by solo singers, both male and female. Some of their featured vocalists were Jimmy Pipkins, Erin Stuart, and Nancy Claire. The 1962 Seattle World's Fair proved an excellent opportunity for the band, which landed a prestigious two-month gig for the local *American Bandstand*–type television show, *Deck Dance.*

The Viceroys' next release was "Granny's Pad," a hypnotic Al Berry instrumental inspired by the band's rehearsals at his grandmother's house. The single was noticed by Seattle DJ Pat O'Day, who featured a comedic character named Granny on his KJR radio show. It was a win-win situation: the high-profile Viceroys coupled with regional powerhouse KJR's radio domination created the best-selling Northwest single to that point. Their follow-up album on the local Seafair-Bolo label, *The Viceroys at Granny's Pad*, was a hot mix of covers and originals. Highlights are Valley's "Tiger Shark," the blistering take on Earl King's "Come On," and four permutations of "Granny's Pad." As expected, the album was quite successful. During its recording, Kim Eggers was brought in on sax and vocals; he would develop into a charismatic frontman.

By 1964, the Viceroys were one of the more popular bands on the Northwest circuit. In addition to playing the three-state area of Washington, Oregon, and Idaho, they performed in Vancouver and Victoria, British Columbia, and in California. The next year founding member Valley was lured away by the Portland band Don and the Goodtimes and replaced by guitarist Greg Beck. By this time the former instrumental band featured four-part vocal harmonies. A pair of 1965 singles, "Bacon Fat" and "That Sound," drew lots of airplay and became local hits. But the band's big national break didn't come through airplay or sales. Mark "Hoss" Amans, a pal of Eggers and former Viceroys roadie, was now working for Paul Revere and the Raiders. Hoss helped convince his new employers to give the Viceroys the opening slot on their 1966 national tour. Raiders producer Terry Melcher was impressed enough to get them signed to Columbia Records.

Their first single for the major label, "Out of My Mind," was basically a reworking of "That Sound" featuring psychedelic studio trickery. Much to the band's surprise, Columbia decided to update their name as well—the single was released under the more contemporary name Surprise Package. As Surprise Package, the band released two more singles on Columbia, played prestigious Los Angeles clubs and national television shows, and opened for such stars as Jethro Tull and Led Zeppelin.

After vocalist Rob Lowery replaced Eggers, Surprise Package released a couple of singles on Lee Hazelwood's LHI label (including a killer version of "MacArthur Park") and the psychedelic album *Free Up* in 1968.

By late 1969 sax player Rogers had been replaced by Gene Hubbard, and the band became known as American Eagle. They released an album on Decca and were quite visible on the ballroom and festival circuit, including an opening stint for Chicago at the Eagles Auditorium, Seattle's hippie mecca. American Eagle ground to a halt in the early 1970s, but the Viceroys of the 1950s had cut quite a swath through Northwest music.

Most members continued in the business. Valley is a successful children's musician ("Rainbow Planet"). Zeufeldt led the megapopular 1970s showband Bighorn, and Eggers plays tasty sax with the revitalized Wailers. Zeufeldt, Beck, and Eggers have played periodic reunion shows as the Viceroys. **NS**

At Granny's Pad

(1963, Bolo)
Full of hot instrumentals, including Jim Valley's killer "Tiger Shark," this album has several variations on the ultra-catchy "Granny's Pad." The album also includes excellent covers of songs by Dave Lewis, Ray Charles, and jazz great Cannonball Adderley.

The Wailers

Formed 1958, Tacoma, Washington

t hey weren't the first or the most famous Northwest band, and their records spent a total of only three weeks on the national Top 40 charts, yet the Wailers remain the quintessential rockers of the Northwest's first golden era.

They were a bunch of Tacoma, Washington, high schoolers who met each other jamming at the Fort Lewis Officers' Club. Taking their name from an old jazz group, the original Wailers were Rich Dangel and John Greek on guitar, Mike Marush on sax, Kent Morrill on keyboards, and Mike Burk on drums. As was common during the era, their early repertoire was mainly instrumentals, although Morrill occasionally let loose with his Little Richard–like vocals. Fooling around on a baby grand piano, Morrill came up with a catchy, jazzy tune they originally entitled "Scotch on the Rocks." The band recorded it at Commercial Recorders in Seattle on August 25, 1958, and their place in history was assured. Retitled "Tall Cool One," the song was released by New York's Golden Crest Records in the spring of 1959. It was a massive Northwest hit and cracked the U.S. Top 40. The high school band was thrilled—they went on a national tour to promote their hit and appeared on several high-profile television shows, including *American Bandstand* and the *Alan Freed Show*. They even played New York's famous Apollo Theater.

The nation's biggest booking agency (GAC) wanted the band to relocate to New York and become real stars. But the young band members preferred to stay in Tacoma with their families and girlfriends. Golden Crest released an album to cash in on "Tall Cool One." Titled *The Fabulous Wailers*, the gritty hybrid of blues, R&B, and rockabilly featured such "tough" cuts as "Shanghaied," "Gunnin' for Peter," and "Tough Bounce." Morrill's Little Richard–influenced "Dirty Robber" would prove a Wailers standard for the rest of their career.

By 1961 Greek had departed and two new members had joined—bassist John "Buck" Ormsby and vocalist "Rockin'" Robin Roberts, formerly of the local group Little Bill and the Bluenotes. This was the lineup that released the song that changed Northwest music history, "Louie Louie." While Little Bill's contemporary version stuck closer to Richard Berry's doo-woppish original, the Wailers' version was abrasive and soulful—in short, a classic. It was also the first release on the band's independent label, Etiquette. It was a Northwest smash but did little nationally, though it was covered endlessly.

The band's second album, *At the Castle*, was a hot live show recorded at the legendary local Spanish Castle nightclub (later immortalized in Jimi Hendrix's "Spanish Castle Magic"). Fifteen-year-old chanteuse Gail Harris sang on a couple of cuts, as did Roberts. The rest of the album was filled with their wiry instrumentals and Morrill's unique vocals.

All of the new Northwest bands were in awe of the Wailers, so finding material to release was no problem. Etiquette was starting to blossom as a label, and the Wailers continued to release material on it, while licensing various recordings to national labels such as United Artists, Imperial, and Bell. But not much clicked outside the Northwest, even though their records sold well in California and other scattered markets. Savvy musicians worldwide did know of the Wailers—such famous bands as the Beatles, the Rolling Stones, the Kinks, and the Who have expressed admiration for their early records.

During the mid-1960s, Dangel, Marush, and Burk all quit the group. The band's first sex symbol, Ron Gardner, was brought in on vocals, keyboards, and sax. Guitarist Neil Andersson brought a more modern style to replace Dangel's bluesy lines. Drummer Dave Roland would remain for the band's duration. Two albums from this era (*Out of Our Tree* and *Outburst*) are classics, producing great songs such as "Hang Up," "It's You Alone," and "Hold," but they sold poorly. The band continued to play many live gigs, appearing with the Beach Boys, the Animals, the Kinks, and the Rolling Stones. They also headlined in San Francisco over such fledgling psychedelic bands as Quicksilver Messenger Service, the Jefferson Airplane, and the Grateful Dead.

Their last album, *Walk Thru the People* (1968, Bell), was evocative of the time. But as an artifact the record (unlike many) has aged well, boasting highlights such as "People," "Smokestack Lightning," and "Busy Man." Guitarist Danny Weaver (Andersson had been drafted) contributes a bluesy/acid rock flavor, Gardner's keyboards add a progressive sound, and Morrill's voice is as haunting as ever.

By 1969 the teen music era was drawing to an end, and the Wailers packed it in. The band's former members are still well represented in Northwest music. Dangel and Morrill have their own bands, and guitar virtuoso Andersson has an instrumental jazz band called Pearl Django. Ormsby has perhaps been the most visible with his twelve-year stint as bassist for the eternally popular Jr. Cadillac (he still runs the Etiquette label). Roberts died in a 1967 car accident. Gardner was a Northwest musical fixture until his untimely death in a fire in 1992. There is still a worldwide demand for the Wailers' music from both listeners and record collectors. The core group of Ormsby, Morrill, and Dangel reunite as the Wailers a few times each year, and their early Northwest magic remains intact. **NS**

Walk Thru the People

(1968, BELL)
While the Wailers weren't thought of as a psychedelic group, their final album is one of the Northwest's best in that genre, full of moody minor-key songs. Kent Morrill's and Ron Gardner's vocals are top notch. "Smokestack Lightning," a blues/psychedelic staple, is presented here in perhaps its definitive version.   CONTINUED...

The Walkabouts

Formed 1984, Seattle, Washington

even as the Walkabouts have layered rootsy Americana and country twang onto their classic folk-rock sound, somehow they still remain a far bigger band in Europe than in their home country. Our loss.

How this eclectic combo became one of Seattle's most noted musical exports in the late 1980s is a story worth telling. Built around singer/guitarists Chris Eckman and Carla Torgerson, the original band in 1984 also included an all-Eckman rhythm section in brothers Curt (bass) and Grant (drums). This lineup recorded the independently released five-song EP *22 Disasters* (1985).

Later that year the Walkabouts signed a contract with a Los Angeles label and were set to beat most of their Seattle rivals to vinyl by about two years. Although recorded, their planned debut album (*Weights and Rivers*) was never released; a single from the sessions ("Linda Evans"/"Cyclone") did come out in 1987. The Walkabouts first long-player, *See Beautiful Rattlesnake Gardens* (1988), appeared in stores as the likes of Green River and Soundgarden were packing local rock clubs. Meanwhile, the Walkabouts were producing songs like "Rotten Tree," a bouncy folk duet by Chris Eckman and Carla Torgerson, and "Breakneck Speed," an edgy low fidelity rocker. The new bass player was Los Angeles native Michael Wells, whose tenure with the band would last almost a decade.

It's tempting to assume the Walkabouts were outcasts in the land of heavy rock, but that was hardly the case. In fact, Sub Pop Records was impressed enough to tender a recording contract, releasing *Cataract* (1989), the EP *Rag & Bone* (1990), and *Scavenger* (1991). The band became a five-piece with the addition of keyboard player Glenn Slater, who joined the band before *Rag & Bone*.

But Sub Pop's troubled finances and disputes between band and label led to a split following the release of *Cataract*. The group signed a European deal with Reinhard Holstein, owner of the Glitterhouse label (Glitterhouse had distributed the Walkabouts' earlier releases in Europe). Ironically, despite the split with Sub Pop (which meant their records were not available in the United States), due to Glitterhouse's contract situation the next few Walkabouts records ended up being released on the Sub Pop Europe label. Their first release under the new contract was *New West Motel* (1993), perhaps their most consistent album. Grant Eckman had left the band by then, and the addition of drummer Terri Moeller and violinist Bruce Wirth made the band a six-piece for the first time. The relationship with Sub Pop Europe continued with *Satisfied Mind* (1993, a collection of cover tunes) and *Setting the Woods on Fire* (1994). Glitterhouse also released the limited-edition live CD *To Hell and Back* (1994) and *Death Valley Days* (1996), a collection of rare tracks. Chris and Carla (a married couple as well as a folk duo) have also released a total of five CDs.

The Walkabouts signed a new contract with Virgin Records in 1995 and released their most ambitious record yet, *Devil's Road*, featuring backing from the Warsaw Philharmonic Orchestra on several tracks. Their 1997 release, *Nighttown*, a suite of songs Chris describes as "a dusk-to-dawn song cycle," also features strings—this time provided by Seattle musicians at the Bear Creek and Avast Studios. Along with the strings, the band retained producer Victor Van Vugt, who also produced *Devil's Road*. The record featured a new bassist by the sole name of Baker, formerly of Mad Season. (Baker, born John Baker Saunders, died in 1999 of a drug overdose.)

Even if Virgin makes a reasonable push for *Nighttown* in the United States, there's no guarantee the Walkabouts will ever become big stars in their home country. But no Seattle band of their era has survived longer, remained as prolific, or shown the consistent musical development displayed by the Walkabouts. **JB**

See Beautiful Rattlesnake Gardens

(1988, PopLlama)
A snapshot of a band still developing its style, but the performances are energetic and the songs interesting. The CD version includes the single "Linda Evans" and three additional tracks from the unreleased *Weights and Rivers* album.

New West Motel

(1993, Sub Pop Europe)
A wonderful band performance behind Chris Eckman and Carla Torgerson's intense vocal outings. Vivid stories from a claustrophobic world—especially Torgerson's album opener, "Jack Candy," and Eckman's gruff "Grand Theft Auto." Thanks to Creativeman Disc for releasing this one in the United States.

The Wipers

Perhaps no other band in Portland's colorful musical history more closely defines the city's stormy vibe than Greg Sage and the Wipers. The music is straightforward and starkly unadorned, while Sage's lyrics hit home like a well-tossed bowling ball. There is no oblique poetry, no secret language to decipher. I'm lonely. It's cold outside. The rain is wet. Welcome to Portland.

The band originally consisted of Sage on guitar and vocals, Dave Koupal on bass, and Sam Henry on drums, though rhythm sections would come and go. When they first began bashing through songs, Sage's inclination was for the band to function primarily as a studio ensemble that would flesh out his songwriting ideas. But friends convinced them to start performing, and soon they were all over Portland—not only at now-forgotten all-ages clubs but at basements and warehouses—wherever someone could wrangle a key to a large space. Tall and skeleton-thin, with his white-blond hair tied up in a sweaty bandanna, Sage was a spectral presence onstage. His piercing gaze seemed to look right through the audience to a better world where he wasn't depressed and miserable.

The first Wipers full-length recording, the now-classic *Is This Real?* (released on Sage's Park Avenue label), is the best and most obvious jumping-off point for the uninitiated. Songs like "Return of the Rat" (later covered by some band called Nirvana), "D-7," and "Windowshop for Love" were towering shards of alienation with chugging, Johnny Ramone–style guitars. Sage's voice yearns and breaks on the title track, as he aches for some kind of comfort and love that remains beyond his reach. These songs show his love for the greats—Iggy Pop, the Buzzcocks, the Sex Pistols, the New York Dolls—but his perspective is as raw and dark as the deep, rainy forests of the Northwest. Still, if Portland ever had a Lou Reed, it would be Greg Sage: an observer/victim who is at once repelled by and vitally part of the street action. Over and over he describes himself as an alien who can't find a place where he's safe and happy.

If *Is This Real?* is an undisputed classic, *Over the Edge* (1983, Braineater Records) is close behind. "Doom Town," "Romeo," and the title cut (later covered by some band called Hole) are even more urgent and grim (if possible) than their predecessors. The Tim/Kerr-released tribute album, *14 Songs: A Tribute to Greg Sage and the Wipers* (1991), is also a necessary purchase; it includes Sage tunes rendered by Nirvana and Hole (as warned) as well as Poison Idea and Napalm Beach.

In the latter part of the 1980s, Sage fell victim to his own restless nature. He started to experiment with different tones and textures, which made albums like *Land of the Lost* (1986) and *Follow Blind* (1987) interesting departures (though distressing to his devoted fans), but when he finally abandoned Oregon and moved to sunny Arizona, the music as well as the weather turned brighter. As one Wipers follower said, "I don't want to hear Greg Sage in a good mood. I can't even conceive of such a thing." In this instance, a growing contentment resulted in increasingly stagnant records.

Sage, who played what he called his last Wipers show at the North By Northwest (NXNW) festival a few years ago, continues to record and occasionally produce other bands from his Arizona studio. In a strange case of fame preceding fortune, he recently sold his custom left-handed Gibson SG guitar to Seattle's Experience Music Project to hang in its museum, intending to use the money to fund another Wipers CD. Despite spotty releases, the man has nothing left to prove. **JC**

Is This Real?

(1979, PARK AVENUE)
The first and still the best. Rereleased by Sub Pop Records in 1993.

The Young Fresh Fellows

Formed 1983, Seattle, Washington

their song list over the years has included such gems as the theme from *The Love Boat*. There were times when certain band members got so drunk that volunteers from the audience had to physically hold them upright so they could finish their set. Guitarist and vocalist Scott McCaughey once took the stage with a loaded deli tray taped to his head. After a few years of this, it began to bug the Young Fresh Fellows that no one seemed to take them seriously.

"The whole rock star thing is really ridiculous, so we would poke fun at that all the time," says Jim Sangster. "I think in the end we might have done it too much. 'Wacky' and 'zany' are two words we never want to hear again." Their wacky antics and zany lyrics do tend to distract from the Fellows' musicianship; they've never gotten the credit they deserve for their instrumental chops.

This doesn't mean they weren't popular. Throughout the 1980s, the Young Fresh Fellows ruled what was then a thriving power pop scene, and they remain one of the only major Seattle bands to emerge from the hype explosion unscathed.

Like many bands, the Fellows began as a group of rabid fans of music who also happened to play it now and then. McCaughey, Chuck Carroll, and Tad Hutchison recorded *Fabulous Sounds of the Pacific Northwest* over the summer of 1983 at their friend Conrad Uno's 8-track studio. Uno originally formed PopLlama Products for the sole purpose of putting out that album. When the record drew unexpected attention from the press and college radio stations, the Fellows decided to make the band permanent and added Sangster on bass. Their early music followed the tradition of mid-1960s garage bands, and the Fellows dressed the part. Scott had a multicolored medieval robe. Their stage shows paid tribute to 1960s music and mocked it at the same time.

In 1987 they released *The Men Who Loved Music*, which signaled a clothing change—the Fellows now wore purple graduation gowns. More important, the album

I Was a Pop Outcast in Sub Pop Seattle (Or Was I?)

In 1986 Seattle had not yet become the world capital of grunge, but it was about to. Two seemingly unrelated events occurred that year: *Sub Pop 100* was released, and I moved to Seattle from the northern hinterland of Bellingham, Washington.

Okay, those two events were entirely unrelated.

However, I came to Seattle for music, and music I got. I joined a crappy pop band, the Elements (not to say they were crappy in general, but they were when I was with them), and played all the usual haunts. The Hall of Fame, the Ditto, even a crowd at the Bumbershoot festival fell under our musical spell—or maybe not. Still, it was fun at the time, and I was playing pop music.

Working in a local record store, I did a lot of hard time stapling Green River promotional slicks to the walls and stocking Mudhoney LPs, but there was also an excellent opportunity to propel *Get the Knack* (the album that brought the world "My Sharona") into the store's Top 10 through in-store play ("Damn, that *was* a pretty good album, wasn't it," was the usual customer refrain). A lot of stuff I would not have otherwise listened to passed over the transom as well.

At night I'd do the same as any other young slacker in Seattle—head out to the clubs. While the next five or six years were a heyday for bands that claimed they couldn't possibly be classified as grunge (even though they actually were), there was a load of poppy goodness to be found. Chemistry Set, Pure Joy, Green Pajamas, Dharma Bums, and more fell under my loose definition of pop.

The popsters were hardly shunned by reigning Sub Pop Records, either. The Posies' Ken Stringfellow sat in from time to time with Mudhoney, and the Young Fresh Fellows often were visited by various scenesters. (A performance of the Sonics' "The Witch" with Tad Doyle at the Center on Contemporary Art stands out.)

The bands did have this . . . fratboy problem, though. In fact, probably the worst part of being a pophead in the late 1980s was having to deal with fifty "brothers" faux-moshing and calling for "Amy Grant" and "Beer Money" between every Fellows number.

Time went by, I joined a good, if slightly less poppy band (Bootleg Howdah—of course you never heard of us—we played a lot of gigs, then flamed out like a good band should), and worked at a second record store. This time I moved lots of English imports and way too many copies of "Doctorin' the Tardis." Then financial reality hit, and I got a "real" job at about the time the scene as we knew it began to peter out, on the cusp of the 1990s.

This bit of synchronicity was once again unrelated, although I'd like to claim responsibility.

—Michael Cox

featured "Amy Grant," a lustful tribute to America's favorite Christian pop singer. Grant turned out to be a good sport about it, but the song did nothing to dispel the Fellows' image as a joke band, especially after it became a nationwide college radio hit.

Grasping for a new image, the Fellows released *Totally Lost* (1988, Frontier), a straightforward rock album with fewer self-consciously jokey moments than any of their others so far. The album was difficult to record; it was the first album they had done outside of Conrad Uno's Egg Studios, and trying to be serious had taken its toll on the band members' nerves.

For their next release McCaughey wanted to book some time at Egg Studios, get drunk, and pound out a bunch of garage rock songs just for fun. Carroll thought it was a terrible idea and didn't show up. The other three band members recorded the *Beans and Tolerance* "bootleg" LP (1989) in a single day under the name *3 French Fellows 3*, and "ended up spending the night at Egg passed out under the mixing board," recalls Sangster. Carroll left the band shortly afterward. Fastbacks guitarist Kurt Bloch, a local punk rock veteran known for his over-the-top metal riffs, soon stepped in as his replacement.

Adding Bloch signaled a change in musical direction for the Fellows, who began to incorporate more punk rock crunch and less country twang. This influence is apparent on their next LP, *Electric Bird Digest* (1991, Frontier), recorded with Butch Vig. At that time, Vig was best known for his work with Killdozer and Urge Overkill, but he couldn't stop talking about the young Northwest band he had just gotten through recording, Nirvana.

Unable to decide what single sound they wanted for their next domestic release, the Fellows ended up recording *It's Low Beat Time* (1992, Frontier) at five different studios in Seattle, Memphis, and Madison, Wisconsin. Hutchison's inexplicable passion for cheesy mid-1960s instrumental twist records led the Fellows to Memphis to seek out the producer of the records, Willie Mitchell, best known for his work with Al Green and other 1970s soul artists. The band laid down some tracks at a nearby studio where ex–Flaming Groovie Roy Loney hung out. From there they traveled to Madison and recorded more tracks with Vig; then, back in Seattle, they recorded some more at Egg Studios with Uno. And because they're all big Northwest garage rock fans, they tracked down Kearney Barton, the original producer of the Sonics, the Wailers, and Paul Revere and the Raiders, and recorded live to 2-track for that classic, raw Sonics sound. The results of all this are uneven, but at least the Fellows can never be accused of letting themselves get in a rut.

These days the Young Fresh Fellows are on hiatus. Bloch continues to play with the Fastbacks. McCaughey toured with R.E.M. as their guest guitarist and then went on to form the Minus 5 with R.E.M.'s Peter Buck. Sangster plays in the Picketts, a country and western alternative band. **DA**

The Men Who Loved Music

(1987, PopLlama/Frontier)
This record would be annoyingly clever if it didn't rock so hard. Contains "Amy Grant" and lots more lovable stuff.

It's Low Beat Time

(1992, Frontier)
From space-age bachelor pad to garage rock trash, this CD is all over the place. For the most part, it's worth the journey.

Zeke

reinventing punk rock is always a capital idea. Zeke may be exhibit 9,000 in this category, but there's no question these ratboys gave Seattle a jolt when they emerged in the waning days of arena grunge rock. Playing speedy thrash numbers, Zeke capitalized on wild live shows and an excellent twenty-song debut CD, *Super Sound Racing* (1994), with All's Stephon Egerton and Bill Stevenson producing. Zeke's original lineup—the creatively self-named Blind Marky Felchtone on guitar and most vocals, Dizzy Lee Roth on bass and "singing," and drummer Donny Paycheck—dished up tunes about cars ("Holley 750," "Hemicuda"), altered states ("West Seattle Acid Party," "Schmidt Value Pack"), and sheer hostility (most everything else). On the follow-up, *Flat Tracker* (1996, their second release on the Seattle independent label Scootch Pooch), Roth was gone, the band was a four-piece with two guitarists, and the topic of the day was motorcycles. The new members were Mark Pierce on bass and Abe Zanuel Riggs III on guitar.

The best of Zeke was yet to come, however. The band signed to Epitaph and went into the studio with Seattle producer Jack Endino. The result, *Kicked in the Teeth* (1998), had the same shake-the-house intensity of their earlier work, but with a clearer vocal mix and the best bass/drums sound yet. You still can't understand what Felchtone is saying half the time, but that's part of the fun. When the band isn't calling for a revolution (twice, on "Revolution" and "Revolution Reprise," which oddly enough are two completely different songs), it's up to no good with tunes like "Kicked in the Teeth" and "Zeke You." Shades of *Super Sound Racing*'s "Highway Star," the band pulls off a note-for-note cover of the Kiss classic "Shout It Out Loud." **JB**

Kicked in the Teeth

(1998, EPITAPH)
The record that forced *Seattle* magazine to choose them as Coffeetown's next big band. Inspirational line: "Ride with Zeke / The future's uncertain and bleak."

Jazz

NORTHWEST JAZZ

Jazz

azz is music of the city, which explains why this section focuses on Seattle and Portland, with only a few excursions elsewhere in the two-state area. Of course, there are factors beyond concentrations of cars and office buildings—Seattle has excellent jazz professor/performers at the University of Washington and the Cornish College of the Arts. Consequently, the area is a haven for young musicians, exhibiting a range of talents from the avant-garde acts at Seattle's intimate Other Sounds performances to the region's hottest young traditionalists, the Marriott Jazz Quintet. And due to the work of pianist Barney McClure and saxman Bud Shank, little Port Townsend on Washington's Olympic Peninsula has become the third capital of Northwest jazz, hosting a popular yearly jazz festival and several major workshops.

We've brought along a piece of the region's jazz history in Seattle writer Norm Bobrow. In an attempt to establish the genre's legitimacy as high art, he staged the city's first concert hall jazz performances starting in 1939, including a legendary 1940 show by the Lionel Hampton Trio and Fats Waller's first American concert in 1941. In the mid-1950s, Seattle jazz lovers trekked to Bobrow's Colony, a downtown dine-and-dance club whose house band was fronted by singer Pat Suzuki, soon afterwards to earn fame on Broadway in the musical *Flower Drum Song*. Most of the modern and avant-garde jazz artists are profiled by noted Northwest jazz writer Andrew Bartlett, whose work has appeared in many local, regional, and national publications.

As in all sections of this book, the artists profiled were selected by the writers, with attention paid to general popularity, historical importance, and impact on their musical peers. Norm Bobrow lamented the limited number of profiles, saying "There are at least fifty worthy jazz musicians in the Seattle area," but he agreed to perform "this impossible task of exclusion" by choosing only musicians who function as group leaders. (For an example of the region's plethora of great sidemen, note how often the name of bassist Phil Sparks appears in the following pages.)

The Northwest's contributions to jazz have been great, from underrated innovators (Portland tenor sax player Jim Pepper) to international stars (singer Ernestine Anderson); from noted transplants (the aforementioned McClure and Shank) to local kids made good (bandleader-turned-producer Quincy Jones). Jazz is the soundtrack of the region, whether heard at the biggest Port Townsend festival or the smallest Portland jazz club. The Northwest is home to one of the country's largest concentrations of jazz listeners. Sit back and enjoy the music.

Clarence Acox

I t's not a palpable stretch to liken Clarence Acox to Wynton Marsalis in his role as developer and encourager of young jazz talent. As chairman of the music department and, for the past twenty-seven years, director of bands, Acox has built the national reputation of Seattle's Garfield High School as a center of teenage jazz education. The school's jazz bands have become a year-in, year-out treat wherever their travels have taken them, and in competitions on jazz bandstands in foreign countries they've invariably brought home the gold.

Acox is also one hell of a big band drummer. As a regular on the club scene, he is the drummer of choice for visiting celebrity artists: Benny Carter, Charles Brown, Hank Crawford, Diane Schuur, Marlena Shaw, the great Ernestine Anderson, and the late Billy Eckstine, among others. As a teacher and player, Acox sticks to the fundamentals of classic jazz drumming in constant homage to the masters who shaped his taste and big band style.

Acox was born in New Orleans in 1947, and no jazzman from there ever severs his roots. At Garfield, coincidentally, his almost-next-door neighbor is fellow Louisiana transplant Robert Knatt, who works with younger jazz students at Washington Middle School (most of whom continue their jazz education at Garfield). Just in the 1997–99 school years, Acox's Garfield Big Band won competitions at the Lionel Hampton Jazz Festival in Idaho, the Reno Jazz Festival, Oregon's Mount Hood Jazz Festival, and the Northwest Invitational Jazz Band Festival in Fullerton, California. Overseas, the Garfield group won standing ovations at Switzerland's Montreux Jazz Festival and at festivals in Amsterdam, Paris, and Luxembourg. Garfield's jazz programs under Acox are as much a source of school pride as the school's renowned Bulldog basketball teams.

Lamenting the cul-de-sac of diminishing career opportunities that brilliant young jazz musicians face, Acox takes pride in influencing many graduates to take their education to the next level. One, Clark Gayton of the illustrious Seattle Gaytons (father Carver and uncle Gary), is a "trombone monster" working out of New York. "Sting took Clark on tour, where he was probably the highest-paid trombonist ever," says Acox. "Like I say, rock stars make the money, jazz stars make the music. Clark's doing both."

Despite Acox's reputation as a no-frills backup musician, on his two solo CDs he exhibits drum subtleties appropriate to small groups, such as his own recording sextets, and displays perhaps the most creative of his talents—as a composer. Unlike so many, if not most, of today's self-styled writers in the various jazz idioms, Acox's compositions are original and retainable. Johnny Mercer, if he were still around, would fancy putting lyrics to several Acox melodies that course through more than a dozen tracks of his two CDs. Rather than write for a fixed number (a quintet or sextet), Acox uses musicians "as needed" for each of his compositions. From a collection of five or six hired for a studio session, he'll muster a few trios and a couple of quartets, as well as using his full complement. Live and swinging with the famous Floyd Standifer Quartet, Acox anchors the Standifer rhythm session with bassist Phil Sparks and pianist Billy Wallace during the group's regular Wednesday night gig at the New Orleans club in Seattle's Pioneer Square. (Standifer, by the way, cites his solos on Acox's CDs *Joanna's Dance* (1995, CAM) and *Indigenous Groove* (1997, CAM) as some of his own best work.)

A new source of excitement for Acox is his role as player and cofounder (with Michael Brockman) of the Seattle Repertory Jazz Orchestra. With the pick of Seattle-area musicians, the orchestra focuses on specific periods of time in America's big band history—such as "New York 1935 to 1945" or, more recently, "Monk and Mingus." In the excellent acoustical setting of the Broadway Performance Hall in Seattle's Capitol Hill neighborhood, the orchestra's concerts have been sellouts. **NB**

Joanna's Dance

(1995, CAM)
Almost exclusively comprising lyrical compositions by Acox, this album and its successor, 1997's *Indigenous Groove*, features a variety of small groups constituting the Clarence Acox Sextet.

Ernestine Anderson

assigned to review a jazz concert in 1947, *Seattle Post-Intelligencer* music writer Joe Miller took issue with the remarks of the enthusiastic emcee about a young singer named Ernestine Anderson. "It was a great concert," he wrote, "and the singer certainly sounds as though she may have a future, but to call her 'another Ella Fitzgerald?' Well, that really seemed a bit much."

Ernestine Anderson had just turned 18 and, in the glow of a reception that prompted five encores (which fully spent her repertoire at the time), probably didn't mind any comment that placed her name in conjunction with that day's jazz goddess, La Fitzgerald. After that 1947 performance at Seattle's Metropolitan Theater (since become the main entrance to the Four Seasons Hotel), the slender whisp of a teenager blossomed into one of a handful of jazz singers who have attracted massive audiences beyond the confines of jazz.

Anderson was born in Houston, November 11, 1928, into a musical family. As a preteenager, she joined her father and grandmother singing gospel music. At age 12 she entered a talent contest and so impressed trumpeter Russell Jacquet that he gave her a chance to sing with his band. When Anderson turned 18 and was legally old enough to travel, she left Seattle to tour with the Johnny Otis band, then a major name in the world of big band swing. She joined Lionel Hampton's orchestra in 1952 and settled in New York the following year. A saxophonist named GiGi Gryce recorded her in 1955 and, as a result of that exposure, she was taken on a Scandinavian tour (where her instantly adoring Swedish fans nicknamed her "Stina").

1958 and 1959 were Anderson's breakthrough years. Through Mercury Records executive producer Quincy Jones, her first album, *Hot Cargo* was released in 1956. At her first Monterey Jazz Festival appearance, she was named Best New Vocal Star in *Down Beat*'s 1959 Critics' Poll, and the singer delivered a command performance at the White House for President Eisenhower.

After living a few years in Europe in the mid-1960s, Anderson returned home and went into semiretirement. It was bassist Ray Brown who in 1976 urged her to resume her career. She signed with Concord Records, and has made some twenty recordings for the label, two of which, *Never Make Your Move Too Soon* (1981) (whose 10-minute title track is her favorite closing number) and *Big City* (1983), received Grammy nominations—as did *Now and Then* (1994, Qwest).

In the summer of 1998, the year she turned 70, Anderson released *Isn't It Romantic?*, the latest of more than thirty albums and clearly one of her most exquisite performances. Her friend and onetime Garfield High School classmate Quincy Jones has described her voice as sounding "like honey at dusk."

Although Anderson belongs to the world now, she regularly returns to her Seattle roots, and accepts regular invitations to all the major regional festivals. She's also received international invitations, appearing at the jazz festivals in Bern, Switzerland (1994), in Ottawa, Canada (1994), and São Paulo, Brazil (1996). Other recent major performances have included the Seattle Symphony Orchestra's "Tribute to Gershwin" (1994), "A Salute to Lionel Hampton" at Kennedy Center for the Performing arts, Washington, D. C. (1995), and "A Tribute to Ella" in Carnegie Hall, New York (1996).

Perhaps Anderson has invited the qualified praise she has received throughout her career. Unlike the other three who make up the most successful foursome of jazz singers (Ella Fitzgerald, Sarah Vaughan, and Carmen McRae, all of whom she admires), Anderson has gone it relatively alone in her career. Even when she's visited the major centers for music promotions-Los Angeles and New York-she's made only short stops, always heading back to the Northwest to be with her family.

Anderson was one of seventy-five women profiled in the book *I Dream a World: Portraits of Black Women Who Changed America* (1989), by Pulitzer Prize–winning photojournalist Brian Lanker—together with Rosa Parks, Leontyne Price, Barbara Jordan, and Toni Morrison. With an impish, often devilish sense of humor, Anderson betrays a certain secret fabric that makes her as a singer the most fascinating of them all.

And, then there's her latest record, with the extraordinarily compatible Netherlands Metropole Orchestra, *Isn't It Romantic?* Indeed it is. **NB**

Live from Concord to London

Live from Concord to London

(1978, Concord)
Includes tracks from Ernestine Anderson's legendary appearance at the Concord Jazz Festival and at Ronnie Scott's in London.

Isn't It Romantic?

(1998, Koch Jazz)
There may be some who wouldn't think Ernestine Anderson singing Rodgers and Hart and Sammy Cahn accompanied by sixty-two members of the Netherlands Metropole Orchestra could deliver a five-star gem. But this CD somehow captures a special side of the singer—a warm, unadorned simplicity, an enrapturing treatment of superb songs in a manner that would delight their composers.

Billy Tipton Memorial Saxophone Quartet

In perfect harmony, you might say, with the big band traditions set by the Count Basie and Duke Ellington Orchestras, where the ensembles continued playing long after their namesakes passed away, the Billy Tipton Memorial Saxophone Quartet has lived through cycles of members. Fitting, this fact, because the all-female quartet is named for the now-famed Billy Tipton, a woman legendary for passing as a male big-band saxophonist for years. Fitting also because rather than set themselves up as a mere tribute outfit to either Tipton or any element of ages past, the quartet has fostered a simultaneously clear and expandable identity.

Formed in late 1988 by Amy Denio, Marjorie de Muynck, Babs Helle, and Stacy Loebs, the group toiled in the fairly fluid musical scene of the Seattle area for years before reaching the international stature they now enjoy. Because of Denio's ties to the art-punk Tone Dogs, the quartet drew from various crowds, bringing punks and art scenesters to their shows, each of which combined the avant-garde material listeners came to expect from all-saxophone groups in the 1970s and 1980s with a great many Eastern European elements. The band's mix was immediately kinetic, without dropping the more cerebral, abstract possibilities of combining four reed instruments. Their debut CD, *Saxhouse*, was released by the estimable Knitting Factory Records to near-unanimous critical acclaim. Containing the *Bus Horn Concerto*, the CD caught on tape one of the best displays of the quartet's grasp, a modular performance in which band members, stationed on top of a city bus, played concerto movements while bus sounds (horns, opening doors, stop bells) punctuated the performance.

The Tiptons quickly found a niche for themselves, garnering grants from state arts commissions, the National Endowment for the Arts (for the Goodwill Games in 1990), Seattle Metro Transit, and, later, from Artslink International for a trip to

Tallinn, Estonia, to perform and record with Ne Zhdali, a similarly difficult to pigeonhole art-jazz-punk ensemble. The quartet's recording since the 1994 debut has been a tad sporadic, offering only *Make It Funky God* (Horn Hut), a brief 1995 follow-up to *Saxhouse*, and the explosively creative *Box* (1996) on New World Records. Since the mid-1990s, the band has undergone numerous personnel changes.

Alto and tenor saxist Jessica Lurie, who joined in 1992, has taken on a strong leadership role in the group, allowing both of her other ensembles, Living Daylights and BOLT, to develop mutually with the Tiptons' exploration of rhythmic, pulsing Eastern-flavored music. Preceding Lurie, Barbara Marino joined the band on baritone saxophone. Marino's background is exceptionally strong in rock, folk, and jazz circles, and she boasts an extended period with Melissa Etheridge and the Indigo Girls. Later in the 1990s, cofounder Amy Denio left to focus on her proliferating solo and group-related projects—the (EC) Nudes, an opera, and international performances. Annelise Zanula replaced Denio, bringing to the Northwest her healthy experience in playing the music of Duke Ellington, Fats Waller, and Fletcher Henderson and in cofounding the group After the End of the World Coretet. Her big band chops have lent the quartet a wider orchestral palette. In 1997 Sue Orfield joined on soprano and tenor saxophones, having studied in the Midwest and performed with Clark Terry, Dizzy Gillespie, and Bo Diddley. But the addition of drummer Pam Barger is what helped propel the group into a new creative era. Once a guest in live sets, Barger joined the group in the mid-1990s and now supplies new rhythmic force.

There are precious few all-saxophone ensembles in any country plying their trade away from the concert music repertoire. The Billy Tipton Memorial Saxophone Quartet ranks easily with World Saxophone Quartet, ROVA, and others in North America and Europe. As of early 1999 the group was recording a CD of new material. **AB**

Michael Bisio

On every list of the best Northwest jazz recordings, bassist Michael Bisio's name crops up. Of the six CDs ranked "Best of" by Seattle's *Earshot Jazz* magazine in September 1998, for instance, two were Bisio's recordings and a third featured his bass. Hailing from Troy, New York, Bisio came west to Seattle in 1976 to attend the University of Washington. He studied with James Harnett, then a bassist with the Seattle Symphony Orchestra, and performed in William O. Smith's Contemporary Group, which fused improvisation with postclassical new music. His classical training led Bisio to a level of reading proficiency that made him a quick "first call" player for numerous concert music organizations. After graduating from the University of Washington, he studied and toured with the Northwest Chamber Orchestra, the Seattle Symphony, and the Pacific Northwest Ballet, among other units.

As the Seattle jazz scene heated up in the 1980s, Bisio was present, front and center, egging it on. The scene welcomed avant-garde innovations and adventurous

Jazzy City

When I moved back to Seattle in the mid-1990s after seven years in New York, I was immediately struck by one thing: this sure is a jazzy little town. Despite the fact that New York is the jazz capital of the world—home to, oh, 90 percent of the world's great jazz players—I almost never *heard* jazz unless I specifically went out to *see* jazz at a *jazz club*. The average bar, cafe, or deli never had jazz playing. It was all club music or greatest hits of the 1950s, 1960s, and 1970s. Only in movies made by French directors can jazz be heard accompanying daily life in New York.

But here in Seattle, jazz is everywhere. I have a few vivid memories of my first months back: pulling up at a little Middle Eastern deli in my neighborhood one afternoon and finding, as I walked in, that they were tuned into the same local jazz station—and blasting the same McCoy Tyner solo—that I'd been enjoying in the car. Aaah. Another time I remember sitting on one of the downtown piers and digging the sound of Mose Allison as it drifted from the outdoor speakers of Elliott's Oyster House. Maybe it seems like nothing to you, but in seven years in New York, during which I was subjected to all manner of awful music in East Village cafes and Upper East Side pickup bars, I never once heard Mose Allison coming from any public speaker anywhere.

Here in Seattle, jazz is inescapable. It provides the just-audible background to nearly every commercial establishment I set foot in, and it seems to be on the CD player at every social gathering I attend. But as a result, the music is now, finally, starting to get on my nerves. Jazz is so much the automatic soundtrack to a certain comfortably affluent Northwest lifestyle that the overexposure is sapping all its meaning.

Now that my beloved 1960s Blue Note records have become just another marketing tool for pushing Starbucks coffee, and now that I'm constantly hearing these same records inside the plush locker room of the Seattle Athletic Club, the music has really started to lose its guts—and, even worse, become a reminder of the loss of my own.

—Mark D. Fefer

talents, both of which suited Bisio. He worked on trumpeter Barbara Donald's vaunted *The Past and Tomorrows* (1993, Cadence Jazz). Donald, who had been a strong force outside the mainstream in the late 1960s with her improvising partner Sonny Simmons, brought Bisio to new levels of performance. His work was spreading to other Northwest jazzers: pianist Bob Nell, trumpeter Jack Walrath, and reeds maestro Bert Wilson all looked to Bisio in creating a fresh jazz language that interjected avant-garde notions of tonal and rhythmic freedom into a strong bank of postbop notions, which were routed through soulful, rich playing best exemplified by Charles Mingus's music.

Bisio's celebrated debut album, *Ours* (1983, CT), laid the groundwork for the rest of the 1980s. Recorded with Nell on piano, the record was surprisingly strong in rhythmic drive and melodic power, winning acclaim from critics across the country. In 1987 his 1-year-old quartet drew upon the strengths of *Ours*, bringing saxophonist Rick Mandyck and trumpeter Ron Soderstrom in for a more loose-limbed,

Ornette Coleman–inspired CD. This release, *In Seattle* (Silkheart), also won acclaim and a place on many critics' Top 10 lists. Bisio's presence on the scene in the late 1980s waned, but only until he began playing first with Buddy Catlett and then with newly transplanted pianist Wayne Horvitz. In short order, he was on tour with tenor sax firebrand Charles Gayle, who is said to have proclaimed Bisio his favorite bassist.

Bisio's next group turned back to pianist Nell and also included Portland-based trumpeter Rob Blakeslee, violinist Eyvind Kang, and drummer Ed Pias. In 1996 the Michael Bisio Quintet released *Covert Choreography* (Cadence), which later won a Golden Ear Award from Earshot Jazz for Best Northwest Jazz Recording of the year. Within a year, Bisio and Joe McPhee, multi-instrumentalist and free jazz founding father, were touring the East Coast and recording their intimate, far-reaching series of duets on *Finger Wigglers* (Creative Improvised Music Projects). A follow-up CD is expected in 1999. He has also won two grants to compose and record new works. Bisio is an adept performer at all levels, from his blistering solo barrages to his more intricate larger ensemble work. **AB**

In Seattle

(1987, SILKHEART)
In Seattle has the distinction of being Michael Bisio's inarguably finest statement. His quartet (with the esteemed Rick Mandyck on tenor saxophone and Ron Soderstrom on trumpet) revolves limberly around his bass playing, even on the tunes Bisio did not himself compose. The music steps roundly up to the "free bop" plate, hammering when the energy is high and hibernating in sonic forests when the energy turns slower.

Covert Choreography

(1996, CADENCE)
Because it's so readily available—and because it's so damn fine—*Covert Choreography* is the place to start with Michael Bisio's recordings. The large composition is long, but not so long that it does anything but continually impress with its richness of contours and depth of execution.

Rob Blakeslee

Of the jazz-inclined natives of Portland, Rob Blakeslee stands out for his keenly developed compositional and improvisational languages. A trumpeter since he was 9 years old, Blakeslee began playing professionally while in college and by 1971 was on the road, where he remained almost continuously for the next dozen years.

Blakeslee's touring days were spent playing a variety of circuits, from musical shows to more extensive engagements with Top 40 and R&B ensembles. By 1983 Blakeslee had settled in Dallas, Texas, where he made serious progress in the city's avant-garde jazz and new-music scenes. He started performing with fellow trumpeter Dennis Gonzales and the Dallas Association for Avant-Garde and Neo-Impressionistic Music; their work culminated in a theoretical big band and short-lived record label, both called "daagnim." In addition, Gonzales enlisted Blakeslee to record as part of his Dallas-London Sextet on the thrilling *Catechism* (Music and Arts), reissued in 1996.

Blakeslee's rich tone and improvisational patience energized *Catechism*'s frequently languid, free-leaning performances, explaining in part his importance to the Dallas avant-garde jazz scene. With *Bitches Brew*–era Miles Davis and avant-garde jazz pioneers Don Cherry and Bill Dixon as key influences, Blakeslee cultivated a midregister range and tonally explorative aesthetic that reflected the "neo-impressionistic" portion of the Dallas collective's name. Blakeslee's influences are rolled into a playing approach that seeks a clarity of sound over and above exactness of notes, harmonic structures, or rhythmic speed. And these qualities certainly struck saxophonist Vinny Golia, who met Blakeslee in the mid-1980s at a gig in Austin, Texas. Blakeslee and Golia's relationship has been vital since 1988, when the trumpeter returned to Portland to take a position as director of the Oregon State University jazz program. In recent years, the two have worked together as part of Golia's quintet, in Blakeslee's groups, and in other contexts.

Having forsworn extensive touring since the early 1980s, Blakeslee returned to Oregon to settle. But his composing, playing, recording, and performing have all continued at what seems an accelerated pace. Blakeslee's musical kinship with Golia has led to wonderfully creative results for both artists. Golia, who owns Nine Winds Records, has helped invigorate the avant-garde jazz and music scene in his hometown of Los Angeles. He has also enlisted Blakeslee's pliant trumpet for a host of recordings and even more live performances. Furthermore, Golia has released Blakeslee's three stellar CDs on Nine Winds.

What the music consistently shows is that Blakeslee is in the first order of creative trumpeters, focusing steadily on his compositions as they serve to investigate both jazz band interactions and the intricacies of extended improvisation. He has performed with a host of marquee avant-garde jazz talents, including Andrew Hill, Oliver Lake, John Carter, Marty Ehrlich, and Anthony Braxton. For his part, he composes music that is unerringly patient, often striking out far away from exact tempos and stretching into wide-open sonic spaces. Blakeslee has taken his groups—mainly a quintet and a quartet—throughout the Pacific and Southwest regions of the United States. Their performances at the du Maurier International Jazz Festival in Vancouver, British Columbia, have won critical accolades. He has recorded for labels such as Nine Winds, Music and Arts, daagnim, Black Saint, and Cadence. **AB**

Lifeline

(1992, NINE WINDS)

Rob Blakeslee dedicated this CD to the late pianist Richard Grossman, and the performances brim with Grossman's energy. Though things develop slowly and with consummate explorative inquisition, Blakeslee creates territories of excitement that jump in surprising clusters. This is spectacular jazz, humble and yet fully engaged.

Long Narrows

(1994, NINE WINDS)

For those seeking another revealing glimpse at Rob Blakeslee's accomplished composition and group-leading improvisations, his *Long Narrows* has lasting impact. The tunes are all taken leisurely, evincing Blakeslee's musical identification with wide-open landscapes. His tone is big and merits the extra space these tunes allow. Pianist Tad Weed's contributions will make jazz listeners yearn to see more of his recordings in the marketplace.

Jack Brownlow

t he emergence of the user-friendly CD format allows us to learn significantly more about an artist than we'd otherwise ever know. This is especially true in jazz, which the daily press virtually ignores. The biographical notes provided by one of jazz's noteworthy historians, the highly regarded journalist Doug Ramsey, are a major bonus on Jack Brownlow's first CD, *Dark Dance* (1996). Ramsey prefaces his bountiful comments by saying, "These notes are informed not by objectivity and dispassionate analysis, but by friendship, admiration, and joy. The joy will be shared by hundreds of Jack Brownlow's friends, fellow musicians, students, and admirers who for decades have been urging him to record." The result of this encouragement, *Dark Dance* features twelve tunes and two rhythm sections divided between two supporting pairs: bassist Andy Zadrozny and drummer Marty Tuttle (son of David Tuttle, the distinguished trombonist and Latin percussionist), and bassist Clipper Anderson and drummer Mark Ivester.

The CD may be recent, but anyone who's dined at Seattle's luxurious Canlis restaurant since 1965 knows of Brownlow. His piano has lured music lovers back again and again (pianist and bandleader George Shearing and composer Alan Hovhaness went frequently to hear his piano at Canlis). Brownlow is a rare jazzman whose music somehow transcends an atmosphere that one might expect would restrict creativity. Brownlow suffers no such restraints, and people love him for it wherever he plays.

Wenatchee, the Central Washington city where Brownlow lived from the age of 10, never had a sufficient population to be a jazz center, but it did produce three memorables: Brownlow, Ramsey (mentioned above), and the legendary Don Lanphere. Brownlow's natural gifts might have emerged without his year and a half of study under Wenatchee's outstanding piano teacher, Eleanor Scott, but he credits her as a significant early influence. It was during his high school days that he acquired the nickname "Bruno," when the little girl next door who liked to visit him but couldn't pronounce "Brownlow" would ask, "Could I see Mr. Bruno?"

Brownlow joined the Navy during World War II, playing in bands at the Farragut Naval Base in Idaho, where he distinguished himself with his impressive ability to play any song in any key. During a jam session, trumpet player Ray Blagof suggested a Harry James tune, "I Had the Craziest Dream." He asked to play it in E, like the original recording, and Brownlow accommodated the unusual key. Only later did he tell the trumpet player, "Harry James recorded that tune in E-flat [a more common key]. Your turntable must have been running fast." Blagof, later a lead trumpet man in Hollywood, frequently told this story to attest to the phenomenal musical ear of this piano player from Wenatchee.

Brownlow's career as a traveling jazzman was fairly short. A regular at the famous Kansas City club Tootie's Mayfair, he relocated to Los Angeles to play in Anson Weeks's dance band (the bandleader's son, bassist Jack Weeks, was Brownlow's good friend). In the following year, he played several high-profile substitute gigs, including appearances with the quartet of tenor sax giant Lester Young (subbing for legendary pianist Dodo Marmarosa) and with Boyd Raeburn's big band, a group still remembered for its intricate arrangements.

Brownlow left Los Angeles in 1946 to join his father, Ty, in the printing business in Wenatchee. But he continued to study and perform music in Eastern Washington before moving to Seattle and returning to music full time with his regular gig at Canlis.

A penchant for sharing is a significant factor in a total appraisal of Jack "Bruno" Brownlow. His generosity has figured in his teaching—both formal and informal—and his special influence on singers. Many of Seattle's best young jazz talents have studied with him or visited his home for casual sessions. Recently a singer by the name of Kat performed with Brownlow on the local jazz station KPLU. Her repertoire of tunes—all of them written well before she was born and largely offbeat—reflected the obvious influence of the man at the piano.

As Paul Desmond, the alto-playing mainstay of the Dave Brubeck Quartet, said after working with Brownlow the first of many times: "If I played piano, that's how I'd want to play it." **NB**

Dark Dance

(1996, BRUNO)
Jack Brownlow's music finally appears on CD, with help from several noted Seattle jazz players.

Jay Clayton

ince her arrival in Seattle, vocalist Jay Clayton has been known mainly as a jazz singer and a professor at Cornish College of the Arts. Her jazz recordings, however, have attested to her jazz chops and her far more varied background. Clayton began performing on the New York music scene around 1963. She was an important presence in an era when jazz vocalists were fast becoming stultified signalers of historical genres while the "new thing" (the 1960s name for free jazz) was sweeping the music into the civil rights era's second decade.

But Clayton was hardly just another jazz singer. She was widely revered, often by composers whose works were being developed on the avant-garde music scene—peripheral to jazz and most other genres but drawing audiences from almost every musical style imaginable. Using her voice as an instrument, Clayton developed methods for shockingly fresh improvisations, taking timbral liberties as well as elongating or collapsing lyrical structures into wordless sounds.

Clayton performed compositions that delved far into the new music world. The godfather of the postclassical avant-garde, John Cage, enlisted her to perform—and later record—his works, as did Philip Glass and Steve Reich. Her vocal style suited a kind of panstylistic vanguard. Frequently eschewing words altogether, she instead intoned with instrumental pitches, whether improvising lines with horn players or singing scripted parts. The heralded singer landed teaching jobs at New York City College, the Banff Centre (Canada's celebrated bastion of vanguard musical exploration), the Bud Shank Jazz Workshop on Washington's Olympic Peninsula, and the Naropa Institute in Boulder, Colorado. Clayton's wide-ranging abilities, not surprisingly, are also keenly appreciated by European audiences, and she has taught in Cologne, Berlin, Munich, and Austria. These teaching positions have been bolstered by public performances throughout the Northwest that highlight Clayton's students and her work with other regional jazz luminaries. Working diligently to develop her students' careers, she expends considerable energy to teach young performers about the musical profession.

Clayton's recorded music is spread across a variety of composers. Her work with Vocal Summit, a supergroup consisting of Urszula Dudziak, Norma Winstone, and Michele Hendricks, bristles with an energy that peels away any resistance to vocal-driven improvisation. Vocal Summit is one of only a few first-class groups in the Northwest to rely on the voice as the prime instrument. In her work with Klaus Konig on *Song of Songs* (1994, Enja), Clayton jousts with British free improvising vocalist Phil Minton and the Montreal Jubilation Gospel Choir. Her floating, atmospheric work with Steve Reich enriches the composer's *Music for 18 Musicians* (1978, ECM/Nonesuch).

Clayton shines brightest, though, on her own, or at least reasonably close to her own. Her teaching at Cornish focuses trilaterally on improvisation, jazz standards, and electronics, and each of these areas remains a core strength. Her *Live at Jazz*

Alley (1995, ITMP) is splendidly couched in bebop's energies, yet Clayton manages to swallow up segments of the music and dance around them in skittering displays of percussive, entrancing vocals. At one and the same time, Clayton is a skilled avant-gardist and an equally skilled neotraditionalist expanding vocal jazz one small uttered loop at a time. **AB**

Quartett

(1988, NEW ALBION)
Jay Clayton's manipulation of the voice with *Quartett* is a brilliant extension of what her new-music years have brought to bear on her jazz world.

Beautiful Love

(1995, SUNNYSIDE)
A collection of Jay Clayton's lovely, intimate duets with noted pianist Fred Hersch.

Tom Collier

At the age of 9, Tom Collier made a guest appearance on *The Lawrence Welk Show*, wearing a tuxedo while simultaneously tap dancing and playing the marimba. Today, in a not altogether unpredictable career progression, Collier is a permanent lecturer on the history of jazz and the American pop song as director of percussion and jazz studies at the University of Washington.

Born in 1950, Collier teamed up with West Seattle neighbor (and fellow musical prodigy) Dan Dean for vibes-and-guitar duets when both were in their early teens. Known as the Whistling Midgets, the quartet (with Ernie Watts and Don Grusin) earned national attention.

"Percussion" for Tom Collier incorporates a wide variety of drums as well as gadgets, a fact that has won him some extraordinary assignments, such as playing two garbage can lids for a date with Frank Zappa at UCLA's Royce Hall. At the Los Angeles County Museum of Art, Collier wore boxing gloves and "boxed" against a thunder sheet to produce the sounds of a raging storm.

"Vibraphonist/composer" is how he bills himself on his résumé. In the first category, *Los Angeles Times* jazz critic Leonard Feather wrote of him in 1976, "He's so well-equipped that his sleight-of-hand solos are a fascinating study." In 1996, Scott Mercado wrote in *Modern Drummer*, "Tom Collier is one of the best jazz vibraphonists on the planet." As a composer of published works, Collier has won fifteen ASCAP Popular Panel Awards over the last twenty years.

What a loss for local jazz fans that Collier has virtually retired from playing dates, except, on rare occasions, those challenging enough to lure him out of town. His most notable local performances these days are at the University of Washington faculty's annual concert, which features instructor/musicians including Michael Brockman, Marc Seales, the renowned Bill Smith, Doug Miller, and Roy Cummings. Since 1980, Collier has presented more than three hundred jazz concerts in public schools for the Arts in Education program of the Washington State Arts Commission, and in that same year he received the Outstanding Service to Jazz Education Award from the National Association of Jazz Educators.

Although virtually all of Seattle's top jazz musicians have worked with many jazz legends on local dates, Collier's fifteen-page musical résumé is unique in that more than half of his studio and live dates have involved him being singled out and flown to New York or Los Angeles. A few of his employers: Howard Roberts, Cal Tjader, Diane Schuur, Peggy Lee, Herb Ellis, Ernestine Anderson, Natalie Cole, Mannheim Steamroller, Sammy Davis Jr., Barbara Streisand, Johnny Mathis, Olivia Newton-John, the Beach Boys, the Mills Brothers, and Della Reese.

Oh yes, that time he was 9, strutting his stuff on *The Lawrence Welk Show* ... the tune was "The Sheik of Araby." **NB**

Jazz

(1987, WARNER BROS.)
This 1978 Ry Cooder session took almost a decade to get onto CD, but it was worth the wait. Collier is heard on vibes and marimba with Earl "Fatha" Hines on piano.

Virtuoso Guitar

(1990, LASERLIGHT)
Collier's vibes work is prominently featured on this recording by jazz guitarist Laurindo Almeida.

Dee Daniels

She's that statuesque beauty with the four-octave range. She's given command performances for royalty, appeared at international festivals, and recently shattered chandeliers throughout North America, Europe, Africa, Japan, and Hong Kong. She exudes a rare sincerity, taking more interest in you than in herself, a quality that's won her new friends wherever she's traveled.

At the age of 9, Daniels sang her first solo in her father's church in Oakland, California. A talented pianist, she also accompanied the church's three choirs. In college at the University of Montana (working on a degree in art education), she helped found and performed in that school's Black Ensemble Gospel Choir. Moving to the Seattle area in the early 1970s, she took a job as a high school teacher.

Daniels made her first musical mark in the Northwest in 1972, when she joined Dynamite, an established local group. Throughout the 1970s, she was a regular on the Seattle jazz circuit, performing as a soloist and with small groups, though she briefly relocated to Los Angeles in the mid-1970s.

In her performances in Seattle clubs Daniels established herself as an up-and-coming jazz singer. She became such a rage at her regular gig at Anthony's in Bellevue, Washington, that she was given regular air time on KING-TV, which provided Seattleites with an opportunity to see and hear her without having to make reservations weeks in advance. In 1982 Daniels traveled to Europe for a three-month tour that turned into a five-year residency. A special favorite of Scandinavian audiences, Daniels performed for the king and queen of Belgium in 1986 and was twice teamed with jazz legends at the Netherlands' Jazz Inn Party—Ernestine Anderson in 1986 and Sarah Vaughan in 1987. One major success was chronicled by esteemed *Los Angeles Times* critic Leonard Feather, who wrote: "Dee Daniels earned a standing ovation for her offering of soul-fried jazz, first vocally and then at the piano."

Daniels has released several CDs, including *All of Me* (1991, September), and *Close Encounters of the Swingin' Kind* (1991, Timeless). A third recording, *Let's Talk Business* (1993, Capri), shows a remarkable merging of her gospel roots and her adult devotion to jazz. *Let's Talk Business* features a small swinging group with John Clayton, Jeff Clayton, Jeff Hamilton, and Larry Fuller, and runs the gamut from gospel to blues to readings of several jazz classics.

A more recent release, *Wish Me Love* (1996, Mons), was recorded in the Netherlands with the world-class Metropole Orchestra. It displays an extraordinary change of focus, representing her emergence as an unqualified star singer. While celebrating the poignancy of Billie Holiday's "God Bless the Child" and the traditional "Sometimes I Feel Like a Motherless Child," Daniels plants new roots with distinctive, lyrical readings of "Time After Time," "How Long Has This Been Going On," "Our Love Is Here to Stay," and "Here's That Rainy Day."

When not on major tours, Daniels lives with her husband and young daughter in Vancouver, British Columbia, frequently visiting her family in Seattle. She is still a favorite with Seattle audiences, most recently playing Jazz Alley with the Seattle-based big band Roadside Attraction. Her legions of Seattle followers should be proud, knowing, along with the rest of the planet, that Dee Daniels has made it big time, yet has only just begun. **NB**

Wish Me Love

(1996, Mons)
Focusing for the first time on jazz standards, Dee Daniels bears favorable comparison with the most famous of singers who've covered the same territory.

Amy Denio

Since moving to Seattle in 1985, composer, singer, and instrumentalist Amy Denio has seen every facet of her musical career blossom, much of it internationally. A Boston native, Denio began impressing her mentors and teachers at an early age. She was singing in school groups in the Detroit area when she was 10 years old and electing to become an autodidact at 12. By 13, she was scoring through-composed (completely scored without improvisation) music using a variety of rhythmic structures, and beginning in 1976 she was performing professionally. Denio spent time in Dublin—studying Irish revolutionary songs—while in secondary school.

At Hampshire College in Amherst, Massachusetts, she devoted her time to art music composition, writing for stringed instruments and ensembles, prepared piano, and reed instruments. While attending Colorado College for two semesters, Denio developed what she calls "Spoot" music, comprising "active listening and empathetic collaboration." She has used the term and its intended operational aesthetic throughout her music. After graduating from Hampshire in 1983, she composed in earnest for dance and theater companies, founding the multi-instrumental duo the Entropics before moving west to Seattle.

In each case, Denio has melded her intense interest in the dramatic dynamics of performance with the timbral and rhythmic dynamics of the actual music. Denio's voice is often the main instrument, and she has tailored it to be a weave of floating harmonies and witty juxtapositions of tone and execution, using a variety of learned approaches to vocalizing. To this end, Denio received sponsorship from the Jazz India Vocal Institute to study Hindustani vocal techniques with a master instructor in Bombay.

Denio has since toured internationally on a rigorous schedule. She cofounded the Billy Tipton Memorial Saxophone Quartet and played alto saxophone with the group until her departure in 1997. The Tiptons, as they came to be known, shared with Denio's other musical projects an ability to bridge the worlds of art music, alternative rock, and avant-garde jazz, drawing crowds from each scene. In the late 1980s, she collaborated (on bass guitar) with Soundgarden drummer Matt Cameron and Cryptkicker 5 guitarist Chip Doring in the "loud and cute" trio Couch of Sound. Denio was a cofounder of Seattle's angular funk-pop band the Tone Dogs, who mesmerized crowds and fans until the early 1990s. She also cofounded Japanese American avant-rock groups FoMoFlo, the (EC) Nudes, and the Pale Nudes, each of which has spent time touring in North America, Europe, and Japan. Denio further contributed her stylized, singular vocals to the jazz group Curlew's stunning CD *A Beautiful Western Saddle* (1993, Cuneiform). Thus it is that Denio could, on any given night, be found in a punk rock club, a more folk-oriented venue, or at Seattle's Westlake Center mall, where she premiered "Hurry Up and Wait" with the Tiptons.

Denio's troika of careers—artist, composer, band member—assures her a constant work schedule. By 1999 she had issued three solo CDs and played on 11 others by her various bands. Among those who commissioned her work as a composer: a Seattle production of Jean Genet's play *The Maids* (1997), the Berkeley Symphony (1995), the American Museum of the Moving Image (1994), Seattle's Pat Graney Dance Company (1992), a handful of independent filmmakers and dance troupes, and, in 1998, the Seattle International Children's Festival. The lattermost commission calls for music to be performed with Lorenzo Pickle, a clown. There are persisting touches of avant-garde new music, Eastern European modalities and melodic contours, jazz elements, and creative interpolations of the postoperatic voice in her creations. In addition, Denio seems to constantly use her familiarity with tricky, avant-garde pop and rock to enhance her work. She has performed more than five hundred concerts around the world. **AB**

A Beautiful Western Saddle

(1993, CUNEIFORM)
Not really an Amy Denio release, but that of George Cartwright's left-of-center jazz band, Curlew. But this CD rattles with both Denio's sometimes flowering, sometimes floating, sometimes jarring vocals and the band's pretzeled take on avant-garde jazz in a post–Sonny Sharrock vein.

Tongues

(1993, PONK)
An oddly calibrated songwriting venture, rippling with adventurous structures and loopy, witty narrative atmospheres.

Greatest Hits

(1999, UNIT CIRCLE REKKIDS)
This collection makes it astonishingly clear how disparate Amy Denio's areas of genius are. From her wavering vocals on the later pieces to the stumbly avant-rock of Tone Dogs, with important stops along the way for such staples as "Salvatore," this is essential Denio.

Bill Frisell

When he moved from New York to Seattle in 1989, guitarist Bill Frisell was not exactly a huge presence in jazz. He had recorded some lovely, explorative music for Manfred Eicher's ECM Records beginning in 1982 (including his first album, *In Line*) and had even been a house guitarist at ECM. But as he discovered his own voice on the guitar, it became clear that he wasn't an exact fit for ECM. In fact, Frisell is a maverick in the world of jazz guitar. He's neither subdued strummer nor foggy harmonic hazemaker nor lightning-quick virtuoso. And although he has unmistakable roots in the avant-garde "downtown" New York jazz scene of the late 1970s and the 1980s, Frisell is also not one to romp on his instrument and hasn't really hammered his guitar since his days in John Zorn's aggressive jazz-punk hybrid group, Naked City.

Born March 18, 1951, in Baltimore, Frisell was raised in Denver, where he began his study of music with clarinet lessons. His education included a short stint with jazz guitarist Jim Hall and studies at Boston's Berklee College of Music in the 1970s. It wasn't until he formed his trio with drummer Joey Baron and bassist Kermit Driscoll in the mid-1980s that Frisell began to blossom as a composer and inventive player. His use of volume pedals and shimmering acoustic tones came to define a sound that by now is unmistakable, even without the pedals and effects. A twangy country style is ever present in Frisell's playing, but he is also an adept manipulator, bending notes and chords to give all his songs a warpy, liquid quality that has beguiled and fascinated jazz fans and many other listeners. His recorded scores for several silent films starring Buster Keaton introduced new audiences to his wry wit and self-deprecating sense of humor. On the mid-1990s Keaton soundtracks, he makes funny, almost bodily sounds with his guitar, then wrings from the instrument the sonic equivalents of Keaton's facial expressions.

Most of Frisell's 1990s recordings have been released on the Nonesuch label (the exception being *Live on Gramavision*, 1995). His Nonesuch recordings include *Have a Little Faith* (1991), *This Land* (1992), *Quartet* (1996), and *Gone, Just Like a Train* (1998).

After moving to Seattle, Frisell was asked by Gary Larson, the creator of the cartoon "The Far Side," to create a soundtrack for a televised special Larson was writing. To do this, Frisell formed a groundbreaking quartet—with violinist Eyvind Kang, trumpeter Ron Miles, and trombonist Curtis Fowlkes—that mixed chamber-music dynamics with the usual yearning qualities that mark Frisell's articulate quirkiness. His panstylistic interest in the music of America, from Madonna to Aaron Copland, Charles Ives, and John Hiatt, had appeared in concrete forms as he played their music with Baron and Driscoll in the mid-1980s. With the quartet, Frisell rolled the influences translucently into his works, giving them a clear harmonic bounce here and an extended-range wail there.

Frisell characterizes his playing with elliptical modesty, saying, "A lot of what I play exists because I can't play . . . . Years and years ago I'd be practicing, practicing, trying to play faster and faster, and listening to people like John McLaughlin and getting really, really bummed out and discouraged. There came a point where I was either going to have to stop playing because I couldn't do that, or try to just imply." This "implying" and pushing against his limitations has led to the formation of his individual style, he says.

Limits or no, Frisell has a genius powerful enough to place him in awe-inspiring company. He's recorded with a roll call of jazz and rock greats, from Living Colour's Vernon Reid to Pat Metheny, John Scofield, Gary Peacock, drummer Paul Motian's quirky trio with saxophonist Joe Lovano, and the trio of former Cream drummer

Ginger Baker with bassist Charlie Haden.

In 1997 Frisell recorded *Nashville* (Elektra/Asylum), a stunning CD with blue-grass and old-time country music artists in Nashville—bringing "alternative country" to new heights. He also formed a new trio with bassist Viktor Krauss (whom he met recording in Nashville) and seasoned rock drummer Jim Keltner. Describing his position in the jazz community, where he is revered for having not only boundless creativity but an adventurous record label, Frisell says, "I've made ten or eleven records for Nonesuch. They have little bit higher hopes for each one. It usually doesn't live up to what they hope, but it's enough . . . . And they always like what I'm doing musically—and they trust me. I feel really lucky." **AB**

Have a Little Faith

(1991, NONESUCH)
Bill Frisell is one of the only jazz artists in existence to flawlessly accomplish cover tunes by Madonna, John Hiatt, and Aaron Copland in the space of a single CD. He does so here with an expanded band, including clarinetist Don Byron.

Gone, Just Like a Train

(1998, NONESUCH)
Frisell reinvigorates his once-familiar trio format on this dynamo. The band includes veteran rock drummer Jim Keltner, who lays down a stronger, crisper beat than was found on Frisell's earlier trio recordings. The rhythms give Frisell lots more room to bend around corners and see with his guitar through opaque surfaces.

Kenny G

t he smooth sound of his soprano sax is as recognizable as the solos of any guitar hero or the pipes of any singer. Jazz-trained, funk-fired, and pop-crafted, Kenny G is the Northwest's most popular recording artist. The Recording Industry Association of America charts him as the twenty-fifth best-selling artist of all time, with more than 37.5 million records sold.

Not bad for a Seattle kid who first caught sight of the saxophone watching the *Tonight Show* at age 10. Seven years later, in 1976, Franklin High School student Kenny Gorelick was a good enough player to score his first professional job, as a soloist for a local performance of Barry White's Love Unlimited Orchestra. Gore-lick's next stop was the University of Washington, where he studied accounting. He didn't totally drop music, however; he picked up gigs backing touring artists and recorded with the funk band Cold, Bold & Together.

After college he joined Portland's Jeff Lorber Fusion, recording an album and impressing label representatives enough to get a solo deal with Arista Records. His first three solo albums, *Kenny G* (1982), *G Force* (1983), and *Gravity* (1985), were reasonably successful given the limited market for instrumental music. Arista stuck with him, perhaps partly because a rising number of radio stations were adopting the instrumental-based adult contemporary format.

The G Man turned the corner in a big way in 1986. His album *Duotones* roared into the Top 10 of the pop charts, peaking at no. 6 and eventually selling five million copies. The instrumental "Songbird," on which Kenny played all the instruments, climbed to no. 4 on the singles charts. A second single, "Don't Make Me Wait for Love," with Lenny Williams of Tower of Power on vocals, also made the Top 20. His next record, *Silhouette*, (1988) was also a huge success, again making the Top 10 (no. 8) and spawning another instrumental hit single (the song "Silhouette," which charted at no. 13).

Kenny G's next studio album didn't come for another four years (his concert album, *Live*, was released in 1989), but it was to be his most successful outing ever. *Breathless* jumped to the no. 2 spot on both the pop and R&B charts and sold over seven million copies during the more than six months it spent in the Top 10. To date, more than twelve million copies of *Breathless* have been sold in the United States alone, making it the top-selling instrumental album of all time.

Among the Kenny G hardware: a Grammy Award (for his hit instrumental "Forever in Love"), numerous readers poll awards (he has been named top instrumentalist by the readers of *Playboy*, *Down Beat*, and *Rolling Stone*), the 1994 American Music Award for Favorite Adult Contemporary Artist, and recognition as *Billboard* magazine's Jazz Artist of the Decade (for the 1980s). Another well-known sax player, President Bill Clinton, invited Kenny to play at his first inauguration in 1993—a feat he reprised at the 1996 Democratic National Convention.

Whether impressed by his lyrical sax lines or his limitless commercial appeal (or both), top vocalists have lined up to guest on Kenny G records and to have him play on their own recordings. Michael Bolton and Kenny had a Top 20 hit in 1992 with "Missing You Now." Such singers as Smokey Robinson ("We've Saved the Best for Last"), Aaron Neville ("Even If My Heart Would Break"), Peabo Bryson ("By the Time This Night Is Over"), and Toni Braxton ("That Somebody Was You") have been featured on Kenny G records. Others, including Whitney Houston, Natalie Cole, Dionne Warwick, Celine Dion, and Johnny Gill, have recruited the popular saxman to play on their albums. Funk/rap producer Babyface also played on two songs on Kenny's record *The Moment* (1996). Throw in the first Christmas album to reach the top of the *Billboard* charts in more than thirty years (*Miracles—The Holiday Album* in 1994), and you've got a multiplatinum career. **JB**

Breathless

(1992, ARISTA)
Twelve million Kenny G fans can't be wrong. CONTINUED...

Tom Grant

In December 1997, the Portland club Jazz de Opus celebrated its twenty-fifth anniversary as a venue the same way it opened in 1974—with a set by native son Tom Grant. In the intervening years, the pianist, vocalist, composer, and producer went from sideman to one of the country's most popular artists in the smooth jazz or adult contemporary format.

Grant, a devotee of such jazz greats as Thelonious Monk and Miles Davis, played in jazz bands during high school and as a student at the University of Oregon. As a sideman in Portland saxophonist Jim Pepper's band, he left behind his postcollege day job as a teacher when trumpeter Woody Shaw hired the band for a Canadian tour. Tours with big names such as Joe Henderson, Charles Lloyd, and Tony Williams followed.

Although Grant had released an album, *Mystified* (1976), while still working as a sideman, he decided to devote himself seriously to a solo career with the 1980 release *You Hardly Know Me*. But despite the aid of established musicians Williams, Patrice Rushen, and Jeff Lorber, the project didn't quite gel. Grant teamed with guitarist Dan Balmer and formed a band, which landed him a contract with the Pausa label and his third album, *Tom Grant* (1983). On this third try, he scored a hit on the adult contemporary charts.

Despite his "serious" jazz background, Grant was attracted to fusion because it allowed him to incorporate his love of rock 'n' roll and dance beats. Although a large number of his songs are strictly instrumental, Grant's laid-back voice is often featured chiming along with the notes of his piano.

After recording three more albums for Pausa—*Heart of the City* (1984), *Just the Right Moment* (1985), and *Take Me to Your Dream* (1986)—Grant recorded six albums for the Verve label from 1987 to 1994. Four of these reached no. 1 on the adult contemporary chart: *Night Charade* (1987), *Mango Tango* (1988), *In My Wildest Dreams* (1992), and *The View from Here* (1993). On *In My Wildest Dreams*, Grant worked for the first time with an outside producer (Wayne Braithwaite, who also produced records for Kenny G).

Grant's next three albums, all on Shanachie, included some of his best work. On *Instinct* (1994), he recruited producer Aaron Walker for his tape loop expertise; as a result, the album has an upbeat, danceable sound. Grant also manages to lure talented musicians to his projects: "Lovely Little Dreamer" on *Instinct* features trumpeter

Randy Brecker, sax player Patrick Lamb, and guitarist Jay Koder.

The 1996 Christmas album *Have Yourself a Merry Little . . .* was a popular collection of reinterpreted seasonal songs. *Lip Service* (1997) continued his string of hits, landing the top spot on the play chart of New York's adult contemporary giant WQCD-FM. **JB**

Instinct

(1994, SHANACHIE)
Aaron Walker's tape loops and guest appearances by the likes of guitarist Peter White liven up this collection, which includes several songs worth of Tom Grant's taffy-smooth vocalizing.

Jeff Greinke

With nearly twenty recordings to his name as either a solo artist or a pivotal collaborator, Jeff Greinke has earned an international reputation as a first-rate ambient music composer. Greinke is a consummate performer as well, using his talents as a visual artist to make his performances multimedia events in even the smallest or least likely venue. As a meteorology student at Pennsylvania State University, Greinke began composing and playing music that ever since has seemed to grow toward a kind of extraplanetary soundtrack. Using keyboards and digital samples as well as rhythmic loops and vocals, Greinke creates an instrumental palette that far exceeds the standard—or even nonstandard—ensemble's range.

Greinke originally garnered acclaim as an acolyte of Brian Eno, especially the rhythmically complex but still "ambient" music Eno made in the mid- and late 1970s. The comparison with Eno, while helpful to Greinke's career, was always slightly inappropriate, given Greinke's more developed compositional language and fondness for playing live shows with various local and nonlocal ensembles. That said, Greinke has cited Eno's *On Land* and avant-garde vocalist David Moss's *Terrains* as germinal to his own work.

More crucial for Greinke's development has been his longtime association with Rob Angus. A music student at Pennsylvania State, Angus took Greinke's interest in weather watching and helped direct it toward sound. Greinke and Angus relocated to Seattle in 1982, shortly thereafter forming the Intrepid record label, which issued Greinke's earliest recordings, *Before the Storm, Cities in Fog,* and *Over Ruins* between 1984 and 1986. In the early 1990s Greinke developed a keen interest in more rhythmic music and, to that end, founded LAND, possibly his most adventurous ensemble. Consisting of trumpeter Lesli Dalaba, guitarist Dennis Rea, bassist Fred Chalenor, drummer Bill Rieflin, and Greinke, LAND veers headlong into looping rhythmic places that pair live percussion with electronic rhythms. Although it is no easy feat to separate instruments in the band's complicated, sensuous mix, Dalaba, Greinke, and Rea do in fact improvise and perform "over" the rhythms. When playing live, LAND incontrovertibly mixes up its members' traditional functional roles, combining avant-garde jazz, traditional international music, and ambient sounds. In November 1996, LAND toured China, using a performance at the esteemed Beijing International Jazz Festival to push themselves into Macau, Hong Kong, and numerous Chinese municipalities.

Greinke says his key influences include historic ethnomusicological field recordings as well as early jazz. Further, he says that although his studio recordings are frequently "solo" affairs, in which he handles all the instrumental elements—sampling, rhythm tracks, found sounds—he performs live without the aid of prerecorded tracks. During his tenure in Seattle, he has remained singular enough to be a wholly individual artist, even as he influenced the development of ambient music both within and outside the region. In late 1998 Greinke was working on LAND's third CD; a solo effort, *Swimming* (1998, Prudence); and a collaborative CD with Anisa Romero of the alternative rock group Sky Cries Mary. **AB**

Archipelago

(1996, PERIPLUM)
Jeff Greinke, while endlessly innovative as a solo artist, really outdid himself with LAND's sophomore CD. The recording melts through the air with its soundscapes but also keeps track on slowly propelled rhythmic energies and a killer combination of Dennis Rea's part abstract, part high-energy guitar and Lesli Dalaba's blurts and liquid runs on trumpet.

Swimming

(1998, PRUDENCE)
This is classic Jeff Greinke, immersed in the watery element to the point that his keyboard atmospheres have a genuine washing feel. They might trickle, they might rumble, but they always hold one's attention.

Rich Halley

aving come of musical age in the 1960s in his birthplace of Portland, tenor saxophonist, bandleader, and composer Rich Halley has always devoted himself to a regional identity as well as sonic adventurousness. He has played a pivotal role in the crossover between mainstream postbop and the jazz avant-garde. As a youngster, Halley was influenced by the usual litany of musical styles of the late 1950s and early 1960s. By age 11, however, he was playing clarinet, and at 14 was taken by the tenor sax—and by jazz. In his teens Halley played Portland's coffeehouse circuit, struggling with bop's advanced harmonic language and as he explored improvisation.

The 1960s took Halley around the world, specifically to Cairo, where he played dance pop; then in 1965 he went to college at the University of Chicago, where he witnessed and performed with the nascent Association for the Advancement of Creative Musicians, an organization he credits with influencing his compositional development. In Chicago, Halley was particularly influenced by then-little-known tenor saxophonist Fred Anderson and played professionally with blues great Otis Rush. By the late 1960s, Halley was back on the West Coast, traveling and, for part of 1969, living in Berkeley, where he jammed with saxophonist Bert Wilson (from Olympia, Washington), Lenny Pickett, and powerful avant-garde jazz figures like Sonny Simmons and Smiley Winters. Halley's trajectory, from bop education in coffeehouses to dance pop in Egypt to blues jams and avant-garde jazz in Chicago and then Berkeley, foreshadowed his musical development after his return to Portland in 1973 to finish college.

Halley identified with the Northwest, he recalls, in part on an ecological basis. He studied biology, lived in New Mexico while studying rattlesnakes, and, after another return to Portland, formed the Multnomah Rhythm Ensemble in 1977. His debut LP, recorded in 1981, bore the title *Multnomah Rhythms* (Avocet) and conjured mixed evocations of tree-crowded, verdant autumnal haze with wide-open, sandy-dry rhythmic hop. The sophomore LP, *Song of the Backlands* (1986, Avocet), further explored the mix, and Halley noted that he enjoyed a regional character in the music. After disbanding the Multnomah Ensemble, he formed a group that more clearly aggregated his experience in music: the Lizard Brothers have remained Halley's vehicle for his recordings and live performances since about 1982. The group mixes Halley's recognizable jumps in saxophone register—from gutbucket blues-type grit to whistling jabs—in a matter of seconds.

Enlisting longtime collaborator William Thomas on drums, Phil Sparks on bass, and Rob Blakeslee on trumpet, Halley has come upon a vibrant ensemble that beautifully pulls together his often lengthy compositions. A computer programmer by trade, Halley writes complex, intricate compositions that swing very hard, showing off his blues chops and funky sense of rhythmic time. Given that Ghanian percussion master Obo Addy was an early Multnomah Ensemble member, it is not surprising that Halley has demonstrated an affinity for African, Caribbean, and Latin percussive grooves in addition to a distinct translation of the grooves into his horn-rich jazz band. Halley's CD recordings *Saxophone Animals* (1988, Nine Winds) and *Umatilla Variations* (1993, Nine Winds) feature a strong four-horn front line that creates harmonic density without the overt direction of a pianist.

Halley serves in the Northwest scene as a purveyor of music rooted in the Northwest experience, and part of that experience is knowing such music is a woodshed affair. Music like Halley's—decidedly not mainstream, though when heard, it invites widespread favor—is something people work day jobs to support. Indeed, Halley works a steady job so that he can explore the development of a unique musical language. **AB**

Saxophone Animals

(1988, NINE WINDS)
This release catches Rich Halley and his Lizard Brothers band in sharp form. The four-horn front line follows a fairly loose but still exciting head-solo-head format while getting a huge amount of soloing space. Halley shows, as always, his command of roiling midtempo avant-garde jazz and a serious knowledge of both hard bop and R&B phrasing.

Umatilla Variations

(1993, NINE WINDS)
The powerhouse sax trio of Rich Halley, Vinny Golia (who founded Nine Winds Records), and fellow Northwest scene mainstay Troy Grugett perform with trumpeter Rob Blakeslee. They offer a rich, bright-hued brass atop the tumbling rhythms of bassist Phil Sparks and drummer William Thomas.

Wayne Horvitz

It might seem a little weird to claim Wayne Horvitz as a Northwest musician, despite his long residence here. Born in New York in 1955, he grew up in Washington, D.C. and San Francisco, but made a name for himself in the early 1980s on New York's Lower East Side. As soon as he finished college, he took off for New York with pianist, singer, and composer Robin Holcomb, now his wife.

Horvitz's jerky fingered style of improvisational Hammond organ playing got him involved with John Zorn, the famously petulant improv sax player. After contributing to four Zorn albums, starting with *Pool* (1980, Parachute), the two collaborated in the group Naked City with Seattle transplant Bill Frisell. Counting their 1989 debut, *Naked City* (Elektra/Nonesuch, released under Zorn's name), the group has put out five albums: *Absinthe* (1993), *Radio* (1993), *Heretic* (1994, all on Avant), and *Black Box* (1997, Tzadik). After this taste of New York fame, Horvitz formed the all-star New York–scene band President of the United States of America or the President (no relation to the Seattle combo with a similar name), whose mix of jazz, rock, and improv was as close to rock as Horvitz's playing gets.

A Seattle resident since the late 1980s, Horvitz finds plenty of improv jazz folks to play with. His five-year-old combo, Pig Pen, includes bass player Fred Chalenor, drummer Mike Stone, and saxophonist Briggan Kraus. The group recorded *Miss Ann* (1995) and *Daylight* (1997), both for Portland's Tim/Kerr label. Horvitz continues to record solo records for various labels, most notably *Bring Your Camera* (1991, Elektra) and *Brand Spankin' New* (1998, Knitting Factory). His compositions range from Vince Giraldi-inspired, sad Charlie Brown songs, to wacky pogo-stick numbers, to beautifully lilting songs that take on new shades of love when performed with Robin Holcomb singing.

Horvitz is also active with Zony Mash, a side band including Fred Chalenor (later Keith Lowe), Tim Young, and Andy Roth, whose rock-oriented music he compares to the President, and which has gotten enough attention to make it Horvitz's best known Seattle group. He also recorded *Monologue* (1998), a solo record of music for dancers, on Portland's Cavity Search label.

One recent project, the Four + One Ensemble, is so known because the five members never thought of a real name. It's a concert hall quintet with a twist, adding multiple influences with violinist Eyvind Kang, keyboardist Reggie Watts, and Julian Priester on trombone. Tucker Martine mixes the music through a soundboard directly as it's played. This group released a self-titled album in 1998 on the Intuition label. Horvitz is also an active producer, whose credits include First Takes, almost every Holcomb project, singer/songwriters Cathy Croce and Karen Pernick, gifted kids, jazz ensembles, and guys with guitars.

At this stage of his career, Horvitz is quite capable of playing anything and has done a great deal to add cohesion to the Seattle improv jazz scene. The best time to catch him is in a casual get-together between his old cronies like Zorn, with Bobby Previtte drumming, Elliot Sharp playing every shape of guitar, and fifty effects boxes at their collective disposal. But really, any chance to hear Horvitz play is worthwhile because you never know when glossolalia will grip his fingers and you'll be taken where you don't usually get to go. **KS**

Cold Spell

(1997, KNITTING FACTORY)
Wayne Horvitz's best-known side project is this spacy, bachelor-pad electro band. Highly recommended.

Human Feel

While rock fans and musicians were moving to Seattle in droves in the late 1980s, three-quarters of Human Feel were headed in the opposite direction: east to Boston. Saxophonists Andrew D'Angelo and Chris Speed and drummer Jim Black optimistically migrated in what has become a jazz trope for Seattle. To wit: native talent heads east to sharpen skills and broaden horizons, then returns and puts that knowledge to use. D'Angelo, Speed, and Black all grew up in Seattle, playing big band gigs together in high school and jamming more intimately as a prototype for Human Feel. Each picked up on the convergence of avant-garde jazz, punk, and other peripheral genres. And they became exceptionally talented players and composers.

The Northwest members of Human Feel took giant steps and left giant footprints along the East Coast. For Speed and Black, the 1987 trek to Boston was prompted by their enrollment at the Berklee College of Music. D'Angelo, their longtime collaborator, headed the jazz department at Boston's prime record store.

Human Feel developed an edgy sound while in Boston, with D'Angelo's and Speed's saxophones sounding like differently pitched Siamese twins and Black's wobbling, jumping off-center rhythms creating delightfully avant-garde instrumental shoving matches. Initially a quintet, Feel (as the band's members call the group) was rounded out by bassist Jon Fitzgerald and guitarist Kurt Rosenwinkel. The group grabbed critics' ears with their self-produced debut CD in 1989 and were quickly picked up by jazz impresario Gunther Schuller, whose GM Recordings released their sophomore effort. That album, the thrillingly broad-based *Scatter*, boasts as much free-jazz saxman Albert Ayler as it does rock innovators Captain Beefheart and, say, Pere Ubu. By 1994 Feel had relocated to New York, where the group shared a Brooklyn brownstone and released one of that year's finest jazz CDs, *Welcome to Malpesta* on the renowned New World Records label. Their sound had only grown more incisive, artfully deconstructive in the face of both mainstream jazz's ascendance and New York's Knitting Factory–fronted jazz scene. Human Feel still returned to the Northwest for recording sessions and shows; in 1996 the Songlines label, based in Vancouver, British Columbia, released their powerfully progressive punk-jazz *Speak to It*, again to critics' raves.

Human Feel has done far more than simply play as a powerhouse group. All the members have toured the world, usually as side players in other people's bands. And each Feel member has taken an active role in the New York scene, playing on more than twenty recordings—always lending overtly beguiling colors and emotions. Speed and Black are charter members of the lauded group bloodcount, led by alto saxophonist Tim Berne, and Black is also a member of Dave Douglas's phenomenal avant-Balkan ensemble, Tiny Bell Trio. Further, Speed and Black now play as part of the quartet Yeah/No, which toured the United States in 1997–98. Human Feel's core sound generously displays the reasons its members have become so pivotal to an entire jazz scene. They borrow the energy of Balkan music without sounding Eastern European, and they claim the thorniness of art punk but never become attitude laden or tawdry. Extremely talented jazz improvisers all, Human Feel invokes the experimentalism of post-free-improvisational music without veering into indulgent obtuseness or oblique complexity. **AB**

Welcome to Malpesta

(1994, New World)

Quite simply, this CD is not only Human Feel's finest moment but also among the best phenomena of 1990s jazz. Bracingly herky-jerky and teetery, it's also nervy and intense, with hard knocks plying through choppy streams of pliant guitar and weavy saxophones. The 3-minute closer, "Yesterday I Passed," is a traditional religious tune arranged by Chris Speed for his and Andrew D'Angelo's saxes. Its mournful beauty aches so energetically that this CD is a must-have for any well-rounded jazz collection.

Speak to It

(1996, Songlines)

Very little can approximate the level of creative success Human Feel reached with *Welcome to Malpesta*. But they certainly grew into their core sound even more after that venerable release, coming out with tough swings on *Speak to It*. It's a grittier record and one that bites deeply in spots. More frantic than other Feel, it's a stellar album when considered in the wider world of jazz.

Edmonia Jarrett

You get a hint of how long Edmonia Jarrett has been growing young by the wink on her 1998 CD cover: her driver's license and the title *Legal at Any Age* (MNOP). Born equally to educate young minds and to make music, she's done each in its time, first as a schoolteacher and principal, and more recently as a jazz singer.

Born in South Carolina on March 11, 1933, Jarrett grew up in a society where little girls with poor but hardworking parents could aim to become teachers or nurses. She chose education, and had a long career that brought her to Seattle, where she served as assistant principal of Wilson Middle School and then principal of Cleveland High School.

But in the early 1990s, Jarrett's world was rocked when she was diagnosed with breast cancer. Her fight for survival was aided by jazz vibes player Elmer Gill, staging his own comeback from cancer, who proved a musical soul mate, lending spiritual support and encouragement to the music that had soared inside Edmonia from birth. She began to pursue work as a singer, finding appreciation and encouragement from the musicians she met along the way, including local blues singer Duffy Bishop.

Seattle audiences also liked what they heard; in less than a decade, she became one of the city's most popular jazz performers. Other musicians showed their appreciation as well: her first CD, *Live, Live, Live!* (1996, MNOP), featured contributions from such top local players as Barney McClure, Bill Ramsay, Billy Wallace, Floyd

Standifer, and Clarence Acox. The song selection ranged from jazz standards to several new compositions.

Her next release, *Legal at Any Age,* showed this same love for standards, with tunes by Jerome Kern, Johnny Mercer, and Harold Arlen prominently featured. A particular highlight is "Too Good to Be True," a duet with Freddy Cole (Nat Cole's gifted brother).

Although Jarrett's days as an educator are over, aspiring jazz singers can still learn from her respect for a lyric and her choice of super songs that stand the test of time. **NB**

Quincy Jones

lthough he was a good enough trumpeter to form a band with Ray Charles at 14 and join Lionel Hampton's big band at 17, Quincy Jones always felt what he did best was inspire and present the work of other musicians, singers, and songwriters. Jones more than proved his point, becoming a prominent arranger/composer, a noted bandleader, and one of the preeminent producers in popular music.

Born in Chicago on March 13, 1933, Quincy Delight Jones, Jr., moved to Seattle at age 10. He took up the trumpet a few years later, and was a veteran of the city's jazz clubs by his midteens. He continued his schooling in Boston briefly after graduating from Seattle's Garfield High School, but departed to join Hampton's big band. He later played with Dizzy Gillespie's big band as well, but by that time he was already well known as an arranger in New York studios. After touring with Gillespie in 1956, he signed on as staff arranger and conductor for ABC Paramount Records.

The most celebrated period of Jones's life as a bandleader began in 1957, when he moved to Paris as a producer for Barclay Records. Inspired by his studio experience, Jones returned to New York to work for Mercury Records, but immediately focused his attention on setting up an orchestra for both studio sessions and touring. Originally founded as the pit orchestra for the touring Harold Arlen show *Free and Easy,* the group included at various times such heavyweights as Count Basie trumpeter Joe Newman, alto sax ace Phil Woods, and pianist Patti Bown. The band's debut album, *The Birth of a Band* (1959), featured an all-star tenor sax section of Zoot Sims and Benny Golson. But despite the participation of numerous top musicians, successful tours, and well-regarded albums, Mercury's budget creaked under the pressure of maintaining an eighteen-member orchestra. By the end of 1961, Jones was so heavily in debt to Mercury that he was forced to sign on as a staff producer, working on jazz, blues, and pop records. He continued to make studio recordings with the orchestra, most of which were organized around a central musical concept, including *Around the World* (1961), *Big Band Bossa Nova* (1962), and *Hip Hits* (1963).

Jones quickly ascended in the Mercury hierarchy, becoming a vice president in 1964. He also began writing and producing scores for movies and television, including the films *The Pawnbroker* and *In the Heat of the Night.* In 1969 he moved to A&M Records and continued to make albums as a composer and bandleader, including the Grammy Award winner *Walking in Space* (1969) and the big-selling *Body Heat* (1974). He collaborated with Ray Charles on *Black Requiem*, a 1971 musical production depicting the struggles of blacks in America, which Charles performed with a symphony orchestra and eighty-voice choir.

At the height of his career, Jones was struck down by two brain aneurysms and underwent major surgery. But he returned in 1976 and began working as a pop producer in earnest, working on records for the Brothers Johnson and Michael Jackson, including Jackson's massively popular albums *Off the Wall* (1979), *Thriller* (1982), and *Bad* (1987). In fact, Jones produced both the best-selling pop album (*Thriller*) and the best-selling single ("We Are the World," performed by a group of musical superstars on the *USA for Africa* album in 1985) of all time. He wrote the score for the television miniseries *Roots* in 1977.

Jones's own pop music career continued as singers lined up to perform with the master. Six times since 1978 he has hit the Top 40 with singers such as Chaka Khan and James Ingram providing the vocals. His last two releases, *Back on the Block* (1990) and *Q's Jook Joint* (1995), continued this trend of big-name guest stars. In 1999 Jones released *From Q with Love*, a two-CD, twenty-five-song collection of the favorite love songs he has recorded as a producer.

Although Jones has won dozens of awards and honors, one stands out: he is the most nominated artist in the history of the Grammy Awards, with seventy-seven nominations and twenty-six wins. In recognition of his career accomplishments, he was honored with the Grammys' Trustees Award in 1989 and their Living Legends Award in 1990. **JB**

Q's Jook Joint

(1995, WARNER BROS.)
An eclectic mix of musical biggies (including Bono, Stevie Wonder, Ray Charles, and Phil Collins) visit Quincy Jones in the studio for this all-star romp.

Pure Delight: The Essence of Quincy Jones and His Orchestra

(1995, RAZOR & TIE)
This well-chosen twenty-song collection includes highlights from Jones's early orchestra sessions, his touring big band, and his subsequent Mercury albums.

Primo Kim

Primo Kim has played every smart Seattle lounge and has been the star singer at many a Seattle concert—at the Paramount and Fifth Avenue theaters, the University of Washington's Meany Hall, the Seattle Opera House. He's also performed at all the major Seattle hotels, San Francisco's Masonic Temple Auditorium, San Jose's Frank Lloyd Wright Performing Arts Center, Las Vegas's Tropicana and the Sands, New York's Latin Quarter, and in Hawaii.

So why is Primo Kim reevaluating the use of the professional name that has served him so well, providing constant employment and a comfortable living in Seattle all these years? The change has to do with his personal decision to publicly identify with his Filipino roots. As Primo Kim, he has been working nonstop since he moved from San Francisco to Seattle in the late 1960s. But his 1997 CD, *To Be Near* (RKK), was released under his full name—Primo Kim Villarruz.

Kim has long been the consummate lounge attraction—Seattle's Bobby Troup, Buddy Greco, or Bobby Short, but with a voice more like Mel Tormé's. He's charming, debonair, and professionally generous to a fault (the mixed blessing of his career). Part of his attraction has been an open invitation to virtually anyone who wants to sing accompaniment. Step right up, folks!

Kim's open-door policy is a little like Picasso inviting passersby to paint with him. Not to worry: knowing the lyrics of just about every song ever written, this impeccable singer remains a spellbinding balladeer—even with that generous offering of karaoke on the side.

When Kim can take a break from lounge performances, he jumps at the chance to just play piano. Among his favorite escapes to jazz playing are the occasional gig with Buddy Catlett, a Seattle bass player of world fame (including years with Count Basie). It's a pity that there are only a couple of tracks on *To Be Near* that show off Kim's jazz piano playing. If you purchase the CD, rush to track nine, a magical treatment of Johnny Mandel's "Emily."

Perhaps Kim's recent decision to publicly reclaim his full name will provide the kind of freedom that can produce a rush of fresh creativity. Maybe as Primo Kim Villarruz, he'll develop on his own terms and bring out more of the great jazz that's in him. And if he continues to work in lounges, he'll do so on jazz piano-playing terms. To be invited to sit at his microphone, an audience member would have to be in his league as a singer.

Here's a trivia question for jazz fans: Who in 1994 was the only Seattle musician to perform among all the jazz greats at the prestigious Lionel Hampton Jazz Festival in Moscow, Idaho? It was Primo Kim, born Primo Villarruz. **NB**

To Be Near

(1997, RKK)
Primo Kim Villarruz's first CD benefits from its mixture of trio performances and big band numbers; the big band assembled for this project includes a roster of Seattle jazz talent, including Bill Ramsay, Floyd Standifer, and Denney Goodhew.

EDMONIA JARRETT

BUD SHANK

featuring:

Milo Petersen   drums
Jay Thomas   trumpet
Rick Mandyck   tenor sax
Marc Seales   piano
Phil Sparks   bass

MILO PETERSON AND THE JAZZ DISCIPLES

JEFF LORBER

TOM GRANT

JEFF GREINKE

TOM COLLIER

BARNEY MCCLURE

BERT WILSON

DAVE PECK

HUMAN FEEL

Jim Knapp

J im Knapp's contributions to Northwest jazz are, to say the least, multifaceted. An accomplished trumpeter, Knapp has devoted considerable time and energy to arranging and composing music for ensembles that he also leads—he sees his role as a member of a group, not a soloist. He has drawn together legions of Seattle musicians as members of several ensembles, including the lauded Jim Knapp Orchestra and Jim Knapp Quintet. He has taught many of his band members during his lengthy tenure at Seattle's Cornish College of the Arts, where he has been a faculty member since 1971.

Knapp himself studied at the University of Illinois, where he received his bachelor's degree and a master's in music composition during the 1960s, a time when jazz performance, composition, and improvisation were under the scrutiny of adventurous, independent players. All of this clearly colored Knapp's vantage point on music, as did the intense late-1960s focus on community development. From teaching music theory at Illinois, Knapp advanced to develop Cornish's now-celebrated Jazz Arts program by recruiting a first-rate faculty. Some of the luminaries that have taught beside Knapp are Jay Clayton, Carter Jefferson, Gary Peacock, Julian Priester, and Jerry Granelli. Knapp's formative role in the school's jazz development has ensured that the mainstream is not the dominant language, and as a result, former students including pianist Myra Melford, violinist Eyvind Kang, and the members of BABKAS ably reconstitute languages of improvisation from late-1960s avant-garde jazz and an array of other eras' characteristics.

Knapp spent almost a decade, from the late 1970s to 1986, directing and performing with the Composers and Improvisers Orchestra. The ensemble similarly arched over stylistic differences, performing pieces by avant-garde composer Anthony Braxton alongside Bob Brookmeyer's straight-ahead California jazz works. Knapp's recording career does not fully capture his range of expertise for a few reasons. His stunning recorded debut, made in 1981 with the collective free-improvisation group First Avenue (including Denney Goodhew and Eric Jenson), remains out of print. In addition, some of Knapp's most adventurous works are for the dance medium and therefore not issued as audio recordings. His work *Lush Rites* was commissioned by Seattle choreographer Stephanie Skura in 1994 and received rave reviews for the music's shape-shifting alongside the dance. One year later Knapp newly arranged two of his compositions for the New York Composers Orchestra West and a set of Andrew Lloyd Webber tunes for the Teo Macero–produced *New Brew* CD on Emerald Records.

Knapp's more recent—and possibly best—vehicles are his orchestra and quintet. Holding court with great regularity around Seattle, the Jim Knapp Orchestra features a roll call of local musicians, many of whom have studied with the bandleader at Cornish. The group's debut CD, *On Going Home* (1996, Sea Breeze), hit high marks with Northwest listeners. But Knapp has also been an in-demand side player and collaborator, known particularly for his skill in arranging complex jazz scores. He has worked extensively with vocalist Jay Clayton, spending the years 1990 to 1994 in the Jay Clayton–Jim Knapp Collective and releasing *Tito's Acid Trip* (ITM) in 1990. He also led the Latin jazz ensemble Ohio Howie (1987–90) and the jazz quartet Looser Futures (1983–88). His performance work has gone beyond dance to include ambient music composed to accompany an installation at Seattle Center's International Fountain as part of the 1987 Bumbershoot arts festival.

Knapp came to that work thanks to such ventures as Meister Eckhart's 1986 dance and theater piece *Airborne*, which itself came into being in relation to Knapp's dance, theater, and music hybrid *Who's When Where*, written for the Composers and Improvisers Orchestra and the Skinner Releasing Dance Company in 1984 and commissioned by the National Endowment for the Arts. More recently, Knapp won the King County Arts Commission Special Projects Award in 1996 for new compositions, in collaboration with singer Clayton and Brazilian pianist and composer Jovino Santos Neto. Members of the Seattle organization Earshot Jazz voted the Jim Knapp Orchestra the Best Acoustic Jazz Group in 1995. Through all the accolades and eventful career moves, Knapp has remained remarkably tied to the community of players that gather in his big band. He can similarly boast a close-knit relationship with jazz audiences. **AB**

On Going Home

(1996, SEA BREEZE)
Saxophonists Hans Teuber, Greg Metcalfe, and Jon Goforth all make this CD a delightful mix of old-school postbop big band charm and teethy, maplike intricacy.

Don Lanphere

books are written and movies made of such lives as Don Lanphere's. When Seattle's premier jazz club, Jazz Alley, hosted a celebration of Lanphere's seventieth birthday, the event sold out, and the club even had to turn away some of those who had come to honor the vigor and creativity of this jazz saxophone marvel.

Born June 26, 1928, in Wenatchee, Washington, Lanphere started his career in promising innocence. He received a scholarship to study music at Northwestern University from 1945 to 1947. The college town of Evanston, Illinois, was just a few steps from Chicago, a jazz center in its own right, and Lanphere's experience there prepped him for his ultimate destination, New York. It wasn't easy to break in, even in small club jazz sessions, but Lanphere never wanted for moxie. When several of his new black jazz friends were determined to put this white kid in his place, Max Roach set an eight-bar breakneck tempo that he probably thought was impossible for a white kid to grab onto. Piece o' cake. New York, meet Don Lanphere.

By 1949, Lanphere, still in his late teens, was making records with Fats Navarro and Max Roach. Unfortunately, the raw kid from Washington's apple country had already become a heroin addict. But during the year or two before his addiction took over, this white jazz prodigy was adopted by black heroes he'd heard only on jazz records. He'd absorbed the best tenor saxophone influences—Coleman Hawkins (whose landmark recording of "Body and Soul" Lanphere could replicate note for note) and Lester Young.

Drug use was the norm among jazz musicians at the time. "One of my high school teachers back home had said to me, 'When you get to Chicago, bring me back some of that light green [marijuana],'" Lanphere recalls. "I didn't know what that was, but since my teacher had recommended it, I started into it right away. It wasn't more than a year and a half before I got talked into needles in the arm, and I was off and gone."

Although he was a junkie from 1947 to 1951, Lanphere landed good gigs making records with Navarro and Roach and playing in Woody Herman's band. But while he was touring with the Bob Hope show, his side trip from a Toledo, Ohio, gig to buy heroin landed him in the Detroit County Jail. "My parents came and got me," he says. "It was the first they knew of my addiction. We went to New York and got my phonograph, my tape recorder, and my clarinet out of the pawn shop—all the things I'd hocked to get money—and we went back to Wenatchee."

At this point Lanphere came close to hanging it up, even with the good fortune in 1952 of meeting Midge Hess and marrying her. For Midge, life in Wenatchee, with Don working in his father's music store, would have been fine. But, putting Don first, she encouraged her crestfallen husband to give New York another shot.

Woody Herman was happy to see Lanphere again in 1959, all cleaned up and married. For two years Don served as a mainstay in the rhythm section of Herman's Second Herd, taking side trips in the bands of Claude Thornhill and Charlie Barnet. But Lanphere again ran into trouble, this time with alcohol: "They were pouring me into bed every night." Once again he got busted, this time in New York with pockets full of marijuana. So it was back to Wenatchee for Don and Midge, and for eight years he was in and out of jail. Midge had already accepted Christianity at a Billy Graham Crusade in 1950, says Lanphere, "so when I met my Lord Jesus in 1969, it was relatively easy for Midge to reverse my direction, and that night we flushed everything down the toilet."

This spiritual revelation is responsible for the Don Lanphere of today—playing as brilliantly as ever, and teaching the art and craft of good American jazz to young people at his invitational jazz clinics. For almost thirty years his teaching and encouragement have produced jazz musicians by the score. He continues as a performing legend, playing the tenor, alto, and soprano saxophones in concert and on recordings, mainly in quintet and sextet structures. Singularly notable is Lanphere's role in the career of trumpeter Jonathan Pugh, who talks of his mentor as one of Michelangelo's sculptures might speak of the sculptor. Pugh is featured on three of

Lanphere's CDs on the Scottish HEP label, *Out of Nowhere* (1982), *Into Somewhere* (1983), and *Don Loves Midge* (1984). Also recorded for HEP were *Don Lanphere/ Larry Coryell* (1990) and *Lopin'* (1992).

The eminent Seattle pianist Marc Seales has been a regular on most of Lanphere's later works, as both composer and arranger with the group New Stories. Most recently the Lanphere/Seales recordings have included bassist Doug Miller and drummer John Bishop. Lanphere's two latest releases on HEP have been collaborations: *Don Lanphere/Bud Shank/Denney Goodhew* and *Don Lanphere and Tenorman Pete Christlieb.* **NB**

Don Lanphere/Larry Coryell

(1990, HEP)
Larry Coryell, the famous jazz guitarist with Northwest roots, teams up with Don Lanphere on this fine release.

Lopin'

(1992, HEP)
Lanphere again shares the solo spotlight, this time with sax player Bud Shank and multi-instrumentalist Denney Goodhew.

Jeff Lorber

today, he's best known as a producer who has worked with such nationally known artists as Kenny G, Herb Alpert, Tower of Power, Nu Shooz, Michael Franks, and Karyn White. But keyboardist Jeff Lorber is also a pioneer of jazz fusion (and consequently its offshoot, "contemporary jazz" or "adult contemporary" music). More recently he's been in demand as a remixer for 12-inch singles.

Born in Philadelphia on November 4, 1952, Lorber began playing piano at the age of 4, also taking lessons on guitar, bass, and violin. He moved to Boston in 1970 to study at the Berklee College of Music. Unimpressed with the local jazz scene, he relocated to Portland, where he formed the Jeff Lorber Fusion, featuring a young sax player from Seattle named Kenny Gorelick. "What I did was to create a more mellow style of fusion that used bebop harmonic ideas, a more pop approach to form and melodic content with R&B and jazz grooves," explains Lorber in a statement posted on his Web site.

The group's first two records, *Jeff Lorber Fusion* (1977, Inner City) and *Soft Space* (1978, Inner City), helped define Lorber's mellow fusion sound (as well as assisting Kenny Gorelick, who would become better known as Kenny G, in launching his solo career). Lorber recorded seven more successful records for Arista during the first part of the 1980s (including *Wizard Island*, which rose to no. 1 on the *Billboard* jazz chart), culminating with *Step by Step* (1985), which earned him a Grammy nomination for Best R&B Instrumental for the track "Pacific Coast Highway."

By this time, Lorber had moved to Los Angeles in order to capitalize on his success as a producer. He released one more album in 1986, *Private Passion* (with his biggest pop crossover success, the Top 30 single "Facts of Love," sung by Karyn White), and shifted his focus to composing and producing. He has remixed songs by U2, Duran Duran, New Order, and Jody Watley, sometimes adding his own keyboard lines. Among his production successes are the first two Dave Koz albums, John Lucien's *Listen Love*, and Eric Benet's *Benet*. His compositions have been featured in the movies *Sideout* and *The Super*.

After deciding to renew his own recording and performing career in 1993, Lorber released *Worth Waiting For* (another no.1 on the *Billboard* jazz charts) and toured nationally. His next album, *West Side Stories* (1994), spawned another hit, "Say Love" (with vocals by Eric Benet). *State of Grace* (1996) featured a superband (under the direction of producer Mickey Petralia, who has worked with Beck and Cypress Hill), that included Dave Koz and Gary Meek on soprano sax, Art Porter on alto sax, Benet and Sue Anne Carwell on vocals, Nathan Phillips on bass, and guitarists Marlon McClain and Michael Landau. Lorber makes a rare appearance as a guitarist, playing on three songs. He also reprises a couple of the Jeff Lorber Fusion's biggest hits: "Katherine" of 1979 and "Pacific Coast Highway" of 1985. Lorber's 1998 CD, *Midnight*, was his first for the Zebra label. **JB**

Step by Step

(1985, ARISTA)
The album that made Jeff Lorber a staple on adult contemporary radio. Both the title track and "Pacific Coast Highway" can still be heard on soft jazz stations.

West Side Stories

(1994, VERVE)
The interplay between Lorber's keyboards and Gary Meek's soprano saxophone drives the better cuts here ("Grasshopper," "Iguassu Falls").

Marriott Jazz Quintet

d avid Marriott, Jr., trombonist/arranger and brother of trumpeter Thomas Marriott, boldly traces the family roots back 900 years to three Marriott brothers who were warriors in the service of William the Conqueror. But with the release of the Marriott Jazz Quintet's CD *Open Season* (1999, Red Raspus), the young Marriott brothers—only 25 (Thomas) and 23 (David) years old—seem poised to overshadow all nine centuries of the family tree.

The two bear unmistakable Northwest jazz bloodlines. They spent their high school years in Clarence Acox's Garfield High School jazz program in Seattle and continued on to the University of Washington's noted jazz studies program. Both have been influenced by the region's best players: Thomas has studied privately with Floyd Standifer, Marc Seales, and Jay Thomas; David has made eight trips to Bud Shank's Port Townsend jazz workshop.

Besides the brothers, the Marriott Jazz Quartet features a who's who among world-class Seattle musicians: pianist Joe Doria, bassist Geoff Harper, and drummer John Wicks. Also appearing on *Open Season* is tenor saxman Rob Davis. The Marriotts have developed impressive individual resumés as well. David's opus for jazz septet "In the Beginning," based on the biblical seven days of Creation, was first performed live in December 1997, then recorded the following summer, with David as producer and Thomas as one of the perfomers (*In the Beginning*, 1999, Red Raspus). Thomas is a performing dyanmo, a member of eight other groups in addition to his duties as a member of the Marriott Jazz Quintet.

While there are numerous brothers in jazz (the Heaths, the Breckers, the Marsalises), you have to go back decades to find brother bandleaders—Jimmy and Tommy Dorsey and Les and Larry Elgart. And these pairings proved short-lived, with each brother quickly going his own way except for the rare reunion concert.

Music has always been a family affair for the Marriotts. Father David Marriott, Sr., played both trumpet and jazz records as a radio DJ. David Marriott, Jr.'s bountiful liner notes for *Open Season*, painstakingly generous in praise of everyone he could think of, suggest that the brothers (and their kid sister, Becky) used horns as teething rings.

The Marriotts' seemingly imperishable family tie makes us wish the brothers will do as many things as a team as they do alone. Their blockbuster debut CD bodes well for a long togetherness. **NB**

Open Season

(1999, RED RASPUS)
Prominent among the many outstanding solos generated by David Marriott's arrangements are his brother Tom's rich, relaxing trumpet lines on "Foolish Things" and David's gentle reading of the Johnny Mandel composition, "Close Enough for Love."

Greta Matassa

greta Matassa's singing is touched by genius—maybe more genius than mere pop songs can handle. Take her signature release, *Got a Song That I Sing* (1991), an album that will be prized among the many recordings she will no doubt make in her career. The album cover is charming, with childlike ink-sketched song titles, track numbers shaped like little boxes, and a photo of the artist barefooted and wearing a quizzical expression. But the cover art gives little indication of the kind of singing in store. After a single listen, knowledgeable collectors made space for Matassa on their CD shelves, moving aside other jazz women.

It was in a nonmusical setting that Matassa first came to public attention—as Greta Goehle, on a bleak Sunday afternoon in 1990, at a Seattle Sounders soccer match in the city's old Memorial Stadium, to be exact. Even in the acoustically impossible setting of an outdoor sports arena, there was no mistaking the sound of a powerful orchestra—the Jazz Police (with whom Matassa recorded two CDs in the late 1980s)—and the robust jazz expressions of the singer.

Not long after the outdoor performance, Greta met Mark Matassa, a former award-winning political writer for the *Seattle Times*. He became her best friend and biggest booster, and is now her husband and the father of their two daughters. He is also the namesake of her own record label, Mark Likes Jazz, which released Matassa's second album, *If the Moon Turns Green,* in 1994. That album also features accompanist Joe Baque, who accompanied Matassa in her triumphant early-1999 performance at Seattle's Cabaret de Paris, where she sang the compositions of Kurt Weill.

Got a Song That I Sing, however, is the album that staggers jazz intelligentsia. It's not uncommon to hear traces of role models in any new singer, but Matassa boldly refers to a surprising number of influences. Encompassed in three songs—"Zing Went the Strings of My Heart," "I've Got the World on a String," and "The Lady Is a Tramp"—are unmistakable evocations of Dinah Washington, Sarah Vaughan, Ella Fitzgerald, Billie Holiday, and on "Zing" even Ray Charles. Downtown critics have fancied they detected Judy Garland; this writer hears the red-blooded sensuality of Della Reese in her prime. Heard at a rehearsal of the Pacific Northwest Ballet, Matassa's singing—lush and full of angst—echoed the voice of Lotte Lenya. (Did anyone hear Edith Piaf?) There may be no mistaking Matassa's many musical heroes, but to thoroughly enjoy this extraordinary singer, the listener must appreciate her free-spirited sense of fun.

Maybe this amazing singer wasn't born a musical genius. Maybe one day she'll admit to being an amalgamation of the many role models she generously acknowledges. And maybe someday she'll soar to the level of success accorded to those famous predecessors. Meanwhile, Matassa is one of Seattle's few working musicians who is offered more jobs than a happy wife and mother of two little girls can handle. As she says, "That's the best of all worlds, at least until the girls are grown up." **NB**

(1991, MARK LIKES JAZZ)
Greta Matassa's first album features magnificent solo passages by trumpeter and tenor sax player Jay Thomas, and on the tour de force "The Lady Is a Tramp," the brilliant soloists are Barney McClure (organ), Denney Goodhew (baritone sax), Craig Hoyer (piano), and Jay Mabin (harmonica). There's also a thoughtful singing duet with Andy Shaw, a merging of the two compatible tunes "A Sinner Kissed an Angel" and "Polka Dots and Moonbeams."

Barney McClure

Where do you start writing about the mega-gifted Barney McClure? He was born April 9, 1941, in Columbus, Ohio, where father Barney Sr. was a big band trumpet player, living a life that caused his mother to leave and seek refuge in California. She raised Barney and his brother, Mickey, in the small desert town of Needles. In his earliest years McClure played the instrument of his paternal heritage—the trumpet—but was still not fully married to music. As a high school student, he focused on mathematics instead and even dreamed of being an astrophysicist. It wasn't until college at San Diego State University that McClure, still playing trumpet, worked the neighborhood clubs. There he succumbed to the temptations of the piano—the one instrument capable of producing all ten notes at once—on which he has since performed in combination with some of the nation's most celebrated musicians.

Like so many young jazzmen, McClure took day jobs such as pumping gas and delivering mail. Then, in the early 1960s, he was drafted into the Army and served as trumpeter and arranger for U.S. military bands in Germany. After returning to the United States and the piano, McClure stayed in New York long enough to enjoy a warm reception among the upper echelons of East Coast jazz musicians. Yearning to return to the West Coast lifestyle, he moved to Los Angeles, where he put his Army experience to good use, writing intricate arrangements and playing with the best in the West. But his total absorption in the jazz world destroyed his health, threatened his life, and cost him his marriage. In despair, he drove northward with two lifelong drummer buddies, heading to "anywhere but LA."

He ended up settling in the small community of Port Townsend, Washington. With the financial support of his father-in-law, McClure founded the annual Port Townsend Jazz Festival (now known as Jazz Port Townsend). The distinguished reed player Bud Shank was lured north from Los Angeles to the action Barney had begun. Shank lives in Port Townsend to this day and runs a summer jazz camp in conjunction with directing the annual festival which has nationwide recognition. McClure and Shank teamed up on the 1984 album *Transition*.

The festival's success brought McClure city-wide prominence, resulting in his election as mayor of Port Townsend in 1979. In 1982 he ran a successful campaign to become a Democratic representative to the Washington State Legislature, playing prized jazz gigs all the while. He describes the triumphs of these years as a mixed blessing. "They were rewarding but difficult times for me," says McClure of the political success, which cost him a second marriage. He remains politically active and even flirted with the idea of running for mayor of Seattle.

Today's Barney McClure, the pianist, credits his father as his strongest musical influence: "He taught me how to think music, and my final switch to the piano notwithstanding, he was my most powerful mentor." Although critics cite Art Tatum and Oscar Peterson as clear influences on McClure, the high-speed dexterity and avalanche of notes that typify his play invite unwarranted oversimplifications. While not hiding the vast reach of his technique, in his more contemplative solos McClure displays warmth and poignancy; consider his treatment of the Johnny Mercer/ Johnny Mandel ballad "Emily" on *Among Friends* (1994, MNOP). Asked which musicians he feels influenced his playing, he cites Nat "King" Cole, the underrated George Shearing, and Horace Silver, who McClure says pushed "soul and gospel into me."

McClure also teaches workshops at high schools and colleges along the West Coast, ever reiterating, "There is no such thing as a mistake." He still tours internationally, most recently making a swing through Australia with saxophonist Red Holloway and touring Japan with trombonist Bill Watrous. McClure has released several superb CDs on his MNOP label, including *Tidings of Comfort and Jazz* (1995), *Not a Day Goes By . . .* (1995), and *Photographs* (1998). In 1999 he was working on producing two CDs featuring the unforgettable Seattle singer Jan Stentz: a reissue of an old LP treasure with Herb Ellis and Seattle multi-instrumentalist Jay Thomas entitled *Profiles*, and, in its entirety, her memorable final concert which she gave only days before her death in 1998, on a CD to be called *Forever (1999, MNOP).* **NB**

Among Friends

(1994, MNOP)
A broad-spectrum showing of Barney McClure's busiest and most relaxing piano moods.

Bob Nell

Pianist and composer Bob Nell falls into the generation between the 1960s veterans and the neobop "young lions" who have captured so much mainstream media attention since the late 1980s. Add to that Nell's remove from virtually all the jazz "centers," and you have the perfect recipe for obscurity and, worse, withering talent. But Nell defies such predictions. The Bozeman, Montana, native has not only stayed in the jazz fan's purview—albeit peripherally—but he has also churned out inventively original and highly distinctive postbebop jazz piano.

Nell got his start as a child virtuoso, playing piano by ear with perfect pitch. He remained in Montana throughout his childhood and adolescent years, eventually settling on a Fender Rhodes electric piano and various gigs with local rock bands. He discovered jazz by way of his brother's record collection, and soon developed adventurous listening tastes. In 1993 Nell told *Piano and Keyboard* magazine that fusion and the 1960s avant-garde were pivotal for his jazz education. "When I heard Eric Dolphy," Nell remarked, "that was it. I didn't see how music could get any better than this."

After beginning his college education at Montana State University, where he played with the school's jazz ensemble, Nell moved to Seattle in the late 1970s to study at the University of Washington. His studies of piano performance and composition led to a string of scholarships and eventually to his first major accolade. As a performer in William O. Smith's Contemporary Group, Nell entered the Contemporary Group Performance Competition in 1979. He played the staggering *Piano Sonata No. 1* of Pierre Boulez with such skill and accuracy that he was awarded first prize. His first jazz session was recorded that year with vibraphonist Fred Raulston and Open Stream.

Returning to Montana in 1980, Nell cut *In Montana* (Jazz Alliance), a dynamite, hard-blowing session with trumpeter Jack Walrath. A fellow Montana native, Walrath had moved to New York years before and played with renowned musicians such as Charles Mingus and Ray Charles. By 1981 Nell's chops were acknowledged by Cadence Jazz Records with the issue of *Chasin' a Classic*, a trio recording of outstanding maturity. He received a Montana Arts Council fellowship in 1989 and, after bassist Kelly Roberty secretly submitted a cassette of the pianist's solo playing to the 1991 Dewar's Profiles Performance Competition, Nell won a $10,000 prize. This honor led to the release of his astounding CD debut, *Why I Like Coffee* (1992, New World). Joining Nell were his Montana rhythm section, bassist Roberty, and drummer Brad Edwards (the trio plays as NRE throughout the Northwest), plus trumpeter Walrath and Ray Anderson, who remains one of the ten best trombonists on earth. *Why I Like Coffee* did wonders for Nell's reputation, cementing his talents as unmistakable for the cadre of listeners willing to take a chance on a musician they never read about in mainstream jazz (or music) publications.

In the years since that CD, Nell has received numerous commissions from Meet the Composer and the New Forms Regional Initiative, and has performed throughout the Northwest. He appeared on Michael Bisio's CD *Covert Choreography* (1996) and frequently joins Bisio for live performances.

Nell's playing melds assertive, clear articulation with keenly sculpted solos, which can slowly take shape and then speed through chordal displays and brilliant clusters. His compositions similarly come across as structurally complex and yet entirely warm, while also bringing consistent challenges to the fore. **AB**

In Montana

(1980, Jazz Alliance)
Reissued in 1996, this record by jazz trumpeter Jack Walrath is a crisp mix of a 1960s Blue Note–era hard-bop toss back and a complete stylistic scramble of snappy, tight postbop with searing avant-garde-touched solos and execution.

Why I Like Coffee

(1992, New World)
Probably one of the region's best jazz recordings ever, this CD has the peculiar power to compel mainstream and neophyte listeners to the same extent that it captures the ears of committed avant-gardists. Nell plays with such conviction that his compositions hit hard and solidly even when they take form at midtempo and with slow, patient clips.

Dave Peck

he could have enjoyed a career as an astronomer, or become a world-class chess player, or applied his mad genius to all sorts of life's adventures. But music, and jazz in particular, offered him a greater opportunity to share his creative gifts with a broader audience, and we should be grateful for Dave Peck's choice to become a pianist and composer.

The Oregon-born Peck's first instrument was the cello, which he took up at age 10. At 14 he attended a traveling summer jazz camp where, having turned to the piano, he came under the brief but stimulating influence of Marian McPartland. She took a fancy to Peck's potential, and from her home in New York corresponded with continuing encouragement. Peck recalls receiving a blues chorus she wrote out for him, and later some voicings for John Coltrane's "Naima." Several years passed, during which he served double duty playing trumpet in one high school band and piano in another. A major boost came from Seattle trumpet and sax player Floyd Standifer, in whose band he played and whom he describes as a "great teacher as well as a player."

Ever since Peck met and married Jane Lambert, who was enjoying a promising singing career, jazz has been paramount for the couple. Jane became chair of the music department at Seattle's Cornish College of the Arts, where Dave, an associate professor, teaches jazz composition and piano.

Seattle has an abundance of resident pianists who can be recruited to share the bandstand with visiting celebrities traveling without their rhythm section, but Dave Peck has always been in the front rank of the chosen. Together with longtime playing mates bassist Chuck Deardorf and drummer Dean Hodges, Peck has enhanced the shows of such jazz luminaries as Chet Baker, Ernestine Anderson, Joe Williams,

Sweets Edison, Lockjaw Davis, and Art Farmer, to name a few.

Bud Shank, the revered alto saxophonist, found a kindred creative spirit in Peck, prompting a professional association that has remained in place ever since Shank became the director of the annual Jazz Port Townsend festival in the mid-1980s. Shank, now a permanent resident of Washington State with his nationally acclaimed festival and teaching center, dedicated one of his CDs to Peck's compositions, *The Bud Shank Quintet Plays Tales of the Pilot: The Music of David Peck* (1989, Capri). The fifth member of the quintet was guitarist Dave Peterson.

Nothing, however, has brought Peck as much national attention as his current best-selling first recording as leader, *The Dave Peck Trio* (1998, produced with Jane Peck on the whimsically named Let's Play Stella). The growing number of serious Northwest jazz fans and the many fellow musicians who have long waited for Peck to boldly step out front will not want to miss this recording. But surprisingly this first CD by a composer of many published works features seven familiar classics, tunes often yawned off as "standards" in the self-conscious world of jazz. In the Seattle jazz chronicle, *5/4*, Peck explained his choice: "I prefer standards in trio and solo formats. I write a lot, but those pieces tend to be for larger groups. The writing is thick, and the long pieces don't lend themselves to free exploration. What I get out of composing is done when I'm finished with a piece." In fact, he adds, "sometimes when I hear other people play my stuff, it hurts."

The name Dave Peck, now echoing wherever jazz is appreciated around the country, attaches itself once again to standards in his new piano-only CD. In addition to his CD *The Dave Peck Trio*, Peck can be heard at the piano with Bud Shank's group on *Live at Jazz Alley* (1986, Contemporary), *Tomorrow's Rainbow* (1988, Contemporary), and *The Lost Cathedral* (1995, ITM). His arranging and composing commissions include works with Marco Silva, Ernestine Anderson, and Diane Schuur. **NB**

The Dave Peck Trio

(1998, LET'S PLAY STELLA)
Dave Peck, Chuck Deardorf, and Dean Hodges amaze with new versions of works by such venerable composers as Irving Berlin, Frank Loesser, and Jerome Kern.

Jim Pepper

Perhaps the most poignant Northwest document coming from the region's extensive jazz annals is not on a recording. Instead, a likely candidate for the honor is *Pepper's Pow Wow*, Sandra Sunrising Osawa's video portrait of tenor saxophonist and longtime Portland resident Jim Pepper. This well-filmed documentary thoughtfully insists on the weave of music and life as it reveals Pepper's honed artistry. *Pow Wow* also inadvertently illuminates the way traditional jazz reference books have ignored artists such as Pepper. Only one major jazz guide makes note of his career, while Osawa's documentary shows how important Pepper was to at least three developments in jazz since the mid-1960s: he was a founding member of the legendary jazz rock fusion pioneers Free Spirits; he advanced musical developments that combined jazz improvisation with world and folk music in the 1970s; and he threw light on the periphery of traditional forms like the jazz ballad, which merged into more adventurous forms such as free improvisation.

Born in 1942, Pepper moved with his family to Portland when he was a child. Of mixed Native American descent (his father was Kaw, his mother of Muskogee Creek ancestry), he was marked in Portland by his overarching Indianness. His father notes in *Pepper's Pow Wow* that the boy was "the only Indian in school" and experienced discrimination. Nonetheless, his family emphasized tribal ceremonial dancing, which spurred Pepper's interest in music and expressive performance. They also cross-pollinated the traditional dancing by encouraging Pepper to take up tap dancing. This mix of rhythms and executions certainly helped him define his saxophone technique as well as his cross-genre interests.

Pepper picked up clarinet first and saxophone second, eventually settling on tenor for his career instrument. In his early 20s, he left Portland for New York and attempted to work in the jazz world. By the mid-1960s, he had hooked up with young drummer Bob Moses, guitarist Larry Coryell (who lived in the Northwest in the 1950s and early 1960s), and bassist Chris Hills. Although their band, Free Spirits, is often named among the founders of jazz-rock fusion, Moses points out that Pepper's opening salvos for the band's dates were frequently Coltrane-inspired free improvisations running 20 minutes in length.

After Free Spirits issued *Out of Sight and Sound* (ABC) in 1967, Pepper played with Coryell on a handful of recordings, guesting also on *The Belle of Avenue A* with the unrepentantly irreverent Fugs in 1969. By 1971 Pepper had his own solo debut, *Pepper's Pow Wow,* and his hit single "Witchi Tai To" nearly placed the saxophonist in the odd position of Native American music superstar. With its melody taken from one of his grandfather's chants, "Witchi Tai To" broke the jazz Top 10. The song's success, however, left Pepper confused about his direction and led to an extended period of inactivity and difficulty. His few recording opportunities failed to produce another hit.

When the 1980s opened, Pepper returned to more favorable music projects by playing on Moses's *When Elephants Dream of Music* (1983, Gramavision) and with bassist Charlie Haden on the Liberation Music Orchestra's classic *Ballad of the Fallen* (1982, ECM). Shortly thereafter he recorded his own *Comin and Goin* (1988, Antilles). The remainder of the decade saw Pepper playing dates in Europe and the United States with, among others, drummer Paul Motian, trumpeter Don Cherry, and pianist Mal Waldron. He recorded extensively with Waldron and Motian as well as with trombonist Marty Cook. Pepper was compiling an impressive discography of his own when lymphoma cut his life short in 1992 at the age of 50.

Future generations might well remember Pepper for his consummate, though seemingly effortless, skill at melding different musical forms. He infused his improvisations with chants and dance patterns from Native American traditions. This technique might not have cracked the sacred jazz canon in the way that bop's architectural complexity and free jazz's mix of energy, spirituality, and politics have, but the musical advances Pepper made were considerable. His death represents a great loss to jazz. **AB**

Pepper's Pow Wow

(1971, EMBRYO)
Jim Pepper's solo debut, featuring his songs constructed around Native American musical themes, is still available only on vinyl as a collector's item.

Dakota Song

(1988, ENJA)
A fine Pepper CD, coming late in his career and displaying his prodigious command of jazz and other musical vocabularies.

Milo Petersen

It may be the first time a jazz CD nurtured and produced exclusively by Seattle musicians has rushed so quickly up the Gavin charts, the radio version of TV's Nielsen ratings. It took less than a month for *Visiting Dignitaries* (1997, Passage) by Milo Petersen and the Jazz Disciples to climb to no. 12 nationally in the summer of 1997, where it remained for weeks, all the while earning heavy radio airplay on jazz stations. Petersen's debut project as a bandleader—at a youthful 45 years of age—came on the heels of a remarkable career as a jazz drummer, guitarist, composer, and music educator.

Petersen's first influence was his grandfather, who played harmonica and accordion in his native Denmark. When 5-year-old Milo showed an interest in the harmonica, he remembers being told in a thick Danish accent, "First, you have to learn how to whistle." From the harmonica, young Petersen went to the violin at age 6 and graduated to the guitar at 8, eventually studying with such legends as Herb Ellis, Tal Farlow, and Joe Pass. Drums came later, with teachers such as Victor Hart, Steve Ellington, and Jeff Hamilton providing instruction.

The best Northwest jazz musicians have a star collection of touring jazzmen they've worked with; Petersen's list includes Eartha Kitt, Julian Priester, Joe Sample, and Herb Ellis. While much of his work has been as a drummer, Petersen is also held in high esteem as a guitarist; he recently played guitar on a Steve Griggs project with famed drummer Elvin Jones.

The Jazz Disciples are an all-star quartet of top Seattle players—tenor saxman Rick Mandyck, bassist Phil Sparks, trumpeter Jay Thomas, and pianist/composer Marc Seales—each a recording artist in his own right. Playing subtle drums, Petersen wasn't just another one of the guys; he composed and arranged nine of the ten tracks (the tenth was a John Coltrane composition).

Jazz critics, notoriously tough as a group, have unanimously praised *Visiting Dignitaries*, one describing the CD as "a stylistic throwback to the Miles Davis Group of 30 years ago." Petersen acknowledges Davis, Coltrane, Thelonious Monk, Charles Mingus, and Wayne Shorter—all considered at least thirty years ahead of their time—as the inspiration for his jazz.

The sudden success of his quintet has brought Petersen several management offers, meaning he will likely leave behind his Northwest roots for New York or Los Angeles recording sessions and national tours. But there's more to the music of Milo Petersen. He will doubtless share a long future with Valerie Illman, a gifted singer/pianist. Already the duo is enchanting lounge audiences, as her sultry, laid-back treatment of carefully chosen songs interplays with his seven-string guitar notes, inviting comparisons to the partnership of Cleo Laine and Johnny Dankworth.

In addition to his work as a drummer, guitarist, and composer, Petersen has been an educator at Western Washington University in Bellingham, the Centrum Jazz Workshop in Port Townsend, Cornish College of the Arts in Seattle, Olympic Community College in Bremerton, and the Friends Seminary in New York, where he spent four years leading trios and quartets before returning to Seattle. He was honored with a composition grant from the Seattle Arts Commission in 1993.

Petersen describes jazz first as music, and music as "a universal language capable of transcending international and cultural barriers. It should be an integral part of our educational process, a constant influence on our culture, the present and future of which lives in the hearts of today."

Most jazz sidemen have remained in that role by choice, resisting the lure of more money in order to maintain the pleasure of simply playing (and to avoid the headaches of leadership). Petersen has enjoyed his sideman adventures and professional growth through his association with numerous jazz luminaries. The success of Milo Petersen and the Jazz Disciples seems destined to rocket him to new levels as a musician and composer—and leader. **NB**

Visiting Dignitaries

(1997, PASSAGE)
This hailing of the spirit of innovators Charles Mingus, Miles Davis, Thelonious Monk, John Coltrane, and Wayne Shorter propelled Milo Petersen and the Jazz Disciples into the contemporary jazz mainstream.

Julian Priester

In the mid-1990s, trombonist Julian Priester made it clear that he preferred to be known as a recording artist residing in Seattle, rather than a de facto Seattle artist. Fine point, perhaps, but for Priester, fine points are the point. His decades of accompanying roles in jazz and improvised music have brought him to a position where he can chime in with the subtlest of pinpoint notes or textures, and people will pay close attention. He often plays with a reserve and economy that belie his vast talents. During his tenure as a professor at Seattle's Cornish College of the Arts, he has rarely recorded his own works or presented his own bands, but when he plays guest gigs with the late Sun Ra's Arkestra or Kosmic Crewe, led by Sun Ra collaborator Michael Ray, fans and musicians alike listen intently to what the trombonist has to say.

Priester has been playing jazz and improvised music since the mid-1950s. A Chicagoan by birth (in 1935), Priester began his longstanding association with the Chicago-based Sun Ra in 1954, after stints as a sideman with numerous local blues legends, including Muddy Waters and Bo Diddley. It was as an early member of Sun Ra's groups that Priester gained considerable notoriety. From the beginning Sun Ra's music was either heralded as unequivocal brilliance or reviled as unbearable nonsense; Priester helped keep the emphasis on the former description. While he spent a relatively brief period as a full-time Arkestra member, Priester recorded on what music historians believe is the inaugural Arkestra recording; *Sun Ra: The Singles*, a two-CD collection of rare releases from the bandleader's Saturn Records, presents two sessions Priester cut when he was with the group in its earliest Chicago days. "Medicine for a Nightmare" may be the Sun Ra Arkestra's first release; it moves with a poignant power made formidable by Priester's ever-reserved midregister trombone work. And the earliest version of the Sun Ra classic "Saturn" (also on *The Singles*) burns even brighter, anchored keenly by the warmth of Priester's sliding scales and delightfully shaded notes.

After stints with Lionel Hampton's band and vocalist Dinah Washington, Priester relocated to New York, where he played in a succession of great bands. He left his mark on the Max Roach Orchestra and Chorus's steamrolling paean to civil rights protest, *It's Time*, as well as on Roach's *Percussion Bitter Sweet* (both on the Impulse! label). In the late 1960s Priester played briefly with the Duke Ellington Orchestra and performed scores of gigs as an accompanist. Some of his best work dates from 1967, when he was recording with saxophonist Sam Rivers's sextet (not released until 1977). With Rivers, as with so many others, Priester's playing provides vivid contrasts: where the band's other members favor exactness in phrasing, Priester revels in his slide's penchant for blurry phrases and smears. He also shows an orchestral touch, taking high-note roads when necessary and, at other times, slip-sliding his way around the melodies and harmonies.

In the early 1970s Priester joined yet another visionary band, Herbie Hancock's

Mwandishi sextet, in which the trombonist took the Swahili name Pepo Mtoto. The electric, free fusion of Hancock's group was elastic to a great degree, allowing Priester lots of space to spread his sound around. Throughout the decade Priester played an array of gigs, many of them after his relocation to the West Coast in the mid-1970s. He took on another largely full-time association in the early 1980s, with the fantastic groups of British bassist Dave Holland, with whom Priester cut some truly remarkable recordings for the German ECM Records label. Into the 1990s Priester recorded on several CDs for saxophonist Ralph Simon's hip Postcards label, including a reunion with Sam Rivers, *Hints on Light and Shadow* (1997), on which Tucker Martine, a Priester associate and fellow Seattleite, backed the duo on electronics. On this CD Priester once again shows he has a clear vision of a trombone artistry that veers away from pyrotechnics and revels in nuance and collaborative dynamics. **AB**

It's Time

(1961, IMPULSE!)
On this Max Roach classic, Julian Priester's trombone leaves its most discernible and memorable swath on "Another Valley," where his sublime lines carry the melody and solos.

Hints on Light and Shadow

(1997, POSTCARDS)
A gently exciting display of talent. The music is eerily free of traditional structure, at times moving ambiently and then showing off latticework levels of improvisational detail between Priester and fellow avant-garde alum Sam Rivers—not to mention the creaky, billowy electronics talent of Tucker Martine.

Bill Ramsay

benny Goodman could have had any tenor saxman he wanted for his octet's U.S. tours. In 1979 he accepted a friend's recommendation and chose Washington native Bill Ramsay. The following year Goodman needed no middleman as tout, and Ramsay was the man again. Bill was surprised when Goodman called on him a third time, for a 1982 tour that included Carnegie Hall and two Playboy Jazz Festivals at the Hollywood Bowl. As the single constant in the octet's three tours, Ramsay wasn't just a big band sideman (especially difficult for a player three thousand miles removed from the group's New York comfort zone), but *the* tenor man under Goodman's demanding leadership. He took solos in virtually every number.

Other jazz adventures have found Ramsay with the Maynard Ferguson band and with Count Basie during his final playing days. He has since continued with the

Basie bands, first when Tee Carson replaced the Count at the piano, and then under a succession of leaders—Eric Dixon, Thad Jones, Frank Foster, and, most recently, Grover Mitchell. Ramsay last appeared with the band in Seattle at the 1998 New Year's celebration at the Westin Hotel. Frank Wess, premier Basie flutist, recruited Ramsay for his big band tour of Japan.

When leading a band of his own, Ramsay enjoys the fun of experimentation: a few years ago he chose the name Tenor Madness for his band, which features four tenor saxophones and a rhythm section. Later he took the saxophone up a register and formed the group Los Altos, with Denney Goodhew, Jay Thomas, and Jim Coile. He now favors alto and baritone. In addition, Ramsay has become an arranger of note, contributing three tracks to Jay Thomas's epic CD *360 Degrees* (1995, HEP), on which his alto solos are prominent throughout. In the Seattle Repertory Jazz Orchestra, Ramsay's baritone anchors the reed section.

Coinciding with a career as a full-time famous jazzman, a lifetime hobby has kept Ramsay busy. He's been an enthusiast of all kinds of model and full-scale trains ever since he discovered the roundhouse in his hometown of Centralia, Washington. We're talking N-gauge, Lionel, G-gauge—and Amtrak. He and Frankie, his wife of forty-seven years, rarely miss an opportunity for a long train trip. A lifelong member of the Garden Railroad Association, he's building an imposing layout in the ample backyard of his Tacoma home.

In recent days Ramsay and Milt Kleeb, the distinguished arranger/saxophonist, have enjoyed a highly respectable alliance as cobandleaders of the Bill Ramsay/Milt Kleeb Band. In 1998, with tenor artist Pete Christlieb, they delivered the exciting CD *Kelly's Heroes*, a tribute to Red Kelly, the renowned bass player who played with Woody Herman, Stan Kenton, and Harry James. **NB**

Kelly's Heroes

(1998, CARS)
Credited to Pete Christlieb and the Bill Ramsay/Milt Kleeb Band, this CD is dedicated to Red Kelly, the best friend Northwest jazz ever had. (Kelly and his wife, Donna, have been feeding and hosting jazz fanciers for years at their Tacoma, Washington club.) The album includes Kelly's poignant, husky vocals on "Teach Me Tonight," the first time his voice has been recorded since a tune called "George" on a Stan Kenton LP in the 1950s.

Diane Schuur

J azz purists may sniff at her love of the blues and fondness for loading her albums with pop songs and jazz standards, but audiences thrill to Diane Schuur's familiar repertoire and three-and-a-half octave voice. Grammy Award voters like her too: they gave her top jazz female vocal honors in consecutive years for *Timeless* (1986) and *Diane Schuur and the Count Basie Orchestra* (1987). Not bad for a singer who was "discovered" at age 35, in her twenty-sixth year as a performer. Born in Tacoma on December 10, 1953, Schuur was blinded just after birth in a hospital accident. She began singing as a child (her earliest musical memory is awakening to Dinah Washington's "What a Difference a Day Makes" on her clock radio) and was performing by age 9.

The teenage Schuur recorded a single ("Dear Mommy and Daddy"/"The Sun Is Shining") for Decca Records in 1971 and two subsequent singles for small labels, but her first major career break was a successful audition in 1975 for *Tonight Show* drummer Ed Shaughnessy. With the Shaughnessy band, she performed several times at the Monterey Jazz Festival.

Since her first trip to the White House, Schuur has performed in concert with the Seattle Men's Chorus; dueted with Barry Manilow on the song "Summertime" (on both his television special and his album, *Swing Street*); sung tributes at Carnegie Hall to Irving Berlin and Ella Fitzgerald; and toured the United States, Europe, and Japan. A particular favorite of former *Tonight Show* host Johnny Carson, Schuur appeared eleven times on the show from 1986 to 1992. **JB**

Love Songs
(1993, GRP)
Diane Schuur, two orchestras, and ten lovely ballads—a winning combination.

Heart to Heart
(1994, GRP)
A simply charming collaboration featuring Schuur's talents along with the vocals and guitar of blues master B. B. King. The two share the spotlight marvelously (King's smoky lead vocals are prominently featured), and there is a tone of mutual admiration and fondness here that can't be faked.

Marc Seales

If Claude Debussy were alive today and found himself in jazz, he'd remind people of Marc Seales. And given his present perch as head of the jazz studies division at the University of Washington, a tenured position, it wouldn't be surprising if one day conductor Gerard Schwarz commissioned Seales to write a major work for the Seattle Symphony Orchestra. This pianist seems destined to take today's concepts of jazz to new levels that call up, with no rhythmic limitations, the creative latitude usually associated with classical music.

Seales was born in Tacoma, Washington, where his father's journeys as an Air

Force man had led the family. He remembers with ease the first recordings that influenced him, and still plays them now and then: Mahalia Jackson, Duke Ellington, and Johnny Hodges together in an LP entitled *Back to Back*; Charlie Barnet doing "Eastside Westside"; Dave Brubeck; the Modern Jazz Quartet; and Ahmad Jamal.

More in demand as a sideman than he usually has time for, Seales, who lives in Seattle with his wife, Mary Kay, and daughter, Maddie, has worked with virtually all the premier jazzmen in the region and sometimes accepts recording dates in New York. At the constant core of his creative work is the trio New Stories, which Seales insists is not his group but an equal effort with bassist Doug Miller (who, with Seales, contributes much of the group's original music) and drummer John Bishop (whose composition "Circled by Hounds" is the title track of their first CD). New Stories released *Remember Why* (Origin) in 1997, participated on three recent CDs by the prodigious saxophonist Don Lanphere, and shared billing by name on two: *Lopin'* (1992, HEP) and *Don Still Loves Midge* (1997, HEP).

Apart from New Stories, Seales anchors a rhythm section that includes bassist Phil Sparks, drummer Clarence Acox, and guitarist Robin Kutz in the hugely successful concerts given by the seventeen-piece Seattle Repertory Jazz Orchestra, founded by Acox and University of Washington faculty member and saxophonist Michael Brockman. As Professor Seales (he's called "Professor" only during his lectures on the history of jazz), he focuses on teaching jazz piano and jazz improvisation, as well as participating in the formation of student groups.

Many people have noted that Seales exudes an aura of well-being while playing. Whether he's smiling in appreciation of a colleague's instrumental solo or deep into his own playing, all seems well as long as he's at the piano. **NB**

Don Still Loves Midge

(1997, HEP)
This Don Lanphere/New Stories release features fine compositions and piano solos by Marc Seales.

Bud Shank

after logging four decades in the professional jazz world, alto saxophonist and flutist Bud Shank has built a career that merits a lengthy treatise. Not only was he an exemplary, if often overlooked, figure in the West Coast jazz scene of the 1950s, Shank is more recently the purveyor of an internationally recognized annual workshop and festival held in his adopted hometown of Port Townsend, Washington. His career has spanned innumerable legendary points, from playing road dates with Miles Davis to being famously summoned by Duke Ellington—who couldn't convince Shank to leave California for a place in the Ellington Orchestra.

Born in Dayton, Ohio, in 1926, Shank was already a multi-instrumentalist as a teenager. He studied clarinet, flute, and alto and tenor sax at the University of North Carolina. His West Coast days began in the late 1940s, when he studied under trumpeter and arranger Shorty Rogers in 1947. After a stint in the big band of tenor sax player Charlie Barnet, Shank joined Stan Kenton's forty-member Innovations Orchestra. He was one of several key soloists in Kenton's sprawling ensemble (Art Pepper and Maynard Ferguson were among the other big names), a group that included a full string section and used innovative and (not surprisingly) extremely complicated arrangements. He later played in Kenton's other performance groups, including the Neophonic Orchestra.

Shank did not become a West Coast icon, however, until he joined up with Howard Rumsey's Lighthouse All-Stars for several years in the mid-1950s. Former Kenton bassist Rumsey managed the Lighthouse club at Hermosa Beach, and performances by the All-Stars there helped solidify the fluid, rounded edges of what became known as "West Coast Cool." Shank had neither the angular fire nor the controversy-fueled temperament of fellow alto sax player Art Pepper; instead he had a strong penchant for Stan Kenton's protoclassical ambitions, favoring more through-composed works over the bop and cool-jazz workhorses popular with other players of his generation. Shank's compositional chops, while excellent in almost any jazz space, drew him toward chamber music and infused each of his works with a sense of structure that owed much to classical music's traditions without altering his solid jazz core. Shank began releasing his own recordings as a bandleader while still a member of the Lighthouse group, and he was a well-admired talent on flute and alto sax through the 1950s and 1960s.

Shank's work with Brazilian guitarist Laurindo Almeida was some of his finest and certainly his most famous. Almeida's peaks with Shank happened in 1953 and later, in 1958, as the two became synonymous with a kind of easygoing hybrid of bebop and bossa nova that would help push West Coast jazz toward Brazilian popular music—just as bebop had pressed the flesh with Cuban music a decade earlier. Shank and Almeida were both talented enough to become first-call players for Hollywood studio sessions. Countless episodes of nameless music for the entertainment industry subsidized the more compelling jazz careers that, alas, rarely paid the bills. Shank's association with Almeida came full circle when the pair cofounded the L.A. Four and played with bassist Ray Brown and a series of drummers in the 1970s. In the late 1970s Shank began doing solo sessions, all but dropping the flute to concentrate on his alto sax. He developed a more aggressive style and cut several albums for the Concord Jazz, Muse, and Contemporary labels, including *This Bud's for You* (1984, Muse) and *That Old Feeling* (1986, Contemporary).

As of the 1980s, Shank was no longer an L.A. Four member and no longer an Angeleno. He relocated to the small Olympic Peninsula town of Port Townsend, where he's headed up Jazz Port Townsend and the Bud Shank Jazz Workshop ever since. Each year, he brings a mixture of world-class touring talent and Northwest creative musicians to the peninsula for a week of solid training and teaching sessions followed by several days of live performances. Possibly the most important jazz event outside a major North American metropolis, Shank's workshop provides unparalleled access to musicians and composers, and then supports the training with legendarily long after-hours sessions that draw on the full gamut of visiting and local talents.

It comes as no surprise that Shank is also recalling his past work with Stan Kenton and various classical music ensembles to fuel a creative burst in the 1990s. The Bud Shank Sextet plays sinuous West Coast bop with a daunting front line of four horns and only a bassist and drummer for harmonic and rhythmic moorage. And Shank's multimedia extravaganza *The Lost Cathedral* demonstrates that he can challenge listeners with wide-ranging explorations of tone and execution, not to mention structure and expansiveness. As the annual Port Townsend events become more ambitious each year, Shank plays a few carefully chosen live dates with selected ensembles, including West Coast all-star aggregates. He is, however, strongly drawn to arranging and composing his own works in the wake of *The Lost Cathedral*. **AB**

Blowin' Country

(1958, BLUE NOTE)

As members of Stan Kenton's Innovations in Modern Music orchestra until 1951, Bob Cooper and Bud Shank had the ideal venue to explore different sonorities, especially in their winning combinations of flute (Shank) and oboe (Cooper). *Blowin' Country* catches Shank and Cooper in two sessions, the first in 1956 and second in 1958. They duel in every combination—two tenor saxes, flute and oboe, flute and bass clarinet, alto and oboe, and more. The recording has a laid-way-back vibe that belies the utter expertise with which the band tackled the fifteen tunes.

New Gold

(1995, CANDID)

For all his mid-1950s West Coast bop shimmerings, Shank's best recording to date remains *New Gold*, which introduced his four-horn sextet. Shank plays a strong leading role, taking the group toward an unmoored sound that bears traces, oddly enough, of Thelonious Monk and even more avant-garde ensembles. The CD's tracks, however, infused with a tremendous warmth and tonal richness, remain unmistakably West Coast.

Wally Shoup

an improvising alto saxophonist and Alabama native, Wally Shoup has been given several occasions to write about his uncompromising music. In an article in Seattle alternative weekly, *The Stranger*, he says simply, "Music is an infinite game: it reflects both the human world of understanding (and all the subtleties contained therein) and the non-human world of what remains to be understood. To use music as an imaginative means to understand the new and unfamiliar is what separates the artist from the entertainer." As an artist, Shoup has always been aware of that dichotomy. A former schoolteacher, he came upon improvised music in 1974 and shortly thereafter began his sometimes hardscrabble career of organizing, performing, and promoting freely improvised music and avant-garde jazz.

Shoup emigrated to Seattle in 1985 and quickly began playing at the center of the avant-garde music scene. In such ensembles as the Catabatics and the Pulsation Crew, Shoup drew crowds from diverse musical audiences in part because of his fierce intensity and strenuously explorative saxophone performances. Following in the shoes of Anthony Braxton, Steve Lacy, Evan Parker, and other well-known jazz musicians, Shoup records himself on solo alto sax and sells cassettes to fans at his performances. He toured England as a solo performer in 1993 and has performed throughout the United States and western Canada both as a soloist and with his ensembles. In addition, he began supporting other musicians in the Seattle and Northwest scene by helping arrange the respected Seattle Festival of Improvised Music, in its thirteenth consecutive year as of 1999. The festival has attracted legions of Northwest improvisers as well as international figures like soprano saxophonist John Butcher and pianist Fred van Hove.

Shoup was crucial in the launching of the Other Sounds series in late 1995. The continuing series invites musicians to perform to solid, if intimate, crowds at regularly scheduled concerts in Seattle. Shoup's most vaunted ensemble is Project W, whose debut CD of the same name on the Apraxia label has become the stuff of legend. Project W is a lean trio, placing Shoup's alto sax and Brent Arnold's cello in front of various drummers' percussive bedding while the group simultaneously discovers musical paths. They play entirely free music, with no notation or prior structures. Defying the common practice of free improvisers simply playing at length until they exhaust an idea, Shoup's model springs from the musical short form, much as opera draws on the art song. Project W's performances are built on kernels of energy that expand for comparatively brief spans, most often just a few quick minutes. The band has played numerous times throughout the Northwest, once as an opening act for alternative rock innovators Sonic Youth. Also a painter and costume designer for dancers (he toured Europe with dancer Mary Horn in 1985), Shoup displays an elegantly adventurous sense of music as a constantly evolving series of brushstrokes. **AB**

Project W

(1995, APRAXIA)
A wonderful adventure, exemplifying Wally Shoup's insistence on constant musical newness. The CD is heated on all sides by three veteran free improvisers (Shoup, cellist Brent Arnold, and drummer Ed Pias) playing in smart bursts of creative excitement.

Floyd Standifer

I f Floyd Standifer had been born, raised, and married in New York, he might have become the most famous jazz musician in America. As it turned out, even a celebrated 1959–60 world tour with Quincy Jones's big band couldn't hold him in New York. Instead, he returned to his hometown and his family and remains only the most famous jazz musician in Seattle playing trumpet and sax. At the New Orleans club in Pioneer Square, a very good sound system that cancels out the room's imperfect acoustics has made the Floyd Standifer Quartet's Wednesday performances a churchlike ritual for countless jazz fans.

Born a minister's son in Wilmington, North Carolina, Standifer moved with his family to the Portland area, and then Seattle. At his Gresham, Oregon, high school graduation, he gained dubious recognition as a band member when he fell off the stage, entangled in his sousaphone.

Standifer's performance history is numerous and deep: he was a company member of the Harold Arlen–Johnny Mercer blues opera *Free and Easy*, a principal musician in a poetry and jazz evening with avant-garde poet Kenneth Patchen, the musical director for a three-play stint at Seattle's Black Arts West Theater, and with Stan Keen composer of original music for poet Theodore Roethke's presentation of "Nonsense Poems." And Christmas after Christmas, Standifer, along with the popular accordian player Frank Sugia, was a musical troubadour parading the aisles of the Frederick & Nelson department store before its closure in the 1990s.

His trumpet has been featured in numerous jazz festivals; recently Standifer has split his solos among trumpet, flugelhorn, and tenor saxophone. He credits Fats Navarro as a model and inspiration for his trumpet technique (Navarro died at age 27, about the age of Standifer's many music students). He's been a featured jazz soloist with the Seattle Symphony Orchestra, and a contract teacher at the University of Washington music department, and has performed in Italy and Switzerland with vibes player Elmer Gill.

Standifer's work on both trumpet and saxophone can be found on Clarence Acox's CDs *Johanna's Dance* (1995) and *Indigenous Groove* (1997). His extended tenor sax solo on his CD *How Do You Keep the Music Playing* (1996, Nightflight) stamps him, in the words of one critic, "a tenor man to be reckoned with." And Standifer sings the Michel Legrand–penned title track with a rich vocal poignancy that matches the high quality of his trumpet solo.

Although his playing has been featured on many recordings, it says something of Standifer the man that he waited until 1996 to release a CD in his own name. Refreshingly, he remains the epitome of geniality, a characteristic in short supply in the highly competitive jazz world. **NB**

(1996, NIGHTFLIGHT PRODUCTIONS)
This CD is a celebration of Floyd Standifer's regular gig at the New Orleans club in Seattle's Pioneer Square, where Standifer is Seattle's number-one jazz tourist attraction every Wednesday night. Bebop standouts Billy Wallace (piano), Phil Sparks (bass), and Clarence Acox (drums) join him.

Jay Thomas

You'd hardly suspect just by talking to Jay Thomas that he has received worldwide acclaim for his performances on six instruments: trumpet, flugelhorn, flute, and alto, tenor, and soprano saxes. He exudes a boyishness that belies years of playing around the globe with jazz musicians whose names (like his) draw crowds. Even in his native Seattle, Thomas is recognized as one of the greats, no matter what instrument he's playing.

Thomas speaks freely of a reckless period in his youth, when he was successful too soon to maintain control. While still a student at Shoreline High School in a suburb of Seattle, Thomas won a *Down Beat* magazine scholarship to Boston's Berklee College of Music. Discovering he was a gifted musician fortunately led him to recognize the advantages of study. From Boston, Thomas moved to New York, where he studied with famed trumpet teacher Carmine Caruso. Instantly accepted by far more experienced musicians, he was a welcome player at Greenwich Village jam sessions and worked one summer with Machito's Latin Band. Three years of playing in New York seasoned his talents. Returning to Seattle, Thomas added flute and tenor sax to his collection of fine musical hardware (his first exposure to the flute was hearing his sister play the instrument).

Through the mid-1970s, Thomas was the rage of jazz musicians in the Bay Area. After coming home again to Seattle, he became a frequent member of the house band at the jazz club Parnell's. Jazz icons such as Zoot Sims, Sonny Stitt, George Cables, Sal Nistico, and Chet Baker insisted that Thomas sit in with them on their Seattle visits. He toured Great Britain with the hilarious jazz satirist Slim Gaillard.

Singers love Jay Thomas. Jan Stentz, Diane Schuur, Jay Clayton, Greta Matassa, Ernestine Anderson, and Becca Duran have all called upon Thomas's talents. Duran, his longtime companion and musical collaborator, has toured Japan five times with his group; their new group, Evolution, blends sung and instrumental jazz with many South American and African rhythmic traditions.

Thomas describes his music as eclectic, drawing on all the musical situations he's encountered in the whirlwinds of his mostly enjoyed life. His career highlights are many. Two CDs by the exquisite pianist Jessica Williams, *Joy* and *Jessica's Blues*, feature especially noteworthy Thomas contributions as trumpeter, tenor saxophonist, and flutist. *Easy Does It* (1989, Discovery), his first CD, also featured Cedar Walton and Billy Higgins. The song "Blues for McVouty" (from the album of the same name released by Stash Records), dedicated to Slim Gaillard, was selected by *Village Voice* in 1993 as one of the year's top jazz recordings. Thomas's CD *360 Degrees* was the nation's recording event of 1995 and belongs on the shelf of every jazz collector. He also made important contributions to the highly praised CD *Visiting Dignitaries* by Milo Petersen and the Jazz Disciples.

Thomas is a regular guest on the jazz festival circuit. He was chosen Jazz Musician of 1996 by members of the Seattle organization Earshot Jazz, and the national magazine *Jazziz* selected him as one of the top ten players in its 1997 "Brass on Fire" search. His more recent CD, *Live at Tula's* (1998, McVouty), is another recording high spot of the caliber Seattle has come to expect of him.

Says critic Mike Shera of London's *International Jazz Journal*: "He has a superb full sound, wonderful time, a delightedly relaxed and confident approach that stems from a superb technique, and is full of fresh ideas. He reminds me a little of both Clifford Brown and Kenny Dorham, but only a little. Mainly, he is his own man." **NB**

360 Degrees

(1995, HEP)

A showcase of top jazz arrangers, including Bill Ramsay, Jim Knapp, John Wikan, Travis Shook, Jack Percival, and Jay Thomas himself. It also shows the multi-instrumentalist at his best. On this CD Thomas gives a full measure of attention to all six of his instruments.

Ralph Towner and Oregon

Of all the esteemed members of the jazz group Oregon, guitarist Ralph Towner has amassed the greatest critical acclaim and most identifiable aesthetic. When Oregon formed in 1970, the group relied almost exclusively on Towner's inventive compositions, which combined the several musical paths he had traveled: classical guitarist, jazz pianist, and member of the eclectic Paul Winter Consort.

Towner was born in 1940 in Chehalis, Washington. He was an exceedingly fast learner: by his early teens, he had played piano and trumpet for years. He earned a bachelor of arts in composition at the University of Oregon in the late 1950s. Shortly after his university days, he immersed himself in the classical guitar, studying in Austria at the Vienna Academy of Music in the 1960s before settling in New York and joining the jazz scene around 1969. He worked as a pianist with a roster of well-seasoned jazz veterans before joining the Paul Winter Consort, where he met the others who would cofound Oregon: bassist Glen Moore, reed player Paul McCandless, and original percussionist Collin Walcott.

Moore, a Portland native, shared a strong jazz past with Towner when the two began playing with Walcott and McCandless, an exceptional talent on bass clarinet, English horn, oboe, and soprano saxophone. The quartet's proficiency at international music—especially East Indian rhythms and compositional ideas—melded with their similarly broad backgrounds in jazz and classical music. Part chamber-music ensemble, part panstylistic world group, and part postbebop improvisational vehicle, Oregon defied multiple musical codes in the 1970s and later: they didn't play atonal abstractions, high-energy free jazz, or electric fusion; but neither did they play polished, nostalgic straight-ahead jazz. The group found a niche in the jazz world, attracting fans of the avant-garde as well as those yearning for a smoother sound, a more agreeably calm music than bop or its various offshoots. McCandless's double reeds and Towner's guitar in particular made the group sound gorgeously full and lithe at once. When Walcott died in 1984, the group pressed on, first with Trilok Gutu as their percussionist and then continuing as a trio. Most agree that Oregon peaked during Walcott's tenure, but in 1997 the group reemerged with percussionist Arto Tuncboyaciyan adding a firm rhythmic touch.

For his part, Towner has been the busiest member of Oregon in terms of recordings and collaborations. Critics have often remarked that Towner plays guitar like a pianist, extending chords beyond the usual bounds and making his tones sing extravagantly without ever seeming pretentious. His twelve-string and classical guitars cut a magnetic path through virtually all the Oregon recordings, but instead of grabbing attention with virtuosic lightning, he does so with a warmly burnished sound and an impeccable classical ear for tonal exactitude.

Towner has worked his guitar magic on many solo and intimate duet recordings, most notably *Diary* (1973, ECM) as a soloist, *Sargasso Sea* (1976, ECM) with guitarist John Abercrombie, and *Slide Show* (1985, ECM) with vibraphonist Gary Burton. He performed with trumpeter Kenny Wheeler on the fiery *Old Friends, New Friends* (1979, ECM), and of course is heard on Oregon's numerous fine recordings. Of particular interest in the Oregon catalog are their debut, *Music of Another Present Era* (1972, Vanguard), its successor, *Distant Hills* (1973, Vanguard), and the powerful *Northwest Passage* (1997, Intuition); which hearkens back to the group's early, heady days when they seemed to effortlessly combine subtle and driving rhythms with McCandless's swirling double reeds and Towner's painterly, imaginative, and genre-bending compositions. His guitar stretched every notion, too, reaching for acoustic clarity beginning in 1972 and staying focused for decades on a more classical approach. **AB**

Music of Another Present Era

(1973, VANGUARD)
Oregon's first album was a momentous, if not overtly powerful, debut. The band showed its floating capabilities over an easily missed rhythmic intensity. Oregon has long held the tension between corralled energy and mellow textures in high regard, and on *Another Present Era* and its immediate successor, *Distant Hills* (1973, Vanguard), they made that tension the hub of their creative wheel.   CONTINUED...

(1998, ECM)

This collaboration between Ralph Towner and bassist Gary Peacock in their late-1990s prime poignantly captures the most stately, delicate moments of an intimate duo—then follows with jumping, sonorous energy that clearly shows the pair's collective history in jazz's postbop movement.

Paul West

Paul West hasn't missed a day at the piano for forty-four years. He wasn't old enough to buy a drink legally when he got his first professional job at the now-legendary Seattle dine-and-dance spot the Colony. This was also the career birthplace of a singer named Pat Suzuki, a former classmate of West's at San Jose State University in California—the Suzuki who went directly from Seattle to the cover of *Time* and stardom on Broadway in Rodgers and Hammerstein's *Flower Drum Song*.

Paul West has been best known (and often honored) for his creativity as an advertising executive. Yet he's somehow combined that career with one as a jazz pianist with the encouragement of both the women in his life—his wife, Ingrid, and their daughter, Lindy. His daughter's own interest in music (she's a pianist with Clarence Acox's jazz ensemble at Seattle's Garfield High School) has inspired West's renewed dedication to the piano.

A unique aspect of West's success as a professional piano man—with three albums and a biweekly gig at the College Club with bassist Lee Phelps—is that he is a four-key piano player—C, F, B flat, E flat. These are the keys he had mastered before the heavy demands of his advertising career obliged him to quit his deep study with his demanding teacher, the hermitic Jerry Gray. This four-key limit sticks in Paul's craw, yet every jazzman who knows West is delighted to work with him. One renowned Seattle horn player says, "Hell, I love to work with Paul in any damned key—he swings and he's tasty."

West made his first recording in 1968 in the hot trio BLT, with Phelps, bassist Rolf Johnson, and singer/guitarist Gail Clements. That same year, he also recorded an album featuring his own compositions, *Married to the Blues*. Both are collector's items. West's first solo CD, *Lucky So and So* (MNOP), was released in 1999. He takes occasional gigs with his bass-playing, jazz-writing son, Jason.

A distinctive singer as well, West covers a broad spectrum of vocal music, from Cole Porter to Tom Lehrer to a treatment of "Georgia on My Mind" with discernible leanings toward the style of Mose Allison. Among fellow jazz pianists, he often speaks admiringly of Dave McKenna.

About ten years ago, while West was working for an advertising firm in Los Angeles, he came upon a startling ad in the classified section: "Smart new restaurant looking for jazz-minded piano player. Must know showtunes and be willing to wear a tuxedo." As Paul was leaving the audition, the owner ran after him and asked, "Do you know 'The Folks Who Live on the Hill'?" West answered in the affirmative but was puzzled by the question. Halfway through his opening night, a man whispered in his ear. "Say guy, d'you know 'The Folks Who Live on the Hill'?" Glancing up from the keyboard, West looked right into the face of Mickey Rooney. The actor, a friend of the proprietor, showed up every night for a couple of weeks and discussed music production deals with West. Before anything developed, a business offer brought him back to Seattle. But this brief episode playing solo jazz piano cemented West's determination to do his first solo CD, where his four keys would be plenty. And he'd never have to worry about a horn player calling out, "Let's take that in D." NB

Lucky So and So

(1999, MNOP)

One of Microsoft's recent retirees, West plays in all keys at last on this CD. An unforgettably soaring performance—in words and music both.

Bert Wilson

Saxophonist Bert Wilson continually surprises nearly all who attend his performances. Some people are impressed by Wilson's multioctave range on the sax (soprano, tenor, and alto) and mastery of the bass clarinet; others (who should know better) might be surprised that such an inventive musician is confined to a wheelchair. Born in 1939, Wilson has lived onstage since his early childhood, when he became part of his grandfather's song-and-dance show in Florida. A student of tap dancing as a 2-year-old, Wilson was a professional by his fourth year. Before he reached 6 years of age, however, he was struck by polio. His nascent performing career was rechanneled into musical study, as he began learning music theory at age 8. His clarinet studies began five years later, and shortly thereafter, he was hipped to Charlie Parker.

Wilson's first foray into the saxophone tradition came when he moved to Los Angeles to study at Santa Monica City College. Before long he was an avid saxophone student, playing gigs at Los Angeles clubs and, as he recalled in a 1997 *Earshot Jazz* magazine interview, performing with pianist Andrew Hill, Howard Rumsey's Lighthouse All-Stars, and Rahsaan Roland Kirk. At the time, Wilson fell into the avant-garde scene in jazz, mainly because he could take his notes to such soaring levels, a talent he would later use in abundance on recordings. He studied, performed, and recorded with alto saxophonist and "new thing" firebrand Sonny Simmons and, like Simmons, maintained an abiding interest in bebop saxophonists and their more mainstream approach to harmony and melody.

Wilson moved to Olympia, Washington, in 1979, instantly giving the city's jazz scene a boost. Since his arrival, Wilson has acted as a conduit between the modest-sized city and the wider contemporary jazz community, not to mention the continuum of jazz composers and performers from the 1960s. After all, Wilson shared the stage with John Coltrane in Los Angeles just before Coltrane's death in 1967: with trumpeter and improvising collaborator Barbara Donald, now an Olympian as well, Wilson joined Coltrane, drummers Rashied Ali and Ray Appleton, and bassists Donald Rafael Garrett and Jimmy Garrison for an extended take on "Blue Train."

His band, Rebirth, has been playing together since the 1970s, coanchored by Wilson and his partner, flutist Nancy Curtis. Rebirth shows traces of all his career developments, including the early knack for showmanship. Wilson's multioctave reach on saxophone, especially his tenor, is an awesome feat, capable of taking the most swollen ballad to breathtaking heights in one leap. Although it might seem like gimmickry, especially to more traditional jazz fans, Wilson's way with a skating, free jazz solo is illustrative of sheer genius. His style has likely had a strong impact on such younger, better-known musicians as the World Saxophone Quartet's David Murray, who as a child lived near Wilson in Berkeley, California. Wilson's Rebirth has, since its inception, been pushed far into the vanguard by this very talent, though the band's position there has not always worked to its benefit. Wilson told Seattle's *Earshot Jazz* magazine that his not being played on jazz radio was quite painful: "I cannot pretend it doesn't hurt. It cuts me to the quick. It hits me in the bottom of my soul." Nevertheless, the band and its leader can play poignant, widely appealing straight-ahead jazz as well as the wilder, avant-garde material.

At the 1995 Earshot Jazz Festival in Seattle, Wilson cut an impromptu, unforgettable swath across the Northwest jazz scene. He joined the trio of Grammy-winning saxophonist Joe Lovano for a loose jam, amazing Lovano's trio and the crowd. Also in the mid-1990s, Wilson used his own record label, FMO, to issue an early quartet session with famed West Coast drummer Smiley Winters. Fortunately for the jazz world, New York's well-distributed and respected Arabesque Recordings issued Wilson's 1997 CD *Endless Fingers*, which elevated him to a new, long-overdue level of exposure. **AB**

Endless Fingers

(ARABESQUE, 1997)
Perhaps the only widely available CD by Bert Wilson, *Endless Fingers* shows off Wilson's grandly postbop compositional touch. He dashes off purple-heart ballads as easily as spring-loaded, soulful hipster tunes, but the saxophonist also careens with lofty free-improvisational solos bearing traces of Albert Ayler and late-period John Coltrane.

American Roots/World

AMERICAN ROOTS AND WORLD MUSIC IN THE NORTHWEST

acoustic folk performers might augment their sound with electric instruments, the blues might become "blues rock," and country music shifts into "alternative country"—what remains the same is the common love for the roots music of America.

The Northwest blues tradition is largely of the electric variety, born in Portland's clubs and Seattle's Pioneer Square, and in the minds and flying fingers of guitarists like Isaac Scott and Robert Cray. Although they started off paying homage to their idols, Northwest blues performers have created unique styles, stretching the genre and cross-pollinating with great performers from other regions, such as Portland blues harp master Paul deLay's recent collaboration with several Chicago blues greats and Cray's albums recorded with Memphis soul masters. Burnside Records in Portland has established itself as one of the country's stellar blues labels.

The spiritual godfather of Northwest folk music, singer/songwriter Woody Guthrie, lived in the region for all of one month, coming to Portland in May 1941 to write songs for a planned documentary by the Bonneville Power Authority. In a letter to a friend, he said his charge was to "walk around up and down the rivers, and to see what I could find to make up songs about." Taken by the concept of cheap public power as a benefit for the common worker, Guthrie produced twenty-six songs that month, among them some of his greatest compositions, such as "Hard Travelin'," "Roll on Columbia," and "Oregon Trail." Guthrie's revival of classic folk music has never been forgotten; Jim Page, the modern Northwest folk singer who best exemplifies Guthrie's populism and positive attitude, has even updated his predecessor's most famous song, "This Land Is Your Land," into a call for action. ("Let's take this song back/Let's take this country/Take back our future/It's our duty/Let's stand up tall so that everyone can see/Then this land will belong to you and me.")

Even country music, seemingly the sound of another region, has taken root in the fertile soil of the Northwest. Mark O'Connor, a prodigy from the Seattle suburb of Mountlake Terrace, went on to become the toast of Nashville before moving his musical experimentation to the classical concert hall. Alternative country groups such as the Picketts merge all their favorite American musical styles in a honky-tonk hybrid.

The region's performers take cues from outside this country's borders—Seattle's Laura Love is often considered a world music artist because she mixes influences from African and Caribbean traditions with her American roots sound. Harp and hammered-dulcimer duo Magical Strings is one of the region's many groups to draw from the well of Gaelic music. Gamelan Pacifica starts with a standard Indonesian percussion orchestra and folds in many years and styles of musical experimentation. Northwest artists practice musical traditions founded thousands of miles away, but produce results that cannot be called anything but authentic.

American Roots/World

Ron Bailey

a s an Army brat whose family was stationed in Germany, Ron W. Bailey was introduced to rock 'n' roll by a doo-wop-singing GI working at the base's teen club. With the help of their GI mentor, Bailey and three friends formed their own singing group—the Mellowtones. "The big event among the teens was waiting to get word on what new hit rock 'n' roll songs were happening back home, because the Army radio stations were always a month behind on what was on the air stateside," he recalls.

In the early 1970s, after graduating from the University of Oklahoma, Bailey began playing in rock bands around Norman, Oklahoma. On a trip to visit family members in Seattle, he went to a club called the Walrus and found the local music scene to his liking. The band that night was a country rock group called Lance Romance, but what really impressed him was the music of a folk singer who played during breaks and passed the hat for tips—Jim Page. Bailey returned to Oklahoma and told others about what he had found in Seattle. One eager listener was a folk singer named Annie Rose De Armas—she proposed to Bailey that they start a country rock band and move to Seattle.

Their group, Rose and the Dirt Boys, found a vibrant music scene. In the mid-1970s, most Seattle clubs hired bands for four consecutive days, and crowds turned out even on weeknights. The groups also ventured outside the city to Portland; Spokane and Ellensburg, Washington; and Vancouver, British Columbia. Rose and the Dirt Boys appeared on a sampler album produced by Ned Neltner (of Seattle's Jr. Cadillac) entitled *Collector's Item: Songs from the Taverns of the Pacific Northwest.* Also featured on the record were an interesting selection of Northwest bar bands of the era: Portland's Clamtones, Vancouver's Dirt City Cowboys, and the Seattle contingent of Lance Romance, Earthquake and the Tremors, Kidd Afrika, folk duo P. K. Dwyer and Donna Beck, and folksinger Barbara Hempleman. After Rose and the Dirt Boys broke up in the late 1970s, De Armas went on to form Annie Rose and the Thrillers, whose R&B and Motown covers remained a major club draw through the mid-1980s.

Bailey's next band was the Dynamic Logs. Assembled in 1978 from a rotating group of street musicians and club-band performers, the Logs served as a showcase for several vocalists, including Bailey, Orville Johnson, Al Kaatz, and Kathy Moore, and melded together the members' folk, country, and blues influences. Many fine musicians played in the Logs at various times, including Tito Fuentes, John Goforth, Don Kammerer, Lou Martin, Jeff Mason, Carson Michaels. Valerie Rosa, Mark Sanders, and Walter Singleman. "This was a great time in the Seattle music scene," recalls Bailey. "Clubs were hopping five nights a week, and insanity did abound." Bands would double-schedule gigs and run from one club to another, playing a set on another group's equipment before returning to their original club. The Logs lasted several more years, breaking up, holding reunion shows, and issuing their posthumous 1986 album, *The Vinyl Reunion.*

Earlier, in 1980, Bailey and fellow Logs member Lou Martin had joined with singer P. K. Dwyer and three female performers, Cathy Sutherland, Bekka Chase, and Jennifer Collins, to form the Royale Famile du Caniveaux (literally "royal family of the gutter"), an all-star group of street performers. They spent a year in Europe, living in Paris, Amsterdam, and Barcelona. This group still performs annually at the Oregon Country Fair in Veneta (a town near Eugene) and now includes Dave Conant, John Olufs, Bill Shaw, and Walter Singleman (all veterans of the rock band Red Dress).

Since 1993, Bailey has organized Hank Williams Wednesdays at the Tractor Tavern in Seattle's Ballard neighborhood, featuring a roll call of local artists, including veterans of the Royale Famile du Caniveaux and the Dynamic Logs. The tribute to the music of Hank Williams is held every Wednesday night from November to February. Most recently, Bailey contributed a trio of songs to a record of lullabies sung by local folk performers. **JB**

The Vinyl Reunion

(1986, SELF-RELEASED)
Good luck finding a copy of this vinyl-only release, the Dynamic Logs' only record. Ron Bailey sings two of his compositions, "They Can't Keep Their Minds off Murphy" and "Long Walk Down to Dibble Street," and contributes to the production and mixing on several tracks.

Duffy Bishop

S eattle's queen of blues rock has headed south to Portland, but Duffy Bishop has been a fixture at Northwest clubs and festivals for more than fifteen years and shows no signs of slowing down. Her latest band is known as Duffy Bishop and Her Palace of Culture, but a few constants remain, chief among them ace guitarist Chris Carlson, Duffy's chief accompanist, songwriter, companion, and, since 1994, husband. Also unchanged is Duffy's love of rock-edged blues, her playful stage antics, and her double helping of vocal charisma—enough to electrify any venue.

Born in Los Angeles, Bishop grew up in the Sacramento Valley. She began singing onstage with bands as a high schooler, but married young and moved to Los Angeles with her first husband, whose band had scored a recording deal. Relocating to Seattle in 1979, she sang with a punk/blues outfit called Skeezix and performed in a pair of cabaret shows, *Eine Kleine* (with songwriter Chad Henry, who would later have a Seattle hit with the long-running musical *Angry Housewives*) and *Champagne Express*. In the mid-1980s, Bishop met Carlson when both were members of the Motown soul band Cool Ray and the Shades.

In 1985, Duffy Bishop and the Rhythm Dogs debuted their blues rock act. Built around a nucleus of Bishop, Carlson, and bassist Keith Lowe, the hardworking band played clubs around Seattle and the Northwest. The Rhythm Dogs released two albums "on wonderful vinyl," reports Bishop: *Dogs Run Cheap* (1986) and *On a Journey* (1989). Although a proven draw and a popular act at blues and rock festivals, the Dogs folded in 1991 to allow Bishop to begin her theatrical career in *Janis*, a locally produced musical about the life of Janis Joplin.

The production seemed a natural for Bishop, a full-throated blues shouter who was undeniably influenced by (and is still often compared to) Joplin. Carlson was the musical director of *Janis*, and Lowe was featured in the onstage band. Bishop both portrayed scenes from Joplin's life and performed her songs, and received rave reviews from Seattle critics and audiences. Among Bishop's fans was guitarist Sam Andrew, who had played with Joplin in Big Brother & the Holding Company. "Bishop has a lot of the same spirit as Janis," Andrew was quoted as saying. "It's a spirit of freedom. It makes you feel good." Duffy would later perform with the re-formed Big Brother at a pair of Northwest shows and on a Japanese tour. The production of *Janis*, however, was forced to close after a few months, when the Joplin family filed a copyright infringement suit.

After the play's closure, Bishop reunited with Carlson and Lowe in a band called Cupid and Psyche that, in Duffy's words, "lasted about ten minutes. We were trying to do kind of a harder rock thing and it was . . . an interesting experiment."

So it was back to the blues with a new band composed of Bishop, Carlson, Lowe, drummer Dave Jette, and guitarist Henry Cooper. The Duffy Bishop Band signed a deal with Portland's Burnside Records and released a pair of fine CDs: *Bottled Oddities* (1994) and *Back to the Bone* (1996). Both relied heavily on the excellent one-two guitar combination of Carlson's driving rhythms and lead lines and Cooper's deft slide work. A few highlights of this period include the band's cover of Howlin' Wolf's "Evil" and Bishop's original songs "Ten Minute Kiss" (both on *Bottled Oddities*) and "Convince Me" (from *Back to the Bone*). The band expanded in 1996, adding Norm Bellas on organ and a horn section.

During all phases of her career, Bishop has appeared onstage and on records with other bands, often in a background-singing role. She was voted Best Female Vocalist in 1996 by the Cascade Blues Association; the band also was honored that year as Best Contemporary Blues Act.

The Duffy Bishop Band split when Lowe left to play bass for Fiona Apple's touring band (a fine adventure that included a European tour and an opening spot at the Rolling Stones' Madison Square Garden show) and Cooper formed his own group. Bishop and Carlson had, by this time, wed and moved to Portland, where they formed Duffy Bishop and Her Palace of Culture with Willie Barber (bass), Michael Partlow (drums), and Jon Goforth (sax, former member of Seattle's Dynamic Logs). In 1998 the Palace of Culture issued a CD, the live set *The Queen's Own Bootleg*. **JB**

Bottled Oddities

(1994, Burnside)

The Duffy Bishop Band's two Burnside releases (the other being *Back to the Bone*) are well played, professionally recorded, and available at local record stores. *Oddities* includes more cover tunes, but there are some killer versions here, including the aforementioned "Evil" and a great take on Jeff Hudis's "Lonely."

Robert Cray

I n the late 1970s a reviewer for the *Oregon Journal* enthused that the Eugene, Oregon, band the Nighthawks were talented enough to blow away big-name national acts. What seemed charming boosterism at the time turned out to be prophetic, as the bar band became the springboard for the career of not only Curtis Salgado but guitarist, singer, and songwriter Robert Cray.

Born August 1, 1953, in Columbus, Georgia, Cray was the son of a military man and spent many of his formative years in Germany before the family moved back stateside. After graduating from high school in Tacoma, Washington, the guitarist relocated to Eugene, where he met singer and harp player Salgado and formed the Nighthawks, which later became the Robert Cray Band.

When *Animal House* was being filmed in Eugene in the 1970s, the band was a favorite of college students up and down Interstate 5 (perhaps no other Northwest act is claimed by so many "hometowns"). Cray scored a small part in the feature, as the guitar player in the fictitious bar band Otis Day and the Knights.

The movie launched a Blues Brothers craze that helped Cray build a devoted following across the Northwest. Many a club has never seen an act break Cray's attendance record, even after twenty years. With Salgado as the vocal focus, Cray concentrated on his playing and writing. Over the years, blues purists and skeptics alike were won over by the man's ability to expand on clichéd blues runs by using jazz and pop influences but not sacrificing the integrity of the music.

Impressive support throughout the region, along with strong word of mouth in the industry, prompted Tomato Records to take a chance on Cray. The independent blues label released his first two albums, *Who's Been Talkin'?* (1980) and *Bad Influence* (1983). A label change soon followed; *False Accusations* (1985) appeared on the High Tone label, and *Strong Persuader* (1986) was released under the combined Mercury/High Tone imprint. *Strong Persuader* was the album that earned Cray his first of four Grammy Awards and gave the world the hit single "Smoking Gun." In an age of lightweight new wave groups like A-Ha, Cray's single hit the airwaves like a blast of crisp Cascade mountain water washing away badly mixed Kool-Aid.

Soon Cray was heavily in demand as a guest on others' records, appearing with B. B. King, Tina Turner, and Chuck Berry. Guitar legend Eric Clapton has been an especially visible fan of Cray's; Clapton invited the guitarist to play on three of his albums, and the two cowrote the song "Old Love," on Clapton's 1989 album *Journeyman*. "Old Love" became a staple of Clapton's live sets and was featured on his live albums *24 Nights: Live from Albert Hall* (1991) and *Unplugged* (1992).

In Cray's subsequent albums for Mercury/PolyGram—*Don't Be Afraid of the Dark* (1988), *Midnight Stroll* (1990), *I Was Warned* (1992), *Shame and a Sin* (1993), *Some Rainy Morning* (1995), and *Sweet Potato Pie* (1997)—he changed band members and experimented with adding soul-style horn arrangements and expanding his range as a writer. In 1999 he teamed with the Memphis Horns for *Take Your Shoes Off* (Rykodisc), a full-on tribute to the Memphis soul sound of the 1960s and 1970s. The one constant throughout the years has been the joy Cray brings to the stage every time he plays, and the good feeling fans get from hearing him sing the blues. —DD

Strong Persuader

(1986, MERCURY/HIGH TONE)
Robert Cray's breakthrough album, and for good reason. In an era when music was finding its way, this solidly self-confident statement proved that blues could be slick and melodic, and still convey intense feeling with impressive guitar work.

Midnight Stroll

(1990, MERCURY/POLYGRAM)
Arguably the best of Robert Cray's soul-influenced albums, and his first collaboration with the Memphis Horns.

Paul deLay

hubert Sumlin, a guitarist who has shared a Chicago blues stage with most of the greats, has said of Paul deLay, "For my money, deLay's the best harp player in the world." It is certainly true that no one else on the blues scene plays a chromatic harp with such invention; deLay has been winning fans on both sides of the Atlantic for almost two decades.

Portland native deLay was born on January 31, 1952, and raised in the suburb of Milwaukie. Along with Portland blues guitarists Jim Mesi and Lloyd Jones, deLay cut his musical teeth in the band Brown Sugar, which heated up Oregon bars from 1970 to 1979. At that point, Mesi and deLay set out on their own, with bass and drums, to form the Paul deLay Band, a group that went on to become one of the Northwest's most consistent draws. DeLay began recording and releasing albums on the Criminal Records label (started by the band's drummer, Jones). When Mesi chose to split from the group in the late 1980s, deLay and the band kept going strong, with deLay earning a 1989 nomination for the W. S. Handy Award for Best Blues Instrumentalist.

Just after that, however, his life took an important turn.

In January 1990 the bluesman was convicted on a charge of dealing cocaine in 1988. After the bust, deLay had made the decision to get clean and sober, and while waiting for his trial he and the band recorded *The Other One* (1990) and *Paulzilla* (1992), both on the now ironically named Criminal Records label. DeLay was sentenced to serve time at the federal corrections facility in Sheridan, Oregon. While incarcerated, he met and became engaged to his wife, Shelly. In prison, deLay got other musicians together to jam, and was allowed to write and practice on a Casio keyboard.

During deLay's incarceration, the other members of the band (guitarist Peter Damman, bassist John Mazzocco, tenor sax player Dan Fincher, organist Louis Pain, and drummer Mike Klobas) decided to stick together and began performing as the No Delay Band (later simply No Delay). Fronting the band during deLay's absence was Linda Hornbuckle, a gospel-based blues siren who made a name for herself with the group. By the time deLay was released in January 1995, the band had honed and polished their group groove to a razor-sharp edge.

Rejoining the band, deLay played clubs and festivals around the West Coast, soon reconnecting with his old fans and winning over many new ones. At live shows deLay proved not only that he still had his edge, but that his vocals were stronger and more versatile. His songwriting, revealing new maturity and depth, moved beyond "bar blues" and into sophisticated R&B.

The Philadelphia label Evidence Records signed deLay to a three-album deal in 1996. The first release on the new label was a combination of *Paulzilla* and *The Other One*, entitled *Take It from the Turnaround*. In late 1996 the first postprison album was released, *Ocean of Tears*, followed in 1998 by *Nice and Strong*. His 1999 album, *DeLay Does Chicago* (Evidence), is a special, one-time-only collaboration with Chicago musicians, including the Rockin' Johnny Burgin Band and guitarist Jimmy Dawkins.   **DD**

Nice and Strong

(1998, EVIDENCE)
A showcase for Paul deLay as both a harp player and a songwriter; he wrote ten of the eleven tracks, including "14 Dollars in the Bank," which was nominated for a W. C. Handy Award for Best Song.

Gamelan Pacifica

Formed 1980, Seattle, Washington

amelan Pacifica, based at Seattle's Cornish College of the Arts, champions contemporary music for the gamelan (an Indonesian percussion orchestra made up of chimes, gongs, and wooden mallets) and involves itself less with the traditional indigenous repertory. Two of the six works on its gorgeous first disc, *Trance Gong* (1994, Nonsequitur/¿What Next?), are collective compositions by members of the variable-sized ensemble. Other composers represented are Jeff Morris, Jon Keliehor, Gamelan Pacifica founder Jarrad Powell, and John Cage, whose "In a Landscape" for piano or harp Powell arranged masterfully for gamelan with the composer's approval.

The title track is a driving *moto perpetuo* that adds roto-toms (modern tuned drums) and Chinese cymbals to the traditional gamelan instrumentation. Powell's "Gending Erhu" is a pensive concerto-ish work for erhu (two-string Chinese fiddle) and gamelan—spare of texture, with very long soulful lines for the soloist, here Warren Chang. In "Small of My Back," distant bamboo-flute calls, electronically processed, float over a light, gently chugging supporting layer. Morris's "Rain," both ebullient and haunting, features some catchy hooks. An urgent backbeat and an almost symphonic richness of texture helps Keliehor's "Peaches of Immortality" take flight. **GB**

Orville Johnson

m ulti-instrumentalist Orville Johnson is the guy Northwest musicians call when they want that perfect dobro part on their latest recording. But although he plays guitar (also lap steel and pedal steel), mandolin, banjo, and fiddle, "instrumental gunslinger" Johnson considers himself first and foremost a singer.

It was singing that first attracted Johnson to music. He was born in 1953 in the southern Illinois town of Edwardsville, to a family active in the Pentecostal Church. "I never completely bought their ideas, but I did like the singing part of it," he recalls. The young singer ventured outside the church when he reached junior high school, after being recruited as a vocalist by one of the thousands of teenage bands formed in the wake of the Beatles' success. But even as a budding rocker, he was forming an affection for traditional American music. One friend had a collection of blues records, including works by Robert Johnson and Mississippi John Hurt. Another group of friends was taken with the harmonies of bluegrass music, and Johnson began playing the guitar when he joined a bluegrass trio. He got his early performing experience in the folk clubs and taverns of St. Louis, Missouri— including a stint with a bluegrass band called the Steamboat Ramblers, whose regular gig was on the Mississippi riverboat SS *Julie Belle Swain*.

In 1977, Johnson moved to Washington State, settling in Seattle the following year. Johnson formed a group—the Dynamic Logs—with several street veterans he met while performing as a street musician in Pike Place Market. Their music started with the traditional folk sound of the busker, but the Logs also dragged country, blues, and rock into the mix, adding horns and keyboards on some numbers. With a rotating membership that hovered at about ten, they were favorites at the Rainbow

Tavern, the G-Note, and the Buffalo Tavern. In addition to bar shows, the band played street sets at Pike Place Market. "That was back when they didn't have all the rules," recalls Johnson. "When the police would tell us not to do it, we'd run away and do it somewhere else." The Dynamic Logs lasted until the mid-1980s. He says, "Idiotically, we made a record in 1986 [*The Vinyl Reunion*] after we were completely defunct."

While still in the Dynamic Logs, Johnson also spent time with the Torpedoes, a standard four-piece rock 'n' roll band. In the mid-1980s he left Seattle to travel and met his wife, Parry, while visiting Virginia. After returning to Seattle, he formed the "classic jug band" Strangers with Candy, joined by Larry Vanover, Reggie Miles, and Walter Singleman. This musical endeavor lasted from about 1988 to 1990 and produced two cassettes of original material.

In recent years Johnson has worked as a session player and guitar teacher (at the Country Blues Workshop and Puget Sound Guitar Workshop in Port Townsend, Washington), while performing in duos with Scott Weiskopf and Mark Graham. He released four albums in the 1990s: *The World According to Orville* (1990), *Orville Johnson and Scott Weiskopf* (1993), *Kings of Mongrel Folk* (with Mark Graham, 1997), and *Blueprint for the Blues* (1998). Johnson is putting the finishing touches on a CD of his own dobro music.

The versatile musician says he keeps his interest in music alive through his varied activities: he has worked as a producer (including on Jim Page's excellent *Whose World Is This*) and in theater. His big film debut was as a band member in *Georgia,* shot in Seattle and starring Mare Winningham. "I got one big close-up," he says. "I was 30 feet tall for about 2 seconds." **JB**

Orville Johnson and Scott Weiskopf

(1993, SELF-RELEASED)
The key to a great folk duo is two singers with equally good but recognizably different voices, good instrumental chops, and an equal skill for writing great songs and spotting songs that are great enough to steal. This record has all that and more. Of special note are Orville Johnson's awesome original "The Sleeper" and the great cover of Jim Page's "Stranger in Me."

Blueprint for the Blues

(1998, SELF-RELEASED)
Johnson's take on blues songs by Willie Dixon, Son House, Wilson Pickett, and—of course—Orville Johnson.

Laura Love

rocker or folkie? Singer/songwriter Laura Love calls her style of music Afro-Celtic and has been known to perform accompanied only by her own lines on electric bass guitar. Since her groundbreaking performance at the 1994 New York Singer-Songwriter Festival electrified the Carnegie Hall audience, Love has released two albums on Mercury Records and has been a featured performer at music festivals across the country.

Born in Omaha, Nebraska, in 1960, Love is the daughter of two musicians—alto saxman and bandleader Preston Love and singer Winnie Jones. Although her father was quite well known in jazz circles (he played alto sax in Count Basie's band and later coordinated the West Coast orchestras that backed touring Motown stars), Laura didn't realize he was still alive until she attended a concert of his at age 16 and ventured backstage to meet him. That same year, she performed her first professional gig, making $50 singing for a band playing jazz and pop standards for a captive audience—inmates at the Nebraska State Penitentiary.

Love took up the bass guitar in her mid-20s and relocated to the Northwest—first Portland, then Seattle. In the mid-1980s, she played bass and sang with the new wave band 'e.' She was strictly a bass player when she joined Seattle blues rockers Faiye West & the Bleeding Hearts in the late 1980s. When the band's singer quit and try-outs began for her replacement, Love asked to audition. Her fellow band members were amazed by her vocal ability and hired her on the spot. The band changed its name to Boom Boom GI and released two albums, *Slide a Little Closer* (1988) and *Don't Know What I'll Wear* (1989), the latter produced by Seattle studio maven Jack Endino. But the band, led by songwriter/guitarist Scott Barr, was heavily influenced by 1970s-style British rock (think the Rolling Stones or the Faces) at a time when punk rock or heavy grunge was the accepted style. Rather than play up their bluesiness and seek an audience outside the narrow music scene of the time, the band instead tried to court the hipster elite—unsuccessfully.

Love found herself at a career crossroads when a reviewer for the Seattle music magazine *The Rocket* criticized her for wasting her talents in the "annoyingly point-less" Boom Boom GI. She split from the band and began working on her own music, releasing *Z Therapy* on her Octoroon Biography Records in 1990. Her second solo album, *Pangaea*, was released in 1992. Love was already creating her eclectic musical style: punctuating songs with chants, jumping into the higher registers at will, even yodeling.

After her Carnegie Hall experience, Love expanded her touring schedule and firmed up her band, adding guitarist Rod Cook and percussionist Linda Severt. This version of her band played on her third and final Octoroon Biography release, *Helvetica Bold*, in 1994. She also began a collaboration with former Ranch Romance singer Jo Miller; the two released *Jo Miller and Laura Love Sing Bluegrass and Old Time Music* (1995).

In 1997, Love released her first major label CD, *Octoroon*, whose title is a word meaning a person of one eighth African American ancestry, and a term that has always intrigued the mixed-race Love. Her band—now comprising Cook, drummer Chris Leighton, and multi-instrumentalist Julie Wolf—plays a mix of African and Caribbean rhythms. The combination of unusually constructed harmonies and largely acoustic instrumentation has made them a popular draw at world music and folk festivals. Love released the album *Shum Ticky* in late 1998. **JB**

Helvetica Bold

(1994, OCTOROON BIOGRAPHY)
Laura Love shows real development as a songwriter on the third—and best—CD released by her label.

Octoroon

(1997, MERCURY)
As in her earlier self-released albums, Love tells the tales of a confused searcher, but the music is rock solid. Although Love's songwriting is strong throughout, two covers are among the standout cuts: a version of Nirvana's "Come as You Are," with Love's voice accompanied only by her bass, and a soaring "Amazing Grace," beginning with a lovely a cappella segment.

Magical Strings

Formed 1978, Seattle, Washington

Philip Boulding's love of stringed instruments began early. At age 6 he was studying classical violin. At age 12 he not only began playing guitar but shortly afterward started making guitars as well. While in high school, he was exposed to the sound of the hammered dulcimer and built one for himself. When he moved to the Northwest in 1974, he fell in love again—this time with the Celtic harp. Becoming a student of Celtic music, he traveled to Ireland and Scotland to learn more about the culture and the instruments.

Pam Boulding's early interest was art. She studied painting, sculpture, and art history at California's Pitzer College and has taught music and art at various colleges and Waldorf schools. But she, too, was fascinated with the sound of the hammered dulcimer and decided to study the rare instrument. She signed up for a class; Philip was the instructor. The two began a musical collaboration combining the sound of harp and hammered dulcimer that continues to this day. Magical Strings is a romantic collaboration as well; Philip and Pam have five children, ages 15 to 26, who perform in their annual Celtic Yuletide concerts. The family quartet (with daughter Brittany Boulding [violin] and son Brenin Williams [cello] joining their parents)

American Roots/World

toured Japan in early 1997, performing sold-out shows from Sapporo to Okinawa. The other musical family members are sons Geoffrey, Morgan, and Marshall Williams.

At performances, Pam introduces each song by telling the story of the travels that served as its inspiration. Then, with Pam on hammered dulcimer and Philip on Celtic harp, hammered dulcimer, tin whistle, and valiha (a Madagascar bamboo harp), the pair create the seamless, stunningly beautiful sounds that have entranced audiences for more than two decades. Unlike many Celtic folk performers, who concentrate on traditional material, the Bouldings are prolific songwriters.

The first Magical Strings album, *Glass Horse* (1980), was self-released, but the group soon signed to Flying Fish Records and released a string of seven albums: *Spring Tide* (1982), *Above the Tower* (1985), *On the Burren* (1987), *Philip Boulding— Harp* (1988), *Crossing to Skellig* (1990), *Good People All (A Celtic Yuletide Tradition)* (1992), and *Bell Off the Ledge* (1993). Their ninth album is *Islands Calling (1996)*. Philip and Pam have toured extensively, playing folk and Celtic festivals across the nation. They accompanied Dan Fogelberg on a thirty-city summer tour in 1988 and performed on his album *River of Souls*. Their music has been featured on Garrison Keillor's *A Prairie Home Companion* and on television advertisements for the Saturn automobile. The Bouldings have also maintained their interests in building instruments and teaching music (at their School of Magical Strings in Seattle). **JB**

Islands Calling

(1996, EARTHBEAT! TRAVELER)

A sonic trip through the islands of the world with the Boulding family and musical guests, including cellist Eugene Friesen and guitarist Alex de Grassi. This amazingly diverse instrumental collection ranges from the steel drum–decorated "Jamaican Port o' Call" to the traditional Irish "Winter into Spring." Brittany Boulding's marvelous violin work on "The Holy Island" carries on the family tradition of virtuoso playing.

Lila McCann

ike all overnight successes, Lila McCann's was a long time in the making. Just 15 when her 1997 debut album, *Lila*, was released, McCann provided a refreshing contrast to LeAnn Rimes, the reigning teen country songstress at the time. In contrast to Rimes's show biz image, the energetic McCann was a decidedly normal teenager, a cheerleader at Steilacoom High School (near Tacoma, Washington) whose parents sharply limited her touring until high school graduation. She played a New Year's Eve date with Billy Ray Cyrus with a cast on her arm, courtesy of a cheerleading spill.

Born December 4, 1981, McCann was just 5 the first time she joined her father's band, the Southlanders, onstage at the local Eagles Club to sing "You Are My Sunshine." By age 8, the little girl with the big voice was a regular at Southlanders shows and was spotted by manager Kasey Walker. With years of shows at county fairs and festivals behind her, she signed with Asylum Records in 1995.

Lila could almost be described as a collaboration between McCann and producer Mark Spiro (Boys II Men, Julian Lennon), who wrote or cowrote more than half the songs on the album. It was the Spiro–penned (with cowriter Buddy Brock) "I Wanna Fall in Love" that gave McCann her first Top 10 hit. The song also made it to the top of the Gavin radio-play charts (the radio verson of television's Nielsen ratings) . While McCann sings about love and heartbreak, the songs are properly oriented to the star's ingenue status. "Just One Little Kiss" celebrates the transition from friendship to romance; "Almost over You" (a 1984 hit for Sheena Easton) is a moody breakup tale. The bouncy "Yippy Ky Yay" is a primer of new country, a sassy, in-your-face message to a boy who just isn't trying hard enough to woo little Lila. And the best song on the album, "Down Came a Blackbird," the third-person story of a shattered romance, was the tune that convinced Asylum executives to kick off what should be a memorable recording career. Ironically, the song was originally McCann's least favorite of the bunch, although she gradually developed a fondness for it. McCann released her second album, *Something in the Air,* in early 1999.

Lila

(1997, ASYLUM)
A fine set of well-chosen songs and mature vocal performances.

Jim Mesi

If you ask any blues player in Portland or Seattle which guitarist they would most like to have in their band, the name Jim Mesi will inevitably appear near the top of the list. His compact stature and affinity for Italian suits make the onstage Mesi look like a character in a Martin Scorsese movie. Selecting from the dozens of guitars in his legendary collection, Mesi spins out solos that dizzy and delight the listener.

Portland native Mesi got his start in Brown Sugar, one of the two leaders of that city's thriving 1970s blues scene (the other top band was Sleazy Pieces). Brown Sugar was the springboard for the careers of vocalist and blues harp maestro Paul deLay, guitarist/vocalist Lloyd Jones (the drummer then), and Mesi. When the group broke up in the 1980s, deLay and Mesi continued as the Paul deLay Band. Throughout the decade, the deLay Band played to audiences of three hundred to five hundred people virtually every weekend.

A substantial addition to the Mesi reputation came during this period, when the Paul deLay Band was opening a show for blues guitar legend B. B. King. Toward the end of their set, Mesi looked out at the audience and noticed an especially familiar face up front. It was King himself, smiling, holding his hands as if praying, and bowing toward Mesi. Word quickly spread around the Northwest that the deLay Band had a guitar player personally blessed by the great B. B. King. In 1988 Mesi broke away from the group, upset over "creative differences" and the band's hard partying. In 1994 the Mesi Band, featuring singer Lily Wilde and guitarist Steve Bradley, released the live-performance CD *Hot Night at the Candlelight* (1994, Candlelight), rereleased in 1998 by Just Ducky Records.

In the early 1990s, Mesi and his wife, Jamie, became the parents of a son, Christopher, who was born with a life-threatening congenital defect of the esophagus. An operation was advised, but the Mesis (like most musicians) didn't have adequate health insurance. Rallying around one of its most respected members, the Portland blues community raised money to help the boy, but Christopher died before the operation. In 1996 Mesi named his first solo CD *Blues for Christopher* in honor of his son. The album showcases Mesi's versatility and mastery of the classic styles of American electric music. From a Link Wray reverb twang to spicy pedal-steel guitar, and blues solos that roar and wail, Mesi plays with an inventiveness and tone that few in the region can match. Mesi's second CD, *Shut Up and Play* (1998, Just Ducky), is composed entirely of instrumentals.

Watching other guitarists watch Mesi is a favorite pastime in Portland bars. When Mesi plays, other guitarists' jaws drop at the melodic adventurousness of his soloing. As a measure of this respect, Mesi was named to the Cascade Blues Society's Blues Hall of Fame in 1995.

Since becoming a bandleader himself, Mesi has gone through a host of players, and his band seems to have a slightly different lineup each time one sees them. Instead of joining another collaborative venture like the deLay Band, Mesi is determined to bring his gutsy guitar sound to the world on his own terms.   **DD**

Blues for Christopher

(1996, JUST DUCKY)
The likes of Mark Proulx, Dover Weinberg, Duffy Bishop, and Curtis Salgado handle the vocals on this showcase for Mesi's musicianship.

Mark O'Connor

S tories of child prodigies often have sad endings. Not so for Mark O'Connor, the talented teenage fiddle player and guitarist who has become a solo artist, Nashville session star, noted composer, and collaborator with musicians ranging from Vince Gill to Yo-Yo Ma.

Born on August 5, 1961, the young O'Connor won a Washington State classical/

flamenco guitar contest at the age of 10. But he was taken with the idea of playing the fiddle—so taken, in fact, that he first tried to construct a fiddle out of cardboard. He quickly got good enough to capture the under-12 division at the National Old Time Fiddler's Competition. At that competition, he met 64-year-old fiddle master Benny Thomasson, who became his musical mentor. By age 14, O'Connor had won the Grand Masters Fiddling Championship in Nashville and the National Guitar Flatpicking Championships in Winfield, Kansas. (His bring-down-the-house rendition of "Dixie Breakdown" in Winfield is included on *Retrospective*, a 1987 compilation of early O'Connor recordings.) By the time he graduated from high school, O'Connor had won every significant fiddle competition in the United States and recorded four albums for Rounder.

Although his first three solo records consisted mainly of traditional country and folk songs, O'Connor began to branch out with *On the Rampage* (1979) and *Soppin the Gravy* (1980), both of which included many tunes he'd penned. The climax of his six-album Rounder career was the ambitious *False Dawn* (1983), on which he played every instrument and composed every song. During this period, he had the opportunity to tour with another of his idols, jazz violinist Stephane Grappelli.

In the mid-1980s, O'Connor moved to Nashville and became one of the city's most noted session musicians, appearing on some 450 releases. He was named top fiddler by the Academy of Country Music in 1986, skipped a year, and then won the award the next seven years in a row. O'Connor also continued to release albums, including *Elysian Forest* (1988) and *On the Mark* (1989).

Despite the many accolades he received, O'Connor felt he was a lesser musician than the masters to whom he was constantly being compared. The problem, he decided, was that he wasn't giving full attention to his own music. So in 1990, O'Connor quit session playing cold turkey and began to work on his own songs. His declaration of independence, *The New Nashville Cats* (1992), paid tribute to his session days by reuniting him with an all-star cast of more than fifty Nashville musicians. O'Connor wrote ten of the fifteen songs. Among the highlights are "Restless," on which Vince Gill, Ricky Skaggs, and Steve Wariner trade off verses and guitar solos; "Sweet Suzanne," which starts out as jazz fusion and morphs into almost classical lines at the end; and an extended "Orange Blossom Special" with O'Connor mixing in quotes from television themes and Bach's *Partita in E*.

His next album, *Heroes* (1993), found him trading lines with fellow fiddlers Grappelli, Thomasson, Jean Luc Ponty, and Charlie Daniels. His interest in classical music grew with *The Fiddle Concerto* (1995), an album-length composition for string quartet and orchestra, and *Appalachia Waltz* (1996), a collaboration with Yo-Yo Ma and double-bassist Edgar Meyer. *Appalachia Waltz* was the country's no. 1 classical recording for sixteen weeks. O'Connor is now on the faculty of the Blair School of Music at Nashville's Vanderbilt University and is the founder of the city's twice-yearly Mark O'Connor Fiddle Camp, which welcomes fiddlers of all ages and abilities.

These days, O'Connor is most likely to be found playing with symphony orchestras, although he is also in great demand for solo recitals. *Midnight on the Water*, a recording of one of his recitals, was released on Sony Classical in 1998. The country world hasn't totally forgotten him, however, as O'Connor has been named the Country Music Association's Musician of the Year for a record six consecutive years. **JB**

Retrospective

(1987, ROUNDER)
An eighteen-track selection of songs from Mark O'Connor's six solo albums on Rounder, from the Texas-style fiddle of his 1975 debut to the multi-instrumental flash of *False Dawn* (1983).

The New Nashville Cats

(1992, WARNER BROS.)
Matchless playing by O'Connor and a studio full of Nashville aces won this gem the Grammy Award for Best Country Instrumental Recording.

Jim Page

I t seems that singer/songwriter Jim Page is always being compared with Northwest folk legend Woody Guthrie. ("If Jim Page ain't the bastard son of Woody Guthrie, I'm T-Bone Walker," quipped Grateful Dead lyricist Robert Hunter.) Perhaps it's the conversational style of his singing, which feels as if you're listening to an old friend—a witty, opinionated old friend, mind you). Page obviously was influenced by the artists of the 1960s American folk revival as well. His playful rhymes and relentless wordplay spotlight a social consciousness that shows no signs of cooling with time; there's no major difference between the guy who wrote "Song for Leonard Peltier" in 1979 and the one who penned the pro-hemp crusade song "Righteous" in 1996.

Born in 1949 in Palo Alto, California, Page grew up listening to all types of music, especially folk and blues. "I barely graduated high school," he says. "The guitar kind of took over my life." His first foray out of the Bay Area was his move to New York City in 1970. "I had to go to New York," he recalls. "The backs of all the record jackets all talked about the Village." He would go on to play at Greenwich Village clubs before relocating to Seattle the following year. By 1971, the Seattle folk music scene had largely come and gone, and Page recalls bemoaning his fate in a Fremont tavern. Someone asked why he didn't go over to the club across the street. "I said, 'Well, they have rock bands'—they said, 'They take breaks, don't they?'" So Page and his acoustic guitar journeyed to rock clubs across Seattle, playing a few songs between rock bands' sets and passing the hat for his pay.

The challenge of getting the attention of an audience that had come to drink and dance, rather than to hear him sing, changed his music. "I was thinking, 'How could I get their attention—ideologically, how can I get off the stage and sit with them?'" The answer was to bring more politics, more street-level issues, into his new songs. Topical songs also proved a hit in another regular gig, singing on the University of Washington campus. Page would station himself on "Red Square" (the main plaza) or at the student union building and wait for the class break. "When people would come out, I'd kind of make up verses as they went by." Once a crowd gathered, he would play an hour-long set. Page also played downtown Seattle street corners, until a motorcycle cop informed him he couldn't do that without a permit, and under city law he couldn't get a permit unless he was blind. Page and others convinced the Seattle City Council to hold a public hearing, and he distributed handbills inviting people to see Jim Page play live in council chambers. The "gig" was a hit, and the council passed a law allowing performers to play on the street.

Page's album of 1976, *A Shot of the Usual*, was funded by his royalties from an instrumental called "Busted Down Around O'Connelly Corners," which old Bay Area buddy Pat Simmons included on the Doobie Brothers' 1973 hit album *The Captain & Me*. Page also started getting recognition outside Seattle through his triumphant performance at the 1977 Cambridge Folk Festival in England. He traveled overseas for several years, releasing four more albums along the way: *On the Street Again* (1977), *Hot Times* (1979), *In the Act* (1980), and *This Movie Is for Real* (1982).

Back in Seattle in 1983, Page admits he didn't know what to do with himself. He played in an assortment of duos and trios and in 1986 released another album, *Visions in My View*. In 1989, he founded the group Zero Tolerance with Dale Fanning (drums), Larry Klein (bass), and Hal Brooks (guitar), which played numerous gigs over the next three years. In the 1990s he released three more albums—*On the Sidewalk Again* (1991), *In the Mean Time* (1991), and *More Than Anything Else in the World* (1993)—and brought his album count to an even ten with *Whose World Is This* (1996).

The 1996 album sets aside Page's usual guy-with-a-guitar approach for a series of full-band arrangements, care of producer Orville Johnson. "I really wanted to help him make a record that you might hear on the radio," says Johnson. The new songs demonstrate Page's range and songwriting skill, from a sentimental tale of his grandfather ("Shiny Bright Silver Dollar") to a whimsical tribute to diehard "Deadheads" ("Down to Eugene") to a sharp rebuke pointing out right-wing talk radio's role in the bombing of the Oklahoma City federal building ("Only Talkin' on the Radio"). As the world keeps moving along, there's no doubt Page will be there to watch it all—and weigh in with his opinion. **JB**

Whose World Is This

(1996, LIQUID CITY)
Jim Page maintains his spot in the forefront of Northwest folk music with this gem.

ORVILLE JOHNSON

CURTIS SALGADO

SHEILA WILCOXSON

MAGICAL STRINGS

PAUL DELAY

JIM PAGE

LILY WILDE

Kelly Joe Phelps

lready an accomplished jazz guitarist at 17, Kelly Joe Phelps had played in a number of jazz and fusion bands in Portland, and was growing tired of the emphasis on technical brilliance in those musical genres. In 1989 Phelps discovered country blues and holed himself up (musically speaking) for a while, exploring a new artistic voice and approaching his technique with fresh ears and eyes. Mississippi Fred McDowell was his biggest influence. Phelps saw in the rough framework that supported country blues a greater emotional range than the one expressed in the music he had been playing—and he felt at least as much freedom to create on the spot. When the guitarist reemerged, he immediately began to catch people's attention with his heartfelt, soulful growling vocals and totally unorthodox approach to blues guitar.

Phelps adopted a manner of playing a standard acoustic guitar by laying it across his lap, like a dobro guitar, and both picking and strumming it. His jazz background aided him in experimenting with new tunings and specially cut-out capos, which expanded the possibilities of playing a guitar with a slide instead of fingering chords and notes with the left hand.

Gigs in Portland began in 1991, and Phelps performed at every covered structure that would have him. At the same time, he continued his day job as one of Portland's most noted guitar teachers. His tireless efforts paid off, rewarded by not only a loyal local following but a CD from Burnside Records, *Lead Me On* (1994). In promoting the album, he began touring and earned a national reputation; he played solo and with Greg Brown on Garrison Keillor's radio show, A *Prairie Home Companion*, and opened for B. B. King. After the success of the first CD, other labels came with offers. True North signed the musician for Canadian recordings, and Rick Rubin's American Records claimed him for the United States. In a shuffle at American Records, Phelps was released and subsequently signed by Rykodisc, which put out his second album, *Roll Away the Stone*, in 1997.

As a vocalist, Phelps tastes his stories of pain and redemption before delivering them in a whisper, rumble, or shout. Not only do the guitar lines swoop and scream, as expected from a slide guitar, but the accompaniment from a regular finger-picker is there as well. The combination mesmerizes audiences by the end of the first song, and Phelps's low-key stage manner and obvious sincerity win over new fans wherever he plays.

At present, the guitarist from Vancouver, Washington, is playing solo concerts around North America and Europe, and collaborating with kindred acoustic spirits like Keb' Mo' and Alvin Youngblood Hart. With rising younger stars like this, the blues are poised to enter the next century with an infusion of new energy, enthusiasm, and individualism that the U.S. scene has been lacking. **DD**

(1997, RYKODISC)
Absolutely thumbing his nose at the so-called "sophomore curse," Kelly Joe Phelps produced a second album with all the strengths of the first but put even more emphasis on originality and expressiveness. A truly hypnotic experience.

The Picketts

Formed 1989, Seattle, Washington

Led by singer Christy McWilson and drummer/singer Leroy "Blackie" Sleep, the twangy sounds of Seattle's alternative country top dogs proved authentic enough to get them signed to Rounder Records, the well-known folk/country label. In a perfect world, this record alone would get the label of "alternative country" deleted from their file permanently.

McWilson is perhaps best known as a former member of retro "girl group" revue the Dynette Set and the wife of Young Fresh Fellow Scott McCaughey (she contributed vocally to three Fellows albums and McCaughey's solo records). In the late 1980s, she met up with singer Sleep and decided to form a group based on their common interest in rockabilly. But personnel problems sank that band, which was called the Power Mowers (like many Seattle bands, they had a noted inability to retain drummers). In mid-1989 the two singers joined with former Mowers bassist Steve Marcus and guitarists Gerald Collier and Brian Kenney (then also playing with the Best Kissers in the World) to form a band known as Chester's Garage. Sleep handled drum duties, but on a stand-up kit at the front of the stage, rockabilly-style.

By the end of 1989, Collier was gone and the group was known as the Picketts (not after the Confederate general, but in an obscure tribute to singer Wilson Pickett). The band played around Seattle for a while, recorded an EP (which, unfortunately, went unreleased), and switched members, resulting in a lineup of McWilson, Sleep, bassist Walt Singleman, guitarist John Olufs (also with the band Red Dress), and guitarist (and Young Fresh Fellow) Jim Sangster.

The Picketts finally released their first album, *Paper Doll*, in 1992. It was produced by Seattle's Conrad Uno and released on his PopLlama label. The combination of swinging honky-tonk numbers and country ballads was a hit with many critics. The band recorded a second album with Uno, but wanted the advantages a national label release could provide. Through an appearance at Austin's SXSW music festival, they got signed to Rounder, and *The Wicked Picketts* was released in 1995. Never stiff or self-conscious like some of their alterntive country brethren, the Picketts put forth a good-timey barroom feel. Critics had to reach for new labels, the best being a play on the grunge sound of the band's hometown—"grange rock."

American Roots/World

For their next record, *Euphonium* (1996, Rounder), the band resurrected a cover of the Clash's "Should I Stay or Should I Go," which they had performed on an early PopLlama single, and added their Byrd-ish take on the Who's "Baba O'Reilly." Both songs had long captivated audiences (among their other countrified covers is a version of Yoko Ono's "Walking on Thin Ice"). But they managed to temper the novelty flavor: McWilson has a fine country voice, and the traditional instrumentation (and capable musicianship) on songs such as "Just Passing Through" and "House Made from Cards" gives them a timeless quality. **JB**

Euphonium

(1996, ROUNDER)
The Picketts show the whole repertoire on their second Rounder release: rockin' dance-floor stompers, pure country ballads, and imaginatively reworked cover tunes highlight this disc.

Ranch Romance
Formed 1986, Seattle, Washington

althm they were Seattle's most beloved country troubadours, Ranch Romance never quite found a place in the country music pantheon. Seattle's urban cowgirls played a blend of western swing and bluegrass, with a touch of rockabilly. Led by singer Jo Miller, the band recorded three records and toured with singer k.d. lang, who proclaimed them her favorite band. Ranch Romance grew out of the All-Star Cowgirl Revue, a one-shot musical/variety production featuring almost thirty women performers. Singer/guitarist Jo Miller, one of the revue's organizers, decided to capitalize on its popularity by forming a smaller performance group, dubbed Ranch Romance after a 1930s pulp magazine. The six-member band first played under the name in late 1986.

The band gradually trimmed down to four members: Miller (guitar, vocals), Lisa Theo (mandolin, vocals), Nancy Katz (bass), and Barbara Lamb (fiddle). Lamb had been a fiddle prodigy as a teen: she recorded an album with veteran Seattle fiddler Vivian Williams (their 1975 collaboration, *Twin Sisters*, has been rereleased on CD) and even gave fiddle lessons. (One of her early students was fellow prodigy Mark O'Connor, whom she soon had to drop as a student because he quickly learned everything she knew.)

The early Ranch Romance punctuated their sets with a campy humor. Cowboy hats and sequined western wear were the order of the day, along with intricate harmonies and tight acoustic instrumentation. This version of the band released the album *Western Dream* (1989), featuring the lead vocals of both Miller and Theo. The band got a major break when lang hired them as the opening act on her twenty-day U.S. tour.

Ranch Romance soon underwent a transformation. When Theo left the band, Miller became the sole lead vocalist, and the band started to trim the novelty aspects of its act. On their second album, *Blue Blazes* (1991), the urban cowgirls went urbane. The cover photo tells the story, showing the band (now including Nova Karina Devonie on accordion) posing in subtly western-influenced clothing, their unsmiling faces signifying their more serious musical direction. Miller's lovin'-and-losin' songs still hit home, but without the well-chosen novelty numbers, *Blue Blazes* proved a bit too grim in places (the sex-and-murder tale "Buckaroo" was a bit much for some fans of the formerly chipper cowgirls).

But Ranch Romance was changing again. Multi-instrumentalist David Keenan, who had previously played with Lamb, ended up sitting in with the band. He proved such a good fit, personally and musically, that he was tabbed as Ranch Romance's first male member. Both Lamb and Keenan performed on the third and final Ranch Romance album, *Flip City* (1993). This record found the band lightening up a bit and tossing in some variety: vocal turns for Lamb, Keenan, and Devonie, more cover songs, and a lively production job by Tim O'Brien. After Lamb moved to Nashville to work as a session player, the band went on tour in Australia and New Zealand in 1994. They continued to be a popular attraction at music festivals up and down the West Coast but decided to call it quits in late 1995. Their last gig (in January 1996) was a show at a grange hall on Bainbridge Island near Seattle—a fitting finale for the urban cowgirls.

Lamb has since released two well-received solo records, *Fiddle Fatale* (1993) and *Tonight I Feel Like Texas* (1996), in addition to appearing on many records by other artists. Miller has continued as a solo artist, in addition to collaborating on *Jo Miller and Laura Love Sing Bluegrass and Old Time Music* (1995). **JB**

Western Dream

(1989, Sugar Hill)
Their debut record is hard to find, but it features wonderful vocal performances by Jo Miller, Lisa Theo, and the band.

Flip City

(1993, Sugar Hill)
A set of tight, varied performances from Ranch Romance for their longtime fans to remember them by. The addition of David Keenan's vocals gives a new richness to the harmony mix.

Curtis Salgado

ortland-based blues singer and chromatic harp player Curtis Salgado has seen his influence spread further beyond his performances and recordings than probably any other Northwest blues artist. (The only possible exception would be former bandmate Robert Cray.) While playing in Eugene, Oregon, in the 1970s, Salgado gave a lesson in "Blues 101" to John Belushi when the actor was in town to film *Animal House*. This eventful meeting resulted in the Blues Brothers phenomenon, and both Cray and Salgado are credited (in small type) on the first Blues Brothers album.

By the time of the meeting with Belushi, Salgado had already been a blues fan for more than a decade. Born in Everett, Washington, on February 4, 1954, he grew up in Eugene. His father was a music lover and singer, and his older brother and sister were also avid record buyers, so singer-to-be Curtis grew up surrounded by jazz, folk, and the blues of Howlin' Wolf, Muddy Waters, and the other giants. Salgado's first musical performance was in kindergarten; his teacher was so impressed she sent him home with a note pinned to his shirt saying he could sing. In high school Salgado formed his first band, Three-Fingered Jack. The band played professionally for two years before Salgado hooked up with another Eugene-based bluesman, Robert Cray. The two played together from 1974 to 1982, first as the Nighthawks, then as the Robert Cray Band.

In 1982 Salgado set out on his own with his band In Yo' Face. Although a strong draw in the Portland and Seattle clubs, the group lasted only two years, and the singer left Portland for the East Coast. He became the lead singer for the noted Roomful of Blues, an association that also lasted only a couple of years, after which Salgado returned to the Northwest in 1986.

Back in Portland, he formed the band that would become Curtis Salgado and the Stilettos. With his friend John Mazzocco (who had been playing in John Lee Hooker's band) on bass, Jeff Minneweather on drums, and local jazzmen Joe Heineman on piano and Jay Koder on guitar, Salgado had an outfit with vast technique and experience to match the singer's gutsy soul treatments of songs. This was the band that really took charge in the Northwest club scene in the late 1980s and early 1990s, packing houses and attracting national attention. When a local timber heir, Tim Blixseth, decided to start a record company, he signed Salgado for the new BFE Records' flagship album release. Titled simply *Curtis Salgado and the Stilettos* (1991), the album featured a slick urbanized version of a song by the Portland band the Razorbacks, "More Love, Less Attitude." Although the single drew some notice around the country, its heavy reliance on urban R&B at a time when grunge ruled no doubt contributed to the album's spotty acceptance.

In 1995 Salgado followed with *More than You Can Chew* (Priority). By now Salgado had disbanded the Stilettos to go on the road; by singing lead vocals for a Santana tour, he gained new visibility around the country. When not on the road, the singer worked steadily in Portland. He decided to record a gritty, rootsy album next, and went into the studio with the awesome Terry Robb on guitar. The duo released *Hit It and Quit It* (Burnside) in 1997. Robb's one-man-band acoustic guitar and Salgado's funky harp playing and arresting vocals make this the Northwest album no blues fan should be without. In 1999 Salgado released *Wiggle Outta This*, his first album for the Shanachie label. **DD**

Hit It and Quit It

(Burnside, 1997)
One of the best acoustic-blues and rag-guitar players in the country, Terry Robb, pairs up with Curtis Salgado. The singer's power and expressive harp playing are showcased more effectively than on yet another band album.

American Roots/World

Isaac Scott

r ocker turned blues singer Little Bill Engelhart calls him "probably the only true bluesman in Seattle." European blues fans consider him a scandalously underrated original and wish he would return to the recording studio. But Isaac Scott has definitely created his own niche as the Northwest's most authentic—and accomplished—blues guitarist and vocalist.

Scott was born June 11, 1945, in Pine Bluff, Arkansas, the son of a railroad laborer; his family moved west to Portland in the late 1940s. Scott's mother was a devoted fan of gospel music, and her son received his early musical education courtesy of her collection of 78-rpm records and the traveling gospel shows the two attended. When he was only 9 years old, she bought him his first guitar. Young Isaac quickly taught himself to play by ear—when his mother signed him up for lessons a few years later, he could already outplay his would-be instructor.

After moving to Seattle in 1974, Scott decided to concentrate his musical efforts on the blues, first as a member of the Tom McFarland Band (he started as the band's piano player, but switched to guitar), then later with his own group. Scott's rise to fame in Seattle was helped by a pair of popular regular appearances—his late-night sessions in the now-defunct Hibble & Hydes in Pioneer Square (which often featured his good friend, guitarist Albert Collins) and his Sunday night gigs at north Seattle's Jolly Roger Roadhouse. The Isaac Scott Band contributed three tracks to the 1984 compilation *Live at the Roadhouse* (rereleased on CD in 1994; the three songs also appear on Scott's 1997 live retrospective CD, *High Class Woman*).

Scott's band recorded a pair of studio records on the Red Lightnin' label: *Isaac Scott Blues Band* (1978) and the critically acclaimed *Big Time Blues Man* (1983). He has appeared at Seattle's Bumbershoot arts festival as well as major blues festivals in San Francisco and Portland. His bands have always featured top local blues talent, including keyboardist and harp player Dick Powell, guitarist Mark Malloy, and the late Tony Thomas, Scott's mainstay on bass for decades.

His major trademarks are soulful vocals and unique lead-guitar phrasing—in a right-hand attack he uses fingers, thumb, and thumbnail, never a guitar pick. "You play the blues off of a feeling—happy, sad, down—whatever you feel," Scott told *Seattle* magazine in 1994. "I never use a song list because I just play off whatever the audience is feeling."

Although Scott has been plagued by ill health—a foot was amputated in 1994 due to complications of diabetes—he has kept playing sporadic gigs, usually with his current trio of bassist Bill Freckleton and drummer Paul Wager. A recipient of the Washington Blues Society's Hall of Fame Award in 1991, Scott is working on a new collection of studio recordings. **JB**

High Class Woman

(SHAKIRA, 1997)

Isaac Scott's only release readily available on CD, *High Class Woman* features material from two early-1990s Pioneer Square club gigs, plus his three-song contribution to *Live at the Roadhouse* of 1984. A good primer on Scott's playing and singing style.

Jimmy Silva

Originally from the Bay Area, Jimmy Silva reached Seattle through his songwriting before he made the journey himself. Silva, an old friend of Young Fresh Fellows vocalist Scott McCaughey, cowrote "Big House," which appeared on the Seattle band's first album. In fact, Silva might be better known through others' performances of his songs than from his own records.

Through four albums of mostly folk-influenced pop, the fragile-voiced Silva was nothing if not a craftsman, reconciling a storytelling ethic with an ear for a catchy musical hook. Early influences like the Who's Pete Townshend and the Kinks' Ray Davies aside ("Big House" sprang from an infatuation with Townshend), Silva described the bulk of his canon as "unabashedly folk." Indeed, the debut *Remnants of the Empty Set* (1986) carries an earthy vibe. Intended as a set of demos, *Remnants* found a home on PopLlama Products, the Seattle label that launched the Young Fresh Fellows. Among the friends backing Silva on the album was drummer Dennis Diken, who took "Hand of Glory" back to his own band, the Smithereens. The New Jersey band recorded the song for their album *Especially for You*, earning Silva a hefty chunk of change.

Silva's second album, *Fly Like a Dog* (1987), was recorded in both San Francisco and Seattle. The resulting grab bag included his own version of "Big House" and backing by the Fellows on some cuts. The Beau Brummels' Sal Valentino added vocals to "Troubled Times," a song about the TV evangelists Jim and Tammy Faye Bakker.

About this time Silva decided to move to Seattle and form a band. Anchored by bassist Walter Singleman, drummer Bill Walters, and multi-instrumentalist Bill "Jed" Jedrzejewski, the Goats helped form a tight, cohesive platform for Silva's songs. Still, it was some time before the Goats recorded an album: in 1991 *Heidi* was released on the Minneapolis label East Side Digital.

The liner notes to the Seattle-recorded *Heidi*, curiously, were signed "Jimmy Silva, San Francisco," revealing that he was once again based in the Bay Area. He returned to Seattle a short time later, however, re-formed the Goats with Jedrzejewski, drummer John Moreman, and bassist Eric Scott, and recorded a new album in fits and starts during 1993 and early 1994.

In December 1994, Silva died suddenly from complications brought on by chicken pox. *Near the End of the Harvest*, muted and country flavored, was posthumously released by PopLlama later in 1995, itself probably the most fitting tribute Jimmy Silva's friends could have made. Leaning more toward country than its predecessors, *Harvest* also features a Jedrzejewski reading of a signature Silva tune, "Tell It to the Raven." MC

Heidi

(1991, East Side Digital)
Silva's songwriting was at a peak for this set, with gems like the martial "Tin Whistle and a Wooden Drum" and the Byrds-ish "City of Sisterly Love," swathed in mandolins and twelve-string guitars.

The Skyboys

Formed 1973, Seattle, Washington

The Skyboys were the premier country rock group in Seattle from the mid-1970s to the early 1980s. Tom Kell (vocals, guitar) and Scott Smith (vocals, keyboard, guitar) formed the band as a duo but gradually added other players, including Dudley Hill (guitar), Linda Waterfall (bass), Leon Edwards Waldbauer (guitar), Gaye Winsor (keyboards), and Pat Bohle (drums). Nearly every member was a fine singer—the Skyboys' sets showcased the band's gorgeous harmonies and a superb mix of electric and acoustic guitars.

The Skyboys were influenced both by straight country singers such as Merle Haggard and by the new country rockers, including the Flying Burrito Brothers and Emmylou Harris. Bursting with creative songwriters (Kell, Hill, Smith, Waterfall), the band gained a devoted following all over the Northwest. Waterfall left in 1977 to start her successful solo career and was replaced on bass by Ken Parypa. The Skyboys finally made it onto vinyl in 1979, with a self-titled release on First American Records.

The band's lineup and sound continued to evolve when Hill departed and Chris Middaugh—a fine guitarist and pedal-steel player—replaced him. This version of the band recorded the 1981 single "Get It Up"/"Backing into a Heartache." The looping hook-laden A-side scored local airplay. The Skyboys continued into the early 1980s, moving toward a more commercial sound. New members Bill Stroum (bass), Chris Leighton (drums), and Mike Elliot (guitar) replaced Parypa, Bohle, and Middaugh. Stroum's brothers Mitch and Jonathan were involved in the band's management and production. This version of the band recorded the Skyboys' final record, the EP *Good Thing Goin'*, which features more excellent songwriting by Kell, Stroum, and Leighton.

The band lasted until the mid-1980s, when Kell left for Los Angeles to concentrate on a career as a songwriter for national acts. He has released several solo albums. Hill now plays with ex-Wailer Neil Andersson in the acclaimed instrumental group from Tacoma, Washington, Pearl Django. **NS**

The Skyboys

(1979, First American)
The all-original set features several great songs, including Hill's "Captain Lonely" and Kell's "Easy Love." The standout is "Lee John Sloaner," a 9-minute Hill/Kell country rock opus about an outlaw.

Uncle Bonsai
Formed 1981, Seattle, Washington

Electric Bonsai Band
Formed 1991, Seattle, Washington

Credit the fates for Uncle Bonsai: a chance meeting between a trio of former students from Vermont's Bennington College resulted in one of Seattle's most popular folk acts.

Andrew Ratshin, an acoustic performer since his high school days, studied music at Bennington before moving to Seattle in 1981. He stayed with friends who had another houseguest, a fellow Bennington refugee named Arni Adler. Although she had attended the school during some of the same years as Ratshin, the two hadn't met. They spotted a newspaper ad placed by another ex-Bennington student named Ashley, who was seeking people to play acoustic music. Ratshin and Adler joked that it was probably a mutual acquaintance, Ashley O'Keeffe. They answered the ad—and that's who it was.

"We got together to sing a couple songs and I wrote a couple songs and a month later, we went outside and sang outside the gates of Bumbershoot [Seattle's Labor Day weekend arts festival]," Ratshin recalls. They made enough money from passers-by to pay their admission into the festival, and a year later, the trio was onstage at one of the festival's largest venues.

The group started writing songs, padding their set with obscure cover tunes. But when they started getting paying jobs, they learned they were expected to perform three 1-hour sets per evening. "Suddenly we're writing a lot of songs," remembers Ratshin, who became the group's major songwriter.

The group's first record was *A Lonely Grain of Corn* (1984), released on the local Freckle label. For this album, the group set aside its usual format of three voices and Ratshin's acoustic guitar and recorded (for the first and last time) with a full studio band. Their second record, *Boys Want Sex in the Morning* (1986, Freckle), was recorded live at the Backstage, a club in Seattle's Ballard neighborhood.

The group's sound was built around their layered vocal harmonies and Ratshin's ringing guitar lines; O'Keeffe and Adler took most of the vocal leads. Ratshin's intelligent, playful lyrics highlighted Bonsai favorites like the haunting character study "Suzie," the self-explanatory "Boys Want Sex in the Morning," and "Cheerleaders on Drugs," which speculates that chemical intervention may be the source of those endless amounts of pep and school spirit.

Both albums sold well (thirty thousand to forty thousand copies each) and received national distribution, allowing Uncle Bonsai to tour the folk circuit. The group performed at summer festivals in the United States and Canada, and sold out shows in Chicago and San Francisco and at New York's Bottom Line. Uncle Bonsai's rapid rise in the Northwest was aided by the regional infrastructure of Chris Lunn's Victory Music organization (which sponsors open mike nights, concerts, and a monthly publication) and KEZX, a radio station with a powerful signal, a good following, and a willingness to play local music in their regular rotation.

In the late 1980s, Uncle Bonsai had their shot at the big time. They were due to fly to New York, sign with Island Records, and begin work on their album, when Ratshin called the label and discovered that the representative who had arranged their concert had suddenly died. "And man, did we not get that contract," he adds.

The next release, *Myn Ynd Wymyn* (1988, self-released), was planned as the group's swan song. Recorded at Seattle's Triad Studios before a live audience of sixty or so friends, this twenty-three-track, double-cassette release was sold mainly through the band's mailing list. *Myn Ynd Wymyn* was intended to make versions of some of the group's favorite late-period songs available to their loyal fans. "We pretty much knew we were going to be wrapping it up," says Ratshin. "The group broke up because we were tired, we'd been together eight and a half years, and we'd pretty much done everything we were going to do."

Ratshin's next project was the Electric Bonsai Band, which was actually his solo act. The name was chosen for obvious reasons, he admits. "Uncle Bonsai was pretty famous for a folk group, and when I went solo, everybody knew me as Andrew from Uncle Bonsai. That way, I keep the word Bonsai in there." He has released five solo records as the Electric Bonsai Band, all on his own Yellow Tail Records: *I Am Joe's Eyes* (1991), *20 Seconds of Pleasure* (1993), *But I'm Happy Now* (1993), *Lounging in the Belly of the Beast* (1996), and *Primal Urge* (1999). Yellow Tail is also the home label of classical guitarist Hilary Field, Ratshin's wife.

In 1992, Yellow Tail Records issued an edited CD rerelease of *Myn Ynd Wymyn* and also produced *The Inessential Uncle Bonsai*, a collection of live versions of most of the songs on the first two albums (the group owned the rights to the songs, but not to the performances featured on the original records).

Ratshin also performs with the vocal group Mel Cooleys, which released the 1993 CD *Live(?) in Seattle* (Yellow Tail) with a lineup including Lisa Theo (formerly of Ranch Romance), Cathy Croce, and Garey Shelton. That group continues with Shelton, Ratshin, and new members including Uncle Bonsai's Adler.

Uncle Bonsai has re-formed for concerts on several occasions, including an August 1998 show also featuring Mel Cooleys and the Electric Bonsai Band, resulting in *Doug* (1999, Yellow Tail), a live recording of songs detailing the continuing story of "Doug," Ratshin's mythical everyman. **JB**

Myn Ynd Wymyn

(1992, YELLOW TAIL)
This is the slightly abbreviated CD release of Uncle Bonsai's 1988 final release. Recorded live in the studio, this eighteen-track album includes fine performances of some of Uncle Bonsai's most amusing songs, including "Folk Song," "Family Restaurant," and "Takin' the Kids to Disney World."

Lounging in the Belly of the Beast

(1996, YELLOW TAIL)
Recorded as the Electric Bonsai Band, this is Ratshin's best solo turn. It features (naturally) some great songs, including "Angry Young Man," "The Airplane: Part II," and the title track, plus instrumental and vocal contributions from members of Mel Cooleys.

Linda Waterfall

With her versatile guitar combinations, counterpoint piano progressions, and crisp, innovative vocals, Seattle songwriter Linda Waterfall delivers a style that is hers alone. Waterfall melds her classical background with the folk sounds of Madagascar, Norway, and Bulgaria, along with American jazz, gospel, and pop. No wonder retailers have trouble filing her recordings.

"My idea of 20th-century American music is . . . blending classical music with the people's music. That's what is really exciting about today's music," she says. Becky Bernson of the *Folk Alliance Newsletter* called Waterfall "one of the finest finger-picking guitar players alive on planet Earth today." In the *New England Folk Almanac*, Bob Franke wrote, "Her musicianship is astonishing, and her lyrical sense is at the cutting edge. I can't see any serious fan of songwriting remaining ignorant of her work."

This musical mistress of the eclectic released her first album in 1977 and followed with seven more by 1998. She is a regular with the Artist in Residence Program of the Washington State Arts Commission and has shared her composing and performing skills with public school students and inmates in correctional facilities across the state.

Waterfall ("It is my real name") started taking piano lessons when she was 8 years old and taught herself to play the guitar as a teenager. But her parents, both professional musicians who had left the business to raise a family, strenuously discouraged their daughter from choosing music as a profession. After earning a degree in visual art—the next best thing—at Stanford University in 1971, Waterfall joined a band that stopped in Seattle for a short period before moving on to Boston. She returned to Seattle in 1975 to settle, and two years later released her first recording, *Mary's Garden* (Windham Hill).

Her producer, Jim Bredouw, hooked her up with the rock band the Skyboys the following year. As the band's bass player, Waterfall was a bit of an anomaly. Fellow members thought it was pretty strange when they found her backstage immersed in a book about spiders during a Jimmy Buffett concert, which the group had opened for. "These guys would come over, look through my record collection, and really be puzzled by not seeing one record they knew," Waterfall remembers.

Although the great artistic influences of her life include the likes of Stevie Wonder, Miles Davis, Joni Mitchell, and the Grateful Dead, Waterfall first lists Stravinsky, Debussy, and Bach. Following the release of her second recording, *My Heart Sings* (1979, Trout), a mix of jazz and classical works, Waterfall was voted Seattle's Best Solo Artist in the *Seattle Sun* Arts and Entertainment Poll (conducted by radio station KZAM). She was invited to teach at the annual Puget Sound Guitar Workshop on the Olympic Peninsula in 1981 and there connected with the local acoustic music community.

Playing both acoustic and electric guitar as well as piano, Waterfall says her work swings back and forth between classical and pop. One of her most popular recordings, *Body English* (1987, Flying Fish), showcases her ability to blend the styles. *A Little Bit at a Time* (1991, Flying Fish) and the spiritually charged *Flying Time* (1994, Trout) carried more pop tunes. *In the Presence of the Light* (1998, Trout/Liquid City) changes the mix again, with a stronger hint of the classical influence.

To fully appreciate Waterfall's musical prowess, it's essential to catch one of her live shows. Believing that performance is an important part of her musical career, Waterfall has been touring nationally since 1983. Connecting with people is her personal measure of success, which is what prompted her to start teaching as an artist in residence. She finds continual inspiration in what she describes as the creative genius residing in everyone. And she expands the scope of her audience each time she shares her music. "It's focusing and channeling the ecstasy—the ecstatic energy between artist and audience," Waterfall says. She's obviously doing things her way—and her way sounds pretty good. **CRH**

In the Presence of the Light

(1998, TROUT/LIQUID CITY)
A lively mix of chant, a couple of fun pop tunes, and a passionate interpretation of the words of Walt Whitman.

Sheila Wilcoxson

Persistence and belief in herself and her music have paid off for Sheila Wilcoxson. Since the 1997 release of *Backwater Blues*, this Detroit-born singer is no longer a well-kept secret in the Northwest, and has finally gained recognition at the national level, earning a W. C. Handy Award nomination in the process.

Moving to Portland in the early 1980s, Wilcoxson first established herself as frontwoman for Sheila and the Boogiemen. The group's repertoire of standard bar-band tunes caused it to be overlooked when its contemporaries such as Quarterflash and Johnny and the Distractions, were being signed by major labels. What the Boogiemen did do for Wilcoxson was allow her to earn a reputation as a powerful blues belter and soul shouter who deserved better.

"Better" came in the form of Backporch Blues, an acoustic quartet—a much different sort of group than the twelve-piece big band Wilcoxson had been fronting. With just guitar, bass, and blues harp, Backporch Blues provided a lighter framework for the singer's vocal dynamics. The Cascade Blues Association voted the group Best New Blues Band of 1989. As a small acoustic band, the group was suited for the growing number of brewpubs exploding around the Northwest, as well as festivals, coffeehouses, and other venues not open to louder, electric blues-boogie outfits.

The quartet's name was completely apropos, as the absence of drums and electric guitars helped the listener feel that the music was being played at a friend's house, almost in private. The rhythm of the bass and guitar nudged audiences into motion, instead of goosing them with a roaring guitar riff. For the first time, people were hearing Wilcoxson's interpretations, and discovering that the woman had charm and smarts along with volume and range.

Backporch Blues recorded two albums, *Down Home* (1990) and *Back to Basics* (1994). Promotion for the second album, on the ubiquitous Burnside Records label, included appearances on public radio programs and at festivals outside the Northwest. The familiar specter of "creative differences" caused the band to break up a year or so after the second album, but Wilcoxson bounced right back with Backwater Blues—both the name of the "band," consisting of guitar and blues-harp backup, and of her breakthrough 1997 album.

Street-smart and college-educated, the singer is ever alert to the importance of passing on a respect for the blues, and Backwater Blues is doing just that. Along with artists like Keb' Mo', Alvin Youngblood Hart, and fellow Portlander Kelly Joe Phelps, Wilcoxson is making younger generations aware of the rich cultural blend that the blues represents.

Playing blues and folk festivals across North America now, Wilcoxson is writing and selecting songs based on her personality and not on how familiar or comfortable they might be to the casual Baby Boomer listener. Instead, the singer's current repertoire is at once spiritual and down and dirty, presenting the singer as, alternately, angel and siren. **DD**

Backwater Blues

(1997, BURNSIDE)
Instead of recording a showcase for vocal gymnastics, Wilcoxson and producer/musician Terry Robb put together a set of fresh blues sounds with plenty of direct references to gospel and African folk music.

Lily Wilde

She may be an icon of Northwest blues, but Lily Wilde was raised in a house "where the blues was a dirty word." The daughter of jazz pianist Calvin Jackson, she grew up watching her father perform with the best musicians Los Angeles had to offer, including Lionel Hampton, Johnny Otis, and Errol Garner. Turning pro herself at age 17, Wilde first found high-profile work as a member of Stevie Wonder's backup band Wonderlove (she performed on his breakthrough 1972 album, *Music of My Mind*). After a short stint in England, Wilde returned to Los Angeles and worked as a backup singer—in the studio and for live dates—appearing with the likes of Rickie Lee Jones and sax player Lee Allen of the Blasters.

Relocating to Seattle, she fronted her own R&B band for about a year before being recruited by Ned Neltner to join the successful band Jr. Cadillac. She sang with them from 1988 to 1991, touring Russian with the band in 1989. Later she fronted Lily Wilde and the Hysterics and performed with Seattle Women in Rhythm & Blues and Little Bill and the Bluenotes. She has also appeared live and on record with Northwest blues chanteuse Duffy Bishop.

Wilde moved to Portland in 1992, where she continued singing the blues with guitarist Jim Mesi, and was prominently featured on the Mesi Band's live 1994 CD,

Hot Night at the Candlelight (credited to "Jim Mesi with Lily Wilde"). She was named 1991 Entertainer of the Year by the Washington Blues Society and 1993 Female Vocalist of the Year by the Cascade Blues Society. In addition, Wilde contributed two songs, covers of Helen Humes's "Be Baba Leba" and Ellen Johnson's "Don't Shout at Me, Daddy," to the compilation album *A Taste of the Blue Rose* (1999, Flying Heart).

Wilde's newest band, the Jumpin' Jubilee Orchestra, pays tribute to the bluesy big-band swing music of post–World War II artists such as Buddy Wilson and Louis Jordan. The band's musical director is drummer Tom Royer, Wilde's husband. Also featured in the thirteen-piece orchestra are top Portland musicians Janice Scroggins (keyboards), Ralph Pritikin (guitar), and Joey Seiffers (bass), and an eight-piece horn section. The group's first CD, *Insect Ball,* was self-released in 1999.

Royer told Portland music writer Virginia Bruce, "I liked [the music] because it had this bluesy, hard-swinging groove and there was also this sophistication to it, like jazz and blues and R&B all rolled into one." "This is the music I feel I was meant to do," agreed Wilde. **JB**

Hot Night at the Candlelight

(1994, CANDLELIGHT)

This live set features Lily Wilde with ace blues guitarist Jim Mesi; in 1998 it was rereleased by Just Ducky Records.

Classical

CLASSICAL MUSIC
IN THE NORTHWEST

t didn't take long to bring classical music to the frontier: the Seattle Symphony Orchestra was formed in 1903 during the growth spurt that saw Seattle become a major city. By that time, the Oregon Symphony had been performing for almost a decade. But it was years before the Seattle Symphony reached national status, by which time the Northwest had spawned a host of other performing groups concentrating on aspects of the classical canon.

The region's two most successful classical groups play a few miles apart in downtwon Seattle. The Seattle Symphony Orchestra performs a full schedule in downtown's Benaroya Hall and has focused on recording, releasing some fifty albums. The Opera House at the Seattle Center is a destination for classical music enthusiasts from across the country, who trek to the Northwest to see and hear the Seattle Opera's famous productions of Richard Wagner's *Ring* cycle.

The Northwest in recent years has seen a surge of interest in early music (Seattle Baroque Orchestra, the Renaissance-oriented Esoterics) and smaller performance groups (the string quartet Bridge Ensemble, the Olympia Chamber Orchestra). And innovators abound: Avant-garde composer/trombone player Stuart Dempster's experimentation has taken him down a deep well to capture the natural reverb, and into the studio with the fanciful long string instrument. In the Seattle clubs, Young Composers Collective has brought the youthful energy and spirit of rock music to its classical fusion repertoire.

Although engaged in a musical genre often focused on its past, Northwest artists are unusually equipped to move classical music into the next century.

Christian Asplund

Composer and impresario Christian Asplund joined forces in 1995 with fellow University of Washington graduate student Tom Baker and avant-jazz violinist Eyvind Kang to create the Seattle Experimental Opera (SExO), which presented its first production that April. Asplund's contribution, with text by his wife, Lara Candland, was *A Girl's Body at Crepuscule*, the first in a series of enigmatic and inscrutable antioperas. The work's central metaphor draws together a woman's shifting sense of identity and the unsettledness of dusk; the main character is echoed aurally by the instruments in the small orchestra or by whispers in dark corners, and visually by a second character who may be her analyst or her alter ego. Later came *The Open Curtain*, a setting of texts by Joseph Smith, which featured Asplund performing on his two trademark instruments: a harmonium that creates a quaint pillowy drone under the voices, and a viola played in a visceral thrash-metal style. *Floralesque* premiered in April 1998; this epistolary opera has a cast of six sopranos and is set in a Victorian walled garden.

Asplund's *The Archivist*, issued on Seattle's Un-Labeled Records, takes place in an underground repository. "Flandro works at his mysterious task in his archive up Provo Canyon. . . . He is visited by the angel Bonting who delivers materials of an undisclosed nature"—that's all the plot summary you find in the liner notes. The dialogue—crisp, poetic, and slightly mannered—is again by Candland. The underscoring and instrumental interludes are played by four strings; Asplund's music for this pocket orchestra is relentlessly dour, repetitive, and absorbing in its simplicity—something like what Satie might have written had he taken *film noir* for his inspiration rather than *le music-hall*. Interspersed with the scenes in the archive are Asplund's contrasting settings of traditional hymn texts for small four-part choir. Though occasionally a bit twisted, the music would not be out of place at any Minnesota Lutheran choral-college concert. Not a note or word too many clutters the piece; it's a marvel what dreamily unsettling effects Candland and Asplund have produced with an (again, Satie-like) economy of means. The close and tight recording of the dialogue adds to the radio-mystery atmosphere. **GB**

Bridge Ensemble

Two Russian men and two American women made up the Bridge Ensemble at its inception in 1993—hence the name, a reference to their trans-pacific origins. The group's concert schedule was somewhat erratic; three of the Bridge—violinist Mikhail Schmidt, violist Susan Gulkis, and cellist David Tonkonogui—were (and still are) members of the Seattle Symphony, and they, along with pianist Karen Sigers, maintained other chamber-music commitments. Their rare recitals were all the more eagerly awaited. Astonishing nuanced technical command in the service of

Classical

high drama is the quartet's hallmark; in the Bridge's hands, music breathes and bleeds, to use composer Ned Rorem's phrase, and sings and dances. The sheer blazing rightness of their performances, in each moment and in the whole, gives the impression of a direct link from the listener to the composer's brain.

A live performance of Brahms's *Piano Quartet in G minor* leads off the quartet's

The Death of Classical Music

Western art music begins, generally speaking, with religious chants of the era from A.D. 800 to 900. The first musical innovation was the invention of polyphony: the addition of another equal or accompanying voice to a single-line chant. Naturally, this development was greeted with an outcry from the church—they were upset that musical complications would distract from the liturgical text.

In other words, classical music has resisted change practically since its very birth. The sole constant in its history is the howls of protest from doomsayers bemoaning the music's imminent demise. In what other art is catastrophe predicted so regularly and with such relish?

Well, classical music's been dying for a thousand years now. Of course, there's no denying that the late twentieth century has been a period of flux, but as we examine the health of the art form, the chorus of Cassandras seems to have a little less to wail about.

Yes, a couple of urban orchestras folded in recent years—but opera attendance is up (thanks largely to supratitles). Yes, there's overwhelming competition from the gargantuan corporate infotainment machine, but classical music has learned a few good lessons in marketing savvy. Yes, classical music seems to have a smaller role in the brave new world of pop culture (remember when even a quintessentially lowbrow artifact like *Gilligan's Island* made references to *Carmen*?), but perhaps now those who follow it are doing so for its own sake rather than as a class-conscious status symbol. Yes, audiences have rejected all those dreadful evil puppy-kicking atonal composers—but there's enough good music being written all across the comfort spectrum that anyone whose brain isn't completely ossified can find plenty to like.

The late twentieth century, however, leaves one major legacy. The growth of the recording industry has obviously been a sea change, comparable to nothing else in music history except the invention of printing and publishing. (Glenn Gould, brilliant aesthetician though he was, has been proved wrong in his declaration that the recording would kill the live concert—another example in the long tradition of deathwatches that never panned out.) Yet the rise of recorded music contains a paradox: it's a change that has changed the nature of change (stay with me), calling into question the whole notion of fashion. What does it mean for a piece of music to be "of" its time, when music from any of the past ten centuries is equally available? Thanks largely to recordings and their welcome disregard of the calendar, musicians and listeners are starting to realize that music is not a zero-sum game; that new music does not have to replace the old, as it used to; that old and new, tonal and atonal, formal and vernacular, European and everywhere else, can all coexist in our culture just as they do within the walls of Tower Records.

—Gavin Borchert

Classical

CD *Live from the Bridge (1996)*. Exuberant and passionate it surely is, but the textural clarity of the Bridge's playing never falters; you can hear every note, even as the musicians work up a visceral whirlwind in the stamping finale. A modern-day extension of the "gypsy" style of Brahms's finale can be heard in Paul Schoenfield's *Café Music*, a sophisticated romp consisting of a fast rag, a slow passage with a waltz interlude, and a neo-Hungarian gallop in Carl Stalling–Warner Brothers style. The Bridge plays with an edge-of-the-seat panache that takes listeners by surprise. Third on the disc is an example of the modern Russian school, favored by the group: a movement from Alfred Schnittke's *Piano Quartet*. The work's lush textures and refracted tonality are reminiscent of a nineteenth-century opium dream (another Brahms connection); its jump cuts and extremes of angst and stasis are the Bridge's specialties.

The quartet makes an exciting contribution to a disc of the music of Daniel Asia (*Ivory*, 1995, Koch International Classics), a Seattle-born professor at the University of Arizona. Asia's *Piano Quartet* is in three movements, the first lyrical and rippling, the others spacious and lightly Copland-flavored. The work's open textures create a meditative mood even in the briskly syncopated dancelike passages. (Gulkis is the violist on both these recordings, though she left the group in the fall of 1997; her replacement is English violist and University of Washington faculty member Helen Callus.)

The Bridge's violinist, Schmidt, is a member of the Seattle Chamber Players as well, with flautist Paul Taub, clarinetist Laura DeLuca, and cellist David Sabee. The chamber group is renowned for its eclectic programming; pianists, percussionists, and other string players are frequent guests, which makes just about any work in the chamber repertory an option. The Seattle Chamber Players take special interest in new music, lesser-known works by the big guys in the canon, and landmark works of early twentieth-century modernism like Schoenberg's *Pierrot Lunaire* and Satie's *Entr'acte* and *Furniture Music*. **GB**

Timothy Brock and the Olympia Chamber Orchestra

Olympia, Washington, composer Timothy Brock has worked extensively in traditional genres: three symphonies, concertos for clarinet and viola, overtures and suites; six string quartets and other chamber music; and two operas, *Billy* and *Mudhoney*. But he is best known for his film scores to ten (so far) classic silents. On CD can be found his scores for F. W. Murnau's *Faust, Sunrise*, and *The Last Laugh*, Robert Wiene's *The Cabinet of Dr. Caligari*, and Vsevolod Pudovkin's *Storm over Asia*. Brock recorded these scores with the Olympia Chamber Orchestra, which he founded in 1989.

Also on CD with the orchestra is a concert suite Brock drew from his music for Walther Ruttmann's 1927 film *Berlin: Symphony of a Great City*. Somewhere between the operas of Kurt Weill and the film music of Dmitri Shostakovich, Brock's intoxicating music is full of period color: jaunty minor-key brass marches, intense percussion, and plenty of ostinatos both ominous and circusy. He reaches for direct pictorial effects—chugging strings and a steam whistle in upper woodwinds to accompany an on-screen train ride, or sexy, smoky jazz saxes for the "Nightlife" sequence—and, with utter conviction but no self-consciousness, he always makes it work. Brock's music for *Berlin* is a counterpart to Guy Maddin's cinematic evocations of the same time and place—he discovered natural and expressive conventions that he didn't hesitate to use, despite their association with a different era. His music is not a matter of pastiche, though, or ironic distance; it calls into question the nature of such an association, and, gratifyingly, exposes the arbitrariness by which we assign a particular set of musical stylistic parameters to a particular point on the calendar. The Olympic Chamber Orchestra plays *Berlin* vividly, and David Beck sounds wonderful in the solo cello part in the elegiac *Largo* from another Brock concert suite on the CD, *Three Cinematographic Scenes from "The Last Laugh."* **GB**

Stuart Dempster

t he earliest recording in Stuart Dempster's discography is the classic Columbia disc of Terry Riley's minimalist milestone *In C*, a 1968 performance that Dempster organized in Buffalo. In the same year, the 32-year-old trombonist joined the music department of the University of Washington. Composer, improviser, and sound inventor, Dempster became known as an advocate for the avantgarde; he is the author of *The Modern Trombone: A Definition of Its Idioms* and a dedicatee of works by contemporary composers Donald Erb and Luciano Berio. In 1987 he released *Stuart Dempster in the Great Abbey of Clement VI* (New Albion). The CD includes his "Standing Waves" for trombone and tape and "Didjeridivish" for Australian didjeridoo, the rich, calm, bodily drones that fascinate him.

Deep Listening (1989, New Albion) was a seminal recording for Dempster, his first of seven collaborations with accordionist Pauline Oliveros and electroacoustic musician Panaiotis (Peter Ward), collectively known as the Deep Listening Band. *Deep Listening* also marked his first trip down an abandoned cistern at Fort Worden, near Port Townsend, Washington, the site for Dempster's most famous and astonishing recordings. The cistern's reverb time could last as long as 45 seconds, and miraculous things happened to the sounds loosed by the trio; each tone of Oliveros's warmly reedy accordion and Dempster's mellow trombone becomes a plane floating in three dimensions, circling and passing through each other with immense grace. The Deep Listening Band's later recording, *Suspended Music* (1997), is less quiescent, more squirrelly, and more haunting. Flutes and electronic processing are brought to the mix, and Dempster's didjeridoo, conch shell, and garden hose add a bit of graininess.

Also heard on this CD is the Long String Instrument, invented, played, and composed for by Ellen Fullman. The network of suspended wires here sounds like the shimmering of a gigantic bowed psaltery. **GB**

The Esoterics

If any corner of the choral repertory is a box-office sure thing, it's the Renaissance: madrigals and masses reliably draw audiences for choirs small and large. But the Esoterics have built an enthusiastic (not to say cult) following with a more difficult repertory, twentieth-century a cappella works. This sixteen-voice Seattle-based chorus was founded in 1992 by University of Washington graduate student Eric Banks to meet his degree requirement in choral conducting; the success of the recitals encouraged the singers to perform regularly outside of academia. In their vocals, the Esoterics offer both fullness and clarity, and a virtuosic mastery of the twentieth-century repertory's tricky rhythms and complex harmony. The group's concerts show an exquisite attention to detail in the imaginative and dramatic use of entrances, exits, and space; their spoken program notes (personal commentary on the music performed) make for a warmly communicative concert experience. Their programs cling to no party line: Giuseppe Verdi and Arnold Schoenberg, Elliott Carter and Philip Glass, Maurice Duruflé and György Ligeti all find a home in their concerts. Banks's detective work on behalf of little-known composers is exemplary, and his organization of programs around a particular theme (elegantly expressed in single Latin-word titles: *Nox, Mors, Lux*) is fresh and clever and deepens the music's impact by providing a context for each composer's tradition.

The Esoterics' first disc, *Beata*, is devoted to eighteen works celebrating the Virgin, performed in Seattle and at Christ Episcopal Church in Tacoma, Washington, where the recording was made in June 1997. The music ranges from Verdi's chromatically luscious setting of the "Ave Maria" from his *Four Sacred Pieces* (an 1898 work that necessitated bending the group's twentieth-century rule) to a brisk setting of a 1990 Russian hymn, "Bogoroditse dyevo, raduisya," by Arvo Pärt. Highlights of the disc include Giles Swayne's setting of the "Magnificat" (1982), which links motifs from West African folksong into a richly rhythmic mosaic. Pablo Casals's "Tota pulchra es, Maria," glowing with resonant simplicity, anticipates the neomedievalism of recent composers like Pärt or John Tavener. In Einojuhani Rautavaara's "Canticum Mariae virginis," sopranos and basses chant long flexible lines over and under ever-shifting tone clouds. Kenneth Gaburo's lovely "Ave Maria, gratia plena," a serenely clashing contrapuntal study, is one of the two American pieces on the disc. Between the sets (six groups of three pieces each), the Esoterics sing strophes of the hymn "O virga ac diadema" by twelfth-century mystic, poet, and abbess Hildegard of Bingen. In concert, these strophes were used to good effect, sung as transition music while the choir progressed through the church. **GB**

Alan Hovhaness

probably the best-known work by Seattle composer Alan Hovhaness is his *Symphony No. 2* from 1955, entitled *Mysterious Mountain*. It contains all the hallmarks of his personal style, which he had fully developed by this time (the piece is his Opus 132). Long, flowing, chantlike lines, either in wind or brass solos or "thickened" in chorale settings for strings, are his most recognizable trait. These lines are often layered fugally, creating rippling or agitated surfaces. His harmonic language is modal, evoking Renaissance music. These traits have practically become, for younger composers, a lingua franca for musical "spirituality," and Hovhaness makes clear the personal beliefs at the core of his art. An air of quiescence pervades every bar he wrote, not incompatible with an occasional urgency—for example, the unflappable, stately brass chant behind the churning strings in the "Double Fugue" movement of *Mysterious Mountain*.

Hovhaness is a true pioneer of contemporary music—he developed his unique personal style back in the 1940s and 1950s, at a time when there were essentially only three options open to composers: Teutonism à la Schoenberg, Gallicism à la Stravinsky, or Americanism à la Copland (and it can be argued that the third is a subset of the second).

The unfortunate fact about Hovhaness is that his personal musical path is so well worn that hardly a living blade of grass is left on it. He is an outrageously prolific and facile composer; current figures are hard to come by, but he composed sixty-three symphonies by 1989 and has written more than four hundred works in total. Once Hovhaness established his idiom, he seemed to forgo any questing spirit or sense of artistic discovery; his music became self-contented almost to the point of being formulaic. Programmatically, his compositions continue to strive for the Infinite and evoke a sort of Eastern-influenced nature pantheism, ensuring that he will remain one of the most popular of living composers, especially in his native Northwest. Comforting consistency, ubiquity and quantity, name recognition, hip Seattle cachet: Hovhaness has become the Starbucks of composers.

The classic recording of *Mysterious Mountain* is by Fritz Reiner and the Chicago Symphony, but probably the foremost CD version belongs to the American Composers Orchestra, led by Dennis Russell Davies. Also on this disc is Hovhaness' *Lousadzak* for piano and orchestra (with soloist Keith Jarrett), influenced by the folk music from his ancestral Armenia. The dance rhythms, spicy clashes, and piano tremolos reminiscent of strummed-string folk instruments add a zing not common in his music.

Another uncharacteristically visceral passage occurs in the "Volcano" third movement from Hovhaness's *Symphony No. 50, Mount St. Helens* (1983). The eruption is represented by a symphonic orgy, undeniably enjoyable, for drums, thunder sheets, and heaving brass. The movement ends with a sumptuous (if typical) chorale of praise. The second movement, entitled "Spirit Lake," foreshadows the tumult with interesting passages of pulsing bell sounds and deep rumblings underneath. Conductor Gerard Schwarz, a champion of the composer, has recorded the work with the Seattle Symphony, along with *Symphony No. 22, City of Light*.

A good overview of Hovhaness's music can be found on a disc by I Fiamminghi, the top-notch Flemish new-music orchestra led by Rudolf Werthen. The most compelling pieces are *Tzaikerk*, another lively folk dance for flute, violin, timpani, and strings, and the second movement of *Concerto No. 7 for Orchestra*, in which figurations on the xylophone, and later on bells and pizzicato strings, bring a flavor of the Indonesian gamelan orchestra. Underneath are querulous glissandos for strings, brass, and timpani. Also on the CD are more fugues (*Prelude and Quadruple Fugue, Alleluia and Fugue*, and the finale of *Concerto No. 7*), more serene brass solos (*Prayer of St. Gregory* for trumpet and strings), and more flowing chant for strings (*Symphony No. 6, Celestial Gate*). **GB**

Northwest Chamber Orchestra

a n uncharitable critic could dismiss the Northwest Chamber Orchestra as purveyors of Sunday afternoon concerts of Classics Lite for Seattle's most conservative audiences. Their self-proclaimed signature piece is, after all, Pachelbel's *Canon in D major*, and their devotion to programming a good deal of drab "Barococo" music has remained firm even as a wonderfully lively period-instrument performance culture has grown up in Seattle around the group, which was founded in 1973 by Louis Richmond.

Still, the Northwest Chamber Orchestra did win a 1979 ASCAP (American Society of Composers, Authors, and Publishers) award for programming contemporary music; and of their six CDs, four are of twentieth-century music, including works by British composers Arnold Cooke, Benjamin Frankel, Gordon Jacob, and Alan Rawsthorne—all favorites of Welsh conductor Alun Francis, who led the group from 1980 to 1985. Another disc is devoted to the music of American iconoclast Henry Cowell, and the orchestra has also recorded Alan Hovhaness's *Symphony No. 38*, commissioned by the group. In recent seasons the orchestra has played, along with Copland's *Appalachian Spring* and Barber's *Adagio for Strings*, non-easy-listening works by Gerard Schurmann and Gerhard Samuel. From these contradictions, the group has carved an admirable niche for itself, with an enthusiastic fan base of Seattle's perhaps not most conservative, but certainly most contented, audiences.

The orchestra has recorded CDs of baroque Christmas music and Vivaldi compositions, including *The Four Seasons*, with concertmaster Marjorie Kransberg-Talvi as soloist. In 1998 the group celebrated its twenty-fifth anniversary by self-releasing a two-CD set of live performances spanning its entire history. But the disc devoted to Cowell contains the most amazing music. Play the first movement of the 1925 *Ensemble* for friends, and ask them to guess the composer. See if they don't name someone from contemporary Eastern Europe, Sofia Gubaidulina, Arvo Pärt, or Peteris Vasks. Then play the *Fiddler's Jig* and *Air*, and they'll say Gustav Holst or Ralph Vaughan Williams. Try another, the third movement of *Variations on Thirds* for two violas and strings. It opens in perfect eighteenth-century style, then goes slowly off the rails: imagine a page of Handel engraved in chocolate just starting to melt. All the music on this disc (four of Cowell's eighteen sets of hymns and fuguing tunes are also included), in whatever harmonic style, is strong, fresh, and a bit rough-hewn. The Northwest Chamber Orchestra plays these grossly neglected works beautifully and convincingly. **GB**

Oregon Symphony

founded in 1896, the Portland-based Oregon Symphony is the Northwest's oldest orchestra, and one of a handful in the United States to celebrate a centennial. James DePreist took over the music directorship in 1980, and in seven years brought the Oregon Symphony to a peak of skill displayed in their recording debut; with marvelous chutzpah, he chose for the CD *Bravura* (1987, Delos) three of the repertory's most extroverted and demanding showpieces: Ottorino Respighi's *Roman Festivals*, Richard Strauss's *Don Juan*, and Witold Lutoslawski's *Concerto for Orchestra*. All receive strong performances; the most impressive playing, deft and wonderfully clean, is in the scurrying second and third movements of the *Concerto*, a traditional but astringent and imaginative work from 1950.

Subsequent Oregon Symphony discs are devoted to Tchaikovsky and Rachmaninoff, coupling well-known and lesser-known works: Tchaikovsky's overtures *Hamlet*, *The Tempest* and *1812*, and Rachmaninoff's tone poem *The Sea and the Gulls*, *Vocalise*, and *Symphony No. 2*. After recording Lutoslawski, the orchestra continued its notable devotion to new music in a disc of two works commemorating Martin Luther King: Joseph Schwantner's *New Morning for the World* and Nicolas Flagello's *The Passion of Martin Luther King* (1995, Koch International Classics). The tautness and polish of the string section are shown off on another disc, in Norman Dello Joio's *Meditations on Ecclesiastes*, a theme-and-variations with an interesting programmatic structure, each variation inspired by a line from the famous verses of Ecclesiastes III, 1–8: "To everything there is a season . . . A time to be born, and a time to die." Also on this disc are a tangy two-movement suite from 1956, *The Masks* by Ronald LoPresti, and the world-premiere recording of Gian Carlo Menotti's 1978 *Apocalypse*, a richly orchestrated work (another showcase for the symphony) with some amazingly banal melodic material.

On a more recent disc, the Oregon Symphony plays, thrillingly, music by film-score composer par excellence Erich Korngold: His *Symphony in F-sharp* from 1954 has as a curtain-raiser the juiciest bits from the 1940 score for the Errol Flynn swash-buckler *The Sea Hawk*, organized into a rousing 8-minute overture. The performance

SEATTLE OPERA'S PRODUCTION OF *DIE WALKÜRE*

YOUNG COMPOSERS COLLECTIVE

BRIDGE ENSEMBLE

THE ESOTERICS

starts out, surprisingly, a bit moderno with clanking xylophones; and throughout the 54-minute work, Korngold's familiar movie idiom (including material borrowed from the scores for *The Private Lives of Elizabeth and Essex* and *Kings Row*) is leavened by darker, harsher effects, a compelling combination. **GB**

Seattle Baroque Orchestra

Seattle's reputation as a center for early-music performance, already strong, was boosted further in 1994 when violinist Ingrid Matthews and keyboardist Byron Schenkman cofounded the Seattle Baroque Orchestra. This ensemble of a dozen or so strings, joined as needed by a half-dozen wind players, recorded their first CD, devoted to Handel, in 1996. The disc contains three cantatas for soprano, "Armida abbandonata," "Tra le fiamme," and "Ah! che pur troppo e vero," along with a miscellany of keyboard and orchestra pieces—and, for dessert, one of Handel's greatest hits: the aria "Ombra mai fu" (known as "Handel's Largo") from the opera *Xerxes*. Soprano Ellen Hargis is the disc's first-rate soloist, exhibiting a pure and lovely tone and an affecting way with vocal nuance and melodic ornament. Written during a stay in Italy under the patronage of a Roman aristocrat, these cantatas exhibit the young Handel's taste for the flamboyant in their extravagant, near-Verdian dramatic effects: Take "Armida abbandonata," the lament of a tormented woman who ricochets between pining for and thirsting for revenge on her unfaithful lover. Hargis has the technique to master the concertolike demands of these showpieces; her style and the orchestra's are bold and flexible enough to turn the pyrotechnics into compelling drama.

Matthews and Schenkman share an equal delight in the extravagant side of the baroque. As a duo, they recorded CDs of the sonatas of French composers Elisabeth-Claude Jacquet de la Guerre and Jean-Fery Rebel (both 1997, Wildboar), and a virtuoso barn-burner titled *In Stil Moderno: The Fantastic Style in 17th-Century Italy* (1995, Wildboar). Notable on this disc are two sonatas from the 1620s by Dario Castello, wildly rhapsodic flights of great rhythmic dash. The first ends suddenly and poignantly, like a thought trailing off, and the convulsive coda of the second is a rhetorical flourish almost four centuries ahead of its time. Marco Uccellini's *La luciminia contenta* is a similar mad scene for violin, its flashing scales no less expressive than the melodic chromaticism, the ornaments, and the vibrato and pitch-bending Matthews applies with élan. On his own, Schenkman also recorded a fine disc of harpsichord music from the court of Louis XIV, preserved in a seventeenth-century collection known as *The Bauyn Manuscript* (1997, Wildboar).

Viola da gambist Margriet Tindemans is a frequent collaborator with the Seattle Baroque Orchestra (her demonically difficult part in "Tra le fiamme" is as dazzlingly performed as Hargis's). Her discography of more than thirty recordings covers repertory from the medieval to the baroque, with one surprising twentieth-century item:

she appears on a CD of music by South African composer Kevin Volans, *White Man Sleeps* (1990, United). Well known as a string-quartet arrangement recorded by the Kronos Quartet, the piece was originally written for two harpsichords, percussion, and Tindemans herself. The viola da gamba's movable frets allow for the tuning changes required in this suite of five dances based on traditional African music. Strongly rhythmic, earthy, and raucous, the suite's second and fourth dances call for Tindemans to produce guitarlike timbres, and in the near-flamenco style of the fast passages, she flat-out rocks. **GB**

Seattle Opera

O ne of the legacies of Seattle's 1962 World's Fair, along with the Space Needle and the Monorail, is the Seattle Opera. Domiciled at the Opera House, which was built especially for the fair, the Seattle Opera gave its first production in 1963. The company's primary claim to fame is, undoubtedly, its productions of Richard Wagner's *Ring* cycle (the four-part epic *Der Ring des Nibelungen*). First staged in 1975 by Glynn Ross, Seattle's *Ring* has been performed fourteen times (the next production is set for 2001); these performances and acclaimed productions of *Die Meistersinger* and *Lohengrin* established the Seattle Opera's reputation as America's premier Wagner company. Keeping up the tradition is director Speight Jenkins, who took over in 1983; his most recent Wagner success was a staging of *Tristan und Isolde* in the summer of 1998 with the title roles sung by arguably the planet's finest Wagnerian tenor and soprano, Ben Heppner and Jane Eaglen. Jenkins has a laudable taste for the offbeat, and his reign has seen productions of Douglas Moore's *The Ballad of Baby Doe*, Sergey Prokofiev's *War and Peace*, and Philip Glass's *Satyagraha*. *Florencia in the Amazon*, Mexican composer Daniel Catán's opulent, Gabriel Garcia Marquez–inspired tale of a mysterious diva on a jungle riverboat cruise, was staged in the spring of 1998; the new work was a co-commission with opera companies in Houston and Los Angeles.

Jenkins also has a fine instinct for singers. In recent seasons, in addition to Eaglen and Heppner, he has brought an exciting stream of splendid leading sopranos (either enjoying major careers or verging on fame) such as Harolyn Blackwell (in *Gilda*), Lauren Flanigan (Violetta in *La traviata*), Sheri Greenawald (Florencia, Mimi in *La bohème*), Angelika Kirchschlager (Octavian in *Der Rosenkavalier*), Nancy Maultsby (Erda in *Siegfried, Carmen,* Charlotte in *Werther*), Carol Vaness (Leonora in *Il trovatore*), and Frederica von Stade (in *Xerxes*). Vinson Cole has been a popular regular, practically the house lyric tenor for the past decade.

The Seattle Opera's regular pit orchestra is a slightly reduced Seattle Symphony Orchestra, whose playing is reliably first-class. Stagings range from traditional to experimental, with no particular party line; a *Carmen* full of chairs and trenchcoats was an interesting misfire, but Stephen Wadsworth's *Xerxes* in an English country house was a delight. Financially successful, the company seems constantly to be breaking box-office records; perhaps the best testimony to its overall high standards is the city's claim to the highest per-capita opera attendance in the country. Unfortunately, the Seattle Opera has shown no interest in recording, so no CDs are available. **GB**

Seattle Symphony Orchestra

O rchestral performances in Seattle date back to 1903, but despite the presence of major figures like Sir Thomas Beecham (who spent two unproductive years here in the 1940s), not until Gerard Schwarz was appointed music director in 1985 did the Seattle Symphony Orchestra rise from provincial to world-class status. Under Schwarz the Seattle Symphony has become a prolific recording group, with over seventy releases to date, mostly for the Delos label.

The Seattle Symphony's unique achievement has been in American music, specifically the nationalistic midwar style and works by the composers who have borne this conservative banner into our day. Schwarz and the orchestra have worked admirably hard to revive and preserve a repertory that has been neglected (frankly, not entirely unjustly) by recording definitive performances of the seven symphonies of Howard Hanson and a large portion of the symphonic output of Walter Piston. Less well-known figures such as Peter Mennin and Paul Creston have also benefited from Schwarz's attention, and he and the Seattle Symphony have cultivated a continuing relationship—on disc and in the concert hall—with composers David Diamond, Alan Hovhaness, and Henri Lazarof.

From the standard repertory, Schwarz favors big romantic and early modern works: Wagner orchestral excerpts, Stravinsky ballets, Strauss tone poems. The recordings of Schumann—the four symphonies, the concertos and other orchestral works—are much acclaimed. Shostakovich has been selected only once, but the recording of *Symphony No. 11* (1997, Koch/Schwann) is a jaw-dropper, and one hopes more Shostakovich is to come. Also on the wish list of many who attended the Seattle Symphony's recent miraculous concert performances are recordings of Mahler's Second and Fifth symphonies. Despite Schwarz's reputation as an eighteenth-century music specialist (he also serves as artistic director of New York's Mostly Mozart Festival and the New York Chamber Symphony), he has recorded baroque and classical works only rarely. The opening in 1998 Benaroya Hall, their superb new concert hall in downtown Seattle, which is much more acoustically suited to this reperatory than their former home, the Seattle Center Opera House, may inspire new work in this direction. **GB**

Howard Hanson, Symphonies Nos. 1 and 2

(1989, DELOS)
Rich and stately readings of these American symphonic classics. CONTINUED...

Grieg, Piano Concerto, Holberg Suite, and Lyric Suite

(1991, Delos)
Bella Davidovich is the soloist for the *Concerto*. All three pieces get sweeping and fragrant performances.

Transformations for Strings

(1993, Delos)
Schwarz has a special rapport with string-orchestra works, evident in the three late-romantic works on this disc by Anton von Webern, Richard Strauss, and Arthur Honegger.

Shostakovich, Symphony No. 11

(1997, Koch/Schwann)
A recording that marvelously captures the work's icy bleakness and barely controlled frenzy.

Seattle Youth Symphony Orchestras

the Seattle Youth Symphony Orchestras, founded in 1942 as a single ensemble, is now a consortium of five orchestras: the Debut Symphony, the Symphonette, the Junior Symphony, the Youth Symphony, and the fifty-member Classical Orchestra. These performing groups involve over five hundred local music students at all levels of experience, from beginners to players approaching college study and professional careers. Jonathan Shames currently leads the 122-member Youth Symphony, a group of near-professional polish that in many respects can be considered Seattle's second orchestra. Shames's programming is ambitious, and the kids rise to the occasion. Since his directorship began in 1994, the students have played, beautifully, some of the more demanding symphonies in the repertory: Rachmaninoff's Second, Shostakovich's Fifth (the Youth Symphony's large string complement was particularly effective in these two), Mahler's First, Schubert's Ninth, Stravinsky's *Symphony of Psalms*, and Leonard Bernstein's *Jeremiah*. Shames has demonstrated a strong commitment to contemporary music in recent performances of works by Daniel Asia, Cindy McTee, Roberto Sierra, and Steven Stucky.

The slow movement of the Youth Symphony's performance of *Symphony No. 2* by Rachmaninoff is available on the disc entitled *Seattle's Most Wanted*, a 1998 sampler of local musical groups released by the classical radio station KING-FM. The performance is most notable for the particular eloquence of the opening clarinet solo, unfortunately uncredited. A 1992 self-released golden anniversary album includes Seattle Youth Symphony Orchestras performances under three previous maestros: founder Francis Aranyi, Ruben Gurevich, and Vilem Sokol. (Unfortunately, this limited release is not commercially available.) The repertory is challenging here too, with overtures by Carl Maria von Weber and Paul Creston, and excerpts from Ravel's *Mother Goose* and Prokofiev's *Alexander Nevsky*. **GB**

Young Composers Collective

J oshua Kohl and Haruko Nishimura, two students at Seattle's Cornish College of the Arts, founded the Young Composers Collective in 1993. The two composers decided to perform their work in Seattle's clubs, striving to break out of the contemporary-music ghetto, escape the mandated formality of the concert hall, and engage audiences beyond their teachers and colleagues. They also wanted to explore improvisation and theater, and most of all to poke holes in the dike protecting the pristine fields of classical music from the rushing waters of jazz, rock, and world music. Cornish offered plenty of like-minded musicians (its thoroughly bohemian atmosphere predates avant-garde composer John Cage's tenure there in the late 1930s as a dance accompanist), and the collective debuted in December 1993 at Seattle's OK Hotel. Not least because their gigs providing live original music at summer outdoor showings of classic silent films, members of the collective have gained a following almost as large and devoted as any non-world-famous Seattle band.

The collective's membership hovers around sixteen; it's a one-of-everything group that simultaneously recalls a traditional chamber orchestra, a collegiate contemporary-music ensemble, a Broadway pit orchestra, and a hotel-ballroom dance band. They sing too, if necessary, and when members collaborate on a theater piece, they're quite willing to do more than work as accompanists. Most important, members of the collective compose: their first disc, from Seattle's Un-Labeled Records, includes works by conductor Kohl and pianist Nishimura, guitarist Timothy Young, and double-bassist (and producer) Ian Rashkin. No stylistic party line here: Kohl's attractive and unassuming chamber music contrasts with Young's manic Zappaesque thrash-collages, while selections from Nishimura's exquisite and vivid theater-dance-music *Yokai* series (based on Japanese folklore) rub against an earthy, if slightly academic, color study by Rashkin, *Lions Cows Gold Dust*. Even within a piece, shocking style shifts appear; Nishimura's *Spinning Wheel Polka* starts out as a brief, boisterous concert closer, but its political subtext leads to the musicians' outburst of justifiable rage.

The Young Composers Collective's 1999 CD for Un-Labeled consists of the members' music (rearranged into a seventeen-movement suite) for Fritz Lang's silent film *Metropolis*. This score displays their widest range yet. A few apropos adjectives: elegiac, fragmented, funky, grungy, hep, manic, mechanistic, raucous, spare. Influences include Zappa (again), Howard Hanson, Alfred Schnittke, and 1970s cop-show themes ("*Metropolis* is a Quinn Martin production"). **GB**

Great Records Not to Miss

Rock/Pop

Alcohol Funnycar *Weasels* (1995, C/Z)

Equal parts power trio and singer/songwriter band, Alcohol Funnycar is built around the vocals and guitar playing of Ben London. Although their debut EP, Burn, was also excellent, *Weasels* is a consistent, forceful sampler of London's tunes, featuring Tommy "Bonehead" Simpson (formerly of Crisis Party and Love Battery) on bass and Joel Trueblood on drum kit. Standouts are "Objects" and the title track, a true tale of a band on tour. (The unforgettable opening line: "Seven weeks in a van / What a long, long time.") JB

AMQA *Mutant Cats from Hell* (1988, Ever Rat/Medusa)

Ah, hardcore. AMQA (it stands for Apple Maggot Quarantine Area, of all things) confirms the timeless wonder of this musical genre with crunching numbers like "Faceplant," "Cop on a Meathook," and, yes, "Crunch." Although the title track is about ferocious felines, this record will always be remembered for its silly novelty number "Cats Are Neat." Meow, meow, meow. JB

Atomic 61 *Purity of Essence* (1995, Cavity Search)

Todd Morey has never lost his fascination with pushing the volume well into the distortion range, which is why *Purity of Essence* will have you checking for blown speakers. Atomic 61's heavy tunes are built around repeating guitar and bass figures with Morey yowling over the din. Each song starts with a sampled bit of dialogue—usually "borrowed" from a movie or television show—and most tunes continue well beyond the time stated on the label. This album was compiled mainly from tracks released as singles, and it features contributions by two guitarists: Jeff Blanston and original Atomic 61 member Trevor Lutzenheiser. JB

Bell *Perfect Math* (1998, Yeah, It's Rock)

A solid six-song sophomore effort from singer/guitarist Vanessa Veselka and Company. Heavy guitar riffs and thundering rhythm-section work frame Veselka's moody wordplay on tracks like "Nice x 3" and "Overwhelming." There are lots of little details here that you catch only on the fifth listen, so be sure to play this one again and again. JB

Beluga *Nuke the Gay Whales* (1996, CM)

Rock 'n' roll comedy is a thankless task and, in most cases, deservedly so. Fortunately, bands like Beluga don't just deliver a poke in the ribs but add a boot in the butt for good measure. Enjoy these brutal but funny stabs at hippies, substance abuse, and Courtney Love. Easy targets, perhaps, but these boys vaporize 'em with nuclear sarcasm. Inspirational tune: "Let's Get High and Read the Bible." JB

Bitter End *Harsh Realities* (1990, METAL BLADE)

A bracing metal onslaught from this speedy and smart Seattle four-piece group. Guitarists Matthew Fox and Russ Stefanovich keep the riffs coming through fast-paced tunes like "Meet Your Maker" and "Waiting for Death." More interesting is "Just Say Yes," the band's slap in the public face of the idiotic war on drugs ("Just say no to Reagan's wife / Just say yes to real life"). JB

The Blackouts *Lost Souls Club* (1985, WAX TRAX)

By far the most talented of Seattle's early-1980s experimental bands, the Blackouts played primal avant-noise that came from the gut, not the brain, and made most of the pretentious New York "no wave" bands sound anal retentive by comparison. Erich Werner's divine caterwauling was never more chilling than it is here, especially on "Writhing." Jagged guitars and slithering sax assault your senses while the drums and bass soothe and beckon you to dance. The Blackouts broke up shortly after releasing this Al Jourgensen–produced three-song EP. Drummer Bill Rieflin went on to join Ministry. DA

Cat Butt *Journey to the Center of Cat Butt* (1989, SUB POP)

If the title alone doesn't make you run out and buy this garage-punk gem, consider powerful songs like "Maximo" and "Three Eyes," the sympathetic Jack Endino production job, or the wild Charles Peterson cover photo. This version of the band featured Danny Bland (also of the Best Kissers in the World) and the ever-prolific Brother James Burdyshaw (64 Spiders, Sinister Six) on guitars (green and black, respectively). A total energy fix. JB

Chemistry Set *Chemistry Set* (1988, ROOD)

There are plenty of unheralded pop bands in Seattle, but Chemistry Set belongs at the top of the list. Born in the midst of the grunge era, this band crafted some of the most haunting, introspective tunes missed by the masses. The Chemistry Set trademark sound mixed thick guitars and lots of drum fills with spacey, enigmatic lines like "I've got the key in the lock / But the chowder it just won't pop" or "When you were young you stared at the sun until your eyes began to burn." Frontman Scott Sutherland's songwriting skills were not lost, however. He went on to play in the Model Rockets and continues to perform in various projects around Seattle. VK

Control Freak *Low Animal Cunning* (1993, CAVITY SEARCH)

Late-period grunge growler Terry Montgomery may someday prove an acquired taste, but guitarist Carlene Heitman, bassist Kelly Wimer, and drummer Mike Mongrain show their mettle here as a powerhouse trio. Heitman's guitar lines steal the show on "What You Need" and "Emma's Thread." JB

Crackerbash *Crackerbash* (1992, EMPTY)

The best early-1990s Portland band that didn't get signed to Sub Pop, Crackerbash played energetic, up-tempo rock spiced with dense, sometimes cryptic lyrics. The band was led by guitarist Sean Crogan, formerly of the Hellcows, and also included bassist Scott Fox and drummer Teddy Miller. On their self-titled debut album the band chose to layer multiple guitar tracks rather than seek a classic trio sound, but the results here are smashing. There are lots of memorable songs, from the ripping opener, "Human Alarm Clock," to more nuanced numbers like "Bite" and "4 LTRS." A great record from an underrated band.   JB

Crisis Party *Rude Awakening* (1989, No Wonder/Metal Blade)

Seattle's uncrowned trashrock kings lasted just one album—fortunately, it kicks ass. Most of the key members had punk backgrounds (singer Kenny D was in Circus of the Stars, guitarist Whiskey Ward an original Refuzor, fellow six-stringer Tommy Hansen a veteran of the Fartz), but the songs here are pure Johnny Thunders/Iggy Pop bump-and-grind. Hansen was an endless font of cool riffs, and Kenny's vocals are, well, unforgettable. They even went out in style, getting ditched for trashing their Los Angeles label's Christmas party. JB

Critters Buggin *Bumpa* (1998, Loosegroove)

A mix of Skerik's avant-garde sax blurts, screeches, and yowls atop a web of drummer Matt Chamberlain's rhythmic pops and Mike Dillon's cosmic, clanky percussions, *Bumpa* veers from rolling jazz beats to hyperpolitical rants on the dangers of sodium fluoride. A true experiment in the art of noise, jazz, and rhythm, this CD proves that the best music is often made when rock stars (Chamberlain and bassist Brad Houser played in the New Bohemians) swim against the current. VK

Daddy Hate Box *Sugar Plow* (1990, New Rage)

They never lost the image (probably accurate) of being just a side project, but Daddy Hate Box provided a rare funky edge to the heavy undertakings of the era. This five-song EP spotlights the vocals of Peter Litwin (sounding quite different than on his work with Coffin Break) and the guitar work of David Goff. The rhythm section of Al Tompkins (Sledge) and Steve Wied (Tad) also acquits itself admirably. JB

Diamond Fist Werny *Enchanted Parkway* (1998, Ruby)

Other folks talk about musical eclecticism—Todd Werny takes action. On this six-song EP, Werny draws from Eastern musical traditions and mixes in odd beats and references ("Fountain Head" seems to be built around a Native American chant) to create music both hypnotic and gorgeous. Also along for the ride is a surprisingly straight cover of the B-52's song "Planet Claire." JB

Diamond Star Halo *Diamond Star Halo* (1996, Regal)

Kinder, gentler trashrock courtesy of sensitive-guy vocalist Bo Bligh, who emotes through numbers with titles like "Peace of Mind." There are simpler pleasures to be had as well: guitarist Aaron Seravo shows off his wah-wah chops on "Old Faces," "Chrome Dolls" is funky in a Stonesy sort of way, and "Mr. JC" and "Firefly" are bona fide trashrock movers, if a bit midtempo. JB

Easy Big Fella *Fruitcup* (1994, SELF-RELEASED)

Like all revivals, the recent ska craze merely reflected the mainstream culture's sudden recognition of a musical style that had long before ventured underground. Seattle's Easy Big Fella played ska during the prepopularity days of the early 1990s and did a darn good job of it, as demonstrated on *Fruitcup*. The real ear-catchers here are the horn arrangements, spotlighted on original songs like "Hit Me in My Head." This isn't just good-time music: Easy Big Fella layers the irony and satire over tunes like "Mom and Dad" and "Surfin' the Trees" (that rarest of birds, a Northwest ska surfing song). And watch out for the "Hell's Kitchen Polka," a goofy cover tune driven by Liam Barksdale's accordion. JB

Fire Ants *Stripped* (1992, DEKEMA)

Brian and Kevin Wood (brothers of the late Andrew Wood of Mother Love Bone) have released two albums on Loosegroove as Devilhead, but this earlier EP contains some of their best work. On *Stripped*, the Fire Ants present five funky rock tunes with compellingly odd lyrics, although the hidden track ("Drove Me Crazy") is the coolest of the bunch. The band also features ex-Nirvana drummer Chad Channing. JB

Fitz of Depression *Swing* (1995, K)

Despite the band's misleading name, this music is huge, chunky, exuberantly goofy punk rock, not depressing in the least. This LP contains more varied tempos and stronger songwriting than your average hardcore punk fare, and some of it does, in fact, swing. Fitz of Depression recorded two LPs for K Records and were about to sign with Mercury (no joke!), but broke up instead. Good call. DA

Five Fingers of Funk *About Time* (1998, SELF-RELEASED)

Who's the star here? Is it frontmen Pete Miser and DJ Chill? The killer horn section? The rock-solid rhythm section of bassist Allan Redd and drummer Talbot Guthrie? All of the above contribute to the total effect on *About Time*, this Portland group's second full-length release. The result is a funky yet laid-back collection of tunes, the perfect soundtrack for a summer barbecue with beers in hand and friends close by. The lyrical mix leans a little heavily to touting their status as rap aces (and every other rapper's status as second best), although "Under Hidden Skies" is a fine slice-of-life tale of one woman's dead-end existence. The final result is a creation whose value far exceeds the sum of its musical parts. JB

The Flies *Alternatoid* (1995, TOO MANY)

The average punk rock record has, out of twenty or so tracks, a total of three brilliant songs. The winners on this release by Spokane punks the Flies are "Austrian," "Queen's Parade," and "Dum Dum Fever." Thank you for your attention. JB

gherkin *ten esperanto love songs* (1994, SCHWA)

Take Skin Yard, cut their hair, dress them better, and make them play pop songs, and you have gherkin. *Ten esperanto love songs* is a thirteen-song collection influenced to a great degree by King Crimson and ranging from the raging "Left Eye

Wandering" to the tense, quirky post–new wave "Valentine" to the thrashy "Sven-gali (love theme from 'gherkin')." It's not just rock with good taste, it's rock that tastes good. To the band's own chagrin, gherkin wasn't nearly as successful as their alter ego, the Dudley Manlove Quartet, who still pack Northwest clubs with renditions of 1960s and 1970s light-pop covers. Go figure. MC

The Gits *Frenching the Bully* (1992, C/Z)

Her tragic unsolved murder made Mia Zapata a Seattle music scene icon and resulted in the formation of the women's self-defense collective Home Alive. *Frenching the Bully*, the single Gits long-player released before the charismatic vocalist's death, is a strong debut containing hints of what might have followed. This is a punk rock record through and through, pushed along by rapid tempos and guitarist Joe Spleen's riff mastery. But Zapata's gritty, uncompromising lyrics put a gloomy luster on the sometimes bouncy music to make this a haunting album. JB

Gnome *Six-Hi Surprise Tower* (1992, C/Z)

Gnome's Loren Evans never got credit for kicking off the Robin Zander revival, but Cheap Trick tendencies notwithstanding, this was a band with a cool, original sound. Despite the hints on their fine debut single ("Up To"/"13 Family"), *Six-Hi Surprise Tower* was still a pop revelation—ten tracks of intense, straight-ahead rock sweetened by Evans's uncanny pop vocalizing. Hits abound: "Watershed," "Freetoy," "On the House," "13 Family." Despite a good follow-up (*Fiberglass*, 1993), Gnome never became a Seattle institution. A pity, that. JB

Goodness *Goodness* (1996, Lava)

A sterling independent release on Seattle's Y Records, *Goodness* was picked up by an Atlantic Records subsidiary, which seemed to lose interest in the band upon signing. Nonetheless, this album is a wonderful showcase for ex-Hammerbox vocalist Carrie Akre and a fine ensemble effort by the band, especially guitarist Danny Newcomb (also Akre's songwriting partner). *Goodness* creates much of its tension with contrasts between sedate verses and intense choruses; in its first minute, "Wicked Eye" goes from zero to sixty and back again. Highlights include Akre's breathy vocal duet with bassist Fiia McGann on "For Lover's Sake" and the singer's unwavering delivery on "Vive le High" as the music rises and falls. JB

Gorilla *Deal With It* (1993, Thrill Jockey)

While most of the Northwest garage revivalists stuck with distorted guitars, the awesome organ artistry of Drew McRoberts let Gorilla send early 1990s rockers through a time warp to a teen dance hall circa 1964. Rather than relegate McRoberts's swirling organ lines to the occasional sweetener, *Deal With It* brings him up front on stompers like "Strange Daze," "Sister and Starman," and "Take a Nap." Bassist Dan Merrick and McRoberts share vocal duties; guitarist Curtis Clark and drummer Brian Nelson hold up their musical end of the band. JB

Gruntruck *Push* (1992, ROADRUNNER)

As many scenesters feared, once Seattle's punk/grunge forerunners learned to really sing and play their instruments, the result was real rock, stuff that sounded great sandwiched between old Deep Purple and Robin Trower hits on FM radio. But aficionados of slow-and-heavy found plenty to love in the music of Soundgarden, Alice in Chains, and their lesser-known contemporaries like Gruntruck. Former Skin Yard vocalist Ben McMillan had, by this time, learned to scream his guts out, and his sinister crooning was never heard again. Speed metal guitarist Tom Neymeyer slowed it down and proved his gift for the big bad chunky riff. There's some solid stuff here, particularly the near-hits "Crazy Love" and "Tribe," the latter being the most convincing tune-in, turn-on, drop-out anthem since Cream first sang about "letting my freak flag fly" (a line Gruntruck borrows). DA

Hammerbox *Numb* (1993, A&M)

Hammerbox's fine self-titled debut on C/Z got them this major label shot, and they didn't waste it. With pro producer Michael Bienhorn sitting in, *Numb* was a triumph. Singer Carrie Akre is center stage, while drummer Dave Bosch offers impressive vocal support, especially on "Hed." The band, with guitarist Harris Thurmond and bassist James Atkins, is tight throughout. Hammerbox didn't last much longer (Akre now sings with Goodness), but this was the high point of their short career. JB

The Hanks *The Hanks* (1990, SELF-RELEASED)

Despite lingering mental pictures of bearded computer programmers playing hackysack on a grassy campus, Microsoft has had little real cultural impact on Seattle. The Hanks, formed via the megacorp's bulletin boards, set out to change that when they recorded this five-song EP with Conrad Uno at the board. It's jangly, atmospheric pop that somehow melds British influence with a hint of country, and Stephen Brown's deep, emotional vocals add an element of pathos. The disc-ending "Dark Panic" may lead one to believe that working for the Empire might even cause gloom. MC

Harvey Danger *Where Have All the Merrymakers Gone?* (1997, ARENA)

The memorable hit single (the catchy "Flagpole Sitta") earned the band national attention, but Harvey Danger's debut was a memorable package throughout. This charmingly off-center indie pop foursome showed smarts ("Jack the Lion"), instrumental prowess ("Old Hat"), and that irresistible new-wave geek sincerity ("Private Helicopter"). John Goodmanson's production is spot-on—smooth enough for radio play, but with enough rough edges to stave off slickness. JB

Hester Pryne *Hateing* (1993, LES)

Just a ferry ride away from the downtown Seattle clubs, Kitsap County, Washington— a land of malls, tract housing, and Navy installations—spawned its own round of grunge-era bands. The best was Hester Pryne, a heavy but curiously pop-influenced trio led by guitarist/vocalist Burt Day and bassist Stace Richmond. *Hateing* collects two album-length collections of Hester Pryne hits, plus four songs from an amazing 1989 session with All's Bill Stevenson and Stephen Egerton. A priceless artifact. JB

The Hit Men *Smashface* <small>(1990, GREEN MONKEY)</small>

Herky-jerky, quirky, and self-conscious, the Hit Men's lone long-player is nothing if not fun. The wackily pseudo-British vocals of Mark Palmer and the instrumental talents of Joe Leonard keep this disc from sinking into anonymity, even on the more mundane tracks. Gimmicks like the chorus on "Ice Age," sung by the Posies' Jon Auer and Ken Stringfellow, the Life's Jimm McIver, and "the Guy from Handful of Dust," would annoy if it weren't for the fact that the band delivers the musical goods as well. MC

Hovercraft *experiment below* <small>(1998, MUTE)</small>

Hovercraft's fourth release marked a departure from the band's previous pleasant ambient noodlings. The key seemed to lie in the replacement of drummer karl 3-30 with dash11, who provided the band with an industrial kick that hearkened back to the early-1980s canister pounding of groups like Einstürzende Neubauten. Closer in form to Hovercraft's live shows than their previous recordings, *experiment below* proved to be the first recording with which bassist Sadie 7 and guitarist Campbell2000 were truly satisfied. VK

Huge Spacebird *Huge Spacebird* <small>(1998, BANDS WE LIKE)</small>

A 1960s-influenced band in the nicest sense of the term, Huge Spacebird showed off their abilities to great effect in this debut album. Guitarist Mark Hoyt and bassist Jeff Taylor sing most of the lead vocals, the harmonies are many and varied, and the guitar work is stellar throughout. This record doesn't sound like a relic, thanks in part to Martin Feveyear's smooth production job, but it's full of the sort of nods and winks to tradition that you'd expect from guys who know and appreciate the rock greats from yesteryear: "If That's Lovin'" would have been right at home on *Nuggets* (the late-1960s rock compilation); "Electric Boogaloo" could have been a great Ten Years After tune. It's nice to hear a band that isn't stuck in the present. JB

Kill Sybil *Kill Sybil* <small>(1993, EMPTY)</small>

Best known for their ex-drummer, Hole's Patty Schemel (who appears on a couple of tracks here), Kill Sybil released this lone CD, a textbook of post-Nirvana Seattle rock. Originally known simply as Sybil, the band was considered Seattle's next medium-sized thing circa 1991. Guitarists Dale Balensiefen and Larry Schemel provide swirly chording and noodling leads, with melodies half concealed under layers of effects and distortion. Singer Tammy Watson's vocals are stylishly buried in the mix, but she manages to push her way to the front occasionally (as on "Die Tomorrow" and "Broken Back," the latter a duet with Treepeople's Scott Schmaljohn). No speed demons here; most songs barely make it to midtempo. JB

Life in General *Life in General* <small>(1982, PANECE)</small>

Kelly Mitchell was the first Seattle punk (and almost the only one) to gracefully make the transition from punk rock (X-15) to new waver. Although far more sedate than the band's exuberant live performances, *Life in General* is a Seattle rock landmark from its wonderfully minimalist cover to intense outings like "Respite Lost" and "One Way." JB

Lois *Bet the Sky* (1995, K)

Stepping back from her electrified turn on *Strumpet* (1993), Lois Maffeo performs most of these songs accompanied only by her guitar and drummer Heather Dunn. You'll find some pretty moments here, especially the lovely acoustic opener "Charles Atlas," the energetic "Shy Town," and the hooky "Transatlantic Telephone Call." The sparse instrumentation has its limits, and the first half of this album is far better than the second, but *Bet the Sky* is a good showcase for this singer/songwriter's talents. JB

Marfa Lights *Tensor* (1998, SELF-RELEASED)

Seattle boy Steve Mack was indeed racking up the rock star props during the last half of the 1980s, but he was doing it miles away from home as the singer for the respected British band That Petrol Emotion. After that band's demise and a few years running a London recording studio, he returned to Seattle to form Anodyne with former Hammerbox guitarist Harris Thurmond. The rock world already having several Anodynes, the band (also including Marcus Pina on bass and drummer Dov Friedman) decided to become Marfa Lights on the eve of the release of their first long-player, *Tensor*. Opening with "Slider" (made for alternative rock radio), *Tensor* shows a band at its best when it tries to be tuneful. The upbeat "Infatuated" and the Beatles-influenced "Silver Spoon" find Mack in fine vocal form; the dense guitar riffs that were Thurmond's trademark in Hammerbox are very much present on the intense "Checkin' Out." JB

The Melody Unit *Wax Cylinder* (1997, SELF-RELEASED)

The EP *Wax Cylinder* features the very complicated musings of a very young band, and that's a good thing. Built around the innocent pop tunes of guitarist/vocalist Kevin Kelly, the Melody Unit adds substance to their songs with three sets of vocals that include the clear soprano of guitarist Amanda Young and the gravelly growl of keyboardist Alex Duff, who adds thick waves of effect rather than traditional melody and rhythm with his Roland piano. Once described as the "best British band in Seattle," the Melody Unit bows deeply to introspective British bands like Lush and My Bloody Valentine. VK

Micro Mini *Get in the Go-Go Cage* (1998, COLLECTIVE FRUIT)

It's a shame you can't see the group members while the record's playing—Micro Mini yields to no band in collective cuteness. Even so, Lance Paine, Nabil Ayers, Amy Barnet, and Jennie Severn ably churn out teen-angst pop on this, their first full-length release. Barnet's keyboards function as an occasional sweetener, but her backing vocals are well integrated into the total sound (especially on "Chemical Girl" and "Putty"). Ayers is the band's most skilled musician by far, and his drumming makes these songs go. Extra credit to the band for resurrecting (and improving) their best song—"Heir Apparent," the A-side of their first single. JB

The Model Rockets *Snatch It Back and Hold It* (1996, C/Z)

There are a lot of power pop bands in Seattle, but most of them just aren't very good. The Model Rockets are a welcome exception. Anyone who loves Cheap Trick will appreciate this CD—it rides the same edge between arena rock and sugar pop. John Ramberg's voice isn't as heart-stopping as Robin Zander's, but it's got the same soaring, melodic quality, wrapping like taffy around each note. Scott Sutherland might not be a great singer, but he'll do, and he contributed one of the most rocking tunes here, "Flame On." Other rave-ups include "Cul de Sac," the obscenely catchy "She's on the Cover," and "Stick It Out," which sounds like garden-variety bouncy pop until the bridge provides an unexpected sugar jolt.   DA

Mondo Vita   *Fins de Paris* (1983, DEAF CAT)

If Seattle wasn't pining away for a new wave comedy showband, then there's no convincing explanation for Mondo Vita, they of the purple hair and bottomless hamper of stage props. This record is Mondo Vita at their silliest, featuring fine vocal performances by Mark Sargent ("Welcome to America"), Jim Santoro ("Idiot Behind the Wheel"), and Eric Wilson ("Technical Difficulties"), plus imitations of Adolf Hitler and Desi Arnaz, a protest against "Horrible Condos," and two songs about teenagers having sex. Ah, those crazy Eighties . . . . JB

Moral Crux   *The Side Effects of Thinking* (1989, POLEMIC)

Earnest Eastern Washington lefties shout about oppression and injustice, but their blaring, tuneful punk rock is about the happiest noise you can imagine. Every song is a fist-shaking anthem, except for the one meandering reggae tune, which could have been taken right from the Clash's *Sandinista!* At the time this record came out, Moral Crux's brand of melodic hardcore was considered outdated beyond redemption, but these days kids would probably lap it up.   DA

Moving Parts   *Moving Parts* (1983, MPI)

Classy, accomplished, and vaguely English-sounding, Moving Parts were the cream of new wave Seattle. This five-song EP catches them in their prime, from the Police-style harmonies of "Blindman Walking" to James Irwin's impassioned vocal performance on "Cities Return to Me." The producer is another Seattle name from the era, original Allies vocalist Steve Adamek.   JB

Mr. Epp   *Ridiculing the Apocalypse* (1996, SUPER ELECTRO)

Mr. Epp and the Calculations were a goofy teenage noise band from Seattle's East-side suburbs that proved to be a breeding ground for alternative rock stars. Mudhoney's Mark Arm, Steel Pole Bath Tub's Darren Mor-X, and Atomic 61's Todd Morey were original members (the fourth Eppster was singer Jo Smitty, who still publishes his legendary Seattle fanzine *Feminist Baseball*). It's all here: the complete EP *Of Course I'm Happy, Why?*, live tracks, studio sessions, and even a few bedroom demos with late arrival Steve Turner (also of Mudhoney). Buy two copies and give one to someone you love.   JB

My Name   *Rocks for the Jocks in '96* (1996, INSTANT)

A critic could easily be faulted for choosing such a late milestone in My Name's career (and for neglecting a couple of great records featuring original guitarist

Trevor Lanigan). However, the addition of a new guitarist, Fred Speakman, revitalized this band as a rock whirlwind. Singer Abe Brennan has never sounded more forceful, and the songs are great. Highlights include "It's a Miserable Life," Green River knockoff (tribute?) "I'm Gone," and ambling guitar tour de force "Keep Me Clean." These guys definitely came here to rock. JB

My Sister's Machine *Diva* (1992, CAROLINE)

My Sister's Machine was among the second-generation Northwest bands to sign with major labels in the early 1990s. Their debut album combined Alice in Chains–like heavy rock (no surprise, given that lead singer Nick Pollock was a founding member) with the bluesier sensibilities of groups such as Guns N' Roses. Far from being pale imitations, though, My Sister's Machine had a more up-tempo attack than their Northwest peers, and songs like "I Hate You" and "Love at High Speed" demonstrated their ability to blend monster hooks, heavy riffs, and agile solos into a sound all their own. MF

The New Flamingos *In the Pink* (1983, SELF-RELEASED)

Reggae influences were all the rage among young rockers in 1983, and the New Flamingos were Seattle's most able practitioners of the genre. On this four-song EP, however, only "Moment of Glory" really hints at the Flamingos' live sound; the other three tracks are basically pop songs ably voiced by brothers Jim and David Keller. The best of the three is "Bo Diddley Didn't Know," a nifty novelty number that notched lots of local radio play. JB

Nu Shooz *Poolside* (1986, ATLANTIC)

This short-lived but extremely popular Portland dance group hit the big time in 1986, when "I Can't Wait" exploded as both a dance floor hit and a top-selling pop record, reaching no. 3 on the *Billboard* charts. The band, built around husband-and-wife duo John Smith (music) and Valerie Day (vocals), had a second Top 40 hit with "Point of No Return" and formed a successful touring band. While their charming dance pop sound never went out of style, the band dropped off the radar screen after the 1988 release of *Told U So*. JB

Peach *Dead Soldier's Coat* (1994, CAROLINE)

Former Posies bassist Rick Roberts picked up a guitar and joined fellow vocalist/guitarist Mark Adler, drummer Shawn Allen, and bassist Nick Lyman to form Peach. Their full-length release *Siesta* (1994, Caroline) is OK, but this four-track EP is more telling. Take their album's best track ("Dead Soldier's Coat"), throw in a spirited rendition of T. Rex's "Children of the Revolution," a non-LP original, and a James Gang cover, and you've got something worth keeping near the stereo. JB

The Pleasure Elite *Hog Tied* (1998, QUIVERING SUBMISSIVE FLESH)

Combining those two American favorites, industrial-tinged rock music and pornography, the Pleasure Elite have gone from obscurity to club-packing local fame and back again. One factor in their inability to cash in on the success of their bombastic theatrical live performances was their so-so debut album, *Bad Juju* (1994), filled with good songs better performed on the band's cassette-only demo, *Candy Ass Goes Stomping*. The Pleasure Elite's later release, *Hog Tied*, is a far more satisfying distillation of their live sound, featuring great rock songs like "Booze Pollution," neat studio manipulations like "Boy Crazy," and other tidbits of inspired weirdness from longtime collaborators Rev V Blast and Lord Hoop De'Luvleggs. JB

Pop Sickle   *Self-Titled* (1995, C/Z)

Pop Sickle's formula of rock songs with pop vocals surprised absolutely no one. Singer/bassist Rob Skinner's contributions to his former band Coffin Break amply demonstrated his pop leanings—Pop Sickle just gave him the freedom to indulge them. Although *Self-Titled* was released after the trio had largely called it quits, the album is a nice set of Skinner pop with significant additions by guitarist Brian Naubert and drummer Shawn Trudeau (Hester Pryne, the Meices). It also features a great double-time cover of Squeeze's "Pulling Mussles." JB

Pothead   *Rumely Oil Pull Tractor* (1995, Orange Haus Empire)

Singer/guitarist Brad (just Brad) was a key player in Son of Man, another grunge-era shouldabeen. With his trio, Pothead, he moved to Europe, where wandering Seattle musicians are rewarded with food, beer, and money. Joyously heavy guitar shuffles and soaring vocals enliven this disc, which includes several classics: "Dead Poet's Society" is gorgeous and inspiring; the thumping, thundering "Threshing Bee" is almost Zeppelinesque in tone (and length). JB

Prose and Concepts   *Everything is Nice* (1997, Status)

Originally known as Six in the Clip, this rap combo bypassed Seattle's dearth of hip-hop performance opportunities by opening club shows for rock bands. A fine album by a racially integrated group with incredible chops and lyrical cleverness, *Everything Is Nice* rambles on through seventeen tracks as Dub, Beatnik, Dope, Rawi, Shark E., and DJ Ace trade off. It's mainly a play-it-through experience, but here are a few highlights for dabblers: "Everything Is Nice," "Salve," and the pass-the-mic hit "Oddballer." Just remember to put on the headphones so you'll hear every word. JB

Psychotherapy   *Tell Me When It Hurts* (1995, self-released)

Just when heavy metal was about to be taken off life support, something like this happens. Psychotherapy would probably argue that they are more of a "rock" band, and guitarists Bob Swanson and Dave King have the chops to avoid being crammed into a genre. But check out the textbook wah-wah attack on "Not Me" or the Aerosmith-like guitar shuffle on "Thin Man." Throw in a fine vocalist in Joe Carolus, rhythm section Eddy Young (drums) and Chris Swanson (bass), and a meaty Gary Thompson production job, and you've got a classic. JB

Running with Scissors *Running with Scissors* (1993, PROCESSION)

One of the more dynamic live acts in the Northwest, Running with Scissors suffered from "Crazy 8's Disease," wherein the band's recordings didn't do their live performances justice. Unlike the Crazy 8's, however, Running with Scissors made dynamic and well-produced records that weren't even close to frat-boy ska. The band's debut featured atmospheric, postalternative mini-epics like "Naked" and "Your Life," the raving "Sold Out," and fan favorite "Piss." In a perfect world, they'd be Radiohead. MC

Sicko *Chef Boy RU Dum* (1996, EMPTY)

Further proof that Josh, Danny, and Ean are secretly the Fastbacks' little brothers—head Fastback Kurt Bloch produced this seventeen-song collection of snappy pop punk hits. It's a good match. Tracks like "I Hate Big Deal People" and "60 Pound Mall Rat" are charming bashers with personality aplenty. "You Are a Space Alien" ably captures the angst of interpersonal relationships. "The Breakfast Song" is just plain perfect. JB

Silkworm *Even a Blind Chicken Finds a Kernel of Corn Now and Then* (1998, MATADOR)

A long title for a long album. This double CD is a rerelease of Silkworm's first album (*L'ajre*, 1992) combined with the Steve Albini–produced EP *. . . his absence is a blessing* (1993) and an archive of vinyl-only releases (mainly scarce singles). Silkworm arrived as a band in Seattle in 1990 (having already played for three years in Missoula, Montana), shortly before the music world recognized Coffeetown as a legitimate destination. Well, Silkworm had little to do with Nirvana's hard-edged pop songcraft or Soundgarden's neometal bombast; they instead practiced a style of atmospheric, rambling guitar rock that would greatly influence postgrunge Seattle. The extra tracks presented here range from the band's first single ("Inside Outside"/"Slipstream," 1991) to a Tom Petty cover ("Insider," from a 1994 tribute album) to a trio of 4-track demos. A historical document, yes, but hardly a "for fans only" release. JB

Sister Psychic *Fuel* (1992, RESTLESS)

Vocalist/guitarist Andy Davenhall gives a songwriting clinic on the first, and best, of Sister Psychic's three long-players. The first line in each song draws the listener into the story ("My old man / Sits at home playing cards" introduces the protagonist of "Birdhouse"; "My sister's psychic" begins the story behind the song "Sister Psychic"). Even when Davenhall is just fooling around, as in "Mind over Matter," he sends signals from the start ("Mind over matter / It matters to me"). Bassist Christian Fulghum and drummer Ryan Vego provide solid support throughout. JB

Slam Suzanne *On the Floor with Your Mom* (1990, SELF-RELEASED)

Fronted by Phil "Intense" Bentz (formerly of the Dehumanizers), Slam Suzanne was one of the hardest-working bands around. They played just about every club in Washington, Oregon, and Idaho to promote this self-financed release. And what a fine release it is: from "Skateboard" and "No Food" to the classic "I Like to Say Fuck," Slam Suzzanne can claim one of the most unpretentious and enjoyable Northwest party albums since the Kingsmen. MF

The Squirrels *Harsh Toke of Reality* (1993, PopLlama)

In their decade-plus career, the Squirrels played about 90 percent covers—not the classic rock hits you all know and love, but brutally butchered versions of songs you tried to block from your mind forever. Frontman Rob Morgan really digs this stuff, and sometimes it's hard to tell where the tribute leaves off and the parody begins. He's supported by a rotating lineup of ace Seattle musicians, the only constant being Joey Kline (Prudence Dredge, Cropdusters), who writes most of the Squirrels' originals. There's no substitute for the live show, but this CD will give you some idea of their schtick. There's a bluegrass version of the Beatles' "Let It Be." Snippets of Gary Glitter and "The Baby Elephant Walk" end their rendition of "Draggin' the Line." More originals appear here than on their two earlier LPs, with mixed results. "Swallowing Tadpoles" is an inspiring Zappaesque moment. The likable grunge parody "Bone of Contention" takes aim at what Morgan calls "that grouchy music." "Bobo" is simply stupid, stupid, stupid. DA

Stagnant Water *What Happened?* (1992, Mope)

Self-proclaimed "prank rockers," Stagnant Water wrote humorous punk rock odes that often descended into downright silliness. This debut CD alone includes the tragic "Salad Bar Psycho," the saucy "I've Been Dating Your Daughter," and the inexplicable "Nut Baby." Extra points for the apt satire of "Sooyside," about the hip band who killed themselves at the end of their lone performance (and disappointed the audience, whose calls for an encore went unanswered). Prediction: Stagnant Water's singer Shane Boday will be elected mayor of Mount Vernon, Washington, by the year 2007. JB

Swallow *Swallow* (1989, Sub Pop/Tupelo)

These guys were known for writing songs with one-word titles and for being kind of short (hey, anything to stand out). But Swallow's major contribution to the world of music was this eight-song blast o' sound released at the height of Sub Pop mania. The standard pop song construction lurking under layers of fuzz-tone drone peeks out on hits like "Guts" and "Foetus." JB

Sweaty Nipples *Bug Harvest* (1994, Megaforce)

By the time Portland's Sweaty Nipples hooked up with Megaforce for this mid-1990s disc, they were grizzled scene veterans, having weathered numerous personnel changes and presented hundreds of famously crazed live shows. Built around the funky bass stylings of Davy Nipples and the band's dual lead vocalists, *Bug Harvest* finds Sweaty Nipples at their hard-edged best, sounding kind of like the Red Hot Chili Peppers' tougher little brothers. The heavy guitars on songs like "Pig Boy" and "Eye Tooth Magnet" are far more metallic than anything the metal boys were churning out at the time (or have since). After ten years the band split in 1997, but it'll be a long time before anybody forgets their legendary fire-breathing, confetti-tossing, groove-laden live shows. JB

Team Dresch *Personal Best* (1994, LESBONIC ACTION)

This record plays better over headphones than on 6-inch speakers (the buried vocals and dense guitar overlays make much more sense). The heavy, distorted electric guitar stylings of Donna Dresch and company help blend a set of very different songs into a cohesive album. Judy Coyote and Kaia Kangaroo trade off on vocals and harmonize to good effect. "Freewheel" is unusually happy sounding, but enjoyable just the same. JB

Teen Angels *Daddy* (1996, SUB POP)

Scream queen Kelly Canary is in fine form on this rare Sub Pop release of straight punk rock. Both Canary and drummer Lisa Smith are alums of the late-1980s all-female combo Dickless. Bassist Julie Ransweiler vocalizes a bit on "Go Away" and "Teen Dream," but Canary's full-throttle shrieks made this band memorable. JB

Truly *Fast Stories . . . From Kid Coma* (1995, CAPITOL)

This is postgrunge: long songs with instrumental flash, lyrics from a dark stretch of the emotional spectrum. The players are ex–Seattle scene guys Robert Roth (Storybook Krooks), Hiro Yamamoto (Soundgarden), and Mark Pickerel (Screaming Trees). The band is tight and energetic, but there are no hit singles here. Fast Stories is clearly an all or nothing mood piece—listening music for those overcast days. JB

Various Artists *Deep Six* (1985, C/Z)

The record that invented the Seattle scene, featuring two songs each from five of the city's soon-to-be-famous underground bands (the U-Men, under contract at the time, contributed just one song). The production is a bit primitive, but the performances are unforgettable. This was the first exposure most folks had to Chris Cornell of Soundgarden, Buzz Osborne of the Melvins, Andrew Wood of Malfunkshun (later of Mother Love Bone), and Ben McMillan of Skin Yard. The best tracks are probably Green River's "10,000 Things" and Malfunkshun's "With Yo' Heart (Not Your Hands)," but it's all classic and educational. Take notes. JB

Various Artists *East Infection* (1995, COMPULSION)

Recorded and released with the goal of exposing the new punk rock explosion in Seattle's Eastside suburbs, *East Infection* stands up well as a telling musical document. No Nirvanas have emerged from this group yet, but there's good music to be had, including Red Rocket's "Reliving the Past," State Route 522's "Worse for the Wear," and a quirky masterpiece from I Fergit? ("Torches"). Of course, in addition to the youthful exuberance, you get a few amateur touches (why do young bands love lengthy song introductions?), but it's all in fun. JB

Various Artists *Seattle Syndrome Volume One* (1981, Engram)

Before Seattle had a sound, it had a Syndrome—that is, the only people paying attention to a given local band were the members of the opening band and their five friends. *Seattle Syndrome* is a sampling of the astonishingly diverse noise resulting from the experimentation of young musicians who had no one to answer to. Back when anything not played on the radio was dubbed "new music," it was all revolutionary. Here we get power pop, pure 80-proof hardcore, reverent rockabilly, unapologetic spaz art, and the Fastbacks. A few tracks verge on the unlistenable, but the electronic musings of Savant and Body Falling Down Stairs are surprisingly catchy, and the Beakers' herky-jerky "Four Steps Toward a Cultural Revolution" is a howling riot. Other highlights include Jim Basnight's Eric Carmenesque "We'll Always Be in Love" and X-15's haunting "Vaporized," a great lost classic. But the album is most brilliant in its abrupt segues between dissimilar songs, barely missing a beat between screeching hardcore and precise standup bass, between the Beakers' strident yapping and Basnight's sugary croon. Moments like these caused much hilarity in 1981, when we were all hard up for amusement. DA

Vexed *Cathexis* (1994, C/Z)

These arty smart guys hovered on the edges of the Seattle scene as the Jet City proceeded from obscurity to worldwide fame. Still, it took until 1994 for this, their first (and only) full-length release, to hit CD. Curiously, at this late point in their careers, the music world had just about caught up with Vexed's dark, instrumentally based trio sound. Alfred Butler's funky basslines and Buzz Crocker's drums provide a framework for Milton Garrison's ethereal guitar lines and understated vocals. "Soulseye" is the most intense standout track. JB

Visible Targets *Visible Targets* (1982, Park Avenue)

Sisters with different last names Rebecca Hamilton, Pamela Golden, and Laura Keane joined drummer Ron Simmons to create this stylish punk/new wave band. Three of the four tracks on this fine EP feature the sibling harmonies and herky-jerky rhythms that were the Visible Targets' trademark. The fourth song, "Twilite Zone," is a softer, moodier composition. The Targets recorded a second EP and toured Canada, but couldn't survive the inevitable schism between Seattle's punk and new wave scenes. JB

Jazz

BABKAS *BABKAS* (1993, Songlines)

When Aaron Alexander, Brad Schoeppach, and Briggan Krauss released their 1993 debut CD, they minted themselves BABKAS (using their initials to form the name). Their lean sound, consisting of guitar (Shoeppach, who recently changed his last name to Shepik), alto sax (Krauss), and drums (Alexander), shocked the ear with exceptional, spinning rhythmic control. Recorded in Seattle, the album made clear their penchant for creating Eastern European–tinged music that found inspiration and energy in avant-garde jazz, Captain Beefheart, and Brahms (whose *Hungarian Dance No. 20* they performed on the CD). Krauss, who made producer Wayne Horvitz's group Pigpen lethal with his piercing runs and scouring growls, gives BABKAS a strong post–Ornette Coleman feel, and Alexander buttresses that vibe with roiling rhythms that occasionally lavish tumultuous rumble on Schoeppach's sandpapery guitar. It's the guitar, oddly, that holds down lots of the Eastern European elements, setting up melodies and playing them with the right mix of up-tempo cheer and tough-minded scree. A fine debut, but the trio's follow-up CDs, *Ants to the Moon* (1994) and *Fratelli* (1996), are equally challenging—and fun. AB

Eyvind Kang   *7 NADEs* (1996, Tzadik)

Eyvind Kang accomplished two of his most outstanding achievements while a Seattle resident, although he spent most of his time touring with various ensembles. *7 NADEs* presents Kang in twelve different settings, from a clangorous sixteen-piece aggregate to a fascinating, hair-raising duo of himself on violin and noted sound artist and producer Scott Colburne doing tape manipulations. This is music that falls radically between the signposts, merging the cacophony of noise and a kind of post-classical instrumental blur, making it a workout to follow the violin. Undulating at times, shattering glass at others, this is a watershed recording for the young musician. Perhaps the best elements on *7 NADEs* are its sonic indivisibilty and organic feel. The electronics, manipulated tapes, and strange analog aura all feed the horns and strings and general tumult, perhaps better than on Kang's locally released *Sweetness of Sickness*. By the way, his other major achievement in Seattle was the dreamy violin he played on Bill Frisell's *Quartet* (1994, Nonesuch). AB

Obrador   *Celebrating Twenty Years '76–'96* (1996, Goiter Muff)

Put simply, Obrador are the longest-living global jazz funk ensemble in the Northwest. They hail from Olympia, Washington, that hotbed of musical creativity, and get considerable charge from overlapping Latin and pan-African percussive layers behind their intricate horn and keyboard charts. This live retrospective catches the group at their onstage best. It complements their LP release on Au Roar Records with strong vocals from Connie Bunyer and furthers a sound that all those years ago was well ahead of the world-music-as-pop-music curve. Obrador's tunes are catchy, and when saxophonist Jim Pribenow is blowing solos or supporting horn parts, the group summons its cool but complex forces and holds them in excited check against the bluesy sax sounds. AB

Michael White and Bill Frisell   *Motion Pictures* (1997, Intuition)

Violinist Michael White, a longtime Cornish College of the Arts mainstay, tore the jazz world asunder way back in 1965 when he played the Monterey Jazz Festival in alto saxophonist John Handy's quintet (and recorded the hugely successful Live at the Monterey Jazz Festival). White helped pioneer a place for violin in the "new jazz" with a stringent style that owed more to East Indian music than to European classical traditions. Yet White played some low-down funky tunes with Handy—

seriously tight, snappy stuff. Motion Pictures is obviously White's CD, Frisell being a serious, respectful accompanist. Recorded in 1995, Motion Pictures is very much a jam session, with Frisell and White taking lengthy looks at "You Are Too Beautiful," "Misterioso," and an aching "My One and Only Love." White plays deliriously perfect fiddle-type violin to sketch many of these melodies, while Frisell takes on broad strokes of texture and displays pinpointy harmonic exactness. The duets are exploratory yet familiar, spare yet rich, and always strike a poignant balance between two players who are distinct stylists and close, close listeners. Frisell and White have delivered a duo session that immerses listeners in intimacy and rich tunefulness, even when things are sparse and patient unto slowness. AB

American Roots/World

Black Cat Orchestra   *Black Cat Orchestra* (1990, Irene Records)

Some traditional and some newly composed music played by the ten-member Black Cat Orchestra, all Eastern European-ish neoklezmer explorations that evoke shtetl, coffeehouse, and the piano lounge at the Budapest Ramada Inn. Rich, seductive, witty, haunting. GB

Kevin Burke   *In Concert* (1999, Green Linnet)

One could pick any of a dozen classic Irish traditional music recordings, and chances are, fiddler Kevin Burke was either in the band or in rotation as a subbing member. He played with classic Irish songwriter Christy Moore before joining the Bothy Band and later cofounding Patrick Street. Bothy and Patrick Street shaped Irish music for the 1970s and 1980s, and Burke's intense fiddle was pivotal in the music. His family came from County Sligo, home to some of the fiercest lyrical music to ever mix moods and speeds, and his playing on *In Concert* speaks to his heritage. The energy is focused, and the playing intensely alert, catering to multiple tones at once and plying jarred riffs as if they were mere frames to beautiful sound paintings between the borders. Of course, the frames are at the music's heart, giving it a push that advances Burke's lyrical sound in chunks rather than arrays of notes. This is contemporary Celtic fiddle music at its most stripped down, and it shines. AB

Citizens' Utilities   *No More Medicine* (1997, Mute)

One of the more impressive documents of the acoustic/roots music revival of the late 1990s, *No More Medicine* reveals a band in love with sound textures, lush harmonies, and instruments of all kinds. The cup overflows on "Call It Your Own," an electrified folk number punctuated first by a straight, country-style guitar solo, then an electric guitar freakout à la Lou Reed. There are many lovely musical moments here, two of the prettiest being the delicate, harmony-laden "Northern Lights" and the sparse "Anderson." JB

Gerald Collier *Gerald Collier* (1997, REVOLUTION)

Onetime frontman of the Best Kissers in the World, Gerald Collier reemerged as a first-class singer/songwriter in the late 1990s. The rebirth suits him well. Gone is the smug cheekiness of youth, and in its place are raw guitar and lyrics that pull no punches. Collier's introspection wanders through graveyards, bedrooms, and bathroom stalls. Throughout the album he dares you to gaze at your own reflection. It's been a long haul, but the honesty of this record proves that Collier has finally come into his own. VK

Cathy Croce *Putting Words in My Mouth* (1996, SELF-RELEASED)

Cathy Croce's confident yet girlish vocals are familiar to Seattle audiences from her time as an early-1980s pop chanteuse with the Connections and her 1990s stint with the all-star vocal group Mel Cooleys, but *Putting Words in My Mouth* is her first full-length outing. The varied repertoire (all written by Croce) shows off her voice to great effect: "Don't Listen to the Colonel" demonstrates a playful side; "Going to Austin" is lovely and wistful; "Nobody's Leaving This Room" re-creates a smoky jazz club atmosphere. Producer Wayne Horvitz and a host of fine guest musicians seal the deal. JB

Elizabeth Falconer *Isshin* (1997, MUSIC AND ARTS)

This recording has a large weight-bearing capacity. Falconer is a stellar performer on the Japanese koto, and she has selected compositions that appeal to both the instrument's tradition and contemporary composition. To the casual listener, much of this music will sound largely in keeping with the flush of warmth typical of traditional koto playing. But Falconer loves the additive, always seeking works that unfurl compacted layers of complexity. The instrument, twangy and warm, can be a stickerbush in Falconer's hands. She's learned to handle times when the music goes way out of tradition's bounds by playing with an array of Northwest (and other) improvising musicians. And since the koto is quite difficult to play quickly, Falconer's task is to maintain her own pacing, as in all of these contemporary works. These performances are indicative of what traditionally rooted contemporary solo music can sound like at its best. AB

Ellen Fullman *Change of Direction* (1999, NEW ALBION RECORDS)

Ellen Fullman explores the possibilities of her aptly named long string instrument on this CD, playing the massive instrument with Elise Gould and Nigel Jacobs. Creating extended harmonic tones and wobbly textural elements, the long string instrument is played by multiple musicians who walk along its 90-foot length and rub or pluck strings for various effects. It sounds like a boundless harp, one that can reach miles high, and miles low. And the instrument can move in lateral directions, with beautiful singing tones and then abstract icicles, or chromatic heat storms that

Records: Roots/World

dazzle and resonate beyond measure. Fullman has been pioneering the instrument since 1981 and gave the first public performances of some pieces in Seattle's Magnuson Park. Her music is delightfully old-fashioned and labor intensive while being unmistakably on the leading edge of expanding tonal ranges (the long string instrument is tuned in just intonation) and compositional methods (all notation is graphical and created by Fullman on a computer). AB

Annie Gallup *Courage My Love* (1998, PRIME)

The talking blues are a recognized musical form, so why not the talking folk song? Annie Gallup's acoustic guitar backs her detailed narrative tales of everyday life: sometimes spoken, sometimes sung, always chockful of the sorts of details that separate heartfelt reminiscence from cliché and platitude. Gallup's repertoire ranges from dead-on tales of her past ("100 Miles from Music City") to the more surreal ("Flood"), with a fine group of backing musicians in support. JB

Martin Hayes and Dennis Cahill *The Lonesome Touch* (1997, GREEN LINNET)

Seattle-based Martin Hayes proved himself a world-class Irish fiddler long before settling in the Northwest. A native of County Clare, Ireland, Hayes won the All-Ireland award for fiddling multiple times while still barely old enough to buy a pint. He did so with what he and other Celtic music aficionados call "the lonesome touch." Comparable to the "high lonesome" core of the best American country music, the lonesome touch flashes in slow, lyrical burns, that pour off this series of duets with Chicago-born guitarist Dennis Cahill. Hayes and Cahill move as slowly as they can, gently unfurling the flag in jigs set a poetic, sublimely crawling pace, and making a whole new map for Irish music. The virtuosity is there, but it's trumped by a higher calling, wider dimensions that will leave even the most fervent jig-ridiculers wide-eyed in amazement. AB

Higher Ground *Better View* (1995, NAIL)

These Grateful Dead–influenced Portland roots rockers build songs around the standard guitar-bass-drums axis, but sweeten things with the contributions of multi-instrumentalist Alan Glickenhaus—who expertly plays guitar, violin, mandolin, dobro, and banjo. The pleasant singing voice of frontman/acoustic guitarist David Kronenberg is also prominently featured. Pick hits: "Timing," "Better View," and all three Glickenhaus-penned instrumentals. JB

David Lanz *Christmas Eve* (1994, NARADA)

Seattle native David Lanz is one of the best-known artists in the "new age" solo piano genre (his *Cristofori's Dream*, 1988, was the top album on *Billboard*'s adult alternative/new age chart for twenty-seven consecutive weeks). *Christmas Eve* features lyrical adaptations of Christmas carols interspersed with short improvisations on the theme of angels. Lanz manages to insert jazzy, minor-key moments into these most straightforward of hymns—his bouncy "Joy to the World," for one, quickly segues into harpsichordlike trills and clever variations. Not all these songs are well suited to his bright, romantic piano style ("Silent Night" is a far too simple melody to carry his meandering five-and-a-half-minute treatment), but *Christmas Eve*'s original take on classic material makes for a holiday rarity.   JB

Kaz Murphy   *One Happy Camper* (1996, LIQUID CITY)

Despite a trademark deadpan to the vocals and a Southwestern twang to the mostly acoustic backing tracks, singer/songwriter Kaz Murphy tucks in a lot of substance with his ample style. Playing the role of the archetypal loner/outsider, he always finds and exposes the human element in each melancholy tale. *One Happy Camper* demonstrates a mastery of song sequence and pacing (the lone cover, Phil Ochs's "Boy from Ohio," follows Murphy's own childhood memoir "Drive Down South"), so this is an album best listened to in its entirety. Even when the point of the narrative isn't clear ("Hit from Buddha"), Murphy's facility with words shines through.   JB

Omar Torrez Band   *Omar Torrez Band* (1997, SELF-RELEASED)

The first release by the Omar Torrez Band, a popular local funk/world music fusion combo, is a five-song EP showcasing the guitar and vocal talents of bandleader Torrez—he is just as adept on a nylon-stringed acoustic as on his electric ax. A finalist in the first annual Jimi Hendrix national guitar competition, Torrez doesn't hesitate to shift between electric and acoustic guitars in a single song (as on the final track, "Tribute"), to scat along with his guitar lines ("Woke Up This Morning"), or to drag along influences ranging from classic rock to Afro-Caribbean rumba.   JB

The Roger Rogers Band   *Good Times* (1996, SELF-RELEASED)

An aptly named release from one of the leading purveyors of the goodtime R&B party music found in the clubs of Seattle's Pioneer Square. Roger Rogers's bluesy guitar licks (notably on "Nobody's Fool") and aggressive vocalizing take center stage, while Dan Davison's tinkly piano and a foursome of guest horn players provide capable accompaniment. Not that it's all good times here; Rogers also wails his misery with the trio of "Tears and Pain," "Cold, Cold Baby," and "Devil Woman."   JB

The Suffering Gaels   *The One-Horned Cow* (1996, FOXGLOVE)

Best known as the house band at fiddler Conor Byrne's Seattle tavern, the Gaels take on any number of reels and jigs on this collection of traditional Irish music. But it's on the four tunes sung by guitarist Finn Mac Ginty that this record really comes to life, especially the American-made Gaelic lament "Jack Haggerty" and the traditional standard "Whiskey in the Jar."   JB

Swamp Mama Johnson   *Wetlands* (1995, BMSA)

This all-female five-piece touring dynamo from Bellingham, Washington, brings a funky dance floor approach to their R&B grooves. Swamp Mama Johnson features ace musicians all; most songs on *Wetlands* give center stage to either guitarist Laurie Miller (the instrumental "Funky Special" is her showcase, but check out the solo on "Gasoline") or tenor sax player Tracy Ferrara (whose lines power their funked-up cover of "Niki Hokey"). But there's some straight blues in the mix as well: on "Evil,

Mean, and Nasty," vocalist Lisa Mills does double duty with an intricate harmonica introduction. All five Mamas contribute songwriting skills on this, their second independent release. JB

3 Track Mind   *Living Room* (1996, JAM & BREAD)

An engaging acoustic act whose songs feature lush harmonies, easy rhymes, and able instrumentation, the group is really a coalition of three singer/songwriters (and percussionist Steve Smith), each of whom gets a turn in the spotlight. Among the highlights are Kristy Gamble's "From the Outside," the story of a family's struggles with alcoholism, Jenn Todd's "The Day (Song for John)," a plea for compassion toward AIDS victims, and Kevin Jones's inspired bit of hero worship, "Martin, Theresa and Me." JB

Too Slim and the Taildraggers   *Blues for EB* (1997, BURNSIDE)

Based in Spokane, Washington, blues guitar giant Tim "Too Slim" Langford isn't worried about being squeezed on record by the limitations of a standard trio. With a guest sax player here and a harmonica part there (not to mention lots of overdubbed guitars, courtesy of Langford), the Taildraggers put together their best album yet in *Blues for EB*. Mixing a few covers into the lineup of original tunes by Langford and bassist Tom Brimm, the group stretches out over a fifteen-song set. Not-quite-purists prefer the party music (cool cover "One More Shot" is a blues rock party classic), but the slower, more intense tracks, such as the slide guitar–powered "Waitin' for the Sun to Shine," also please. JB

Kate Wolf   *Daisy Petals on My Head* (1998, CAKE)

Singer/songwriter Kate Wolf splits her time between Cape Cod, Massachusetts, and Seattle. Wolf splits her musical influences as well, from the jazzy, goofy "Snap Out of This" to the harmony-washed folk of "Lives Within a Life," but she maintains her laid-back, even tone throughout. Among the noted local musicians along for the ride are guitarist Rod Cook, sax player Hans Teuber, and bassist Evan Brubaker, plus singers Cathy Croce, Jen Todd (3 Track Mind), Karyn Schwarz, and Julie Wolf (Kate's jazz-singing sister). The arrangements are clever throughout: "Try Try Fly" starts with Wolf and her acoustic guitar, picks up Teuber's sax along the way, then adds Julie Wolf's piano and a chorus of background voices; drummer Andy Roth is invited in for a couple of tracks, including the up-tempo "I Think I Told You So." JB

Classical

Auburn Symphony Orchestra   *L'Amoureux de l'Orgue* (1996, AMBASSADOR)

The core of this full-size professional orchestra, whose home is a suburb midway between Seattle and Tacoma, is the pit orchestra for the Pacific Northwest Ballet;

it's augmented by members of the Northwest Chamber Orchestra and miscellaneous freelancers. The group's conductor, English-born Stewart Kershaw, decided in 1996 they should be let out of the pit to explore a broader reperatory in a concert setting. This fine first disc features a decidedly offbeat selection of pieces. The best-known work is Francis Poulenc's *Concerto for Organ, Strings, and Timpani* (with organist David Di Fiore), which gets a beautifully crisp and dry performance. Two exquisitely gooey religious songs by César Franck and Charles François Gounod (with tenor Mark Calvert) and two grandiose speaker-testers from the height of the nineteenth-century French organ repertory—Louis Vierne's *Marche Triomphale* and Alexandre Guilmant's *Symphony No. 1 for Organ and Orchestra*—complete the program. GB

Christopher DeLaurenti *Three Camels for Orchestra* (1995, AMERICAN ARCHIVE RECORDINGS)

"Sonic saboteur" Christopher DeLaurenti offers here a jolting, if good-natured, dose of electronic noise-music. His sound sources are primarily the composer himself playing a bunch of traditional, found, and invented instruments, with results that are processed much less than their evocative oddness might indicate. The eight works sound at the same time both homemade and grandiose, especially the title work, a well-paced three-part collage of orchestral fragments (the risk of any collage piece, not quite circumvented here, is that the "name that quote" game distracts from whatever might be going on texturally or structurally). "Loud Weird Disturbing" says the CD cover, but actually DeLaurenti uses a wide and effective dynamic palette, with the subterranean burblings of *Dimming Hope, Rising Ambition* sounding almost serene. GB

Geisa Dutra *Geisa Dutra* (1994, YELLOW TAIL)

Pianist Geisa Dutra, born in Rio de Janeiro and residing in Seattle, offers Spanish and Brazilian music on this 1994 release. She generally keeps a rather dry tone for these works, giving them a snappy, sophisticated air, especially in two Carnaval-esque tangos by Ernesto Nazareth and a crackling, wayward *Toccata* by Camargo Guarnieri. The spacious, organlike sonorities Dutra calls up for the near-liturgical opening section of Albéniz's *Cordoba* provide an impressive contrast. GB

Garrett Fisher *The Passion of St. Thomas More* (16 VISIONS, 1999)

This hour-long liturgical drama by Seattle composer Garrett Fisher (text and music) is a meditation on the final hours of 16th-century theologian Thomas More—his decision, which led to his execution, not to endorse the divorce of Henry VIII from Catherine of Aragon. The CD is most notable for the serene and sublime voice of soprano Anna Burdak, one of three singers joined by an ensemble of guitar, English horn, and harmonium. Combining influences from Norwegian hymns to Middle Eastern arabesques to Gregorian chant, Fisher's somber music provides more ritual-istic atmosphere than theatrical impact. GB

Robert Kyr *Unseen Rain* (1995, NEW ALBION)

The celebrated early music group, Ensemble P.A.N. commissioned *Unseen Rain* from Robert Kyr, whose Ivy League background hardly indicates his musical outcome as a composer. *Unseen Rain* takes full advantage of Ensemble P.A.N.'s prodigious chops in pre-Renaissance music. The composition moves like a medieval vocal work, with elongated rhythms and gorgeous vocal stretches that evoke composers as diverse as Pérotin, Arvo Pärt, Steve Reich, Kyr's onetime teacher George Crumb, and numerous others. The director of Eugene, Oregon's Music Today Festival, the Vanguard Concert Series, and the Pacific Rim Gamelan at the University of Oregon, Kyr is making some of the most compelling twentieth-century music in an aging, if timeless style. His 1998 follow-up CD, *The Passion According to Four Evangelists* (New Albion Records) has all the drama of *Unseen Rain* and is a musical high mark that should be celebrated by fans of the pre-Renaissance era and choral music in general. AB

Maria Newman *The Birthday of the Infanta* (1997, RAPTORIA CAAM)
Maria Newman twists dance rhythms to sinister and capricious effect in her epic chamber tone poem *The Birthday of the Infanta,* based on Oscar Wilde's fairy tale. She wrote the piece for the Kairos String Quartet—composers- and quartet-in-residence at the Icicle Creek Music Festival in Leavenworth, Washington—and they play it vividly. Two other duets, *Le petit due* for violin and viola, and *Deceptio visus* for violin and cello, both tangy yet rather dark, fill out the disc. GB

Northwest Chamber Chorus *Credo* (1997, CHINOOK WIND)
The chorus chose a liturgical miscellany for this CD: mass movements by Bach, Arvo Pärt, Antonio Lotti, and Frank Martin, interspersed with plainchant and culminating in a performance with orchestra of a complete Mass in C by Mozart. Their sound is light and flexible enough to effectively embrace these stylistic extremes. GB

Northwest Sinfonietta *Mozart, Symphonies #40 and #41* (1998, SONIC WINDOW)
Based in Tacoma, Washington, the thirty-six-member Northwest Sinfonietta takes a full-orchestra approach to Mozart's last two symphonies, the exacting program on the group's first CD. Their sound is not crisp but warm and full-bodied, and conductor Christophe Chagnard draws vigorous performances from these musicians. GB

Philharmonia Northwest *Beethoven's Symphony #1* (1996, SELF-RELEASED)
This midsized Seattle ensemble handles chamber orchestra and bigger midromantic works equally well. Conductor Roupen Shakarian's way with classical repertory, informed by the early music movement, is heard to fine effect in this recording of Beethoven's First Symphony—little vibrato, prominent winds and brass, and a brisk, almost Ländler-ish tempo for the second movement. Also on this disc is a poised and atmospheric reading of Ravel's Tombeau de Couperin. GB

Seattle Choral Company *When the Morning Stars Sang Together* (1997, SELF-RELEASED)
The favored repertory of the Seattle Choral Company is broad and serene music of any period, as befits the sumptuous sound-bath sonorities they can produce. This debut CD includes luscious late-romantic works by Bruckner and Rachmaninoff, a near-ecstatic, Alleluia-filled "Apostrophe to the Heavenly Hosts" by Healey Willan, and a clustery "Euntes ibant et flebant" by Henryk Górecki. GB

Music
Festivals

February

Seaside Dixieland Jubilee
SEASIDE, OREGON / LATE FEBRUARY / (888) 306-2326
This Oregon beach city welcomes Dixieland performers from across the country to this weekend-long event.

Wintergrass
TACOMA, WASHINGTON / LATE FEBRUARY / (253) 926-4164 / WWW.HALCYON.COM/HEALEY/WINTERGRASS
A winter bluegrass festival that features worskhops and performances of traditional American music, Celtic, and jazz at several locations in downtown Tacoma.

March

Northwest Barbershop Ballad Contest
FOREST GROVE, OREGON / EARLY MARCH / (503) 357-3006
This two-day battle of the region's best barbershop groups always draws a crowd at Forest Grove, a town near Portland.

Old-Time Music Festival
TENINO, WASHINGTON / MID-MARCH/ (360) 273-5360
Folk, country, and other roots music presented at three major concerts.

April

Old Time Fiddlers Fest
SHELTON, WASHINGTON / EARLY APRIL / (800) 576-2021
A weekend festival featuring several fiddle concerts.

Northwest Guitar Festival
BELLINGHAM, WASHINGTON / MID-APRIL / (360) 650-7712
Classical guitarists from the Western U.S. and Canada are featured in workshops and concerts during this three-day event.

May

Sunbanks Spring Blues Festival
GRAND COULEE, WASHINGTON / MID-MAY / (509) 633-3786
Held on the shores of Banks Lake, this is one of the year's first outdoor events. Camping and RV sites are available nearby.

Northwest Folklife Festival
SEATTLE, WASHINGTON (SEATTLE CENTER) / MEMORIAL DAY WEEKEND
(206) 684-7300 / WWW.NWFOLKLIFE.ORG
Although it also features many ethnic music and dance performances, the three-day Northwest Folklife Festival is best known as the meeting ground for acoustic musicians from around the region. Some of the best performances are impromptu jams which spring up around the 74-acre Seattle Center Grounds. Admission is free.

June

Olympic Music Festival
QUILCENE, WASHINGTON / JUNE TO SEPTEMBER / (206) 527-8839

A.K.A. "Concerts in the Barn," the Olympic Music Festival has grown from a three-week chamber music concert series to a summer-long series of concerts with artists from around the world—all presented in a converted, turn-of-the-century dairy barn in the rustic Olympic Peninsula town of Quilcene.

Spokane Dixieland Jazz Festival
SPOKANE, WASHINGTON / EARLY JUNE / (509) 235-4401

A three-day weekend jazz festival with local, regional, and national acts.

Burns Old Time Fiddlers Jamboree
BURNS, OREGON / MID-JUNE / (541) 573-2863

One of several fiddlers' events held in Eastern Oregon. Also on the fiddle circuit are contests in Enterprise (Fourth of July weekend; 541/ 432-4634), La Grande (late August; 800/ 848-9969), and Irrigon (late April; 541/ 922-4399).

Country Blues Festival
PORT TOWNSEND, WASHINGTON / LATE JUNE / (360) 385-3102 / WWW.CENTRUM.ORG

A weekend of concerts and club performances by participants in the Country Blues Workshop.

Oregon Bach Festival
EUGENE, OREGON (UNIVERSITY OF OREGON) / LATE JUNE / (800) 457-1486 OR (541) 346-5666 / HTTP://BACHFEST.UOREGON.EDU

The music of Bach, Mozart, and other great composers are presented at concerts (most on Sundays), lectures, and recitals. The University of Oregon also presents the annual Vanguard Concert Series of twentieth-century music and the biennial Music Today Festival.

July

Icicle Creek Chamber Music Festival
LEAVENWORTH, WASHINGTON / JULY / (509) 548-5807

An intimate series of weekend chamber music concerts held on weekend nights and afternoons during the month of July. A couple of jazz concerts are usually included in the mix.

Seattle Chamber Music Festival
SEATTLE, WASHINGTON (LAKESIDE SCHOOL) / JULY / (206) 283-8808 / WWW.SCMF.ORG

A month-long series of all-star chamber music performances at the Lakeside School in north Seattle. Concert-goers can picnic before the shows on the school grounds. The festival has recently added a series of mid-January Benaroya Hall recitals.

Festival of American Fiddle Tunes

PORT TOWNSEND, WASHINGTON / FOURTH OF JULY WEEKEND / (360) 385-3102 / WWW.CENTRUM.ORG

Two days of performances close this week-long workshop featuring fiddle players from across the United States.

Spokane American Music Festival

SPOKANE, WASHINGTON / FOURTH OF JULY WEEKEND / (509) 921-5579

A series of twenty free concerts in Spokane's Riverfront Park, featuring performers from many musical genres.

Waterfront Blues Festival

PORTLAND, OREGON / FOURTH OF JULY WEEKEND / (503) 282-0555 / WWW.WATERFRONTBLUESFEST.COM

A Portland institution featuring the best bands from this Northwest blues capital, plus top national acts. Bring a few cans of food along; the festival is a benefit for the Oregon Food Bank.

Oregon Country Fair

VENETA, OREGON / EARLY JULY / 1-800-992-8499 / WWW.OREGONCOUNTRYFAIR.ORG

Held in a wooded setting 13 miles west of Eugene, the Oregon Country fair features acoustic entertainment, mainstage shows, and vaudeville performances.

Walla Walla Sweet Onion Blues Fest

WALLA WALLA, WASHINGTON / EARLY JULY / (877) 998-4748

Two days of "hot blues and sweet onions" at Fort Walla Walla Park.

Yakima Folklife Festival

YAKIMA, WASHINGTON / EARLY JULY / (509) 248-0747

Jazz, folk, bluegrass, and ethnic music are featured during the two days of this arts festival, held at Yakima's Franklin Park.

Kent Cornucopia Old-Time Music Festival

KENT, WASHINGTON / MID-JULY / (253) 939-8436

Held in conjunction with Kent Cornucopia Days, the city's major summer event, the festival features old-time fiddlers, bluegrass, and Cajun music.

Ritzville Blues Festival

RITZVILLE, WASHINGTON / MID-JULY / (509) 659-1936

A one-day event with indoor and outdoor venues.

Winthrop Rhythm & Blues Festival

WINTHROP, WASHINGTON / MID-JULY / (509) 997-2541

A weekend of concerts featuring national and regional R&B and blues acts.

Yachats Music Festival

YACHATS, OREGON / MID-JULY / (541) 547-3530

Two days of classical music performances at this tiny town on the Oregon Coast.

Yoyo A Go Go

OLYMPIA, WASHINGTON / MID-JULY / WWW.YOYOAGOGO.COM

A not-every-year festival of lo-fi rock, featuring performers from Olympia's K, Kill Rock Stars, and Yoyo record labels. Late and early shows are presented Tuesday through Sunday. Organizers have announced that there will not be a 2000 Yoyo A Go Go, but the festival is expected to return in 2001.

Jazz Port Townsend

PORT TOWNSEND, WASHINGTON / LATE JULY / (360) 385-3102 / WWW.CENTRUM.ORG

There's a major mainstage show in McGurdy Pavilion on each day of the festival, but the real attraction is "Jazz in the Clubs," in which every possible venue in tiny Port Townsend features live jazz. The festival is held in conjunction with the week-long Bud Shank Jazz Workshop.

San Juan Island Jazz Festival

FRIDAY HARBOR, WASHINGTON / LATE JULY / (360) 378-5509

All types of jazz are on the menu (plus zydeco, blues, and gospel) at this four-day event in the lovely waterfront town of Friday Harbor.

WOMAD USA

REDMOND, WASHINGTON / LATE JULY-EARLY AUGUST / (206) 281-7788 / WWW.WOMADUSA.ORG

The only American stop of this international touring festival, WOMAD (World of Music, Arts and Dance) brings together music and dance artists from around the globe and celebrates cultural diversity.

August

Marrowstone Music Festival

PORT TOWNSEND, WASHINGTON / AUGUST / (360) 385-3102 / WWW.CENTRUM.ORG

Young musicians from the Seattle Youth Symphony Orchestra come together with a faculty of noted international artists for three weeks of study and performance. Full orchestral performances are held each Sunday afternoon; guest artists/faculty perform on Thursday evenings and Saturday afternoons.

Beethoven in Bellingham (Bellingham Festival of Music)

BELLINGHAM, WASHINGTON / EARLY AUGUST / (800) 335-5550 / WWW.BELLINGHAMFESTIVAL.ORG

This music festival presents nightly performances of the music of Beethoven and other great composers, including some jazz concerts.

Methow Music Festival

MAZAMA, WASHINGTON / EARLY AUGUST / (800) 340-1458 / WWW.METHOW.COM/MMF/

Hear chamber music performed in the barns and meadows of the picturesque Methow Valley. The festival consists of six main events over two weekends, plus intimate recitals, lectures, and "open rehearsal" workshops.

Mt. Hood Jazz Festival

GRESHAM, OREGON (MT. HOOD COMMUNITY COLLEGE) / EARLY AUGUST
(503) 231-0161 / WWW.MTHOODJAZZ.COM

Regional and national acts are featured in this three-day concert series.

Whidbey Island Folk Festival

GREENBANK, WASHINGTON / EARLY AUGUST / (360) 678-1912

A weekend of acoustic music performances at Meerkerk Gardens, a natural amphitheater.

Crescent Lake Dixieland Jazz Festival

CRESCENT LAKE, OREGON / MID-AUGUST / (541) 433-2793

A weekend-long celebration of Dixieland jazz with several concerts.

Northeast Washington Fiddle Contest

REPUBLIC, WASHINGTON / MID-AUGUST / (509) 775-3819

Old-time fiddle music played by competitors ranging from beginners to national champions.

Peter Britt Music Festival

MEDFORD, OREGON / MID-AUGUST / (541) 773-6077 / WWW.BRITTFEST.ORG

A series of concerts featuring jazz, folk, country, and classical music. Held in conjunction with several summer music camps for young people.

Seattle Hempfest

SEATTLE, WASHINGTON / LATE AUGUST / (206) 781-5734 / WWW.SEATTLEHEMPFEST.COM

A day-long celebration of the positive uses of the cannabis plant, Hempfest alternates speakers and music acts on its four stages.

September

Bumbershoot

SEATTLE, WASHINGTON (SEATTLE CENTER) / LABOR DAY WEEKEND /
(206) 281-7788 / WWW.BUMBERSHOOT.ORG

Now well into its third decade, Seattle's Bumbershoot is a four-day affair with dozens of performances by national, regional, and local musical acts at the Seattle Center's many venues. Also included are a film festival and arts exhibits, but the music is the draw for thousands of Seattleites celebrating the traditional close of the summer festival season. A single admission charge gets you onto the grounds and into all venues (except for a few special events).

Lincoln City Jazz Festival

LINCOLN CITY, OREGON / LABOR DAY WEEKEND / (800) 452-2151

A three-day jazz event on the Oregon Coast.

Victory Music's Great Northwest Shanty Sing-Off

TACOMA, WASHINGTON / MID-SEPTEMBER / (253) 428-0832

A songwriting and shanty-singing contest held on the Thea Foss Waterway featuring the best of Northwest maritime musicians. Also features a Saturday night concert.

Earshot Jazz Festival

SEATTLE, WASHINGTON / LATE SEPTEMBER-EARLY OCTOBER / (206) 547-9787 / WWW.EARSHOT.ORG

A series of jazz performances at venues ranging from large theaters to smoky clubs, Earshot draws top national acts from across the jazz spectrum.

Vancouver Wine and Jazz Festival

VANCOUVER, WASHINGTON / LATE SEPTEMBER / (360) 892-6233 / WWW.VANCOUVERWINEJAZZ.COM

A Saturday and Sunday event featuring fine Washington wines, regional cuisine, visual arts, and a full schedule of jazz performances.

October

NXNW (North by Northwest Music and New Media Conference)

PORTLAND, OREGON / LATE OCTOBER / (512) 467-7979 / WWW.NXNW.COM

The music industry types rush to Portland once a year for panel discussions, trade shows, and lots of schmoozing. The real attraction for many are the multiple showcase shows of unsigned bands at local clubs each night of the three-day event.

November

Ocean Shores Dixieland Jazz Festival

OCEAN SHORES, WASHINGTON / EARLY NOVEMBER / (800) 762-3224

A weekend of concerts at five area venues by Dixieland Jazz bands from around the U.S.

Photo Credits

Rock/Pop

Photos by James Bush: The Posies, p. 105; Steve Turner, p. 105; The Moberlys, p. 105; Metal Church, p. 106; Sir Mix-A-Lot, p. 107; Screaming Trees, p. 107; SGM, p. 107; Nirvana, p. 108; Treepeople, p. 108; Inspector Luv, p. 109; Tad, p. 109; The Walkabouts, p. 110; The Cowboys, p. 111; The Fastbacks, p. 111; Layne Staley, p. 112; Coffin Break, p. 113; The Heats, p. 113; Billy Rancher, p. 114.

Photos by Alice Wheeler: Soundgarden, p. 106; Pond, p. 110; Hazel, p. 114.

Photos by Cam Garrett: Green River, p. 110; The Accused, p. 113.

The Young Fresh Fellows, p. 112, **photo by Michael Cox**

Green Pajamas, p. 112, **photo by Rich Hansen**

Chris Newman, p. 112, **photo by Jan Celt/courtesy Flying Heart Records**

Courtesy Neal Skok's collection: The Viceroys, p. 105; The Hudson Brothers, p. 106; The Wailers, p. 106; Pat O'Day and The Kingsmen, p. 107, photo by Forde Photographers; Bluebird, p. 108; Easy Chair, p. 108; Daily Flash, p. 109; Jr. Cadillac, p. 109 (flyer); Paul Revere and the Raiders, p. 110 (advertisement); Don and the Goodtimes, p. 111; Crome Syrcus, p. 111; Merrilee and the Turnabouts, p. 113; Rockin' Robin Roberts, p. 114; City Zu, p. 114.

Jazz

Edmonia Jarrett, p. 205, **photo courtesy Edmonia Jarrett**

Bud Shank, p. 205, **photo courtesy Bud Shank**

Milo Petersen and the Jazz Disciples, p. 205, **photo by Adam Crowley/courtesy Passage Records** (CD jacket)

Jeff Lorber, p. 206, **photo by Loren Hammer/courtesy Jeff Lorber**

Tom Grant, p. 206, **photo courtesy Pacific Talent, Inc.**

Jeff Greinke, p. 206, **photo by Lisa Amorous/courtesy Jeff Greinke**

Tom Collier, p. 207, **photo courtesy Tom Collier**

Barney McClure, p. 207, **photo courtesy Barney McClure**

Bert Wilson, p. 207, **photo by Carl Cook/courtesy Bert Wilson**

Dave Peck, p. 208, **photo by Richard Lewis/courtesy Point Source Music**

Human Feel, p. 208, **photo by Eric H. Antoniou/courtesy GM Recordings**

American Roots/World

Orville Johnson, p. 257, **photo courtesy Orville Johnson**

Curtis Salgado, p. 257, **photo courtesy ODAGLAS**

Sheila Wilcoxson, p. 257, **photo courtesy Sheila Wilcoxson**

Paul deLay, p. 258, **photo by Ross Hamilton**

Magical Strings, p. 258, **photo courtesy Magical Strings**

Jim Page, p. 258, **photo by Dana Schuerholz/courtesy Jim Page**

Lily Wilde, p. 258, **photo by Robert Duncan/courtesy Lily Wilde**

Classical

Seattle Opera's production of Die Walküre, p. 285, **photo by Gary Smith/courtesy Seattle Opera**

Young Composers Collective, p. 285, **photo by Junko Yamamoto**

Bridge Ensemble, p. 286, **photo by Wah Lui**

The Esoterics, p. 286, **photo by Jimmy Malecki**

Every effort has been made to contact the copyright holders of the photographs included in this book. If there are any errors or omissions, please contact the author in care of Sasquatch Books so they can be corrected in any future editions.

Index

Bishop, Duffy, 201, 242–44, 272
Bishop, John, 212
    New Stories, 228
Bisio, Michael, 179–81, 218
Bitter End, 295
Black Cat Orchestra, 310
Black Supersuckers. *See*
    Supersuckers
Black, Jim: Human Feel, 199–200
Black, Lori: Melvins, The, 90
Blackouts, The, 43
Blackstone, Don: Gas Huffer,
    58–59
Blackwood, Morgan: Big Fun, 23
Blaine, Chris: Hocus Pocus, 65
Blake, Braden: Super Deluxe,
    151–52
Blake, Tchad, 31
Blakeslee, Rob, 181–83
    Lizard Brothers, 197, 198
Bland, Danny, 152, 153
Blau, Karl: D+, 7
Bleyle, Jody: Hazel, 63–64
Blind Horse, 88
Blobbo (Kurdt Vanderhoof), 43
Bloch, Al: Moberlys, The, 96
Bloch, Kurt, 58
    Fastbacks, The, 42–45
    Young Fresh Fellows, The,
    170
Bloodloss, 102
Bloom, Don: Some Velvet
    Sidewalk, 141–42
BLT, 236
Blue, Christopher: Ten Minute
    Warning, 44
Blue Horizon, 160
Bluebird, 13–15
Bluenotes. *See* Little Bill and the
    Bluenotes
Blues
    "Great Records Not to
        Miss," 310–14
    in the Northwest, 240
    See also American roots
        music
Blues Interchange, 39
Blues Power Review, 56
Bobrow, Norm, 174
Bodine, 29
Body Falling Down Stairs, 308
Bogdan, Henry: Poison Idea, 123
Bogle, Bob: Ventures, The, 160–61
Bohle, Pat: Skyboys, The, 266–67
Bolme, Joanna: Spinanes, The,
    147
Bolo, 37, 38
BOLT, 179
Bolton, Dan: Supersuckers,
    152–53
Bondage Boys, 92
Boom Boom GI, 249
Bordonaro, John: Touch, 35
Borg, Pete

Dynamics, The, 37–38
    Jimmy Hanna Big Band, 38
    Kingsmen, The, 84
Boulding, Pam, 250–51
Boulding, Philip, 250–51
Bourgoin, Rick: Heats, The,
    70–71
Bowen, Toby: Bighorn, 10–11
Bowling Stones, 56
Boy and His Dog, A, 65
Bradley, Steve: Mesi Band, 253
Brady, Chris: Pond, 124–25
Brady, Jim: Sonics, The, 144
Braeden, Mari Ann: Green Apple
    Quick Step, 59–60
Brannon, Melvin II: Dan Reed
    Network, 29–30
Brecker, Randy, 195
Brenner, Adam: TKO, 157–159
Bridge Ensemble, 277–79
Brill, Rob: Millionaires, The, 37
Brock, Isaac: Modest Mouse, 97
Brock, Timothy, 279–80
Brockman, Michael, 176, 187, 228
Brooks, Dave: Coffin Break, 21
Brooks, Hal: Zero Tolerance, 256
Brotherhood, 120
Brown, Pat: Treepeople, 15–16
Brown Sugar, 245, 252
Brownlow, Jack, 183–84
Brownlow, Paul: Cowboys, The,
    24
Brownstein, Carrie: Sleater-
    Kinney, 139–40
Bud Shank Sextet, 230
Built to Spill, 16–17
Burgeson, Eric:
    Cheyanne/Shyanne, 158
Burk, Mike, 85
    Wailers, The, 163–64
Burke, Kevin, 310
Butorac, Frank: Gabriel, 56

C

Cahill, Dennis, 312
Cameron, Matt, 100, 189
    Skin Yard, 137
    Soundgarden, 145–46
Campbell, Charlie: Pond, 124–25
Candland, Lara, 277
Candlebox, 17–18
Cantrell, Jerry, 130
    Alice in Chains, 5–6
Capps, Andy: Built to Spill, 16
Carlson, Chris, 242–43
Carmassi, Denny: Heart, 68
Carmody, John
    Jimmy Hanna Big Band, 38
    Little Bill and the
        Bluenotes, 87
Carrion Commandos, 72
Carroll, Chuck: Young Fresh
    Fellows, The, 168–70

Cartwright, George, 190
Cat Butt, 295
Catlett, Buddy, 180, 204
Cavender, Joe: Dynamics, The, 38
Cavity Search, 69
Celt, Jan: Snow Bud and the
    Flower People, 115–16
Cerar, Jeff
    Cowboys, The, 22–24
    Moberlys, The, 95
Chainsaw, 139
Chalenor, Fred, 198, 199
    LAND, 195–96
Chamberlain, Matt: Pearl Jam,
    121
Chancellors, The, 39
Chang, Warren, 247
Channing, Chad: Nirvana, 117
Chapman, Tom: Bluebird, 15
Charles, Jack: Quarterflash, 128
Chase, Bekka: Royale Famile du
    Caniveaux, 242
Chase, Ken, 83
Cheaters, The, 42
Checkers, The, 47
Chemistry Set, 295
Cherry Poppin' Daddies, 18–19
Chesterfield, Jack, 158
Chester's Garage, 260
Cheyanne (aka Shyanne), 158
Child, 159
Childers, Kathy: City Zu, 20
Childs, Dave: Don and the
    Goodtimes, 34–35
Chilton, Alex: Big Star, 125–26
Chirillo, James: Heart, 65
Christensen, David:
    Cheyanne/Shyanne, 158
Christenson, Stacy: Gabriel, 56
Christie, Robert; Some Velvet
    Sidewalk, 141
Christlieb, Pete, 226
Christopher, Gretchen Diane:
    Fleetwoods, The, 45–46
Citizens' Utilities, 310–11
City Zu, 19–20
Clack, Wayne: Heats, The, 70–71
Claire, Nancy, 161
    Jr. Cadillac, 82
Clarke, Robb: Bighorn, 10
Classical music, 275–91
    "death" of, 278
    "Great Records Not to
        Miss," 314–16
    in the Northwest, 276
Clayton, Jay, 185–86, 209, 210
Clements, Gail, 236
Clinkingbeard, Les: Jr. Cadillac,
    81–82
Cobain, Kurt, 76
    Nirvana, 116–19
Coe, Charlie
    Don and the Goodtimes,
        35

Donald, Barbara, 180
Doria, Joe: Marriott Jazz Quintet, 214
Doring, Chip, 189
Doubleday, Mark: Dynamics, The, 37–38
Downbeats, 119
Downe, Taime: Bondage Boys, 92
Doyle, Tad, 155–56
D+, 7
Dresch, Donna, 139, 140, 142
Screaming Trees, 132–33
Drewry, Dave: Moberlys, The, 96
Driggs, Carl: Paul Revere and the Raiders, 120
Droge, Pete, 36–37
DTs, The, 43
Dub Narcotic Sound System, 9
Ducky Boys, 62
Dudziak, Urszula, 185
Duffy Bishop Band, 243, 244
DuFresne, Jon: Billy Rancher and the Unreal Gods, 12–13
Dulli, Greg, 51
Duncan, Todd: Crazy 8's, 24–25
Dunne, Roisin: 7 Year Bitch, 134–35
Dust Blair, 99
Dutra, Frank: Little Bill and the Bluenotes, 86–87
Dutra, Geisa, 315
Dwindles, The, 49, 50
Dwyer, P.K., 241, 242
Dyer, Tom, 60
Dynamic Logs, 241, 242, 247–48
Dynamics, The, 37–38, 85
Dynette Set, 260

e

Earl, Scott: TKO, 157–59
"Early Seattle Punk/1977–83," 43–44
Easton, Lynn: Kingsmen, The, 82–84
Easy Big Fella, 297
Easy Chair, 39–41
(EC) Nudes, 179, 189
Eckman, Chris: Walkabouts, The, 165–66
Eckman, Curt: Walkabouts, The, 165–66
Eckman, Grant: Walkabouts, The, 165–66
Edwards, Brad, 218
Edwards, Nokie: Ventures, The, 160
Eggers, Kim, 56
Viceroys, The, 162
Eklund, Greg: Everclear, 41–42
Electric Bonsai Band, 268–69
Elliot, Mike: Skyboys, The, 267
Ellis, Barbara Laine: Fleetwoods, The, 45–46

Elvrum, Phil: D+, 7
Ely, Jack
Don and the Goodtimes, 34–36
Kingsmen, The, 82–83
Emergency Exit, 39
Emery, Jill: Hole, 76–77
Endino Jack, 15, 101, 116, 137–38, 152, 154, 155, 171, 249
Endino's Earthworm, 137
Skin Yard, 137–38
Enemy, The, 23, 43
Engelhart, Bill ("Little Bill"):
Little Bill and the Bluenotes, 83, 86–87
England, Buck: Little Bill and the Bluenotes, 86–87
Enigk, Jeremy: Sunny Day Real Estate, 150–51
Entertainment Authorities, 56, 65, 150, 158
Epicentre, 56
Erickson, Dave: Statics, The, 148–49
Erickson, Duke: Metal Church, 91–93
Erlandson, Eric: Hole, 76–77
Esoterics, The, 281
Estrus Records, 89, 98
Etchoe, Mick: Hocus Pocus, 65
Everclear, 41–42
Everman, Jason
Nirvana, 117
Soundgarden, 145

f

Fags, The, 43
Fairweather, Bruce
Green River, 62–63
Love Battery, 88
Mother Love Bone, 100
Faiye West & the Bleeding Hearts, 249
Falconer, Elizabeth, 311
Fanning, Dale: Zero Tolerance, 256
Farrell, Misty: Sleater-Kinney, 139
Fartz, The, 4, 43–44
Fastbacks, The, 42–45
Seattle Syndrome Volume One, 308
Fat Cat, 49
FDM, 72
Feelings, The, 22
Felchtone, Blind Marky: Zeke, 171
Feldman, Bill: Johnny and the Distractions, 80
Festivals, 317–23
Feveyear, Martin, 152, 155
Fieflin, Bill: LAND, 195–96
Fillmore, Kent: Hudson Brothers, 78

Fincher, Dan, 246
Finn, Jason, 45
Love Battery, 87–88
Presidents of the United States of America, 126–27
Skin Yard, 137
Fire Ants, 297
Firefly Wreck, 72
First Avenue, 209
First Thought, 17
Fisher, Garrett, 315
Fisher, Ian: Cowboys, The, 22–24
Fisher, Mike, 64–67
Fisher, Roger
Alias, 68
Army, 64
Heart, 64–67
Hocus Pocus, 65
Fisk, Steve, 132
Anonymous, 132
Halo Benders, 7–9
Fitz of Depression, 297
Fitzgerald, Jon: Human Feel, 200
Five Fingers of Funk, 297
Flaxel, Billy: Billy Rancher and the Unreal Gods, 12–13
Fleetwoods, The, 45–46
Fleming, Don, 76
Flicker, Mike, 65
Flies, The, 297
Floating Bridge, 47–49
Flop, 49–50
Flower, Wayne: Halo Benders, 7–9
Floyd Standifer Quartet, 176, 232. See also Standifer, Floyd
Flying Heart Records, 115
Flynn, Mick: Child, 159
Flynn, Steve: Jr. Cadillac, 82
Folk music. See American roots music; World music
FoMoFlo, 189
Fong, Nathan: Snow Bud and the Flower People, 116
Foo Fighters, 51
Foos, Ron
City Zu, 19–20
Paul Revere and the Raiders, 120
Forced Entry, 52–53
Fossen, Steve
Alias, 68
Army, 64
Heart, 64–68
Hocus Pocus, 65
Four + One Ensemble, 199
Fowlkes, Curtis, 192
Fox, Dave
Flop, 50
Posies, The, 125–26
Fragile Lime, 158–59
Frantics, The, 29, 47, 53–56
Fraser, Doug: Quarterflash, 128
Freckleton, Bill, 265

Seattle Experimental Opera
(SExO), 277
Seattle Opera, 288–89
"Seattle Power Pop/1979–84," 23
Seattle Repertory Jazz Orchestra,
176, 226, 228
Seattle Scene, definition of, 2–3
Seattle Symphony Orchestra,
289–90
Seattle Women in Rhythm &
Blues, 272
Seattle Youth Symphony
Orchestras, 290–91
Sea-West, 40
Seiffers, Joey: Jumpin' Jubilee
Orchestra, 273
Seigel, Dan: Supersuckers, 152–53
7 Year Bitch, 133–35
Severt, Linda, 249
SGM, 154
Shaar, Casey: Crazy 8's, 25
Shadow, 92
Shaefer, Ray
    Army, 64
    Heart, 65
Shames, Jonathan: Seattle Youth
    Symphony Orchestras, 290
Shank, Bud, 174, 212, 214, 216,
    220, 228–30
Sharp, Elliot, 199
Shaw, Bill
    Pins, The, 95
    Rangehoods, 71
    Royale Famile du
        Caniveaux, 242
Sheila and the Boogiemen, 271
Shelton, Garey
    Big Fun, 23
    Hi-Fi, 23
    Jr. Cadillac, 82
    Mel Cooleys, 269
Shepherd, Ben: Soundgarden,
    145–46
Shikany, Joe: Bighorn, 11
Short, Don
    Heats, The, 70–71
    Moberlys, The, 95
Shoup, Wally, 230–31
    Project W, 231
Shreffler, Ted: Crome Syrcus,
    26–27
Shumway, Alex: Green River,
    62–63
Shyanne, 158
Sibbald, Alex: Accused, The, 4–5
Sick, Jeffrey: Jim Basnight Band,
    96
Sicko, 305
Sigers, Karen: Bridge Ensemble,
    277–79
Silence Records, 15, 16
Silkworm, 305
Silva, Jimmy, 265–66
    Goats, The, 266

Silver, Susan, 145
Simmons, Jeff: Easy Chair, 39–40
Simms, Rick, 153
Simpson, Art, 53
Simpson, Tommy: Love Battery,
    87–88
Sims, Susan: Jim Basnight Band,
    96
Sinder, Josh
    Accused, The, 4–5
    Tad, 156
Singleman, Walter
    Dynamic Logs, 241
    Goats, The, 266
    Picketts, The, 260–61
    Royale Famile du
        Caniveaux,, 242
    Strangers with Candy, 248
Sinners, The, 37
Sinsel, Brad ("Bad Brad"): TKO,
    157–59
Sir Mix-A-Lot, 4, 135–36
Sir Walter Raleigh and the
    Coupons, 47
Sister Psychic, 50, 305
Skin Yard, 87, 137–38
Skinner, Rob, 137
    Coffin Break, 21
    Pop Sickle, 21, 304
Sky Cries Mary, 17, 138–39
Skyboys, The, 266–67, 270
Slam Suzzanne, 305–6
Slater, Glenn: Walkabouts, The,
    165–66
Sleasy Pieces, 80
Sleater-Kinney, 139–40
Sledgehammer, 48
Sleep, Leroy ("Blackie"): Picketts,
    The, 260–61
Slivka, Mike: Jim Basnight Band,
    96
Slyter, Greg: Snow Bud and the
    Flower People, 115–16
Smear, Pat, 151
    Foo Fighters, 51
    Nirvana, 118
Smegma, 72
Smith, Bill, 187
Smith, Brady: Hazel, 63–64
Smith, Carl: Crazy 8's, 25
Smith, Elliott, 68–70, 147
    Heatmiser, 69
Smith, Larry: Dynamics, The,
    37–38
Smith, Mike ("Smitty"): Paul
    Revere and the Raiders,
    119–20
Smith, Scott: Skyboys, The,
    266–67
Smith, Tony ("Tiny"): Statics,
    The, 148–49, 150
Snivlem. See Melvins, The
Snow Bud and the Flower People,
    115–16

Snyder, Gary: Dynamics, The, 38
Soderstrom, Ron, 180
Softy, 21
Solger, 43
Solger, Paul, 43
    Fartz, The, 43
    Solger, 43
Solomon Grundy, 132
Soltero, John
    Bluebird, 14–15
    Punch, 47
Some Velvet Sidewalk, 141–42
Sonics, The, 142–44
Soules, Scott, 10–11
Soundgarden, 144–46
Spaghetti, Eddie: Supersuckers,
    152–53
Spangler, Mark: Johnny and the
    Distractions, 80
Spano, Jim: Statics, The, 148
Sparks, Phil, 176, 228, 233
    Jazz Disciples, 223
    Lizard Brothers, 197
    Umatilla Variations, 198
Speed, Chris: Human Feel,
    199–200
Spike, 72
Spinanes, The, 146–47
Spring Tooth, 33
Springfield Rifle, 38
Squirrels, The, 306
Stagnant Water, 306
Stahl, Franz: Foo Fighters, 51
Staley, Layne
    Alice in Chains, 5–6
    Mad Season, 133
Standifer, Floyd, 176, 201–2, 214,
    219, 232–33
    Floyd Standifer Quartet,
        176, 232
Starr, Mike
    Alice in Chains, 5–6
    Sato, 92
State of Confusion, 15
State Route 522, 307
Statesmen, The, 56
Statics, The, 148–49
Steimonts, Ken: Bighorn, 10–11
Stentz, Jan, 217
Stephens, Jody: Big Star, 125–26
Stepson, 36
Steve Miller Band, 94
Stevenson, Bill: Flop, 50
Stevenson, Don
    Daily Flash, 28
    Frantics, The, 55
    Moby Grape, 55
Stilettos, The, 263
Stone, Mike, 198
Stooges, The, 83
Stotic, Eric: Hellcows, 72
Strangers with Candy, 248
Stricker, David: Billy Rancher and
    the Unreal Gods, 12–13